TOWARD A PERFECTED STATE

A volume in the
SUNY Series in Systematic Philosophy
Robert C. Neville, Editor

TOWARD A PERFECTED STATE

Paul
Weiss

State University of New York Press

Published by
State University of New York Press, Albany

© 1986 State University of New York

For information, address State University of New York
Press, State University Plaza, Albany, N.Y. 12246

Library of Congress Cataloging-in-Publication Data

Weiss, Paul, 1901-
   Toward a perfected state.

   (SUNY series in philosophy)
   Includes indexes.
   1. State, The. 1. Title. II. Series.
JC325.W44   1986   320.1   85-26220
ISBN 0-88706-253-9
ISBN 0-88706-254-7 (pbk.)

FOR JAMES COLLINS

A Man I admire

Books by Paul Weiss

Beyond All Appearances (1974)
Cinematics (1975)
First Considerations (1977)
The God We Seek (1964)
History: Written and Lived (1962)
The Making of Men (1967)
Man's Freedom (1950)
Modes of Being (1958)
Nature and Man (1947)
Nine Basic Arts (1961)
Our Public Life (1959)
Philosophy in Process, Vol. 1: 1955-1960 (1966)
Philosophy in Process, Vol. 2: 1960-1964 (1966)
Philosophy in Process, Vol. 3: 1964 (1968)
Philosophy in Process, Vol. 4: 1964-1965 (1969)
Philosophy in Process, Vol. 5: 1965-1968 (1971)
Philosophy in Process, Vol. 6: 1968-1971 (1975)
Philosophy in Process, Vol. 7: 1975-1976 (1978)
Philosophy in Process, Vol. 7, Part 2: (1985)
Philosophy in Process, Vol. 8: 1978-1980 (1984)
Philosophy in Process, Vol. 9, (forthcoming)
Philosophy in Process, Vol. 10, (forthcoming)
Reality (1938)
Religion and Art (1963)
Right and Wrong: A Philosophical Dialogue Between Father and Son, with Jonathan
  Weiss (1967)
Sport: A Philosophic Inquiry (1969)
The World of Art (1961)
You, I, and the Others (1980)
Privacy (1983)
Creativity (forthcoming)

Principal Contributions

American Philosophers at Work, edited by Sidney Hook (1956)
American Philosophy Today and Tomorrow, edited by H. M. Kallen and Sidney Hook
  (1935)
The Concept of Order, edited by Paul Kuntz (1968)
Contemporary American Philosophy, edited by John E. Smith (1970)
Design and Aesthetics of Wood, edited by Eric A. Anderson and George F. Earl (1972)
Determinism and Freedom, edited by Sidney Hook (1958)
The Dimensions of Job, edited by Nahum N. Glatzer (1969)
Dimensions of Mind: A Symposium, edited by Sidney Hook (1960)
Evolution in Perspective, edited by G. Schuster and G. Thorson (1971)
Existence and Actuality, edited by John B. Cobb, Jr. and Franklin I. Gamwell (1984)
The Future of Metaphysics, edited by Robert Wood (1970)
Human Values and Economic Policy: Proceedings, edited by Sidney Hook (1967)
Law and Philosphy, edited by Sidney Hook (1964)
Mid/Twentieth Century American Philosophy, edited by Peter A. Bertocci (1974)
Moments of Personal Discovery, edited by R. M. MacIver (1952)
Moral Principles in Action, edited by R. Anshen (1952)
Perspectives on Peirce, edited by R. Bernstein (1965)
Philosphers on Their Work, edited by André Mercier (1979)
Philosophical Interrogations, edited by S. and B. Rome (1964)
Philosophy and History, edited by Sidney Hook (1963)
The Philosophy of Baruch Spinoza, edited by R. Kennington (1980)
The Relevance of Whitehead, edited by I. Leclerc (1961)
Science, Philosophy, and Religion: Proceedings (1941-)
Studies in the Philosophy of Charles Sanders Peirce edited by C. P. Weiner and F. H.
  Young (1952)

Edited Works

Collected Papers of Charles Sanders Peirce (six volumes), editor, with Charles Haw-
  thorne (1931-35)

CONTENTS

PREFACE

Almost every way in which humans have been distinguished from animals has been challenged. It has been denied that they have a distinctive kind of mind, will, and language; that they alone have moralities, an ethics, laws, and religions; that only they have creative powers and imagination, or the ability to engage in inquiry, art, and speculation. Each suggested difference has been held by some thinkers to obscure a basic similarity. I think the claims made for a sharp and steady distinction between humans and animals on these and other grounds are warranted.

Humanity's distinctive abilities are discoverable in a number of ways. One is through an examination of individual acts. Another is by attending to the kinds of groupings humans form. Apart from the rest of the world, under conditions which are both accepted and opposed, and sometimes formulated in more restrictive forms, they live in some accord with what they take to be reasonable, right, and good.

Only people compel themselves to refrain from doing what they might tend to do, by subjecting themselves to self-imposed demands. With other types of being, they can and do conform to multiple conditions, but unlike all others they also yield to demands which they impose on themselves. Only they assess themselves in terms of conditions they themselves sometimes defy.

People are together in many ways. They live in some harmony in families, communities, and other complexes, and there achieve what they could not by themselves. Each person there is occasionally blocked or injured and sometimes defeated. None exists in complete isolation. None lives in perfect harmony with, or is absolutely opposed to others; but also, none is necessarily ruined or perfected by being joined with them.

It is eminently desirable to know if and how humans can act together in better ways than they now do. To discover that, one must know how they can be together, and under what limitations. A very extended study, though, would be needed to enable one to grasp all the ways that people are, can be, and should be with one another. It would be enlarged further, were one to try to consider all the conditions to which they were subject. A basis for such a study, though, could be provided could one learn how people can and should interplay with the most common effective conditions, particularly those characteristic of every society and state. It is one of the tasks of the present inquiry to provide this.

The first part concentrates on the constituents, nature, and tasks of society. The second deals with similar issues pertinent to the state. Each could be read without taking account of what is discussed in the other; but each also gains if approached with some understanding of what the other establishes. The work, as a whole, points toward a world of people who, without abandoning their positions in a state, live together under the guidance and control of more comprehensive conditions. Since the proper appreciation and use of actual societies and states, and thus of what should be done by, to, and for them, is promoted by an understanding of what they can and ought to become, only at the end of this work will it be possible to achieve an adequate understanding of what had gone before. But it is no less true that only so far as one has grasped the natures of actual societies and states that one can understand what could and should replace them. This, the Commonhealth, is relevant to all of them, and plays a role in whatever they do.

To function well in or under a government, society, state, or Commonhealth, one must tailor preparations and acts in the light of what other persons and the various complexes are, can be, and should be, and what they will most likely do. The position is gradually won by altering one's course so as to keep in accord with what is encountered and learned. But when an attempt is made to understand and to provide a systematic, justified account of humanity as together in various complexes and subject to conditions that prevail regardless of purpose and desire, something more than such reasonable acts is needed. Otherwise, one would do little beyond recapitulating what had been more or less successfully achieved in the course of daily living. One would go astray, of course, were one to ignore what daily good sense endorses; it would be quite foolish to set oneself firmly in opposition to it. Unfortunately, it is not clear nor steady enough to satisfy the relentless questionings of a persistent inquiry. It must be supplemented and qualified by a consideration of what is being presupposed, what should eventually be achieved, and what crucial tasks are to be performed in private. To arrive at what can withstand criticism one must make use of an intellectually grounded reasonableness, specializing in and justified by a systematic mastery of the principles presupposed by every being and in every act.

This is not the place to present a systematic account of what every reality and inquiry specializes, though that would enable a reader to rectify and order some apparently unorganized and inadequately sifted observations and reflections. I did though keep it in mind. Pivotal ideas are here focused on again and again so as to make evident the warrant for major claims. Throughout and particularly in the footnotes I have also attended to questions discussed at length elsewhere, but which deserve some acknowledgment here in order to make evident what is being presupposed and serves as a guide. The answers to those questions not only offer checks; they enable one to see how people are united with factors having a range not limited to them and of which they are often not aware.

The present work examines the reasons and ways people join in work and belong together; what they require and are required to do; and how what is pertinent to their living well together can best be utilized and improved. The whole exhibits common practice qualified and systematized, speculation specialized, analysis at the service of the very unities it dissects and re-presents. To the degree that the inquiry is successful, the most universal and pervasive of factors will be found to have been wedded to the most direct deliverances of daily life.

The work as a whole exhibits a progression from the most primitive but basic ways people are joined together to more and more effective ways in which they can and do benefit themselves and what governs them — and conversely, can be and are benefited as well. Each stage opens the way to the next, not because there is a relentless dialectic or historic current at work, but because the defects characteristic of each position point the way to desirable remedies. These have sometimes been provided, under the pressure of circumstance, though often in too limited a form. Reasonableness knows them as they are needed; speculation attends to them as purified and their intrinsic natures and essential relations exposed. The present work attempts to weld the two achievements in an adventure at understanding the nature and course of public life and what it could become. Those with some familiarity with *Privacy* could use its discoveries of the different epitomizations of human privacy to alert them to distinctions to be made among the different ways humans are or could be publicly together. But this and that work are not, could not, and should not be treated as needing one another. There are specializations of the person and the self, such as sensibility (with its occupation with nuances in experience and its role in the appreciation and creation of art) and choice (with its concern for the obligatory) which have no adequate counterpart in the progressive move from associated and cooperative humans, with which this work begins, to the Commonhealth, toward which it points. Although the main epitomizations of privacy do lay the ground for ways people can be together, not all of these are in a direct line of advance from the most primitive public groupings to the most advanced. But even if there were such a parallel of distinctions, one would have to make use of it with great caution, since one might otherwise neglect the independent adventures of the different works.

Over the years, I have discussed many of these issues with my son, Jonathan. He is a practicing attorney who has written extensively on jurisprudence and various legal questions. We disagree on some basic topics, a fact which makes me suspect that I may have overlooked or misconstrued some crucial issues. I am most grateful to Robert Neville for his acute and encouraging observations on this and other works, to Robert Castiglione, Aoki Kataoka, Anthony Cua, and Jude Dougherty for their sustaining confidence in the importance of what I have been doing, and to my recent graduate students who have made me meet a continuous barrage of challenges on the issues underlying this and a number of my other works.

Washington, D.C.
June, 1985

PART I

Unions
and
Societies

FOCAL POINTS

1. People take on different tasks, so as to be able to deal collaboratively with common challenges better than they otherwise could or would.

2. Traditionalized practice and guiding objectives fixate some of the tasks and determine what will be done.

3. People are also associated, sharing a common ground.

4. People reach one another through the agency of their common ground; they are then intimate with one another while still remaining publicly distanced.

5. To continue to be together in constant ways, people accept their contrast with all else as definitive of themselves.

6. The contrast between those who are united and all else is maintained apart from them.

7. The contrast, as maintained apart from people, is adopted by them, thereby defining them to be together in contradistinction from all others.

8. The present is enriched by the past and future.

9. When both collaborative and associated, people form a union. They are then intimately involved with one another at distanced positions.

10. A union requires people to act together in consonance with its demands. So far as they do, they act morally.

11. A commune is a union acting primarily as a medium for the demands of a superior reality.

12. When collaborative people are subject to a common tradition and prospects, they constitute a community.

13. A commune has a tradition and prospects to which its people submit, and which interplay with a community's tradition and prospects.

14. A nation is a self-sufficient commune; an organization is a self-sufficient community.

15. The prospect at which a community is directed is an ideal to be realized.

16. A society joins a union and a homeland; it has an inherited past and an ideology, and it occupies a territory.

17. People and unions have values which they partly express by acting in accord with societal demands.

18. People act appropriately so far as they conform to societal demands; they may then also act immorally.

19. There are three basic kinds of truth: embedded, objective, and conformal, each having the others as special cases.

20. All three types of truth are used in both the sciences and the humanities.

21. The sciences and humanities make use of similar methods, but they have different objectives and make a different use of tests, logic, and mathematics.

22. Social study begins with the commonplace, clarifying it through the use of classifications, observations, and other operations.

23. Causation combines a formal necessity with a creative production of determinations in prospective effects.

24. Practice assumes that mathematical probabilities are realized in a finite time, unless an alien factor has been intruded.

25. All beings have the native right to be and to prosper.

26. The use of any being to serve the purposes of others always involves some loss.

27. People and society have rights maintained against one another. Each is to be perfected with the help of the other.

28. The best of societies is to be achieved by reconstructing actual societies, each contributing to a single complex, embracing people functioning excellently, in harmony.

1. Tradition and Purpose

1. Collaborative People

The world is alien, dangerous, and brute, the locus of multiple challenges, some of which are beyond the capacity of anyone to deal with adequately. It is also benign, bountiful, and occasionally beautiful. There is winter but also spring; there are dry seasons and wet, day and night, the compelled and the spontaneous. The one demands collaborations, the other encourages associations. No account of humanity, nature, society, or state can long neglect either. The demands, though, tend to make us stop; they therefore offer a good place from which to begin to act, and sometimes to think of how we do act and should.[1]

Again and again people are forced to respond to other beings acting independently of them. No one is ever entirely freed from the challenges others put in the way of ease, health, prosperity, or continuance. Heat and cold, hunger, thirst, and fear, dangerous turns make some challenges stand out more than others, requiring quick and good responses by those involved, severally and, often enough, together.

Little that anyone does is carried out without regard for what has been taught, or for the expectations of others. None is so alienated from the rest that no use is made of what has been learned from some. All take some account of what others expect from them. Although each individual has a private depth that is not ever fully probed, although each remains a stranger even to intimates, each is also affected, supplemented, and sometimes helped by some of them. Faced by challenges from external objects, each usually acts in ways more or less sanctioned. All the while, no matter what the degree and extent of intimacy with others, each person remains both irreducibly separate and singularly insistent. Individuals must usually rely on what has been learned and must look for help from others. Otherwise what is confronted will often be beyond their capacity to deal with effectively.

Challenged, a person usually makes use of acquired knowledge and skills. These may not be enough to enable effective action to occur. That is possible only if a place can be found alongside others also occupied with that challenge. If able to act sufficiently well alone, a person may still have to make room for others. Occasionally, these will be opposed, particularly when they are seen to preclude the achievement of what is sought. But whether individuals compete or cooperate, allowance must be made for the presence and likely actions of all. Sometimes others are faced as challenging, and thus as existing and acting in opposition to oneself; they may then be dealt with as though they were just objects in the world, and then primarily as obstacles. Presented with a challenge too great to master, a person, though, may share in an effort to which others also contribute. The actions of one will then more or less mesh with the actions of the rest.

Subhumans, too, act in consonance with one another, sometimes even more effectively than humans do. What, among other differences, clearly distinguishes the humans from them is the accompanying ability to preserve, in the form of present, effective traditions and objectives, the pattern of positions and tasks which had been exhibited in successful ventures in the past. Where subhumans can do no more than modify present activities by what they had learned from experience, humans can vary the use to which they put what had been previously done, learned, sought, and achieved. Their undergone past and possible future can be used to enable them to act differently from what they would, were they merely to express the nature of their present tendencies and what they had learned to expect. Because their actions do not simply reflect their previous adventures, and the expectations these warrant, human beings never act simply as creatures of experience.

Subhumans exist in a limited part of the world. There they act both independently of one another and cooperatively. All acquire habits; most adjust their moves so as to fit in with the moves of others. While only a few are acute and well-nuanced with respect to this or that recurrent type of challenge, most act as their encounters and needs dictate. There is no way in which subhumans ought to, but may not in fact act; there are no conditions distinct from them which they more or less accept so as to enable them to act privately, sometimes in opposition to the teachings of experience and inviting prospects. Subhumans do what they have to do. Acting with some degree of liberty, changing stresses to keep in better accord with circumstance and one another, they have no achievements or objectives maintained in the present as part of a condition with which they are to interplay. Only humans have traditions and ideals enriching their present and awaiting their acceptance or rejection in any one of a number of ways and degrees.

A satisfactory study of people who can be in a society, state, and other complexes deals with them in their full concreteness, but still as acting differently from the way they do when just expressing their individual privacies or interacting with others. If the nature, capacities, rights, and promise of humans are to be correctly grasped, account must be taken of them as existing outside as well as inside the complexes, and thus as private and public persons, able to so collaborate that they together deal effectively with what challenges them. If, as here, a study is primarily occupied with society and state, the recognition that each person exists privately apart from all others at the same time that he or she is together with them in a single world, requires one not only to avoid a reduction of human beings to the status of just social or political units, but to make room for evaluations of what is done in and by society and state.

Humans collaborate to meet challenges with a success otherwise not possible. Their collaborative acts rarely coincide with others carried out without reference to a common challenge, but that will not prevent them all from obtaining some of the things they separately seek. If, initially, they had no interest in working together, the discovery that supplementation and support by others can make for a success otherwise not possible will usually lead them to engage in collaborative efforts, adjusting to one another while taking account of a present condition enriched by an inherited past and a distinctive prospect.

A person may or may not make use of what is remembered; subhumans inescapably use what is remembered to modify what they do. An animal might recall what it once underwent; it could conceivably dream about its experiences; conceivably, it could make what it remembered affect its preparations and activities. Its remembrances do not sanction what it does, though they may prompt or back what it is doing, making it continue with a new force and in a modified way. If an animal remembered what a number successfully did together, its memory would still be only part of a cause acting as it must and could not, as it could in a human being, have the role of a because, a reason.

No subhuman insists on carrying out conditions which the rest might reject. They act as functions of what they are and have undergone, not as a consequence of an acceptance or rejection of a justifying condition. Some animals train their young, teaching them how to carry out certain tasks. So far, they seem to be like those humans who demand that others act in various ways. But since the animals have no traditions or accepted common objectives, they can do no more than modify the acts they or some others are readied to perform. Humans, instead, are faced at every moment with conditions embodying a shared past and a prospective future. Unlike the training of their young, which is one among many things that animals unreflectingly do in rather constant ways, human training is in good part a matter of choice, voluntarily carried out in different ways at different times and in different places.

So far as human beings adjust themselves to one another in order to be able to meet present challenges effectively, they are collaborative. Sometimes they are united in only a minimal way, not yet ready to engage in joint, sustained, effective action. There are, though, enough actual and prospective challenges to keep them at least incipiently collaborative, guided and controlled by conditions inherited from the past, some of which may have effectively governed other collaborations.

The more people act collaboratively, the more they are occupied with adjusting themselves to one another under common conditions, and with reference to what acts without regard for them, challenging their ways and sometimes their continuance. Sometimes their collaboration and sometimes the challenges play a major role in determining what is to be done.

The more a collaboration is carried out under a condition that had governed successful action in the past, the more prepared will humans be to meet a present challenge successfully—provided, of course, that they and their world remain rather steady and the challenge is somewhat like others encountered before. Successful collaborations are usually those in which present activities take account of what is beyond the ability of any one to deal with alone, but is like what had been successfully met in the past by people working well together.

Since what is done is not entirely separable from the prospects people seek to realize, a separation of present and future can be only partial and artificial. Indeed, as will become evident, the past can play a role in the present only because the future enables it to do so.

Ongoings pass away, never to be again. What is brought into the present is the fact of past ongoings, and then only because the future so holds on to the past that it is able to play a role in the present. The resulting enriched present is a condition in terms of which people adjust themselves so as to meet challenges beyond the capacity of any one alone to deal with successfully.

If humans had no memory of past successes in meeting challenges, could not benefit from what they had achieved, had no traditions or objectives, if they could not assign or accept assignments from others, or had no concern with mastering what no one individually could, they would not be able to collaborate. Instead, they would engage in a series of unpredictable adventures in adjustment, without necessarily promoting a mastery of what they confront. By acting together in mutually supportive ways, they might even make themselves members of a successful band, but they would not yet be collaborative. Collaboration requires them to adjust themselves to one another at positions and in ways definable apart from them.

Collaborators share traditions and purposes, and adjust to one another in order to take account of differences in tendencies, as reflected in preparations and habits, and the presence of common conditions. The problem that has constantly perplexed political thinkers (and has led to the postulation of imaginary social and other kinds of contract, common wills, deliberate decisions by rational people, individuals with unbelievable power, infallible wisdom or appeal, or a relentless course of history) vanishes with the acknowledgment that present conditions, qualified by the past and future, affect what people otherwise attempt to do.

A challenge is best met when some persons take advantage of their native abilities, established habits, acquired skills, and what had been learned from experience, parents, teachers, and contemporaries in a present enriched by the past and future. Explorations, investigations, study, and experimentation will enable them to become more and more prepared to overcome and perhaps benefit from the presence of what otherwise might compel their submission to its course and insistence, perhaps to their detriment. Conceivably, a person might separate from the rest after having joined with them in a common enterprise. A person may also later come together with the same or other people in fresh ways, particularly when confronted with a new and great challenge.

No one learns much from the past if it serves merely to change subsequent actions. To learn from it, the past must guide and limit an individual and thus function as a part of a present in which that individual's acts must more or less fit. The circumstances, of course, present a challenge of their own. Sometimes they prompt people to neglect what is not of common concern.

If people are not to rely solely on spontaneous responses, in the hope that they will thereby act in consonance, they must take advantage of what had helped them prosper in the past. Since what produced past benefits may no longer be available, they must also avoid just conforming to what previous successes sanction. It is therefore desirable for each not only to make use of what has been learned, but to attempt to discover, through actual affort, what can be done then and there. What had been successfully done is to be used to help determine what is to be done, but it will then be necessary to be on the alert to prevent such determinations from being so effective that an appropriate flexible response is precluded.

When someone's occupation with a challenge is not only supplemented by contemporaries, but is conditioned by a tradition, what before may have been beyond an individual's own powers, or even beyond joint efforts, may sometimes be mastered. What would otherwise have been rough adjustments worked through then and there will be smoothed out and often made effective by being carried out in the light of what the past endorses. The possible conflicts which would be produced were people to try to act together for the first time will be reduced; people may even avoid some conflicts by facing the present as that which is qualified by a common successful past and a desirable future. Such a present is a common condition under which a number deal with what challenges them. [2]

Each individual acts alone. None produces a tradition. Traditions are the product of a number. They exist and are able to be effective because the present is the inescapable locus of what is preserved of the past and is guided by the prospect of what is sought. The way this occurs is a topic to be subsequently explored; for the moment, it suffices to remark that human beings live in an accumulative time. There the past is always a part of a present limited condition in which the future functions as a control. Successful collaborative actions take account of it. [3]

The adjustments people make to one another are their own. And, no matter what the conditions are under which they act, people often enough get in one another's way. Some over-insist, and some do not insist enough. Even when they decide to act in concert, they frequently hinder one another. It is tempting, therefore, for them to look to someone able to see to it that conflicts are avoided or readily overcome. Such a power, of course, would have to take account of the fact that the people, independently of it, adjust themselves to one another. And it would have to be flexible enough to keep them acting as it requires, sometimes even in opposition to its demands. The power would be needed, too, in order to achieve more than the kind of harmony that would be produced by reducing efforts at mutual adjustment to a minimum, with a consequent failure to provide a satisfactory answer to what challenges all. A power acting without regard for the tradition and objectives in terms of which people live in the present will, more likely than not, prompt them to oppose and perhaps even to free themselves from it.

No tyrant is a natural force. Each acts in the light of what people are and might do. If shrewd, a tyrant preserves a tradition directed at realizing a common objective. So far, he will differ from other successful leaders primarily in the nature and extent of the compulsions used to make others accept his decrees. It is one thing though to provide desirable conditions with a backing, and even to require people to function in some accord with those conditions—that, of course, should be done—and quite another to insist on acts regardless of what people in fact may need and deserve, since this would be to explicitly oppose their right to be full human beings.

To act together, people need not be self-conscious. Nor need they suppose that they fit well in the same world with other beings. It suffices if there are external objects which challenge them, requiring them to act under a common conditioning from particular positions and in certain ways, so as to bring about what they could not separately. Conceivably, they may have accidentally learned that they could achieve what benefits each, only by working together. Conceivably, they may have acted independently for a while and belatedly discovered the value of taking on supplementary roles. Conceivably, they may have imitated the behavior of animals in packs, herds, and flocks, or learned from them that there is something to be gained by acting in consonance. In any event, they would still have to reach the stage where positions and tasks are recognized to make distinctive demands on them. The awareness that they together exist in contradistinction from what challenges them, and that they must do certain things from certain positions if they are to be successful, leads humans to collaborate by adjusting their acts in a common present which has been enriched by an inherited past and a prospective future. Not until then could they be like those who exist today.

There never was a time when human beings were just Hobbesean savages, each with a hand raised against the rest. Without help no human being ever gets past infancy. If humans eventually became Hobbesean savages they would do so after they had benefited from collaborations which made it possible for them to continue and prosper in the face of natural threats and disorders. The contract Hobbes thought they might have had to make would require them to take advantage of a common knowledge of what they needed, a common language, and a common understanding of the nature of a contract, sovereign, obedience, and so on.

To avoid frustration and perhaps extinction by the rest of the world, people must collaborate. They can exist and work together long before they are in a position to make a contract or are able to acknowledge the right of a sovereign to demand obedience, not only from them but from posterity.[4] When they collaborate, each need do nothing more than accept a position and tasks directed toward a challenge also being faced by others. Each will then act as a distinct individual, adjusting to others who, under the same conditioning present, confront the same challenge that they, too, could not properly meet by acting alone.

People can act well together even when they do not think about the desirability of collaboration. Each person could be said to act selfishly, to be occupied primarily with benefiting from and overcoming challenges. But, equally, each could be said to be altruistic, occupied with achieving what might benefit others, since they are many and he or she is but one. Neither characterization, though, is alone appropriate, for what each does involves a facing of challenges then faced by others as well, requiring an adjustment of actions to them so as to overcome what otherwise would overwhelm.

There is a hidden truth in Hobbes' view; people work together because that is a good way for them to obtain what they wish to have. But no deliberation or conscious concern for satisfying only themselves or helping others need be supposed. They unreflectingly discover the advantages of collaborating by doing what they can, and seeing that their incidental adjustments under common conditions allow them both to achieve what they seek and to obtain what they need, better than would be possible were each to ignore the ways the others act.

Humans adjust themselves not only to one another, but to animals and things. Whatever is confronted, in fact, requires that some account be taken of its nature and tendencies. This must be done both to make it possible to engage in other tasks and to function independently of what is confronted. The first depends on the second, for nothing can be properly used as an agency unless provision is made for people to carry out appropriate actions by making use of their distinctive powers.

It is not just the kinds of objects, the relations these have to one another, or the ways they stand in contrast with humans which characterize the encountered world. The manner in which objects there insist on themselves determines the kind of challenges which will be met, and therefore the extent to which the world is alien, perhaps hostile, and surely indifferent to human concerns. It has to be dealt with on its own terms, if humans are to act successfully in it and are to make any of it a part of their own limited world.

Obstacles, threats, and invitations all have a status apart from those who face them. Each object insists on itself, helping determine how others must act. To be effectively used, whatever is encountered must be dealt with in some accord with its nature and functioning. No matter how thoroughly people are socialized and civilized, how conventionalized they are, they are forced again and again to attend to problems not of their own making. The weather, the seasons, the changes from day to night to day are due to forces not under human control, though people may and do modify, anticipate, and take advantage of them. Again and again, for their very continuance and prosperity, they must take account of what threatens and what promises to benefit them. Both to gain maximally from the world's bounty and to avoid being crushed by what else there is, they must attend to what the world insistently presents. To do this well, they must set themselves apart from it, take a step back in order to move forward effectively. They must also assume special positions relative to one another. Only then can they deal adequately with what challenges them. Collaboration is an effective way in which they act together toward what they need to overcome.

For some people more than others, but inevitably for all, the world dictates when, where, and how they are to act if they are to continue and to prosper. They can qualify only a portion of it, and then only partly; they can push it aside, but only for moments and then not altogether. Farmers, sailors, and hunters order their lives in accord with its rhythms. At earlier times, more people apparently paid some-

what the same attention to it than is commonly done today. Still,
even today, spring and summer are lived through in different ways,
and day and night are divided for all in considerable accord with the
rising and setting of the sun.

When people act collaboratively, they act together often with the
strength and diversity needed to control what would otherwise overwhelm. The separation from the rest of the world that their collaboration requires and promotes follows on (but never extinguishes) their
being together with whatever else there is. Both the separation from
and their connection with others depends on the possession and
expression of their individual privacies.

The grip one has on one's body may be minimal, but because a
privacy is expressed in and through it, that body becomes the body of
a person. From the beginning, the privacy is expressed in a distinctive way with different outcomes for the body in nature, and as
joined with others. As a privacy, and individual is the equal of others;
all, too, are equal as collaborative units. At the same time, there is a
considerable difference in the way each body is controlled and used,
as well as in what can and will be done when a number of persons act
collaboratively.

An arena of thrusts and counterthrusts, of interactions, oppositions, and concordances, the world goes its own way regardless of
what people decide, cherish, or desire. The differences which mark
humans off from other kinds of beings, their theories, technologies,
and controls, never suffice to free them from its influences. They
distinguish themselves from it, subordinate some of it, redirect its
forces, and make it serve distinctively human demands. Sometimes
they join together and make it serve them. But no matter how they
use or close themselves off from it, the world continues to exist apart
from and to act on them. Subhumans, no less than humans, are
compelled to take account of what is there. But they never face any
thing from a distinguished, separated position. They may band together, protect their young, identify some others as enemies or as
supportive, and take some situations to be inviting or dangerous.
They may respond beneficially to what they confront. But they do
not take themselves to exist together apart from all else. Their activities are determined by their structure, strength, gender, health, age,
location, appetites, lacks, obstacles, and opportunities. Although
many act cooperatively, supplementing one another, none act collaboratively, To do that, they would have had to assume positions from

where they could begin to engage in tasks whose nature and demands are determined apart from them. Even when they vary their positions and activities in relation to one another and are thereby able to meet what challenges all of them, subhumans do not see themselves to be distinct from what they do.

A knowledge of the world's primary rhythms enables people to deal with it with considerable success, both separately and together. But such knowledge is a late achievement, dependent on a detachment and a reflection which await a time of comparative peace and leisure. Well before and apart from such an opportunity, successful action is possible by more or less conforming to insistent present conditions which incorporate the past of successful joint efforts and the future of a common concern. People also know themselves to exist and able to act apart from the roles they fill, and the tasks they carry out. Most know themselves to be persons who may fail to do what they ought, but who can expressly take account of their successful achievements, as well as those due to others, no longer present. Only humans know how to meet challenges with ease and success, by each adjusting acts to others in the light of common, traditionalized, guiding conditions.

Subhumans are intimately joined with one another. So are humans. But the connections that subhumans form are inseparable from their bodily tendencies. Unlike the others, humans can distinguish their roles from themselves and carry these out regardless of the intimate bonds that unite them with one another. As a consequence, the ways in which they jointly act and are intimately involved may not mesh. That danger is more than balanced by the opportunity they then have to bring their activities and bonding together in new and sometimes desirable ways. Risking failure more often than subhumans do, they can so act together that they are able to achieve results which even their own predecessors could not. Still, no matter how well they do this, nature continues to function as it had before, endangering and nourishing them, at once alien and inviting.

People act together to meet challenges too great for any one of them to meet. They also know that they have ancestors and that there are some demands they can best satisfy by taking account of positions and roles successfully filled before. Having acted together to meet challenges beyond the ability of any one of them to deal with well, they can and do use successfully occupied positions and remembered achievements to dictate how they are next to act.

Ants, bees, and other 'social' insects make use of a limited portion of the world to carry out various functions. They exist and act as units in well-knit wholes. They may reject others of their kind, not as humans sometimes do because the others failed to fill ascribed positions or to carry out required tasks, but solely because those others have different odors, shapes, or ways of acting. When some people reject others because they are different in appearence, or because they follow different religions, moralities, or customs, they may still require them to occupy certain positions and to engage in particular tasks. The members of any particular type of living being may act in consonance; only people, in addition, can act in ways which are both sanctioned and avoidable.

There are reasons why subhumans do what they do. Those reasons are not accepted by them as reasons. We attribute the reasons to them. But even when a human's acts, like those of a subhuman, are the product of relentless causes, account can be taken of reasons which are present in what is affecting them. The effective conditions which make a successful collaboration possible for humans provide justifying reasons for their acting in particular ways. Even when the justifications are not recognized, they still play a role, affecting what is being initiated, though usually so slightly that what is done is mainly the result of causes having nothing to do with overcoming common challenges. It is only when humans attend to reasons for their acts that they clearly do what no other beings can.

There are causes which make particular reasons available in the present. There are others which prompt people to engage in voluntary acts. The produced effect, at both times, enjoys a status that other effects do not, since it is accepted or rejected in any one of an endless number of degrees as being more or less appropriate and sanctioned.

By using previously accepted conditions as reasons, people tacitly assume the status of judges legitimizing what is about to be done. As such judges, they stand apart from all reasons, responses, and others—and what else they themselves do. The last is possible, because in judgment a portion of a privacy is used to assess what is being done in the rest. If this were not possible, they would have to act without being able to accept or reject reasons for doing so.

Because use is made of approved past activities to yield warrants in a conditioning present, there is a tendency for people to act as though they were in a stable world. That conservatism makes for efficiency, continuity, and some success. Since no one could be alive and effective if the past were entirely disastrous, and since the world exhibits many recurrent rhythms, the conservatism becomes more and more entrenched. The more the world is brought under control, and the more people are able to live successfully apart from it, the more will that tendency toward conservatism be strengthened. The world and common life have to make quite unusual turns for the tendency to be overcome. A new conservatism will then be readied, using the new successes that are then being achieved to provide warrants for certain later activities, and not others.

To be unreflectingly conservative in responding to challenges, determining acts in accord with the conditions that made success possible in the past, is to function in the present as a justified being. Such conservatism, of course, is quite unlike a political conservatism that insists on enjoyed privileges, refuses to experiment or adventure, and insistently maintains established institutions and practices. That conservatism uses past successes and established objectives as sufficient warrants for what is done; it therefore tends to exclude activities in the present which are not endorsed by what had been effective in the past. While it does not preclude all adventure, it does nothing to assure or prompt any. A good retention of the past and a maintenance of an objective are not incompatible with a freedom to do what is needed in the present.

The sanctioning of present answers to challenges depends on a distinctive human ability to assess what is now done. The assessment depends on past successes being given a present role in combination with a pertinent prospect. The interplay of conjoint activities with an enriched present thereby makes for a collaboration partly justified by what had been and by what may be.

The world about changes considerably over time. Conditions may be imposed, to the detriment of many. Though well warranted by the past and prospective future, those conditions would have to be defied to make possible a better occupation with what is challenging. Whatever is done, the people can be said to be ruled by themselves or, equally, to be ruled by what is distinct from them, for it is by having successfully functioned in the past that the present is enabled to be the locus of an enriched condition, conformity to which promises a successful answer to what is challenging.

Past effective practices provide some justification for what is now to be done. The justification differs from the rules, laws, and other conditions operative in a society or state, primarily in not having any well-defined power associated with or assigned to it, and in being acceptable primarily because it promises success in meeting present demands.

The conditions which govern present efforts at collaboration are yielded to because they supposedly promote successful action. When they are used to benefit only some, they offer presumed warrants for turning others into means. When the conditions are used to benefit all, all are so far treated as termini, which other means are to serve. Although a collaboration avoids both extremes, it does not assure that all will be dealt with equally well. The opposite defect is exhibited when acts are carried out for no other reason than that they are like what had usually been done, apparently successfully. A good collaboration avoids that limitation as well.

Conditions operative in a collaboration, by bringing a tradition (and a prospect) to bear, tacitly assess what people are about to do. The assessment is a function of the degree to which the past is enabled to affect incipient acts and thereby promote their prevention or expression. As a consequence, those acts are positively or negatively qualified. Since they are modified before they are fully expressed and are able to affect what else there is, no study restricted to overt behavior will be able to take adequate account of the role that conditions play in what people do.

Different people give different weights to their acts and to their assessments of these. They may independently minimize the importance of their assessments, allowing these to have little effect on the determination of the acts in which they engage. Or they may give the assessments a primary role and act only in ways which are maximally endorsed. They may accept assessments other than those which their inherited past and desired future provide; they may also act in ways which are unfavorably assessed, sometimes even by themselves. Their past and future are, and should at times be treated, as possibly of minor or even of negative value. Those who keep their acts in close conformity to what had been done or cherished may not later be in a position to act successfully, particularly in a fast changing world. Those who act in perfect accord with what had been done in the past and what they desired, consequently, may find that what they do is not adequate. An inherited past and accepted future might justify what is presently done, but do not do so in every case.

Humans know themselves to be different from all else. It is not clear knowledge or steadily maintained. Sometimes they do not recognize one another as humans; sometimes they destroy one another. Yet, all the while they face what is not human as forming an alien world. Occasionally, some see other humans as enemies, befriend animals, and try to live without any of the available and commonly used appurtenances. With the few items with which they are joined, they seem able to face the rest of the world somewhat as animals do. In fact, they have withdrawn from all others by a special act, while continuing, like the rest of humanity, to live their human bodies more or less successfully.

A manageable challenge, a common tradition, similar training and habits, and sometimes just the need to deal with what is beyond the ability of any to master, when combined with a steady purpose, often suffice to get a number of people to act collaboratively. An inherited, guiding common condition, governing their collaboration, helps determine what will be done. The inclinations, habits, training, and aims that had served them before lead them to engage in different interlocked tasks to bring about what none could alone. All the while, what they confront exists and acts independently of them.

Were external realities to act monotonously, people would gain little more, from a present use of the past and future, than a greater ease in action and an increase in their confidence that they were attuned to the world about. They are able to benefit from their use of the past and future to a greater degree, because they are able to accept or reject what had been and can be. When they do so in ways partly worked out then and there, they are thereby often able to achieve a better accord with changing, contingent occurrences than they had.

The vastness, power, implacable impersonality of the world inevitably makes it formidable. Inevitably people turn away from it, if only to be able to counter it in better ways than they individually could. They do so both as better prepared for what is steady than their predecessors were, and as able to benefit from the guidance of collaborations previously undertaken. The fact that they live in the present, not entirely oblivious of what they had confronted in the past, or of what they want to achieve, means that challenges later faced will be countered in the light of what is remembered and cherished. Animals also live in the present, have objectives, and learn from experience. But, unlike human beings, they do not confront their past and future in the present as part of a condition with which they will interplay as they adjust themselves to one another, and are thereby able to deal well with what challenges them.

People take account of one another and respond to common conditions while acting with reference to a common challenge. What they do, need not be deliberately done or volunteered. It may be enough at times for them to act within the scope of a condition in terms of which they are able to justify what is being done. Because a tradition may falsify or distort the facts, thereby making evident that the justification to which it contributes is not itself wholly justified, it needs supplementation by a separately grasped incipient future. Because that future does not show how it could be realized, it in turn needs supplementation by the past. The two meet in the present and enrich it, thereby constituting a condition which, by interplaying with adjusting men, helps produce a collaborative group of them.

Subhumans can learn from experience, and can act in new ways in the light of past experiences and what they discern of the incipient future, but they do not and cannot face justified positions and tasks. They are therefore unable to act in sanctioned ways. Were one to try to imagine a first moment when humans suddenly distinguished themselves from animals, one would therefore also have to suppose that they remembered something of that animal life, gave it a humanly pertinent form, and had it help justify acts to be carried out in the present. If the idea of a first moment of emergence from an animal stage be put aside as beyond all discovery and undeterminable either by argument or speculation, humans will have to be understood to have always been together in collaborative ways, and therefore to have always ordered their responses so as to interplay with sanctioning conditions. Collaboration will distinguish them from all other kinds, regardless of the size of their skulls, body size, posture, or an absorption in hunting, fishing, or farming.

2. ASSOCIATIONS

Individuals exist apart from one another, each unique and irreducible. When they collaborate, they privately make use of their bodies to carry out conjoint activities under common conditions so as to meet common challenges successfully. Did they do no more than this, they would have their joint activities sanctioned and controlled, but they would have no direct appreciation of one another as having anything in common beyond the ability to act in consonance.

Conceivably, a person could achieve the same degree of success by working cooperatively with animals. A large portion of the efforts made would then be directed toward making the animals function on behalf of or in accord with what people wanted to achieve. Tradition and prospects would still play a role but would so far not be used to make it possible to work together with other humans and thereby be in a position to deal effectively with what challenges all. If people had ever been at that stage, they would have reached it only after they had somehow discovered the advantages of collaboration.

Today, machines and technology could be used by a single person to accomplish what a multitude could not have in earlier times. This is possible because the machines and technology are the products of considerable collaborative efforts in the past. Used in the present, they may be taken account of by separate individuals. Since machines and technology could, in principle be used by others with benefit, machines and technology are evidently able to be treated as conditions enabling people to be collaborative. But such collaborations presuppose others already carried out. If only one person attends to a common condition which makes a collaboration possible, the stage of active collaboration can be approximated only through the individual's representative functioning, so as to bring about for all what they could in principle achieve concordantly. Collaborative action would not yet have occurred. No matter how good a representative anyone is, or how he or she does for others, collaborations occur only if a number together take account of the same conditions in order to deal jointly with the same challenges.

The new romanticism, exhibited by current existentialism, views technology as standing in way of the integrity and fulfillment of individuals. It does, of course, primarily impinge on humans as public beings and, so far, neglects what they are and need privately. But humans are no more private than they are public; all are public while they are private. They need to collaborate because they inescapably live in a public world. Technology provides good means by which this can be done efficiently and well. It is not to be disdained or dismissed. More, of course, is needed if people are to do what they can and should.

People are together with whatever there is, by being related in a common space and time, in other ways, and through a common ground. All originate from and continue to be connected with one another, and eventually disappear into that ground. That ground has been referred to over the centuries and in different cultures in many different ways—'Tao', 'The Receptacle', 'The Collective Unconscious', 'The Will', the *élan vital*, and 'Creativity'. All are somewhat overlapped by what I have called the *dunamis*,[5] to accentuate the fact that what is the ground of all is at once potential, powerful, and dynamic. However it be designated, it is acknowledged by everyone to be internally indeterminate. Some take it to be radically unintelligible. But if it were this, it would be so below the level, where anything could be grasped, as to be undetectable. Always available, it is a flux where distinctions are being constantly made and unmade, without ever achieving the status of separations. Some distinctions there, though, crop out in the form of separate, actual individuals, each with its own privacy. [6]

The different irreducible beings, which exist and act apart in a common space, continue to be together through the agency of their common ground. A portion of this is shared by human beings, enabling them to join together in distinctive ways. While distanced from one another, as surely as they are from nonhumans, they are more closely involved with one another than they are with anything else. A baby and its mother are usually intimately related, not only because they have taken particular account of what each is or might do, but because they have made a limited portion of the common ground their own, directly occupying themselves with one another through it, at the same time that they act through space and over time. And what is true of the mother and the baby is true of other humans, though rarely with such an emphatic stress on a limited portion of the common grounding *dunamis*.

The grip all men have on a common ground is intensified, both when they attend to one another sympathetically and when they face the world as alien. At both times, they adopt a portion of the *dunamis* as common and connecting, and thereby take themselves both to belong together and to contrast with the rest of the world. Because a portion of the ground has been held away from the rest, the surrounding world is seen to be alien, independently of the discovery that it goes its own way and jeopardizes cherished values.

The sympathies of people are not just feelings privately undergone and then brought to play in some accord with what is occurring elsewhere; they are the common ground joined to the relations connecting distinct beings. Members of a family sometimes take more account of the *dunamis* than strangers do, not because they have a more ready or greater access to it, but because when they turn toward one another they relax and thereby open themselves up more readily to the common ground. Whatever part of that ground a number of strangers share makes itself most manifest in crises and celebrations, when they form a single whole contrasting with all else.

Humans associate through their acceptance of a portion of a common ground while separating themselves off from the rest of the world. They set themselves in contrast with all else at the same time that they accept one another as belonging together. It is possible for them to act at cross-purposes, to hate, fight, and even kill, but they will still do so as fellow humans joined through the agency of part of the *dunamis*.

For a person to treat others as just things, that person must first believe he or she is not a thing, all the while continuing to share a portion of the *dunamis* with others, but not allowing this to play much of a role in what is done. This allows retention of a personal, distinctive human privacy, and an ability to act jointly with the others. A person's actions would be hardly distinguishable from those carried out by a number who work well together with animals, were it not that the human and the animals cannot act within the compass of a shared tradition and objective.

At one time, people act well together; at another, they may be in some disaccord. At both times, they are joined in and through a portion of the common ground, making them attuned to one another's presence and attitudes. They are associated so far as they are together in a common public space as well. Because they are together in both ways, they are distanced from one another and more or less intimately related. All the while, each stands apart from the rest as a privacy, acting in and through a possessed body, sometimes without taking account either of the public world or of the *dunamis*. It is because of that very privacy, radically individual and irreducible, though, that an individual is able to be a person together with others. This is only to say that he or she is a human individual, and remains one even when joined to others and merged into a part of the *dunamis* into which those others also merge.

Whether they wish it or not, people share in a portion of the *dunamis* and are thereby inescapably involved with one another. They can make use of it in different degrees and on different occasions, depending on the depth to which they penetrate and the degree to which they are acceptive of what they reach. The deeper they reach into it, the richer the intimacy they sense; the more acceptive they are of what they grasp of it, the closer they feel they are with others. An intimacy, not accompanied by the acceptance, has the quality of a blood-tie; an acceptance, not accompanied by the intimacy, yields nameless fears. The first is defied by antagonisms between those who are supposed to share the tie, and by bonds keeping them joined to others; the second is countered by reason and stable habits.

To focus on a portion of a common gound is to join with others in the acknowledgment of a shared contrast with all else. Were that acknowledgment to occur by accident, it might do so for just a short while, and never be repeated. It is in fact unavoidable. When insisting on themselves as individuals, all persons withdraw from the rest of the world, and at the same time intimately unite with some others. By emphasizing an individual distinctiveness on the way to joining the others, a person becomes part of a singular whole with them.

Because the *dunamis* is shared in by people, they are able to be associated. It is no less true that subhumans are involved with one another, even more immediately and effectively than humans are. The subhumans differ from the humans, though, not in the depth of the *dunamis* they can make their own, but in their openness to it and in its determination of what is done by them. Much of what passes for their mutual concern expresses only the way in which the common ground is diversely, though consonantly, effective in a number. What is appreciated—particularly what is encountered as sublime or awesome—also is more deeply rooted in the *dunamis* than humans usually are. The appreciated objects are encountered at the same time that contact is made with them below the surface, both of the humans and the objects. It is hard to know whether what is then reached is ever met at the depth where a number are intimately together, fighting for their lives or when peace is declared. Apparently it is. People who deeply love and sympathize, or share a common nameless fear or joy, seem sometimes even to be together at a still deeper level. The beautiful, awesome, and sublime never appear to be encountered with the warmth and intimacy that people sometimes emotionally achieve when they join one another unreflectingly and inexpressibly. But since each usually keeps a steady contact with others on a superficial, unnoted level, it is their experiences of beauty, and occasionally the awesome and sublime, that most often makes them take note of the presence of the *dunamis*.

A person can make use of the *dunamis* to achieve intimacy with some animals. When this is done, the animals are reached either at a level only humans can attain, or at one also available to animals. If the former, a human's involvement with them will not be matched by their involvement, and there will be a tendency to anthropomorphize them. If the latter, the person will be with them, but in a less intimate way than they can with other humans; it may then be supposed that people are not united in a distinctive way. If the former, one will tend to speak of a dog or horse loving him as he loves it; if the latter, of a dog or horse loving in a way no human could. At both times it will be evident that the person does not know what love is.

A contrast of humans with all else is no accident, momentarily and unexpectedly produced. It is the inevitable accompaniment of their intimate joining. It may not, though, be maintained long in a particular way. To assure such maintenance, humans must accept the contrast as definitory of themselves. If they do, they will form a distinct association. The contrast, at the same time, could be maintained by what is distinct from both humans and the actualities with which they contrast. If the contrast is then maintained in such a way that the humans are still able to be kept apart from other actualities, they will be able to identify themselves as belonging together. For this to occur, there would have to be a reality apart from both people and that with which they contrast. That reality is sometimes identified with God, and one is asked to take him to be the cause of humans existing together apart from all else. No one, though, really knows whether or not there is a God, or, if there is one, what he does. Nor do all people take themselves to be joined with others within the compass of a contrast accepted by them as definitory of their status as humans in a world where there are other beings.

An objectively maintained contrast is fixated by being embedded in a common place, a land that men together take to be theirs alone. To increase the assurance that such a contrast will be accepted in the same way by a number, it may prove desirable to go further and have some identify themselves, other people, or both, as beings who will maintain the contrast with all else and, so far, enable a number to be associated apart from the shared land.

If some people (or even just one person) were to take an objectively maintained contrast between humans and other actualities to be pertinent only to themselves, the others would have to be viewed as being part of the contrasted world. This would require the neglect of the ground they all share. Actions would then be directed at the others as in a larger world, and nothing more. The others would not be ruled, though they might be dominated and made to do the bidding of those who had accepted the contrast as distinguishing themselves from all else. Absolute tyrants, and those who take themselves to be Gods, set themselves apart in this way. As a consequence, they are unable to form a single group with the rest. At best, they are rulers for, not rulers of, a people, unable to be humanly together with those they govern.

Were a number to accept a contrast of themselves with whatever else there is, they would associate with no one else, thereby allowing themselves never to be intimate with more than a small segment of humanity, even while they joined others in distinctive ways. Both Plato and Aristotle supposed that something like this was desirable. Occupying themselves with the problems involved in having a limited number of virtuous people be effectively together, they viewed the rest of humanity as barbaric, beings of another order, to be treated in a different way, as not complete, true humans. Aristotle credited non-Greeks and females with the same human nature possessed by those he favored, but did not think that this required him to take them to be able to be functioning parts of a state. He could therefore speak of them as living tools, barbarians, or lesser humans, properly used by or subject to the supposed superior male Greeks. Plato's views were not as clear as Aristotle's on this issue, in good part because, apart from a special group which included some women, he took most of humanity not to be worth thinking about.

It is a fact that not everyone accepts the contrast between humans and all other actualities as definitory of a distinctively human association. Only those who do, though, and thereupon take other humans also to belong with them within a single contrastive group, will be able to achieve the status of representative sages, teachers or rulers who have the task of deciding and acting so as to benefit those others, as well as themselves. If they govern the others legitimately, it will not be because these contracted with one another or with them. People who are to become part of a group only through the acts of others are in no position to contract with anyone, since they are not yet sufficiently together to agree on anything. Only if they were joined in their own association before they were brought within some other, would it be possible for them to contract among themselves, or with other men.

People govern with at least a minimal legitimacy when they accept as their right or duty a contrast of themselves and those they govern with whatever else there is. If they accept those they govern as being humans like themselves, they can, together with or on behalf of these, accept the contrast as that which they intend to preserve, enhance, or insist upon. Despite the fact that they set themselves apart, they can then form an association with those they rule, bounding this off from the rest of the world, without precluding interactions with it.

The identification of some people as being subject to the same contrast that is accepted by their rulers may be so emphatic as to exclude other human beings living in the same city. This is the line that Aristotle took when he supposed that Greeks were superior to other human beings. An association limited to only some people, though, need not deny others complete human status, or deny that they all belong together in a single association, encompassing smaller ones. Any number of such smaller associations may have mature people as members, and have them together within the compass of a larger. Aristotle could have and should have distinguished non-Greeks from Greeks—and females from males—without taking them to be natively inferior human beings.

Well before there are governments, some accept as their own the contrast holding between just themselves and all other actualities, and thereby form a single association contrasting with these. The guidance, teaching, disciplining, and control of children is one primary way that process is begun. This is quite different from the training to which animals subject their young. Where the young of animals are molded to increase their chances of survival, children are brought within the compass of a contrast maintained primarily against the rest of the world and, sometimes at some risk to their survival, made more and more aware of what it is to be a human being associated with some others. All the while, the contrast between themselves and other beings will be sustained by some of them—or more objectively and less precariously, by the place in which they exist together with others—and if fortunate, by a place that is both cherished and objectively maintained, while being sustained by a common ground.

A contrast between humans and other beings is objectively and persistently maintained by a common place. To the degree that people are receptive to that sustained contrast, to that degree they are together as associated beings. If there is an emphasis on what is shared only by a few humans, there will be an inadequate sustaining of the contrast which separates all men and other actualities. The spirit characteristic of a few will then be lived through intensely, at the same time that the rest will be taken to be together in a different way.

In the absence of the *dunamis*, nothing would natively belong together with anything else. By accepting the *dunamis* at a depth not reachable by other beings, humans become aware of themselves as belonging together and, so far, to be so associated that they contrast with what is not human. When a number of them accept the objectively located and grounded contrast that separates them and the rest of the world, they form an association. Taking themselves to be able to express and make use of the common spirit better than others can, some among them may not only take the adoption of the contrast as their task, but will seek to alert others to the fact that they are associated. Those who do this are leaders.

Since a contrast is directed in both directions equally, it is distinct from a facing or meeting of a challenge. Collaborations and associations, consequently, are necessarily different. But they are not incompatible. Indeed, because they are not, they can be combined. When this is done by a number, a union may be formed. There, people are both intimately involved with one another and are able to work together, thereby producing an essential constituent of a commune, community, society, or state.

A combining of a collaboration with an association enables people both to work and belong together. They then not only contrast with other beings but may meet common challenges effectively. All the while, as individual persons, they continue to exist and function outside the union, with irreplaceable privacies living distinct, organic bodies. By privately expressing themselves in and through their bodies, they act in a common enriched present in a common place. Those in the union that is thereby formed carry out roles in some accord, and enjoy a kind and degree of intimacy they do not have with others. By combining the two sides, they constitute a common public life carried out as though they were cut off from the rest of the world. Were there no enriched common present and fixated common place, there would be no assurance that they would ever be involved with one another except adventitiously and momentarily.

Sometimes people collaborate very well but are poorly associated; they act effectively but have no feeling of camaraderie, no sense of being part of a single group. Sometimes they are strongly associated but collaborate poorly; appreciative of one another, they do not know how to engage in interlocked tasks. These deficiencies are functions of their failure to benefit maximally both from a past and a future, as well as from a fixated place. The failure could be reduced, as it is with subhumans, were joint activities and a common bond united in rather constant ways, no matter what the circumstance. But again and again people rightly minimize one for a time in order to allow for a good expression of the other. They always form some union, but its two components rarely contribute to its nature to the same extent, for any considerable time.

Occasionally, it is necessary to act primarily as part of a collaboration because a great danger is looming; sometimes it is better to emphasize the fact that people are associated since their shared spirit is becoming indistinct. Technology will sometimes help the one; crises, festivals, and celebrations promote the other. The technology enables rather limited collaborations to yield greater and greater fruits, but each generation has to learn anew how to share a spirit at the level that had once prevailed. It is also true that while people may fail at times to collaborate, they never entirely escape from their common bond. Although enemies are sometimes spoken of as being 'subhumans', 'animals', 'dirt', one still prepares for what they might do as humans, with private thoughts, wills, and plans which will be carried out in distinctly human ways.

People do not first collaborate or associate and then individually combine the two roles. These are always combined, because each person is inescapably singular, functioning in both ways at once. This is not yet enough to enable them to be persistently together. For this to occur a number of people must engage in collaborative and associative acts in ways which are in some accord. And if they are to maintain a steady course, they must use something beyond them all which will help them join their collaborative and associate efforts in certain ways rather than others. Their common enriched present and fixated place must be used to limit what they do together. This is best done when the present is enriched by the acceptance of a common ancestry and a prospective ideal glory, and the place becomes established as theirs.

People are never just collaborative, they are also associated; they are never just associated, being always collaborative. But one or the other may be overwhelmingly dominant at a particular time. Each, too, varies in emphasis independently of the other. As a consequence, the ways people are together will vary considerably over time, but for practical reasons, different variations will be ignored on different occasions as making no appreciable difference to what must be done to obtain what is sought.

Because people are always collaborative and associative they are always together. Because the collaborations and associations are produced by their making use of different determinants of their activities, the ways they are together will vary from time to time, fluctuating from the extreme where they are splendidly collaborative but with little common spirit, to the extreme where they have a strong sense of belonging together but do little to supplement one another's actions. In between these extremes, the two are more or less balanced. Nothing, so far, assures the achievement or continuance of this result. Only if people together are effectively conditioned can one count on them to act associatively and collaboratively in steady ways. So far as conditions are joined to them as together, they form a union. Societies and states depend on the presence of other, more independent conditions interplaying with such a union.

Collaborations, associations, unions, societies, and states arise neither by design nor necessity. Nothing prescribes that they should be present or that they should occur. They are 'natural', not because they are the product of people fulfilling their potentialities, but because people make use of factors already present, without deliberation or thought, to achieve what they otherwise could not—a distinct status as public beings, living together, persistently, effectively, and cohesively. No study of their needs or the course of history explains their groupings; account, instead, must be taken of the fact that people are conditioned by enriched regions of time and space, and inevitably interact with these.

Collaborations are promoted through the use of language, recapturing what occurs by taking the form of reports. Like customs, manners, and family ties, a language also adopts an aspect of the common ground, thereby presenting in a verbal form the fact that people are not only collaborative but associated. As both a means for providing reports and keeping people together, a language reflects the way they steadily unite their collaborative and associative efforts. Because a language is also useful for the expression of claims, experiences, surmises, and knowledge, it invites dissection and the formation of limited units having definite functions. Grunts and cries, shouts, groans, and gestures do not suffice (as they often do the members of athletic teams) to enable people to be in accord for long times, or to deal with issues of great range and difficulty.

The arts offer ways of expressing and introducing people to their common ground. Only incidentally do they promote collaborations. Expressed in a world where people are alongside one another, and subject to a common tradition, they both hold on to the common ground, and provide ready avenues by which it can be more profoundly experienced. Poetry and story are therefore able to do for associated people what daily prose does for collaborative ones, language being used by the poems and stories in somewhat the way paintings use colors and music uses sound.

Daily language fixates the common ground and turns it into a background for what is being said. Because the language is pertinent to much that is done, the background is able to play a role in determining what people do together. By means of the language, also, people are not only able to be associated and collaborative, but can express the fact that they had been associated and had collaborated before and are ready to continue to associate and collaborate in the future. By means of language, they are able to distinguish what is simply present and what has been introduced into this. History and plans are two outcomes of such efforts.

The recognition that a present objective moment sustains and is enriched by the past and future, and thereby enables people to collaborate by adjusting themselves in the light of what had been and can be, makes evident that the effective coming together of people does not depend on their individually making wise decisions to work together. There is no need to invoke some alien force—a sovereign, a market, or chance—to compel them to act in consonance. The recognition, also, that they always share a portion of a common ground, and therefore belong together, makes evident that they do not have to be taught that they are allied in ways and in degrees that other beings are not.

Whether they wish to or not, whether they know what they do or not, people always collaborate and associate to some degree, the one because they face challenges in a shared, enriched present, the other because they are intimately joined in a limited place, and there contrast with all else. Because they both collaborate and associate, whether they wish to or not, they are always joined in unions. This does not, unfortunately, prevent them from acting at cross purposes or from drawing apart, in hate or fear. The one occurs when the challenges they present to one another seem greater than those that nature presents; the other, when they allow what they experience on one level of the *dunamis* to get in the way of what could be experienced on another.

2. UNIONS

1. INDIVIDUALS TOGETHER

Collaborations and associations are separately constituted. Not entirely cut off from one another, they are still produced in different ways; what happens in one consequently may not entirely mesh with what happens in the other. Neither has power either to control the other or to join up with it so as to produce a single product in which both are maximized, or in which the results that each produces are added together.

People are affected by an enriched present and share in a localized common spirit. As a consequence, they can take advantage of what had been achieved and what is prospective, and benefit from the sharing of a common ground. Since they are unities, they are able to unite their collaborative and associative roles. Insisting on themselves, they combine their participation in a collaboration with their participation in an association, and thereupon become interrelated members of a union.

Were people to do no more than collaborate, they would be able to function as mere bodies, fitting their activities together in such a way that they might jointly bring about what none could alone. Were they to do no more than associate, they would be able to function just as privacies sharing a common ground. Because they both collaborate and associate, they are able to act jointly as bodies and as privacies. Equally, by expressing their privacies through their bodies, they are able to act as individuals who belong together and adjust to one another's presence and actions. That they participate in both collaborations and associations, they make evident when they carry out mutually relevant roles. The natures of these is determined primarily by the collaborations; their relevance depends primarily on the associations.

Roles are sustained by individuals and have reference to other roles carried out by other individuals, each making use of his body. A number of those individuals are thereby able to deal effectively with common challenges and to sharpen their contrast with some others. As sustained and quickened by separate, independent privacies, their roles are so many limited avenues through which they constantly make themselves be together as public beings.

Each person is affected by the ways others express themselves through their bodies, under the restrictions that their roles present. As a result, many are able not only to act with reference to something distinct from them, but on one another as already belonging together. To the degree that their roles are supplementary, to that degree are they privately sustaining, interrelated, unit members of unions. Their roles in the unions are agencies through which others are often reached, and of which account must be taken.

Because both collaborations and associations take place at the same time people are able to act through the medium of their roles. Because the roles are carried out by individuals who express their privacies through their bodies, they have a dynamic form. So far as the acts of each are begun and directed at others carrying out pertinent roles, they help constitute a common union. Individuals do not thereby lose their status as distinct beings, each with a privacy, expressed in and through a body.

People act on one another and on what is apart from all of them, in distinct and sometimes even in oppositional ways. Sometimes they remember, believe, think, imagine, and make decisions without providing any clear evidence that they do. Their responsibilities, obligations, inalienable rights, self-control, self-respect, self-mastery, and the like are private acts, which may or may not be given a public bodily form.[1]

The actions of people in and through their bodies occur without their losing the status of independently acting beings. Indeed, were they to lose it, they would not be in a position to assess the nature of the union in which they are together with others. They would also be unable to oppose it, or to act in and through it. As a consequence, they would never be responsible for what occurred there. At most, they would be only accountable, to be rewarded or punished because they were taken to be the sources of publicly desirable or regrettable acts.

Accountability is determined on the basis of whatever system of distribution of rewards and punishments prevails. It might not result in rewards for those who had responsibly begun a desirable public act; it might not result in punishments for those who had responsibly begun acts which were undesirable. Responsibility, with its accompanying innocence and guilt, its enabling people to be worthy of praise or blame, coincides with an attributed accountability, only some of the time.[2]

Infants, the disabled, the senile need to have roles ascribed to them, or must be brought within the compass of roles carried out by others. Otherwise, they would be denied to be together with others, except so far as they made accidental contact with other humans, or made unreflective use of the *dunamis*, their common ground. Although what they did might be treated as of minor importance in a world of significant action, they can still be members of a truncated union and be protected and represented by members of a better one.

Viewed as just a unity of a collaboration and an association, a union has the status of a network of roles in abstraction from the sustainings and vitalizings which originate in individual privacies. If, instead, a union is taken to be the product of individuals, expressing their privacies through bodies restricted to carrying out roles, it will be viewed as being no more than the outcome of a plurality of interconnected, privately begun acts. The former treats a union as a single bloc; the latter looks at the union from the position of individuals. Where the former relates a union to other unions and anything else with which the union interplays, the latter treats the union as the outcome of interlocked roles. Because a union is constituted by both collaborations and associations, it is a pulsating, limited, bounded-off whole of multiply related people defining a common value in which its unit members participate. A person is moral to the degree that his or her actions conform to the demands that that value makes on a particular occasion. At the very least, a union tells each to fit in with others; at most, it tells all to enrich and vitalize it by finding compatible places within it as so many sustaining, harmonized units.

As existing outside a union, a person, from the standpoint of that union, is a source of a unit in it. Whatever else that person does can then be treated as immoral if it goes counter to what the union requires, or as amoral if it is occupied with something else. The attitude is at the root of the views which take a whole to prescribe to all within it what is to be done, assessing every item according to the degree to which this finds a position that supplements and is supplemented by others.

From the standpoint of privacies, a union is desirable to the degree that it enables people to be together in public without loss to their rights or powers. So far as a union falls short of this, it is inferior to another, in which a common good is joined with the good of individuals, other unions, a society, a state, and any other complex of which the union is a component. Each of these goods is limited, requiring support and supplementation. Someone, therefore, who confined actions to meeting the demands of the union, though moral, would not necessarily be as good as was possible. To be that good, a person would have to be ethical as well, living in accord with prescriptions different from those which unions impose. Nothing less than a maximum satisfaction of all limited goods together accords with ethical prescriptions and is therefore good without qualification.

The unwillingness of some to accept the prescriptions their union imposes on them, defines them, from the standpoint of that union, to be so immoral that they are less than the worst of those who fit poorly in it because they do not know how to mesh their activities with those characteristic of others. The union itself may be seriously defective. This it will surely be if it does not contribute to the good of its members and support whatever is able to help it and them. But it will still define what is moral. Though its demands are not formulated explicitly, many of them are effective, and some are known by being expressed in public judgments made about character and acts performed.

Since there are many unions, there are many moralities. To assess them in relation to one another, account must be taken of what is ethically required. This measures the good of a union—and everything else.

A collaboration makes it possible for people to deal with challenges too great for any one alone to meet satisfactorily. A contrast between an association of themselves and others provides them with an identity as humans together. Because a union joins a collaboration and an association, it enables people to be readied both to meet common challenges and to stand apart from all else. And since those in a union are role-bearers, they are so far directed toward one another, with bodies sustained and used by their distinct, individual privacies as outside that union.

The world continues to threaten and intrude, no matter what humans do. It will not be gainsaid. Not until enough of it has been brought within the control of humans, and thereby is made to function as a continuation of themselves, as their sustenance, tools, and material, will people be able to devote themselves to living within a union, and whatever complex this helps constitute. They will then collaborate, not only for the sake of mastering something otherwise beyond their individual powers to deal with effectively, but to take advantage of whatever they can of what is available. They will also accept their contrast with all else, both to mark themselves off from others and to enrich the meaning they already possess as belonging together. If they are not yet at that stage, or if they have to abandon it because of circumstance, they exhibit a comparatively unspecialized meaning of a common humanity, and have to turn toward one another in fresh ways so as to be able to attend elsewhere together.

Only those who have managed to bring within their control all that they need do not have to turn toward one another to deal effectively with various challenges. No one is in that state. Again and again, people must carry out interlocked activities and so far be both mutually supportive and associated. Since, at the same time that they are so together, they exist apart as unduplicable privacies, they are able to insist on and carry out their roles. Each acts independently of the others, expressing an independent privacy; all act in some consonance as well, through roles interdependently vitalized.

What union would be best from the standpoint of those who form it? The question subdivides into several. Two are immediately evident. What union would be best from the standpoint of individuals as privacies; what union would be best for individuals as lived bodies?

Each person, while a member of a union, also stands apart from it, able to carry out an accepted role. As so standing apart, each is able to assess both the morality produced by the joining of a number, and the limitations to which their activities are thereby subject. Evidently, from the standpoint of their privacies, a union should at least preserve whatever values each possesses, and go on to enhance all of those values in harmony. No one, though, exists just as a privacy, standing away from all others. Each expresses a distinctive privacy by living a body. The control and utilization of this enables each to become a public person, enriched to the degree that the union enables him to benefit from the acts of others.

The roles people have, defined as they are as the beginnings and endings of collaborations and associations, may not coincide with the ways in which the bodies are lived. From the standpoint of the lived bodies, a union has value to the degree it enables those bodies to prosper; but the roles in that union may be too narrow, too restrictive, too confused to be correlatives which mesh well with one another.

The value of a union does not depend on the possible or actual benefit people do or can obtain from it. It has an intrinsic value by virtue of its possession of an inherited past, a common prospect, and a common ground. Individuals gain from being in a union because they make their own that part of the past and future the union preserves, thereby extending their experience indefinitely. They benefit from the union, too, by sharing in the ground it demarcates, thereby extending the range of their usual associations. The union, in turn, gains from people living their bodies, since it thereby acquires a plurality of avenues from which insistencies radiate, thereby making that union a vitalized whole. The best of unions enables individuals to supplement one another as effective bodies belonging together, the individuals giving it in turn a strength and meaning reflecting the nature of their mature, joined, and well-expressed privacies.

It is not often that people try to have what from their standpoint would be the best of unions. Sometimes they fear to expose their weaknesses or fear to be rejected or misunderstood. Sometimes they try to reserve energy for other tasks. The value of other ways of uniting also keeps most from devoting themselves to producing or sustaining only one. Quite often they do not promote the best of unions because they do not attend to the issue, or do not know what to do; they just constitute some union or other by unreflectingly more or less fitting in with one another and sharing a common spirit. A union, which allows individuals to express themselves maximally, is obviously superior to one in which people are able to express less of themselves, or to do so less harmoniously.

Different people contribute to their unions differently and in different ways. By virtue of their locations, energies, knowledge, training, and abilities, some of the others are able to provide supplements, thereby making possible the carrying out of particular activities beyond the point and to a degree otherwise possible. The fact prompts the question whether or not all should benefit equally from what is then achieved.[3] Evident injustice is done when differences in their contributions are due solely to differences in interest, to selfishness or malevolence, and the outcome distributed equally. But there is also injustice done when differences in their contributions are due to differences in native capacities or opportunity, and the outcome is divided proportionately to the actual contributions made.

It is not hard to deal with the first of these injustices. Those who contributed less, when this is less than they could have contributed, are not to be treated in the same way as are those who not only contributed more but contributed all that they could have. There is difficulty, though, in deciding what is to be done about the second kind of injustice. If those who contribute less because of lack of ability or opportunity are to receive proportionately less than others who are better favored, inequalities will be hardened and perpetuated; the disadvantaged will be kept in a disadvantaged position, though their initial disadvantage may have been accidently or unavoidably produced.

It does not help much to say that those who are advantaged are to receive benefits, provided that the others are thereby also benefited, unless something is also said about the degree to which these are to be benefited, and at what cost to the others. Since it would be unjust for the less fortunate to benefit only to the extent that they are able to contribute, leaving all in the same relative position as before, it is necessary to conclude that the less favored are to be benefited disproportionately in such a way that the distance between them and the others is shortened, and eventually eliminated. In effect this is to say that a just distribution of what is possessed by a union, promotes an equality of status and opportunity among all those who, within the limits of their relative abilities and circumstances, exhibit the same degree of effort.

The disadvantaged, Rawls rightly remarks, are to benefit disproportionately in order to close the gap which birth or opportunity happened to produce. The idea presupposes that people are intrinsically equal in nature, and that there is a certain amount of effort all will make. It is a viable idea, even if one refuses to follow Rawls in imagining an ideal situation where mature, intelligent, decent people think of such a situation as one they will promote. People of that type are in part the products of unions and societies, not preconditions for them. They are also supposed not yet to be in states with institutions designed to achieve justice through the impartial execution of common laws; they are not even taken to be in actual unions or societies, since these take some account of differences in ancestry, color, gender, and the like. A justice, that intelligent decent people agree should prevail, is not the justice unions define, societies demand, or states do or should concentrate on. It is no more than the justice that is pertinent to a number of separate intellects imagining a world that never was or could be. It would nevertheless not be wrong for those in government to attend to the outcome of such lucubrations when they forge and administer laws.

While avoiding futile efforts at determining the differences in the intent, desire, willingness, and devotion that people might express, one should specify the nature of the contributions that are to be made at determinate positions and on well-defined occasions, and use the result to measure what is to be done. Those who fall short of what they are then required to do are to be treated as not having contributed what they should have, and therefore not to deserve the benefits to which they otherwise would be entitled. This procedure is roughly followed daily, in determining the rewards to be received for performing assigned work. It is partly acknowledged in the slogan, "From all according to their abilities, to each according to his needs," though 'needs' is too odd a term to use for referring to all the goods that are to be received. Knowledge, aesthetic experience, play, self-respect, honors, contemplation, inquiry, friendship, and creativity are not 'needs' in the sense that food, shelter, and health are, but they can still be properly said to yield distinctive and eminently desirable satisfactions. The need for food, shelter, and health, of course, have to be satisfied, if the other goods are to be diligently pursued. To know what all are, and their relative importance, one must have some understanding of human nature and human rights.

Another meaning of the question, what union is best, attends to a union in relation to other occurrences. No reference is then made to its members or to anything else that the union might serve. So far as a union needs something else in order to be or to act, its existence and functioning will depend on what might not work well on its behalf. The best of unions is self-sufficient, possessing whatever power it needs and whatever it must have in order to continue and to prosper. Maintaining itself in the face of external pressures and the demands of privacies, it enters into different situations, not only with minimal loss, but as able to enhance itself.

For utopians, the best of unions encompasses perfect individuals. Yet these are thought to benefit from being together. Together as a consequence of their free activities, they supposedly gain by sharing in a common venture. A paradox is lurking here. Were these individuals truly perfect, they would have nothing to gain from a union. No one who could gain from it can in fact be as excellent as utopians require humans to be.

The best of unions encompasses public persons. These have privacies. Since no union controls privacies, none can involve people to the degree they could conceivably be involved. If it is to be constituted by humans at their best, it will therefore have to encourage them to be together through the realization of themselves in better, mutually supportive ways. The more it gets them to be alert to their private powers, the more is it able to have them come together as they should. It will then not only be self-sufficient, effectively maintaining itself, but will be better than any other union that could be constituted in that place and at that time.

Actual unions are connected disjunctively. That fact, and the fact that people have limited attention spans and energies, precludes them from being fully part of many unions concurrently. The disjunction of unions, though, could be converted into a conjunction, but at the price of reducing the status of one or more of the unions, since the best possible conjunction will at times require such limitations.

Unions operating independently of one another come into conflict, forming a harmonious set only if one or more are there in restricted forms. The best possible combination of the best unions necessarily has some of them reduced in status. One or more may favor a few individuals and require some limitation of all, so that they can coexist harmoniously. At one moment, in some or all of the unions, it may be better for a person to be involved in purely private activities as well, since these will allow for understanding and planning, assessment and the assumption of accountability in ways which could promote better joint activities. At another moment, it may be better to be absorbed in some particular work. Sometimes it is better to be in one kind of union rather than another, or to be there with greater concentration and effort. For all to be all they should be, moreover, excellence must be achieved both privately and publicly. But that outcome is rarely, if ever, attained, and it does not seem likely that it will be attained by many.

"What is the best union?" exhibits another meaning when it is specified as "What is the best union from the standpoint of every union, each occupied with itself being at its best?" No priority is here given to any one of the unions. Since all cannot be satisfactorily occupied at the same time, it is necessary to determine what the best union would be were all jointly but not entirely satisfactorily maintained, or if they were so ordered that the maximization of one promoted the maximization of others, then or later. Conceivably, a large loss to one union at a particular time or on some occasion might make possible greater gains by other unions, with a consequent equal or even greater gain by all—but what is to be sought is such a gain bought without such a loss.

Still another form of the question depends in part on the answer to the last. It asks about the nature of the best union from the perspective of a combination of all the previously distinguished ways of having an excellent union. The answer requires either that the other unions be adjusted to one another, or that a reference be made to some governing measure outside them all, provided perhaps by ethics or civilization. But if some one outcome is preferred over all others, a variant of one of the previous, not altogether satisfactory answers will be needed.

The desired answer requires a reference to a union that encompasses all those unions whose members splendidly carry out essential and desirable activities. Though dependent on, that encompassing union will be maintained in contradistinction to smaller unions where some other people associate and collaborate effectively. Lacking guidance and control by what in principle could keep it at high pitch, such a splendid union would eventually have to look to a society or state for help. This, of course, is also needed by other unions. One kind, a commune, though, seems to need something additional to what a society or state could provide, without its being able to avoid inclusion in and control by them.

2. COMMUNES

A union is formed when a number of people join their collaboration with their association. Some among them may take it upon themselves to determine the ways the others are to collaborate, or they may suppose it to be their function to maintain a contrast on behalf of all—or both together. Whatever occurs, the union will have a distinctive nature and career, and be bounded off from whatever else there is. Those in it will be inter-involved through the agency of the roles they there have, making the union a self-contained whole, functioning in contradistinction to other unions and the private beings which constitute it through their expressions.

A commune is a union in which collaboration is minimized while the contrast that distinguishes those in it from what else exists is accepted by some or all, and the whole maintained in contradistinction with what is faced as having a superior value. It is a union where people are intimately together, primarily in order to focus on that value. In place of an emphasis on a collaboration to enable them to master what is beyond the capacity of any, a commune thus emphasizes the contrast of some with all else, while getting them to attend to what could accept or ennoble, but also could and might destroy or enslave them.

Different kinds of communes focus on different common splendors.[4] In religious communes this is identified with a supreme reality. For scientists, over the ages, despite fundamental changes in theory, it is embodied in a theoretically knowable cosmos. Economists and historians take it to be ingredient in a humanized, intelligible world, able to be well understood within the limits of a common acceptance.

The most common of communes are the religious. Some of these take the value, with which they contrast and to which they owe their presence, to be embodied in a personal God. Others take the value to be sustained by a more impersonal, self-maintained source, or to be the locus of whatever is real or good. Those in each have a common faith in the existence and functioning of a sustainer, and identify themselves as having a value relative to and perhaps dependent on it. If there is no such sustainer in fact, the commune will remain unaffected, since people are together in it only as long as they believe that they are sharing in some great sustained value. The contrast they accept as their own, though, would then have no objective status; it would be both self-created and confined to the commune, revealing the commune to be a union which had embellished its contrast with the rest of the world, with the supposition that it had a value relative to some other reality that, on the hypothesis, does not exist.

In a commune, people focus on a supposed sustainer of a value greater than their own, and act together mainly to carry out common practices. As a consequence, they are parasitical on others who collaborate and thereby effectively get, retain, and transform what is needed, if the commune is to be able to carry on its work. The people in the commune, in reply, may and often enough do claim that what they are able to obtain from their concentration on a sustained superior value will redound to the credit of those who emphasize collaboration, or who are otherwise intimately concerned with one another. There is no deciding the issue as long as each side insists on looking at the other from a vantage point that is peculiarly its own. One way of assessing both of them is to envisage what they are and do from the position of a nation. The superior value that this cherishes answers to a common spirit, but the people there also conspicuously collaborate. Consequently, the activities that it demands are like what they usually produce in unions, but with a greater emphasis put on what sets them off from all else, as having a distinctive, shared, glorious past, and a distinctive, common, idealized future.

Different communes come into conflict because of what they demand on behalf of their distinctive values. These are usually taken to be superior to all others and sometimes even to preclude the values the others cherish. A religious commune, existing within the confines of a nation, requires its members to act together so as to conform to special demands at the same time that they are required to so act that they protect and promote the nation against demands of other nations, and even against the religious commune, so far as what this prescribes is not in accord with what the nation insists upon.

A nation takes a great value to be embodied in itself and consequently acts as a completely self-enclosed whole. This still leaves it able to be brought within the scope of other ways in which people are together. It can be subjected to societal or state control, compelling the abandonment of its traditionally sustained symbols, festivals, dress, cuisine, and language. Its members may nevertheless still continue to emphasize their association, sometimes for long periods, and act together in obstinate opposition to the demands of a dominant society or state.

Since its members' acts may fit well together while they share in a common spirit, a nation may not need supplementation or control. Still, it could profit from well-formulated rules and guides, expressly promoting common purposes, making provision for posterity, and providing neutral, detached agencies for adjudicating conflicts. Other communes, also, could benefit from a governing control, particularly if they have no well-defined direction and are being constantly made and remade. But if a society or state tries to compel a commune to abandon deeply entrenched, traditionally sustained symbols and practices, it will risk a defiance which, if successful, may extinguish the common spirit that so effectively kept the members of the society or state in considerable accord.

Were a commune free of all excesses, were it to deal even-handedly with every one, even those who were lax, who did not participate, or who did not participate fully, constraints externally imposed on it might be as unnecessary as they were undesirable. But just as a commune can provide a desirable check on the values and actions emphasized by a society or a state, so it may need to be restrained by them to prevent it from interfering with the exercise of the people's rights and opportunities to prosper. Rarely, or for long, though, is a commune able to ignore or go counter to what a society or state insists upon, for the one makes provision for collaborations which may sometimes be desperately needed, while the other adds express formulations and an effective control to a commune's acceptances and its members' submission to the commune's nature and course.

A tradition emphasizing great religious and national figures, and pointing toward a glorious ideal future for all, can promote the interests of both religious and national communes. If may even promote their unification and thereby produce a religious nation. This backs national interests with religious commands and gives religious practices a nationalistic tone. The religion will be institutionalized, taking the shape of a church with intermixed worldly and otherworldly concerns, while the nation will be glorified, with its people made to act on behalf of a great destiny. As a consequence, the religion will tend to exist mainly in words and rituals, while the nation will be credited with a future that, most likely, never could be.

In recent times a good number of historians and philosophers have suddenly become aware that scientists, no less than the religious, and those who form a nation, are members of distinctive communes.[5] An overemphasis on the supposed precision of scientists' claims, their controlled use of evidence, and their astonishing successful predictions, prevented earlier thinkers from recognizing that scientists also fit in with one another and share a common ground for a while, thereby affecting the meaning of their major claims. It does not, of course, follow that what scientists together maintain is not objectively so, but only that what they affirm is maintained by members of a distinctive kind of commune, giving a distinctive flavor and value to what is said about what is known.

Just as a religious commune may exist in contrast with a sustainer of a supreme value, so a scientific may exist in contrast with a cosmos, objectively sustaining what is communely maintained. This idea is rejected when the scientific commune is taken to be thoroughly affected by the course of history, and thus to have its truths both confined to a present and qualified by what is accepted from the past. Such a rejection could not, of course, be warranted unless it were more than a reflection of what the members of an historical or philosophical commune had for the time agreed upon. It could therefore be maintained only if, against itself, it allowed that people could formulate objective, constant truths in their commune, or if they could exist and know while outside any. If the first, the fact that inquirers operate within a commune will not necessarily jeopardize the constancy and objectivity of at least some of the truths they affirm; if the second, what they did, as affected by the commune, will not be all that could be achieved.

A similar issue arises when one attends to what can be affirmed in a society, about which the relativity thesis is most persistent and widely held—apparently most persuasively. For the present, it suffices to observe that the contention of the relativists rests on the supposition that scientists (and other inquirers) are together primarily as associated, under limitations determining the range of their collaborations. But even those in a religious commune, where they are intimately associated to a degree they usually are not in others, can affirm objective truths. They may, of course, without sufficient warrant, accept the existence of a sustainer of some supposed supreme value, and may do this as the outcome of the way in which they there associate with one another. But nothing in the way that they associate necessitates that they can only arbitrarily hold that there is something behind a cherished value. The fact that an association differs from the associations of scientific and other inquirers does not endanger the truth of what is claimed in it; there could be a sustainer for the value, and it could conceivably be known or reasonably assumed. [6]

While in a commune, people also collaborate if only to deal effectively with what challenges them. What is there done in act can at times also be expressed in speech. Their association will then affect what they say, all the way from a minimal innocuous degree to one that is overwhelming and able to preclude the clear expression of what they collaboratively seek or achieve.

In the unlimited community of which Peirce spoke, scientific inquirers act concurrently while sharing in a common spirit. He apparently thought that the truth then obtained was a function of the way the scientists supported one another in their investigations, rightly assuming that they maintained that spirit independently of what they happened to discover. If, with Thomas Kuhn, the shared spirit were treated as a common desire to conform to a dominant view, an association of inquirers would be taken to be subservient to a collaboration. That assumption inevitably leads to the denial that scientific truth holds always. Once it is recognized that the spirit common to inquirers is not a function of a collaboration, and can be joined to it to produce a constant union where discoveries can be persistently maintained, one is in a position to affirm that the common spirit of inquirers, instead of necessarily relativizing what is discovered, may help invigorate it, and make it likely that it will be preserved and utilized everywhere.

To this it might be objected that dominant theories and meanings change over time, thereby qualifying and relativising whatever these dominate and govern. That is to overlook the fact that what is dominated has a nature of its own, and need not lose its distinctive nature or meaning because it is joined to those theories and meanings. The result of such a joining is produced by both. Instead of showing what is acknowledged as fact fits in with a theory that happens for the moment to be to the fore, and survives and passes away with it, both what is acknowledged and the accepted theory exist apart, precluding either from being a creature of or wholly subject to the other.

What people learn, through experiments and other inquiries into particular matters of fact, are not instances of the theories they entertain. The same theories joined to different observations, and the same observations joined to different theories will of course yield different results, but that does not necessarily compromise the truth of either the theories or the observations. Even when observations are guided and structured by theories, they deal with what exists apart from those theories. Nothing warrants the supposition that what exists apart is just brute material without an intelligible nature. To suppose that is to suppose one knows what is confessedly not knowable and what (because on the hypothesis whatever was claimed was a function of a theory) would have no being of its own. The fact that what was dealt with yields this result and not that, when confronted with a theory, shows that it has a nature apart from the theory. It is knowable, at the very least, as able to give the theory specificity, and to provide it with an opportunity to have a career in an objective world. What is learned in a scientific or any other kind of commune can be about something existing apart from any theory, even one used to discover and articulate it.[7]

Sometimes the same objects can be approached from the position of different theories and be articulated in quite different ways. Relativism says that there is no way of choosing among the alternatives and that one must be content with accepting what a commune agrees upon. Some theories, of course, will not include what others can. If none encompasses all items, a number of theories must be tentatively entertained, until some more comprehensive one is produced. Both the entertainment and the production will be due to the members of a commune who, while belonging together, attempt to act collaboratively, fitting their ideas of the world together somewhat in the way in which people, meeting a physical challenge, try to mesh their different efforts so as to constitute a single organized joint activity.

The contrast with others that some people in a commune adopt for themselves, and perhaps also for the rest, has a value between that of all members there as belonging together, and of a superior value that is yielded to by them as so associated. Because the members must also collaborate, if only to do justice to what is demanded of them by the accepted superior value, they usually must add to the limited ways in which they collaborate in a commune. What is directly done is then produced through two distinct efforts. The result has the association and collaboration externally joined and, so far, is different from what would otherwise be produced. What is so brought about by associations and collaborations externally joined will, more often than not, differ considerably from what is produced through an immediate merging, as the members mutually carry out roles.

The less that religious and similar communes provide for the necessities of life, the more surely must they overlay the association they unreflectingly produce with the collaborations which circumstances require. To the degree that the collaborations are separately carried out in order to deal effectively with what is needed, to that degree a commune will be produced, not directly by people acting both associatively and collaboratively through the agency of interlocked roles, but by their adding to their association whatever collaboration they happen to engage in.

Self-defined and independent in their ways, religious communes have to keep within the limits a state imposes, or suffer for their intransigence. But their primary concern is to submit to a sustainer of supreme value, and to have their members privately conform their lives to accord with what that sustainer is taken to require of them. Although they may view the requirements that a state imposes as vexatious and wrongly intrusive, they cannot ignore or reject them without risking penalty. On its side, a state can do no more than prevent the carrying out of religiously prescribed activities. So far as it does this it successfully opposes the practices of a religious commune. The denial, though, will not necessarily result in a destruction of the religion, since this can continue to be maintained through the persistence of individual belief.

There are state religions. They express a devotion to a supreme being in ways which meet the requirements of a religious commune and satisfy a state's demands. There are also religious communes which are tolerated so far as what is there done not only does not conflict with what some state requires, but which limit the activities of their members in ways that the state prescribes. Both kinds of religion may satisfy many; neither need pervert sincerely held beliefs. Each, though, risks pollution and the carrying out of irrelevant and corrosive and what may turn out to be self-destructive practices. All religions are forced to yield to political and military pressures; they can survive with something like their initial spirit only by risking rebuke or suppression by powers which demand other expressed beliefs and acts.

A society provides independently determined governing conditions for a union. It may also interact with a religious, scientific, or other commune, particularly if this had added on, to what was directly achieved, supplements taking account of the need of the members for what will enable them to act well together. If the addition is made by the very people who form those communes, they will incidentally produce another commune by joining their initial appreciation to a collaboration, or will be incidentally encompassed within some union primarily occupied with other issues. Monks, with their vineyards, farms, and presses, illustrate the one; scientists, working on behalf of corporations or a federal government, illustrate the other. At the very least, both spend some time acting in accord with the demands of a complex constituted of their original commune and externally determined, demanding governances and, so far, fail to live simply as members of a commune.

An economy, in which goods are produced, interchanged, and utilized in a series of market adjustments of supplies and buyers, functions in radical contrast with associated individuals. But since these may unquestioningly accept the same medium of exchange, trust one another, keep their practices in accord with tradition, and the like, an economy may also function like a commune. But where a commune may allow insufficient play to collaborations, an economy will tend to neglect associations.

When associations are belatedly considered and joined to collaborations, an artificial commune is produced, close in nature to the kind of economically determined class that Marxists take to dominate over all others in a capitalistic world. The Marxists seek to abolish, or expect history to abolish, such limited communes, leaving people primarily associated and their collaborations attuned to the result. What the Marxists seek would approximate the kind of commune that an all-comprehensive religious commune of workers might produce. In place of the religious commune's subservience to a God the Marxists would, though, have people see themselves at the service of a perpetual, peaceful civilization. People today, according to Marxism, live in artificial communes in which limited, favored, economically determined collaborations are externally joined to a universal association, and the available power is used to make every other collaboration yield to what a dominant, economically determined one demands. People are thought to collaborate today primarily in an economy, and on uneven terms, and therefore to be unable to produce a commune appropriate to humanity—a humanity that they already constitute through an at least implicit association. The existent communes—'classes', Marxists call them—in which individuals are today associated and collaborative, are said to wrongly limit the range of proper collaborations and associations. An economically self-sufficient, world-wide union, it is claimed, would result were all people to free themselves from unfair economic practices and freely join the two.

Marxists want people to be freed from the undesirable, limited economic collaborations that now prevail, so as to enable all to act in a way that matches the association in which they in fact participate but which is now partly obscured by self-serving propaganda and debilitating exploitation. Limited communes, for Marxists, are artificial because they are limited. Even the proletariat it is held exists and always will exist in a limited commune and must therefore, after having replaced the capitalistic, have its commune give way to an all-encompassing and more perfect one in which a present, latent universal association is joined to a now precluded universal collaboration. A necessitarian history, it is thought, will bring this about, pushing relentlessly to the point where the universal association already formed but which is now obscured, is joined forever to a universal collaboration now blocked through the selfishness and greed of a dominant few.

The Marxists are surely right in remarking that people are associated, and that economic collaborations are limited to those who compete for common goods against other collaborators. But they join this view to the not altogether compatible suppositions that there is a necessary course to history, and that a dominant commune is to be overthrown through the intelligent use of force. History, though, is more a domain of contingencies than necessities. Nor are violent revolutions always the best ways to clear a path leading to important objectives.

A collaboration, produced through the imposition of force, can yield only an artificial commune, one in which the collaboration is externally joined to an association. A true commune requires the collateral production of both. Were that commune just suppressed and distorted, as some Marxists seem to suppose, the removal of the causes would allow it to appear. But it would then be found that some in it were primarily collaborative, not as economic beings but as scientists, artists, or technicians.[8] Such collaborations, though, are limited in range. But a commune embracing all humanity will never do justice to what people are and need, if it does not also respect the limits of other smaller communes where people work and belong together, guided by great objectives of little or no economic value.

Were the most comprehensive of communes to embrace all humanity acting collaboratively as economic beings, there would still be a need to have smaller communes, where some act together as inquirers or creators, or as religious, social, or political beings. They would be associated in these in intensive, desirable ways, at the same time that they worked together to bring about what could benefit others as well. To the usual complaint that the Marxist does not make adequate provision for the exercise of individual rights, it is therefore necessary to add another, pointing to the failure to allow for the existence of freely constituted limited communes whose members collaborate and associate to realize noble ends which might result in benefits for all.

To this a Marxist might reply that once an economic commune of universal scope is achieved, various subordinate communes would not only be produced but would necessarily flourish. Until then, it is believed, they can be no more than the products and creatures of a dominant economic commune, or of what is distorted and corrupted by this. But other communes have their own origins and careers, and can flourish inside many different larger ones. Scientists form communes within others, and operate across the borders of these. Mathematicians, artists, and even philosophers and historians come to the same conclusions despite their living in different nations, societies, and states. And, as we shall see, there are non-violent ways of getting to the stage where all people are collaboratively together while being well-associated. The defenders of both communism and capitalism credit an economy with more importance and power than it in fact has.

A commune, that is to embrace humanity properly, awaits a time when people will see themselves both to belong together and to need to act in consonance there, as well as to live in more limited, independent ways, all occurring within the compass of the other. An all-encompassing commune, in which a number of smaller flourish, is in fact glimpsed at times. People occasionally contrast themselves with every other kind of being, at the same time that they act together with some degree of harmony, without ceasing to occupy themselves with tasks requiring only a few to share in a common spirit and to adjust to one another.

3. COMMUNITIES

Communities and communes are readily confounded. Both have collaborations and associations joined together. Both define a morality to which people are supposed to conform. Both can be included in and include other communities and communes. Both can occur within societies and states. And the one may sometimes imperceptibly give way to the other. Still, they do differ, and deserve to be sharply distinguished. In a commune, members collaborate so as to serve some superior value. In a community, instead, they do so in order to maintain themselves against what else there is in the world. But there, too, an inherited tradition and a common purpose are used to provide a guide for what is to be done.

Collaboration for a commune involves a distribution of efforts, all valued because sanctioned by a superior value. The members of a community rarely make reference to such a value. And when they do, it is usually because some or all are also already functioning in a commune. The members of a commune are characterized by a common devotion; those in a community put emphasis on what is to be done to have it continue and prosper. A monastery is a commune; a well-run hospital a community.

The members of a community associate in order to be effective. They use their past and prospects to help them in that task, thereby making a good union possible.[9] Since what is primarily sought is to continue the past and maintain the purpose in an indifferent or hostile world, collaborations are there carried out in such a way that what had been is preserved and perhaps enhanced, and what should be is promoted. In place of the largely rhetorical character of the language used in a commune, the members of a community emphasize clarity, accurate reports, and effective interchanges of information. But since they tend to over-emphasize their need to function together successfully, the community readily becomes rigidified and stratified.

A community can coexist with a commune. Indeed, the very people who constitute the one may also constitute the other. That in fact is the ideal cherished by some large Japanese enterprises. But since their purpose is to promote efficient work, they eventually make a commune of workers subservient to a community of collaborators. A reverse emphasis occurs everywhere in times of crises. Workers then yield to exhortations on behalf of communes that they make sacrifices of their time and wages.

In place of a communal camaraderie, a community demands that members fit well together; in place of a commune's acceptance of a superior reality, a community emphasizes a readiness to act together. Supporters of athletic teams are like the one, joined together as members of a commune through their acceptance of its supposed splendor; the members of a team, instead, form a community, devoted primarily to bringing about a successful outcome. Continual defeats may not daunt the one, but will unhinge the other. Displays of temper and poor grace disenchant the first, but may still be accompanied by a maintenance of a community by the second.

A society finds communes more congenial than it does communities, since it need only make a place for the commune's values within the compass of its own. A state, instead, finds communities more congenial, for it is primarily concerned with making possible a more harmonious way in which people can act well together. But just as a state can provide a place for communes, so a society can provide a place for communities. When it does, the society takes the communities to be doing in limited areas what it itself is doing in a larger.

A community's members supplement one another in the light of a past and a common future, and what must be done if they are to exist together, apart from all else. Because there are so many things that require prolonged attention and the mastery of special skills, a community readily breaks up into a plurality of subcommunities, each doing part of what is required by all. If some of the subcommunities demand great abilities and training, meet important demands, and are hallowed by long traditions, the larger community will tend also to order the subcommunities in a hierarchy in which they are to engage in quite different activities. A community may even include a subcommunity of people who do nothing or who waste valuable resources, but who enjoy a preferential status, precisely because they are free from the necessity to do what is contributive to the welfare of the whole. That paradoxical result, so well exploited by Veblen, points up the fact that a community may also find room for communes credited with cherishing great values.

There are tight-knit communities and loosely organized ones. In the former, various subcommunities are well-calibrated with one another and together help promote the functioning of the larger. A greater leeway is given to subcommunities in those communities which are loosely organized. The result may be superior to what is attained in one where requirements are inflexible and the different parts related by a planning committee or an armed force. Sooner or later, though, loosely connected subcommunities will come into conflict, or at least will fail to mesh well, with a consequent loss to the whole. Just as likely, sharply defined and controlled subcommunities can become over-rigid, without much sense of a common purpose. Absence of a direct concern with the whole, of course, need not preclude great contributions to it, any more than sharp definition need preclude flexibility.

A planned community life, carried on within the limits of a larger, must be allowed some autonomy; independently constituted and maintained subcommunities need regulation. Neither will be effective unless the members of the larger and smaller community understand what the other needs and deserves, and act accordingly. Sometimes independence has to be stressed, sometimes regulation. Which and when can be determined only by one who understands the nature of communities and how subordinate ones should function within a larger. That understanding has to be backed by a power able to carry out in practice what reflection endorses. Governments sometimes assume that task. But well before and apart from the existence of such governments, it is both necessary and possible to order subcommunities in relation to one another and to the community in which they occur. Ideally, a tradition of successful interplay will govern what all do, and will be backed by a rhetoric bringing the values and achievements of a commune to bear.

The members of a community belong together through their possession of a portion of a common ground. Because that possession functions in part under the lead and pressure of their collaboration, the members of one community will sometimes act with a stress opposite to that exhibited by those in others. A balance, somewhat like that exhibited by a nation, is achieved by a community in which ranks or roles are so related that what is done in one is supported and enhanced by what is done in others. A team does this, but usually only when composed of a few members, all engaged in well-defined, limited, and interlocked activities. To approach the balance that a well-functioning nation exhibits, one has to interconnect hierarchically ordered tasks and permeate them with a common spirit.

Although both a nation and an organization may unite the same factors, they do so in different ways. A nation is a commune in which people who share a common ground, past, and ideals are able to work well together; an organization is a community in which those who work well together incidentally share a common ground. In a nation, people carry out roles alert to the common spirit that is to be joined to their collaborations; in an organization they focus on hierarchically ordered tasks, and incidentally share a common spirit. In both, the collaborations and associations are joined directly, without reflection, but from different positions and with an emphasis on different factors.

An armed nation and a military dictatorship, from opposite sides, come close to being properly characterizable either primarily as communes or communities. Neither form of commune or community is desirable, since it allows for little or no independent private lives, little or no public liberty, and few, if any, independent, subordinate communities and communes. Such evils can be avoided and their advantages preserved in other societies and states; there, members of various communes, communities, and combinations of these, are better united and both guided and controlled.

Since a commune acts with reference to an acknowledged superior value, in the form of a divine command, a noble destiny, or some other great value, leading the members of the commune to see themselves as belonging together, and since a community faces an ideal prospect yet to be realized, no identification of the two is possible until a good, already sustained elsewhere, becomes the very good that the people jointly incorporate. A commune will then take it upon itself to carry out community functions as well, while a community will treat some great value as being also maintained elsewhere in a better form. There would still be something gained were they to check one another to constitute a social union, under the aegis of a society or a state; they would then be so guided and controlled that their members would be able to act persistently and well together in the light of what is important for them.

In the East there is a tendency for some sages to minimize the community, because of the community's comparative neglect of the common ground its members in fact share. A community is taken by some of them to be only a device or momentary stopping point on the way to extending the range and probing the depth of a commune. A perfect commune would, it is thought, require only minor regulations in order to continue and flourish. Most Westerners are not persuaded. They fear what seems to be the nonrationality, the open-endedness, the emotional appeal made by evoking a shared spirit rooted in a common ground. Reciprocally, there is a disposition in large parts of the East to distrust the rigidifications and formal nature that communities tend to encourage. It is illuminating, though, to note that while Rousseau's and Marx's concern for a commune is expressed across the barrier of an acknowledged community, supposed by them to be wrongly but actually in ascendancy, some Eastern sages treat communities as illusory or distortive, due to the failure of those in them to free themselves from confusions, errors, and self-interest. Eastern political organizations, governments, and required functions, though, prevent Eastern complexes from being viewed simply or even primarily as communes.[10]

People sometimes strongly and effectively refuse to act in harmony. But both communes and communities deny them the right to publicly and independently express whatever they privately entertain, particularly if they do so in order to oppose what they themselves had together helped constitute. A community, with its hierarchy of positions and of tasks that are to be performed, is usually well prepared for that refusal. It is not surprising therefore, to find that deviations are dealt with there by individuals occupying important posts, acting on deviants in effective, prescribed ways. These are so dealt with, not because they do not share in a common outlook, but because they do not act as required.

Both societies and states may encompass communes as well as communities. Both may be encompassed by communes as well as by communities. A commune treats an encompassed society or state as requiring a stable underpinning; an encompassing community demands that they spell out roles and tasks.

Both society and state may intrude into encompassed communes and communities and interfere with their functioning. If they do, the result will be a loss of intimacy and coordination. So far as a commune is denied autonomy, the common spirit that it nourishes will be attenuated. If, instead, a community's integrity is not respected, its efficiency will be reduced. The intensity of a feeling of belonging together is diluted with a growth in the membership of a commune; the establishment of an order of interlocked tasks tends to become rigidified in a community. But it is also true that an uncontrolled spirit makes insufficient provision for the demands of individuals, just as an uncontrolled market makes insufficient provision for the multiple ways in which people joined, even within that limited sphere.

In order to credit corporations with rights and duties and to open them to taxation, a statute of limitations, and condemnations and punishments, the United States has credited them with the status of 'quasi-persons', i.e., units to be treated 'as if' they were persons. The fact provides a good illustration of the way in which a state may both permit and limit what organizations do. Since such organizations are legal entities, they cannot exist in the absence of a state. But that still allows for other organizations—clubs and guilds, for example—not only to exist inside a state but in societies as well.

Both those organizations which are under the jurisdiction of a state and those which exist inside a society may defy these or may function as instruments for them. So far as a defiance is successful, the existence of the state or society is jeopardized, and the organizations are no longer able to benefit from activities which can supplement and support theirs, steadily and deliberately. And so far as a state or a society turns organizations into instruments, these will function mainly as momentary halting places where parts of the work of the society or state are carried out.

Separately maintained communes and communities need to be encompassed with benefit, within separately maintained societies and states. That is not likely if the resulting complexes are not dealt with from a position outside all of them. In the absence of this, the communes and communities, as well as societies and states, soon find themselves in a conflict that usually cannot be resolved except by the exertion of greater force by one of them.

No matter how effective a community or community is, and no matter how completely societies and states control what they encompass, none ever reaches men's privacies. It is from their privacies, though, that people express themselves through roles and in hierarchically ordered positions; from there they assess what they together constitute; from there they attend to what might conceivably harmonize all the different ways in which they are and could be together.

What each person privately begins achieves determinations by being channelled through his body and by becoming adjusted to what others are and do. As together, people become subject to conditions maintained apart from them, and with which their unions interplay. How there could be such conditions, how they could be effective, how they could interplay with the communes and communities people form, and with what result, are central problems which must be mastered before there can be an adequate knowledge of either society or state.

Account must be taken of communes and communities, for these in different ways help determine what it is to be moral. If people form a commune, this will dictate how they are to serve a common focal good. If they form a community, it will prescribe the degree to which they are to act together. When the two different types of demands are joined, people will be moral so far as they accept the guidance of a superior value so as together make this be an integral part of what they jointly realize. No matter how desirable and excellent that result, it will still be less than what should be, since it will still not take full account of people as private beings, each with individual rights and dignity.

There are many moralities. Each falls short of providing an adequate place for the values that privacies possess and which they insist upon in the limited forms that their bodies make possible. But some moralities are better than others, because they are constituted by people who jointly express multiple dimensions in harmony. The best will still fall short of providing a place for the value each person should have as a private individual being. It will also exist in some opposition to the conditions which societies and states introduce. Consequently, it will not conform completely to the spirit and stability that these emphasize and, so far, will be alien and inconstant. If people are to become moral beings who are also well-habituated and effective, they must, while still functioning together in a union, become full members of a society and a state.

3. Society

Social unions are produced by people acting both collaboratively and associatively, with tendencies toward the status of communes and communities kept more or less in balance. Were the people not collaborative, they would not function together. Were they not associated, they would not be joined through a shared spirit. As members of a union, they are consequently together, joined efficaciously and interinvolved. There, they privately live their bodies in some accord with one another, at the same time that they remain distant from and act independently. Each is replaceable and yet unduplicable; each has public duties and private rights.[1]

People form a social union only so far as some of them are connected over a limited space, while being merged with a common ground at a depth below that in which they would be indifferently together. When the space they occupy extends beyond the point where they are intimately together, their union has more and more the character of an aggregate of independent items. Still, living in a limited area does not preclude them from being indifferent or antagonistic. Since the depth at which they are joined is greater than that where they usually interact, they continue to be involved with one another, despite the fact that they may be distant in space, or may not even be acquainted. They never though can become so intimate that they cease to be unique beings, who live independent, privately grounded lives.

When and as a social union is formed, people accept it as theirs, and hold it in contrast with the rest of the world. So far, its separation depends on them, and the union they form has no status of its own. This it can have only if the contrast, that the people provide in the act of forming the union, is maintained independently of them, and is thereupon able to be a contrast with which they can interplay. The tradition and prospects that people collaboratively use are also countered as existing apart from them; there is no society unless the tradition and prospects function as part of a present condition.

Tradition and prospects qualify and are sustained by an objective present moment. Individuals are thereby able to act together toward a common challenge in the light of what had been and could be achieved. Concurrently with and independently of the establishment of such an enriched present, the contrast that distinguishes people from other actualities obtains an objective status by being embedded in the space that the people together occupy. The space is thereby converted from an occupied extension into a territory with which the people interplay.[2]

The enriched present accompanying a collaboration, and the enriched region accompanying an association, together constitute a single governing condition, because and so far as individuals act both collaboratively and associatively and thereby constitute a union. The union, and a governing condition with which it interplays, together constitute a society when the enriched present has an indefinite temporal extent and a place is sustained by a primal ground. The fact deserves closer scrutiny.

Tradition and a prospect are together sustained by a present moment; a contrast is sustained by a territory. Together these sustainers define a condition to which a union is subject, and with which the union interplays. Objectively constituted, but not planned or deliberately instituted, the condition provides a common governance for those in the union.

A tradition is an inherited past joined to a pertinent future, maintained and effective in the present.[3] When joined to a spatially maintained contrast, it provides a condition with which a union can interplay and thereby constitute a society. No examination of the members of the union will make evident the nature of the interplay or its outcome. The union may continue to exist and function apart from the interplay, and the members of that union will continue to act as separate individuals, but some of the things they do will also require a reference to the ways in which they affect and are affected by what functions independently of them.

There is no deciding that it would be desirable to be governed by present, past, future and territory together, or by someone who makes use of these in his own way. People are together subject to a common condition, whether or not they wish it, think about it, or take it to be represented by somebody. Societies exist, not because humans have recognized their desirability or have been forced into them, but because their unions are subject to inescapably effective, pertinent conditions sustained by portions of an objective time and space.

No one, of course, is entirely passive. Each individual is not only insistent but offers some resistance to whatever might act on him or her. Each, too, has habits and expectations, memories and hopes, a personal past and future which preclude any common condition from being simply illustrated in an individual's actions. Space and time also have their own structures, and the bodies in which they are joined have their own natures and modes of action. Each is therefore able to contribute to the nature of what they together produce.

A society is the outcome of the interplay of an insistent union with an insistent condition. Those in the union are affected by the condition at the same time that it affects the ways they there act. All the while, they continue to exist outside the confines of that union, and outside whatever this helps constitute. To find the sources of their individual contributions to the ways they are together with one another, one must trace the maintenance of their roles back to their privacies.[4]

We know of no person free of all social influence.[5] Hermits and the cloistered carry out in limited areas, and sometimes in distorted ways, what had been obtained from society, if only through the mediation of others. Adults, teachers, and peers socialize the young, giving them direction and control, and helping them acquire habits of behavior and speech. Even those whose practices deviate considerably from what others expect from them, continue to remain part of a society, through rejections having various strengths and natures or, more often, through the insistent intrusion of the others into their lives. Because every person lives within a society's confines, each inevitably acts in some consonance with what this requires. Even those who shun the company of their fellows, and find peace in living with animals or in harmony with nature, are part of a human society to which other kinds of beings do not belong.

Almost every kind of union of men, and almost every type of condition to which people are subject, has been called "social", and their combinations "societies". Conforming to that practice would lead to the blurring of important distinctions among such complexes as families, clubs, and teams, on the one side, and states on the other, particularly since all are tradition-bound, have relevant futures, and embrace people who act more or less collaboratively and associatively. The error, though, is not as disastrous as that involved in the nominalistic insistence that all groups are fictions. To suppose that, is to leave unexplained how people could be effectively conditioned, controlled, and governed, as they in fact are. The opposite, idealistic claim that only complexes are real cannot provide for the fact that these could be guided and controlled, and sometimes rightly opposed.

Human beings have their own integrities and abilities to act; unions have their own natures and careers; societies and states control and are resisted. Each is affected and limited by the others. Humans are confined and controlled by their unions, but not without making a difference to them. Their society, too, is a product, constantly renewed through an interplay of an insistent condition with their insistent union. Each side affects the other while yielding to it, if only to make maximum use of it. Were either not insisted on, it would fail not only to make a difference to the other, but would not be able to withstand the other's insistence. Resistance is insistence answering a counter-insistence.

Some views trace all power back to individuals; others locate it in unions; still others credit it to a governing condition. Many more locate it in society. Were individuals alone to possess it, "family", "commune", and other ways in which people are together, would be shorthand for the presence of a plurality of separate, effective, segregated individuals, and no complex of union and condition would have a role in history or outlast the particular individuals who happen to be together at a particular time. Were all power located in unions, people would not be able to oppose or change them, and there would be no contribution that tradition, prospects, or a territory would make to the existence and functioning of a society. Nor could all power be provided by a governing condition, for then both unions and those in them would be unable to resist, interplay with, or qualify it.[6]

The rejection of the supposition, that power is initially possessed and exercised only by individuals requires a rejection of the familiar formula, "All power comes from the people". Were it supposed that the people's power is lent to the condition under which the people will thereupon live, it would have to be a power that the people authorized, and any authority possessed by a union or a condition would be derivative from this. Morality, tradition, and prospects would then be without force except so far as men lent them theirs, and thereupon were able to be used to make the people do things they would not otherwise, and to prevent them from carrying out what they might want to do. People are compelled, but not only by what they delegate to rule them. The claim, therefore, that people are compelled only by what they empowered is not only not supported by history, but is not tolerable as theory. Could it be justified, human beings at one time could make future generations inescapable hostages of decisions which these might regret; or each generation would have to be viewed as freely deciding to be constrained, perhaps along the lines their ancestors followed, since this is what their tradition requires. If "people" be taken to refer to humans collectively, moreover, the contributions of individuals would be ignored, while if it were taken to refer to them distributively, there would be no acknowledgment of what they help constitute. A related, but different set of difficulties follows on the supposition that all power originates with unions or societies, since this implies that humans have no power of their own.

A union makes use of the joint power of individuals as a counterfoil to the power of a common condition.[7] When the latter is used by some to govern others, both the governed and the governors may continue to be members of the same union, but they will carry out different kinds of roles, sometimes in opposition to one another, with the one acting mainly as members of the union, and the other as mediators for the condition.

A weak condition interplays with a union as surely as a strong. In different societies and at different times, either factor may have a leading part. Some of the powers that a union and a condition independently exercise will be combined in the course of and as a consequence of their interplay, to become the power of a society as a single complex. That society may merge with or repel other societies, and qualify the ways in which its own union and condition act apart from one another or from it.

Because the past and future are different moment after moment, conditions, unions, and the resulting societies are necessarily different moment after moment. For short periods, no appreciable change in natures, functioning, or membership may be discerned. And when the differences are great, there often are accompanying constancies or slow changes which lead one to view the society as having a continuous and even an unchanging existence. Related observations are pertinent to other complexes. Although none has an identity excluding changes, any one may persist for an indefinite period. When any is examined at two times far apart, it is likely that what occurs at those times will not be credited to the same entity, unless there is a discoverable constant, operative throughout, or unless it is possible to pass from one to another occurrence over a series of actual or imagined intermediaries, differing only slightly from one another.

We speak of the same family existing over fifty years—even though there have been births and deaths in the interval, some members have moved far away, and the family's fortunes, residence, and style of life have changed radically—because it is possible to pass from stage to stage in its career without appreciable break. Although we are likely to say that a family ceases to exist when the parents die and the other members are widely dispersed, we are not inclined to draw that conclusion if the children continue to live together, or if their parents keep in some contact with them. The decision to draw the line in one place rather than in another is arbitrary. A similar decision usually lies behind the claim that a society has continued or has given way at some particular time to some other. If it is persistently guided and limited by some prospect, the presence of a series of linked stages in it can be accounted for. Whatever the decision, the society will be constituted by the interplay of a union with a condition in which a distinctive present and place are joined.

A number of additions to this observation should be quickly made. People and objects exist both outside and inside unions and the range of social conditions, as well as outside and inside the complexes which the unions and conditions constitute. They may exist for longer or shorter periods than a particular kind of union, a condition, or a complex does. These all have power enough to act and limit one another. The present, too, of each factor is actually indivisible, though of course able to be divided mathematically. This limitation is not as obvious as the others.

Unions and conditions stretch over a plurality of shorter extensions in which specific acts occur. Both the larger and smaller extensions are indivisible. The shorter extensions, as part of a larger, occur together. But, as extensions of particular occurrences taking place one after another, they occur outside the larger.[8]

Outside a union, people have their own distinctive, undivided presents and places. But when they join together, these become part of the indivisible extensions of unions, societies, and states. As members, people are locatable in the single present and place of the unions, societies, and states of which they are a part and, so far, cannot, without losing their membership in them, be separated from those presents or places. Each individual also has a status distinct from what he or she has as a member of these. Located within a larger space and time, each occupies and thereby possesses an individualized present and place. An identification of individuals with members will consequently confound different ways of being and functioning. The classical observation, that no one is truly human outside society (or another complex) needs the addition, "No one is fully human as just a member of a society (or other complex)".

A move away from a particular place to another does not take one away from or toward a condition, though it may take one to a place where the condition does not operate in the same way. Nor does it bring one closer to or further from a union or a society. All three fill out places, but those places are not alongside the places occupied by people. Locating a union, a state, a society, or any other complex, requires a reference to the limits within which these occur in a larger complex, not to places in the public, neutral space (or time) occupied by bodies. One can take a complex to stretch over the occupied regions, but it will do so as an indivisible unit somewhat as an organic body indivisibly extends over the region where its parts are.

Individuals are unit members of unions. On their becoming members of a society, their privacies sustain, possess, and are expressed in new ways, and, as a consequence, they can be identified as publicly determinable origins of what is publicly done. Each, though in fact more than just a unit in a union or a member of society, also exists apart with a distinctive privacy, able to insist on itself and thereupon able to help constitute a union, or pass judgment on both the union and the society of which the union is a constituent.

As a member of either a union or society, a person may be held accountable. But no one is responsible except for what he or she privately begins.[9] Not every act is publicly expressed; even the most cohesive of societies may be privately and adversely assessed. It is in privacy, too, that each person engages in such activities as believing, imagining, and wishing in ways which may have no social import.

Security, stability, planning, and clarity are promoted when a condition dominates over a union. The union is thereby limited. That result may be acceptable to those who provide the units of that union, since the union may have failed to be as protective, steady, responsive, or organized as they need it to be. The condition insisted on against such a union may, so far, be acting on behalf of the individuals who together constitute the union, even though that condition sets limits to what they and their union may do.

A society is constituted by a union of people and a distinctive condition, itself the product of two factors, an ideology and a territory. The ideology provides an ordering for what occurs, in terms of its consonance with what is commonly cherished; the territory enriches a present place with an inherited past. The ideology and territory together constitute a homeland, a valued temporalized region.

In the absence of an ideology there would be no ordering pertinent to a located union; in the absence of a territory there would be no hallowed historic land to which those in the union belonged. The one absence would leave a union without the benefit of a common stable conviction; the other absence would leave it without a needed stabilized identity. Both together enable a union to face a region of space as a conditioning locus of an honored past and an ennobling future.

The homeland (and therefore the society produced through the interplay of the homeland with a union), is located in a rather stable region. The present time of a society (like the presents of other kinds of reality), gives way to other presents, not always of the same magnitude. Whatever their magnitude, the successive presents are always part of a time distinct from the time that is germane to other kinds of occurrences, and is always divided into presents singularly appropriate to the distinctive kinds of beings and occurrences existing there.

Different kinds of occurrence take place in presents having different magnitudes. If all had the same length, some occurrences would be completed and become past before others came to an end; alternatively, some would take so long that smaller episodes within them could not be related as earlier and later. A step occurs in one present; a walk occurs in a larger. As encompassed by the walk, the step is only before or after other steps; dealt with as a single unit with its own beginning and end, the step occurs earlier and later than others.[10] A pure present, an empty moment which gives way to another of the same kind, is an abstraction from a present that is a part of what actually occurs.

The length of a commonly accepted present is determined daily by the positions of the sun. The entire day is also recognized to be an inseparable component in a longer present marking a season or its recurrence. Because these different presents are filled out by distinctive kinds of activity, they have different boundaries. Were they just merged in an ongoing time, there would be no distinguishing those presents, and they would not be appropriate to distinctive kinds of occurrences. Although recurring natural events, like the reappearance of the sun and the return of the seasons, are distinguishable in relation to one another and provide useful measures for a host of occurrences inside and outside society, no society attends to them alone, for they fall short of providing all the stretches which are appropriate to actual social activities.

A society and state are not objects in nature. Astronomical bodies and places on the globe, as part of an indifferent nature, do not play a role in human affairs, except so far as they prompt people to act in certain ways. Such prompting is possible only so far as they are relevant to people,[11] at the same time that they continue to be and act without regard for them.

As long as it is recognized that what prompts people and unions to act in certain ways is an objective condition relative to them and, with them, yields what is other than an astronomical or geographical item, one assumes toward society and state the position of a reasonable human being, which is to say, one who does not believe that astronomy or geography suffice to account for the outcome of private acts or for social or political occurrences. Existing together in a union, people are conditioned there. Some among them may have the task of presenting and urging the condition on others. But whether or not the condition is so utilized or is, instead, taken just to be grounded in nature, it will make demands on the union. Since all the members of the union are subject to the same condition, this must have a status distinct from them, as well as from the union which they constitute.

Those who dictate the times for the beginning or ending of certain kinds of events make use of their memories. The events are also captured in stories and songs, and are aroused by particular symbols. But whether they be located in some occurrence, in the prompting that results, or even in the memories of individuals, they affect a union only so far as they affect it as a whole and, so far extend over its entire range. That present is qualified as well by the future as expected or desired. This plays a role in the minds and affairs of individuals; it is also pertinent to an entire union and so far conditions it.

Unions are in territories which have distinctive values and meanings for their members. Here, too, memories, individual and collective, play a role, leading to the treatment of a particular place as special. Possession and use, and eventually separate claims to portions of the territory, intensify and focalize the memories. What is remembered is that territory as having a distinctive meaning. It is in fact viewed as being particularly relevant to the present, with its inherited past and governing future. A homeland is a territory interlocked with an enriched past- and future-oriented present. When a union interplays with it, they together constitute a society.

When one or more of the components of the condition that interplays with a union to constitute a society is missing or is present only in a minor way, the outcome is defective or truncated. When we speak of a society as "roving", "displaced", "decaying", and the like, we tacitly acknowledge it to be unduly limited, and thereupon open the way to a consideration, and perhaps also to the production of a more comprehensive, perfected society.

A society has a nature and career of its own, distinct not only from the natures and careers of its interplaying condition and union, but from individuals as having the status of units in the union and the status of members of the society. As members, they are more than units, and less than private beings living their bodies; as publicly functioning together with reference to, but not necessarily in accord with what society requires, they are distinguishable from themselves, both as private persons and as units. Although it is better for them to be members of a society than it is for them to be merely units in a union, or to be directly subject to effective conditions maintained apart from and in some opposition to them, they will not be properly dealt with as long as they are not treated as existing in these other ways as well. Even a society from whose presence and operation they gain what they should have and which they could not otherwise obtain, does not give them all that is needed for their prospering, for people cannot be at their best unless, in addition to being members of splendid societies, they exercise mature privacies, expressing themselves fully and excellently apart from, as well as in and through their individualized bodies.

A societal condition is effective, but not to a great extent. It may focus only on crucial activities, without having these stated clearly and well, or without having them consistently backed by well-directed power. The career of a society depends also, and often mainly, on the unions people form, and how these react to a governing condition. If a union yields too much to a governing condition it becomes routinized and dull, inviting individual and joint outbreaks of spontaneity, with accompanying disruptions, possible violence and disorganization, interspersed with rigidities, superstitions, and neglect.

Sooner or later, people make their individual interests and emphases manifest. Even when they act in routine and uncreative ways, they so affect their union that they disturb its course, thereby making evident that they have independent distinctive powers. Sometimes, too, they jointly engage in novel and aberrational activities. None is ever so caught up in a union or so absorbed in a society that he cannot and does not express himself in ways which challenge the roles he has in a union, the union itself, the operation of a common condition, and the functioning of the society.

The manner and degree of insistence that a union exhibits against a condition's, depends on the units people provide, while its effectiveness depends in part on the degree of resistance it encounters in its interplay with the condition. There is, though, no sure knowing how insistent or effective a union will be, and no advance knowing of the result of its actions. In any case, the result is a society, with its own distinctive nature and dynamics.

When a union dominates over a condition with which it interplays, a common morality is in ascendancy. This may be enough to lead people to endorse the resulting society. While their failure to act so as to satisfy the prevailing condition may then be taken to be of little moment to themselves, or even to the society, the societal condition could still be commended for providing a possibly desirable, but perhaps not very important stability.

When a condition is too restrictive, unduly breaking people's spontaneity, and tying them too tightly to the past, a prospect, or a place, it will usually be repelled or modified by the union, even one in which people are together in not very supportive ways. Usually, too, the less people are coerced by social insistent demands which are insensitive to their changing moods, needs, and interactions, the more are they inclined to act as the society requires.

A condition may be distortive or its dominance may be excessive, standing in the way of a desirable morality. And there are times when a union has its units poorly joined or when it dominates over a social condition, with little benefit either to itself or to the condition. Since in a society, in which a union is dominant, morality plays a major role, to approve of that society is to approve of the way in which the morality reduces the alienation that the societal condition might otherwise introduce, and to ignore the loss involved in having the people subject to a common but independently constituted governance.

Those who endorse a society in which a condition dominates over a union and those who endorse the outcome of an opposite emphasis are opposed to one another. Both reject intermediate positions as involving unnecessary and irreparable losses. In some particular cases, no compromise will either be desired or needed. But so far as a society is worth having, both condition and union are to be expressed as fully as they compatibly can be. Neither rightly precludes a full expression by the other.

When the past is made into an integral part of a present condition, thereby enabling the past to be effective as well as pertinent, some sanctioned practices may serve as reminders of what should not have

been done, and are not to be repeated. That is fortunate. Not everything that is long-established is worth preserving. Slavery, child-la-
bor, the subjection of women, and sanctioned bigotry are part of a
regrettable past. They are to be made part of the present only as
having negative values, leading people to act in ways different from
and sometimes opposite to those which their predecessors followed.
The resulting society may be pertinent only to aspects of the individuals and may provide only partial satisfactions for those who express
themselves there, but if the union is excellent, those in it will still be
able to benefit from one another, and often from the society that the
union helps constitute.

There is warrant for objecting to a society in which a condition
dominates over a union, in which a union dominates over a condition,
and even one in which the two are more or less in equilibrium, if
they then prevent individual men from maturing and obtaining what
they need and rightfully claim. On behalf of their right to be and
continue, to express themselves and to be fulfilled, people properly
fault unions, conditions, and society, so far as these do not do all that
these conceivably could to benefit them. To know what is then to be
done, of course, it will be necessary to know what all three are, claim,
and can do.

Conditions and unions are pertinent to one another, with independent existences and ways of functioning, each insisting on itself
and therefore resisting the incursions of the other. Never able to
exclude or reject the other entirely, each inevitably accommodates it
in some way and to some degree. The outcome is worked out then
and there. Sometimes anticipatable in the large, it is never fully predictable; at every moment it contains what never had been before and
will never be again.

Conditions and unions rarely affect one another to exactly the same
degree for any length of time. It is often possible, though, to reduce
or increase the effectiveness of one or the other until neither serves
mainly as an accommodating locus. Interplaying factors may, of
course, mute one another, so that neither is well-expressed. They
may both be at their most effective, thereby assuring that their values
will be respected and perhaps preserved in the new unitary society
that their interplay produces, or they may balance one another at any
one of an endless number of stages in between a full expression and
a radical muting of both. Only if the two are fully expressed and
joined without loss is it possible for interplaying factors to constitute
a perfect society.

A society, even a perfect one, yields less good than individuals need and could have, for these have privacies societies can never fully satisfy. The failure is inseparable from whatever good the society provides, and is to be compensated for by acts carried out there by the people themselves and by what they are able to achieve in other complexes. To be as excellent as a person can be, each must function splendidly—and continue to live a good private life, but since what each needs cannot always be obtained alone, each must act together with others.

In themselves, individuals are privacies; by themselves, they live their bodies; in a union, they are interrelated units; in a society, they interact and belong together under a common present governance as a people with a common homeland. Although there will be some who have advantages and enjoy benefits denied to others, although some will do or need more than anyone else, they can all be members of the same society. Those who are repressed and insurgent, and others who are abused or neglected, are no less and no more its members than are those who fit in well, who are favored, who prosper from it, or who support it. When it is said that the members of a society lack elementary liberties, are lax, rebellious, and the like, a comparison is tacitly being made with the members of other societies, or the society is being measured in terms of a standard requring members of the society to be assessed differently.

Because both conditions and unions have natures, powers, and values of their own, it is desirable to have a society in which their opposing insistencies are so balanced that neither cripples the other. When a balance is achieved through a muting of both insistencies, or by the two meeting in less insistent forms, the resulting society is defective for, though it will have its own nature and members just as surely as any other society does, neither the common morality nor the condition will be there expressed to the degree that is theoretically possible and worth having. A society, constituted by a condition and union in which each is maximally supported by the other, deserves endorsement. It is not to be approved solely because individuals benefit from it.

There is no need to choose between the desirability of having individuals prosper, and the desirability of having a society as excellent as a society can be. Individuals should be excellent; so should their society. People should gain from their public activities, and their society should help them prosper. In addition, a society should be helped to preserve cherished achievements and to be perfected. Each should, without detraction from its own possible success, promote the other's. Since each has distinctive needs, when there is a conflict between what is required by one or the other, some adjustment by both will usually be required.

It is not difficult to see why those in dominant positions demand that others sacrifice themselves for the good of society; they expect to be among the chief beneficiaries. It is not difficult to see why those who are over-restrained or denied opportunities demand that a society serve them; they expect to have some of their neglected desires satisfied. It is, though, hard to see why any theorist concerned with understanding what is and ought to be should ally himself with one side or the other. Either people or society may be favored at a particular time, so as to achieve a better balance between them or as a necessary step on the way to getting such a balance. One justification for such favoring is provided by showing that it brings about what is maximally good for both.

A society has its own nature. People can gain from being its members, even when it is seriously defective. Their joint activities are subject to a common condition at the same time that the society is vitalized by their activities. Ideally, each gain supports the other. By living in a society, its members are in a position to benefit from its persistent, unitary career. If they also help their union to interplay with the societal condition, they provide desirable aids.

A good parent is not without merit. A strong family has a value other than that which is possessed by any of its members, each able to serve as an agency through which the others are enhanced. What is true of the family, is true also of a societal condition insistently acting on, while being affected by, a union. Each can gain from the independent activities of the other. This might not only help improve it but may even add some of its own value to it. It is also true that the individuals, whom Aristotle, Hobbes, and Hegel took to be seriously defective if they existed alone, have values in themselves. If those individuals also have instrumental functions, that will still allow them to have their separate dignities, and even to contribute to the value of what uses them.

When a condition or union is maximally accommodative, it provides a locus for the other. If mutually accommodative, they will give one another a status within themselves under limitations independently provided. Neither side can guarantee that the outcome of the interplay will be a balanced unity, or that this will not limit the other's independent activity or reduce its value. Usually, though, the resulting society is biased toward and will favor one of the factors, largely because this had a dominant role in the interplay.

Conditions and unions make no decisions or efforts; they just express what they are. When, through their interplay, they constitute a society, they may be less than fully effective, and may be joined as though they were restrained. In fact, the rest of the insistencies of each may have been spent in resisting the other. The result might still be approved—even though it is less than what might have been achieved. When a balance is produced, the result may still be found to be wanting, because one or the other, or both factors may have had to be restrained in order to produce it. No matter how excellent the resulting society is, it will have different degrees of importance from the standpoint of the individuals, the union they constitute through their interaction, other unions, combinations of unions, conditions, and more comprehensive complexes.

Objection to a society, even one produced through a combination of factors which act in harmony, is always justified, for it never embraces all that is good. Limiting the insistence of one factor while favoring the other, even in order to produce a better society, will make one lose part of what had been achieved and to fall short of what is still needed. No matter how excellent the outcome, this will therefore not deserve unqualified endorsement, any more than the worst of imbalances deserves unqualified condemnation.

Sometimes people are rather cavalier in their assumption that only humans and what interests them have value. Although other beings do not differ from humans only in degree, some of them are sensitive, many are active, and all are distanced from nothing, with natures of their own, making irreducible claims. To be is to have value. Even what does not benefit others, is not great compared with them, or may injure and destroy, cannot properly be reduced or annihilated without some justification beyond the fact that it or what it does is not wanted. The killing of disease-bearing insects and animals is justified because their destruction promotes the continuance and increase of the values that humans and their health possess. This does not mean that the destruction involves no loss.[12]

Each being blocks the activities of others. Anything used requires its user to attend to it and, so far, to yield to what may not benefit it. The used may in fact preclude its user from doing all that otherwise would or should be done then or later. The value of the used may not be overlooked; the used may simply be denied adequate expression, continuance, or activity. And that is never absolutely right to do. The actions of no human, union, society, or state, no matter how excellent, can be both warrantedly and unqualifiedly endorsed.

Aristotle held that mature people, identified as Greeks, free, and males, were political (or social) beings. What he appears to have overlooked in his political study is the fact that even if such people must live in a society or state, they also exist as privacies apart from their bodies, and can express those privacies apart from their bodies, thereby making it possible for them to be publicly together. Judging from what he said in other works this perhaps is what Aristotle intended to maintain. In any case, a social life, where challenges are jointly faced by those who belong together, is and should be supplemented by private acts.

All persons begin life only dimly socialized, socialized by being cared for, before and after birth, in ways which differ from society to society. But it is one thing to recognize that they are socially affected, and quite another to hold that they are human only so far as they are members of a society. Only gradually does anyone achieve the status of being a full member of a society, with habits which comport with what others usually do. All the while, each person continues to be a member of a union, and to exist as a private being, living in and through a personal body in an individual way. To attain the stage of a social being, each must be trained, admonished, directed, and restrained. None of these extinguishes the privacy or prevents it from being used independently of, and sometimes in opposition to, what society demands or needs.

Were people essentially social beings, the presence of those not fully socialized or hardly socialized—idiots and the insane—would present a serious problem. One would have to deny that these were truly human and would therefore have to hold that they might properly be enslaved, destroyed, and perhaps consumed. To avoid such prospects, one might suppose that asociality was a kind of sociality. Failure would then be understood to be a faint kind of success, and the abnormal a special case of the normal. The maneuver has some merit. It alerts one to the fact that there is some continuity between the most undeveloped and aberrant of people and the most mature, conventional, or routinized. But it also allows for the supposition that social beings are just variant or deviant forms of a more basic, asocial way of living.

Aberrant, uncalculated, and inadequate behavior, though characterized from the position of what is acceptable socially, does not depend for its occurrence on the normal, the required, or the desired. Denials need affirmations to work against, but inadequacies do not depend for their presence on the existence of what is adequate. Ineptitude could be characteristic of all people, demonstrated by the injuries they inflict on themselves and one another.

The attempt to take humans to be just social beings, no matter what they do, leads to a neglect of the speculative mind and the private acceptance of responsibility. No account would be taken of people as able to be absorbed in nonpractical issues, or of them as occupied with envisaging, creating, or appreciating intellectual and artistic works. It would require the neglect of the fact that some artists and sages act in asocial ways and yet not only live rich lives but sometimes produce what is of value to all.

A person's thoughts may reflect what had been taught or what is expected by other social beings, and individual decisions may reaffirm what society prescribes, but the thoughts and decisions of each will be unique. A person's privacy sustains some claims which owe nothing to society and may prescribe what society must do if it is to merit approval. Some of the rights a person publicly insists on, and which a society might help to satisfy, express rights privately possessed and given a specialized and limited bodily form, but some of the rights may not be publicly expressed, and when publicly expressed may be expressed poorly. Also, some decisions, beliefs, surmises, thoughts, fears, and hopes are kept private; others sometimes are not expressed very well. As long as a person lives, he or she has a privacy, never exhaustively revealed in what is publicly done.[13]

Were humans social beings essentially, their privacies would be separately maintained portions of unities of interlocked, mutually supported items. Each individual would be just a part of society who had retreated from or had been disconnected from the rest, and had then been compressed and individualized. Privacies, so far, would be reduced to fragmented and inactive parts of a public world. To account for nonsocial activities, one would then have to allow that some persons become parts of new kinds of situations. This, though, would be both to admit that they had exercised their privacies apart from society, and to make the unwarranted supposition that they had been socialized in a way and to a degree they might not be again. Yet if people are always socialized, it is hard to see how or why they would ever separate themselves off from society, except out of sheer stupidity or perversity—and these would have to be credited with great power. A rejection of the claim that a person was a social being would also require one to suppose that he or she either was not a real human being or was one in a poor disguise. Truth would be what society sanctions, and because society sanctions it. The assertion that people are essentially social beings, moreover, its defender would have to hold, is what society made him maintain. That, of course, will not mean that it is true. Indeed, it must be false. Formulated in privacy, it reveals its falsehood on being offered as a truth to be accepted by other privacies.

The claim that people always have the status of social beings is to be distinguished from the claim that they are essentially or nothing other than social beings. Only the latter need be rejected, since it alone denies that people have private thoughts, make private decisions, have native rights, assert truths, and use their bodies to serve privately acknowledged objectives.

The supposition that human beings are essentially social does not allow that each enters society as an individual. One of the virtues of a social contract theory is that it does not have to struggle with that difficulty. It knows that people are not just social units, and that they must attain the stage of being able to function well in a society. Of course, if people were wholly asocial initially, as some versions of the theory suppose, [14] they would not know how to get together.

People exist apart from a society, at the same time that they are members of one. Were there ever a person who was never detached from society, never exercised imagination, never contemplated or speculated, never appreciated or produced anything through a creative act, never considered anything untried, that person's life would be tedious and pitiful. Yet even such a person could enrich social life by what was privately begun, as well as by what was done together with others.

Through training, practice, discipline, and act, each individual must be helped to move toward the stage where use is made of social goods in distinctive, individual ways. We take someone to be mature when he or she persistently tries and usually is able to function in some harmony with others, a position that can be achieved because each exists and can initiate acts apart from society. On some occasions, of course, a person may be more social than at others.

A good social life for all depends on more powerful or influential people limiting and redirecting the activities of those who conspicuously fall below an accepted level. This is still not enough to achieve. If it were, there would be no need for a state, and ethics would have no role to play. But it may be enough to enable people to function well together for a while. Resistances will sooner or later be encountered by them which are not traceable either to them as individuals or as the members of the society.

Societies remain in existence even when the unions they encompass change radically. At those times, it may not be possible to determine that a societal condition is operative, or what it is. But that there is one becomes evident when different public acts are effectively limited and fitted into common, persistent settings. The presence of privacies becomes evident when the societal condition, despite the long standing tradition and the high ideals which it backs, is rejected, modified, or ignored by people acting separately or when joined in a union.

In a union, people are consonantly together. All the while, nature continues to exist as a possible antagonist. It is the fear of the Lord and not the acceptance of him, the fear of disaster and not the joy of fellowship that keeps humans tightly together. Terror, difficulties, and possible death unite them quickly and effectively. When the challenges of nature are met or forced into the background, or circumstances change radically, nothing is left to keep them in a union together for long, in a satisfactory way, except some externally sustained, insistent condition.[15]

The more tightly people are bound together, the more surely do they find the beliefs, practices, involvements, the Gods, and the values of those in other groups to be not just alien or repugnant, but to tacitly criticize their own. Not only the practices but the people themselves, it is sometimes believed, must be obliterated, since this is the surest way to eliminate the difference. Because people, from the beginning of their lives together, are never free from fear of, nor altogether avoid expressing contempt for those in other societies, war is always in the offing. Although it is states in modern times which declare and conduct wars, some were begun by and, well before the existence of modern states, took place among societies with diverse customs. At the very same time, all shared a common ground. Even during the conduct of the fiercest wars, where supposed civilized people set themselves against those they take to be barbarians or worse, some on both sides recognize others to be human beings like themselves, belonging together with them in a way they do not belong with anything else. Unfortunately, that does not assure that they will ever live in peace. Fights are begun for the most superficial of reasons, forcing awareness of a human bond into the background, where it does not disturb their thoughts or seriously qualify their actions.[16]

The so-called "moral equivalent to war" is too tepid to be more than a slogan invented by a philosopher. What is needed is a willingness for humans to be together in a society with minimal negative thrusts toward other societies. Since no society can count on surviving long if a number of others take a strong stand against it, nothing less is needed than the conversion of the negative thrusts of all into acceptances or at least tolerations, without preventing any from acting in distinctive ways. There is little hope that war will ever be eliminated if people cannot form a single union, and there find a condition with which to interplay, at least as well and as confidently as numbers of them now interplay with more limited conditions.

A societal condition may coincide with one that is characteristic of an economy. The result will be an estate, where people are occupied in distinctive kinds of work, and deal with goods, exchange, control, and consumption in interrelated ways. Over the years, "estate" has acquired a political meaning, not here intended. Since it would be difficult to identify any complex today as a political kind of estate, a reference to an estate should be taken today in a less restricted sense—and thereby enable it to be applicable in every epoch.

Marxists use "estate" to refer to a juncture of economic and social conditions, combined with those which are present in a union. The result of that combination is an emotionally sustained social class having antagonistic relations to other classes. Such a social class joins societal conditions and economic requirements in opposition to others, which it presumably must diminish or destroy if it is to prosper. All the while, the various classes remain part of different societies with their strong insistent requirements. Although it did astonish the Marxists, it should therefore have been expected that the members of depressed and deprived social classes would not, in war time, desert their societies to join the members of similar classes elsewhere.

So far as people conform to the demands of a society, they act properly, and their language, customs, and work will keep in well-established grooves. Since the requirements of their unions and societies do not always coincide, the people in them will often enough act morally but improperly, or immorally though properly. The unions and states may insist on marriage customs though these result in the perpetuation of disease and disabilites; they may insist on differences in rank or status despite the need to overlook these in order to get people to fit well together more efficiently and intimately. One of the functions of a state is to provide opportunities and a means for acting both appropriately and morally, which is to say, reasonably, doing what is right. In the absence of a state, people can do no more than try to promote a society in which a strong union and condition insist on themselves, while making provision for the other.

A society is constituted by factors having power in reserve, able to constitute it in new ways. So far as it is concerned, proper behavior is all that is required. The fact allows one to understand the kinds of truth that can be expressed in and, incidentally, about society, as well as the distinctive nature of inquiries which are to be conducted if one is to learn what occurs within it.

4. SOCIAL STUDY

1. TYPES OF TRUTH

Were someone entirely out of accord with what prevailing standards permit or require, he or she would come into conflict with others and, more likely than not, be blocked. Every one lives in some consonance with established ways. Even eccentrics and rebels, who conspicuously go counter to acceptable practices, do so by fitting in with others, at least linguistically as their speaking attests. What is done is opposed and rejected, in part because it is presented in acceptable contexts and ways. To be most effective, to understand what others say and intend, one has to understand what it is reasonable to expect.

Few know exactly what a situation requires, and exactly what actions would be approved by others. Few know to what extent and with what justification others deviate from familiar forms of speech and action. No one does only what is sanctioned, or altogether avoids what would be condemned were all motives and outcomes known. No one lives in perfect harmony with all others. Even when living with others as a well-functioning member of society, each inevitably adds distinctive rhythms, stresses, meanings, and values to what is done. Still, most of the time, most keep quite close to the established outlook and ways. Those who are very deviant are so only part of the day, just as surely as those who are least deviant follow their own bent now and then. Human existence is more loosely organized than are colonies of bees or ants and much more self-limited than are flocks of birds or packs of animals. Unlike the one, humans can alter the ways they live together. Unlike the other, they subject themselves to persistent, strong restraints of their own contriving.

There is no, there cannot be a completely separated human being whose attitudes and acts are in no way affected by what others have done and might do. At the beginning of life, it has already been remarked, each has to be fed, weaned, and taught. Each is inevitably habituated in ways from which only partial escape is possible and then only after some self-knowledge had been acquired and a strong effort had been made to stand apart. Others, older, more habituated and stronger, slowly but inexorably mold and fit each into ongoing acceptable practices, affecting beliefs, and helping shape fears and hopes. Through admonition, punishment, training, and example, each is led to share in a prevailing outlook and values.

A person puts up some resistance to whatever intrudes, so as to be able to deal with it on individual terms. Each is unique, unduplicable, with an irreducible privacy possessed and used by no one else. Were someone thereby entirely cut off from all others, that person would not be able to communicate or know how to carry out tasks which require cooperative efforts. Nor would such a person be able to benefit from the knowledge that the others had accumulated about what will nourish and what will not. There would be no way to know how to act well when faced with novel obstacles and opportunities, and no preparation for understanding them or for learning from the errors of others. Such a supposed isolated being could not only not know what the rest insist on or require, but would not be able to use much that was needed in order just to continue. Whatever was attempted would be carried out only occasionally in ways not blocked by whatever others there happen to be. A blunt push forward would be pushed back by apparently mysterious forces, and there would be little benefit that could be derived from the experience.

Those unfortunates who are never able to do more than infants can, usually acquire rhythms governing their feeding times. Those who become so eccentric that they must be forever confined and constantly supervised, are influenced in their public behavior and, like others, make evident that what they do is in part a function of what they have been compelled to acknowledge. Like the rest, they also express themselves, though pitifully and distortedly. Immature or mature, fortunate or unfortunate, humans both insist on their unique privacies and are subject to conditioning by others. Each is always alone, and always accompanied.

Behind all intellectual activity, people reflect the influence of a common ground that is inseparable from all. Could one free them from every involvement in practical affairs, they might be able to penetrate deeply into that ground. There is, though, little likelihood that this will be done or that, if it is done, they will then be able to conceptualize what they encounter. Nor is it correct to say that if they probed it they would become ethically good, since this requires them to also be able to know and do what is wrong. Only people, who are joined in other ways as well, are prepared to act properly in the company of others. Only they are able to be ethical beings independently existing and deciding what it would be desirable to do for themselves and others.

All humans are in and are subject to unions and societies, never becoming entirely free of these or other influences. All have indurated and often parochial concerns. To view them as though they were so many calculating machines who decide how to maximize pleasures, is at best to express a hope, and to place its realization in imaginary time. The supposition that they are pure intellects, thinking about what should be, and toward which they will be led by an invisible hand, is no better. Actual human beings are more than machines and more than pure intellects.

Those who turn their backs on established ways, for the sake of discovering what they should eventually do, are like those who take themselves to be in complete opposition to everyone. Both have been affected by the society in which they had lived for a while. Were any one to try to overthrow or ignore that society, this would be done in some accord with what had already been learned in it. Experience is socially conditioned; the truths that people obtain through experience are obtained by them while they are functioning members of a society, subject to its influences.

Although all that is empirically known may be known in a society and affected by it, some truths hold regardless of what the society is, does, or requires. Mathematical truths are not functions of a society, changing as it does, though there are social conditions which affect their discovery, formulations, and use. All remain unshaken by perturbations in social practices, beliefs, teachings, and restraints.[1] Our numerals, to be sure, have associations for us that the numerals used elsewhere do not. We may not know with what the numerals elsewhere are associated, but we and the others are still able to add and subtract the numbers that the numerals signify, and to do so with accuracy. Arithmetic commutative and associative laws are rarely focused on, hardly ever stated, and yet are well-used by people, despite radical differences in their societies.

Were it not possible to know any of the things those in other societies know, were every thought and truth a function of the society in which it is known or uttered, there would be no objective knowledge of what occurred in the other societies. One would not even be able to know the supposed truth that only local, socially determined truths were possible. If all that is said has to reflect the influence of a particular society, all claims made there would tell one only what had to be said by a member of it.

A truth is never just a function of that with which it deals. To be able to be a truth about something, it must not only be related to but be distinct from this, with its own neighbors and consequences. Only if people could stand away from society could they possibly say anything true about it. It would therefore be foolish of them to claim that whatever they maintained was just a social occurrence.

What is simply accepted, justified by, or agreed upon by a society as a whole, or by members of it, does not have the status of a truth. This requires that what is claimed have its own adventures and relations to other claims, even when all do nothing more than mirror that to which they refer. Truths can be reorganized, added to, and subtracted from no matter what occurs apart from them. Were there only a society and offshoots from this there would be no logical rules or inferences, but only socially produced occurrences; nor would there be anyone who had anything to communicate. The view that truths are merely social or (more narrowly) linguistic or historical products gets in its own way.

Knowledge is truth possessed. The truth may be *embedded, objective,* or *conformal:*

Embedded truths are claims involved with that to which they refer. Moral judgments are embedded, acquiring truth by becoming part of what enables them to be true. Usually, though, truths are held apart from what is known. Made available for accommodation and even absorption by the known, they continue to be presented as claims. Such objective truths may be about one's own society, about some other, or about anything else—facts, theories, logical rules, final realities, cosmic laws. Conformal truths, in contrast with both of the others, are set at an extreme of a continuum and are thereby made inextricably pertinent to what is at the other end. They interest those who wish to keep in accord with what they know. All three have their own natures and consequences.

There is warrant for taking any one of the three types of truth to be primary, and the other two to be special cases: An objective truth is an embedded truth that is able to retain what it acquires from the embedment, and therefore can be treated as apart from it; a conformal truth is an embedded truth involved with what it governs, but kept at a distance from this. An embedded truth is an objective truth that is attached to and may be modified by its object; a conformal truth is an objective truth related to its object within an undivided whole. An embedded truth is a conformal truth affected by that to which it is related; an objective truth is marked off from a continuum having a conformal truth as an inseparable part.

Each of these truths shares features with the other two, but has them in distinctive, limited forms. An objective truth is conformal by virtue of a component attaching it to its referent, and is embedded at the terminus of this. A conformal truth is distinguishable from occurrences at the other end of a continuum and, so far, is objective and able to be embedded. An embedded truth is objective as that which is being introduced into some other content; it is conformal because it is there sustained. The triple role of each makes evident that we not only never lose hold of what is being dealt with truthfully, but that the hold involves distinctions between what is being used, the use, and the terminus.[2]

It is an objective truth that one should not eat with one's hands in the United States. It has a conformal role there for all who are about to dine; it is embedded when one in fact dines. When its objectivity is stressed, its conformal and embedded roles are subordinated; when either of these is stressed, the other two are subordinated.

Activists take all truths to be embedded; conventionalists take all to be conformal. Both are opposed to realists, who maintain that truths are all objective. The conventionalists dominate discussions in political, and particularly social, thought. Everyone, they maintain, is affected by his time and place; every affirmation is a function of history, practice, or convention. It is surely an embarrassment for these conventionalists that they wish their view to be recognized as objectively true. Just as they maintain themselves as privacies apart from all else, even while they are being conditioned and limited, so they maintain their claim apart from the situations in which they are expressed. Revealing that embarrassment does not, of course, show that there are any objective truths, or that these have any role to play in the understanding of a society, but it does show that their denial, that other views are tenable, cannot have for them any other status but that of a conformal truth, being offered to others outside, and perhaps also inside, the society as though it were an objective truth. There are, to be sure, various difficulties, facing the view that there are objective truths. Not only does there seem to be no way to make contact with the referent of what is being maintained—since that referent is external to and quite different in being, nature, and career what refers to it—but what is claimed is expressed in universal terms, and limited and possibly radically transformed on being referred to any particular. Though formidable, these difficulties are not insuperable.

The problem of reference is to be met with the recognition that an objective truth is not a self-enclosed, separated item that must leap across a gap in order to have anything of which it could be true. It has a component terminating in what is known. While continuing to exist apart from its referent, an objective truth remains in contact with this through an intensive unifying adumbration.[3] This enables the objective truth to be conformal and embedded as well, without compromise to its objectivity. The adumbrative component unites the parts of the truth in a more and more intensive way, until a limit is reached at the object that is thereby known. An objective truth is thus able not only to express a privately made and maintained claim, but to be joined to what makes it true. Unlike a merely embedded truth, though, it has a status apart from that to which it applies. And, unlike a merely conformal truth, it can be just thought about, and so far be held apart from that of which it is true.

The second problem facing a defense of objective truth is that all its referents seem to be particular and limited, so that no provision is apparently made for the truths of logic and mathematics, or for the nature of words. Logical and mathematical truths hold always and apparently even in the absence of any object. And all terms, even "this" and "here"[4] are universals, able to be applied an endless number of times without ever having their meanings exhausted. The reach of objective truths is unduly narrowed if these are precluded from referring to anything but actual occurrences. But if understood in their full universality, they seem unable to refer to anything that in fact occurs. Adumbration is pertinent to that problem as well.

Adumbration enables objective truths to be inescapably connected with what is both concrete and of a limited scope. Logic and mathematics adumbratively hold of any and every intelligible object. Only if they could be separated from their adumbrative connection with the intelligibility in every thing, would they be freed from all reference to what occurs—but then they would be just empty forms, no longer true. Even "this" and "here" are adumbratively connected with the world in such a way that they are enriched and limited by particular cases. Because they are not just words unrelated to anything but words, it is possible to use them so as to speak of something. What is said through their help is connected with objects outside the linguistic expressions.

The supposition that whatever is affirmed is inevitably confined, and thereby qualified by the language in which it is expressed, or is in some other way determined by the way in which it is formulated, is itself adumbratively connected with what is distinct from the language and the act of formulating expressions in this. Otherwise, what was said would fail to have an application.

No one is completely free from conditioning by society, nor is anyone completely conditioned by it. Our knowledge of the conditioning is usually expressed conformally; it is also presented in an objective form and embedded when we act in terms of the condition. "All knowledge is just a social product", "A truth is of only one type", "What is clear and distinct, well-defined, practically useful, expresses us, or pleases us, alone is true" could be true only if they were false, since each rejects some dimension of truth that it itself exhibits.

If the ways people have been, are, and could be together is to be understood, one must be ready to affirm objective truths of them, without either having to insist on or deny the embedded and conformal roles of those truths. The formulations will, of course, be unavoidably affected by the time, place, practices, standards, and assumptions that prevail. This, though, is not yet to say that objective truths, holding in and of every society, are not possible. Caught up in a society, interplaying and assessing on its terms, people also consider and use what has its own nature, career, and requirements.

Individuals join others from private positions, and from there may take account of what is common to all. Their society affects them, but cannot turn them into just a function of itself without destroying what it needs in order to have something to condition, and to work on its behalf. A person who is through and through social is as much a fiction as one who is not socialized at all.

A society's practice and rhythms can be objectively described, its structures correctly distinguished, its history and tendencies truthfully and impersonally recorded. The achievements require that abstraction be made both from the particular effects that conditions have on the society's members, and from the effects of different biases. Objective truths are maintained at various positions near a midpoint between an insistent society and insistent individuals. If truths are about a society, they are pointed in one direction; if about those who are or can be in it, in another.

An objective truth most appropriately refers to the nature of a condition; a conformal truth often takes account of the way in which a condition governs; an embedded truth may be part of an insistent condition. A society's demands are like objective truths; its insistence is like a conformal truth; and the outcome of its activities is like an embedded truth. A condition matches an objective truth when directed at the members of a society; it becomes conformal and embedded when it affects them.

Defenders of the exclusive use or superiority of one of the types of truth will quickly take the claim that all three types are always present to be a truth of the kind they favor. But that claim is also a truth with a three-fold form. It objectively refers to the other two, is supposed to be conformally attached to both, and to be embedded in each.

Objective truth is here being favored, since we are primarily concerned with attending to the fact that conditions pertinent to all people impose limitations on every society; that complexes are formed within the compass of general conditions which provide governances specializing what is common to all; and that conformal and embedded truths need to be stressed only when we are primarily concerned with unions and their interplay with conditions.

2. Science and The Humanities

The acknowledgment of different meanings of truth makes it possible to bypass the controversy carried on by those who hold that all truth is objective (particularly if formally presented or sanctioned by science) and those who hold that truths in the humanities, in history, politics, sociology, or philosophy, are all embedded or conformal. Both sides assume that objective (and particularly scientific) truths have no social role, with the consequence that both fail to see that those truths can be dealt with in the same ways that other truths are. Both sides also take social roles to be inescapably limited and relative to special interests, and therefore fail to see that what is said in a society about what occurs there may be as objective as any other truth.

The sciences and the humanities are interested in different topics, pursue different methods of inquiry, and provide truths for different purposes. Related observations are to be made about different branches of a particular science, and about the different humanities and their various parts. Biological truths are embedded and conformal in ways which differ from those appropriate to physics or geology. Sociologists, historians, and philosophers make a different use of their different truths. They, too, like the others, seek to understand what exists independently of them.

How can one be assured, or at least maximize the assurance that what interests both sides is properly understood? How can one come to know objective social truths? Philosophical reflections and speculations will not do; they are too broad-gauged, too occupied with what holds always and everywhere to make possible a satisfactory grasp of what occurs in a society and what in it needs remedying. Specialized methods are needed, making possible an effective, objective understanding of actual occurrences, either in their singularity, or as gathered together in revelatory combinations. Are there such methods? Are they shared by other disciplines? What do they enable one to learn and to do?

The questions raise issues of fact whose answers require the use of a sound method. We would be on the way over an endless series of investigations, were it not that the nature of method and the different forms it may assume in different fields can be made the object of dispassionate analysis, reflected on, and objectively known. Whether or not this is done, the actual investigation of what occurs in a society must still be left to dedicated investigators of particular topics, all keeping within the compass of what had been shown to be required and available.

Since humans are social beings, whatever they do occurs within a society and in subordinated groups. All their knowledge has a social dimension. Knowledge of astronomy, physics, chemistry, biology, and mathematics is achieved in a particular society, and bears traces of the fact. That contention, not too long ago, would have been rejected out of hand. Great results in these disciplines have been produced over the centuries by people in different societies and without regard for the particularities of these, and were then presented in precise, quantitative, universally applicable, constant, and often verifiable terms. Despite differences in upbringing, language, custom, and belief, a number were able to engage in the same inquiries, and to come to conclusions which others, no matter where or when, could accept and reproduce. It is, though, also becoming more and more evident that disciplines are pursued by people who belong together and share views for a while. Members of a commune or even of a community of scientists, are evidently not limited by the peculiarities of the different societies in which a number of them happen to live. Their confraternity extends beyond social, national, and political borders. While in these, they continue to function independently of them. And what they then affirm often holds, not only for themselves as belonging within a special group, but for all humanity. Science is pursued, its achievements recognized and practical consequences produced with remarkable success under diverse social and historic conditions. Nor need art or the humanities always be subject to prevailing social conditions, conventions, or acceptances. Sophocles and Dante wrote for all; some French critics understand Poe better than many Americans do.

To show that how scientists act and what they affirm is a function of what they happen to believe or accept, it is necessary to hold that their primary assumptions radically affect and do not merely guide them, and also that those assumptions preclude them from knowing what is objectively true. Every scientist, of course, operates under limitations of unquestioned, because unexamined common suppositions, attitudes, and use. The technological accompaniments of these—telescopes, microscopes, scales, and measures—are produced at distinctive times and under special conditions, often clearly bearing the marks of contingent determinations. These limitations, however, have not made impossible the discovery of what is not limited or qualified by any society, or even by the entire scientific community.[5]

A theory and an instrument lead one to look in one direction rather than another, and undoubtedly make one overlook what would have been to the fore had use been made of different ones. Still, what was not discovered initially might be discovered later. Such discoveries often lead to the replacement of one theory by another, and may prompt the invention of new instruments. There is no necessity that the limitations, under which scientific claims are made and justified, preclude what is maintained from being objectively true, holding independently of the complexes in which they are discovered, formulated, and used.

Just as sociologists assume that what they discover about social conditioning is an objective truth applicable to every supposed objective truth, no matter where discovered or how expressed, and just as historians of science suppose that historic inquiry yields objective truths about the conditioning of scientists that should be accepted by all, so those who hold that there are no objective truths assume that they have found a truth all are to accept. If they, and therefore presumably we, cannot escape from a necessary relativization of such claims, the claims, as we have already seen, will be self-defeating. The discovery that scientists share many historically grounded and linguistically expressed assumptions, procedures, instruments, and tests falls short of showing that what is discovered by them is not objectively true and able to remain so no matter what their commune or community, or how these change.

Some would bypass the supposed opposition of the kind of truths achievable in the sciences and humanities by boldly holding that all inquiries should make use of the methods and concepts of the sciences (often, especially those of mathematical physics). Those who do not do this are then assumed to think "unscientifically", i.e., in ways not appropriate to serious investigations. History, jurisprudence, economics, linguistics, literary criticism, and other humanities, it is thought, are to be carried out along the lines followed by scientific investigations and expositions, or are to be judged as being seriously defective—or at the very best, to be practicing a kind of art, subjectively toned, metaphorically expressed, and unsubstantiatable. The accounts they provide and convey, the emotions they arouse and quiet, it is thought, may produce pleasure but cannot yield anything objectively true or intelligible.

There are two different theses here. One of them takes only scientific procedures and outcomes to be valid, even if inescapably socialized; the other holds that truth is properly found and expressed only in a context-free, depersonalized form. Neither grants legitimacy to any non-scientifically achieved or expressed claim, though this conceivably could be equally well-socialized or depersonalized.

A third, more moderate view, divides all inquiries into two branches, the exact sciences and the humanities. The latter are taken to attend to particular contexts and to identify humanity in the double role of investigators and investigated, or at least as inescapable components of what is discovered. Remarking on how language and emphases have shifted over time and therefore presumably in meaning, this third view maintains that if we are to know the world of which humans are a part, we must make use of a distinctive mode of apprehension, quite unlike that employed by those who presumably look at the world coldly, cosmically, unaffected by humanity's presence or attitude. A study of society, it is held, would be intellectually respectable only if it followed a distinctive method, unlike that used in the inquiries pursued by the exact sciences.

One peculiarity shared by the three views is that they do not allow equal standing to all the enterprises that supposedly conform to the different prescriptions. Physics and history are treated as ideal or model disciplines, with chemistry, biology, and geology, and perhaps psychology, taken to require eventual expression in terms of physical units combined in special ways, while jurisprudence, economics, and philosophy are supposed to be subject to serious perturbations having their origins in history. The arts become inexplicable anomalies for those who accept such contentions. At best, the activities of artists would have to be treated as understandable in purely physiological terms, while their topics and styles were fitted within historically determined changing frames. Such procedures do not capture the creativity of artists or the distinctive nature of their achievements. And all the while, those who were trying to explain the artists and their work in this way, would exhibit some of the creativity for which their accounts make no provision.

Scientists and historians are creative as surely as artists are. The achievements of all three are pivotal points in the career of humanity. But, unlike the others, most artists are engaged in making something, not in investigating and understanding.[6] They are not inquirers but producers. Although they help one get a better grip on the world, and provide insights into the nature of humanity, they do this mainly by affecting awareness, not by adding to factual or theoretical knowledge.

Scientific experiments and historical narration share so many of the features exhibited by the arts that they make a neglect of the distinctive procedures and accomplishments of these, and of the manner and nature of their communications, a self-defeating move. If a reduction of one kind of discipline to another is thought desirable, it would be better to reduce the sciences and the humanities to the arts, rather than the reverse, for the sciences and the humanities require of their practitioners a disciplining, training, devotion, creativity, persistence, and an interest in the excellent, similar to what artists and their works sometimes magnificently exhibit. But such a reduction, too, is not desirable. The sciences are carried out in one way, the humanities in another, the arts in a third, practical affairs in a fourth, philosophy in a fifth, and theology in a sixth. Nor do these exhaust the possibilities.

Work and craftsmanship require activities and reports having one form within scientific and another within humanistic studies. In addition, they use material existing in the very world that concerns both science and the humanities, and do so in distinctive ways. The fine arts are also produced through work and craftsmanship—but not without giving them a new import. And since we learn something from the outcome of artistic and practical—and philosophical and theological—efforts, it is willful to say that these do not help us increase our knowledge.

People try to overcome inadequacies by mastering, both intellectually and productively, what is other than themselves. Their scientific, humanistic, and other enterprises exhibit special forms of a single effort to be in control. At the very least, the sciences and the humanities should be seen to belong together as different but reputable intellectual inquiries, each following its own procedures and making its own type of report, to end with equally justified truths. Specializing a common effort in independent ways, they are in turn specialized by a plurality of different, independently pursued inquiries, exhibiting in limited forms the creativity exploited by artists and others, and achieving results not wholly anticipatable.

Peirce and Dewey were inclined to hold that thinking was never self-provoked. They thought that if a doubt were freely raised it could not be genuine. They were surely mistaken. Intellectual inquiries begin with problems, often self-set. People can, should, and often do raise questions as to whether or not what all agree upon is to be accepted. After all, common agreements may indicate nothing more than the presence of a convention or a state of ignorance, allowing one to rest with what is unwarranted, unreliable, or false. The fact that what one believed is also believed by others, does not make it sacrosanct. Still, no results are acceptable which deny the existence of love, hate, pain, pleasure, or of individuals, their rights, families, and societies. Every quest must at least allow for these and that, apparently, is what Peirce and Dewey wanted us not to forget. The idea, though, contrary to them, allows for self-provoked doubts.

Scientists entertain hypotheses and affirm truths which oppose and extend beyond the reach of ordinary understanding, as surely as artists produce outcomes no one else could have brought about. Over the course of time, the sciences have made evident that the most advanced of their predecessors were mistaken in their belief in the existence of witches, and in their understanding of the causes of disease, the fixity of the species, and the cosmic movement of the sun, while the arts—and the humanities and practical activities as well—have made us acquainted with dimensions of reality otherwise unsuspected. Both types of venture begin with commonplace obser-vations and commonplace acknowledgments; both sooner or later proceed beyond these, freshly and boldly, to discover new truths, new openings, new relationships, and unsuspected depths.

There is nothing that cannot be put to question. But to question, it is necessary that one accept some claims. These may eventually prove to be untenable. Until they are, it is necessary to be content with what is not dislodged. Beginning where we are, questioning what we can, we not only do but should accept what is not found wanting, and then move on. Were it later learned that what had been accepted was in fact untenable, unpromising, or derivative, the dis-covery would be made from a position involved with the common-place, and could be as blunt and final as any affirmed today. What may be discovered is that one had been mistaken on specific issues, or in taking some unnecessarily limited position. All the while, a root outlook will have been shared, in terms of which the nature and value of whatever is claimed was approached. That outlook has a specialized form in a particular society, and less specialized forms in the com-munes and communities of inquirers, artists, humanists, and tech-nologists. All tacitly accept assumptions which apply to more than what holds only for them. When people share an outlook, they would be precluded from saying what is true apart from all of them, were it not possible for them to have what they understand referred to what exists apart from all, and were they not able to recognize that what is affirmed conforms to and is embedded in that referent.

Affirmations which no one can properly reject are reinstated when-ever they are denied. Progress in knowledge is in part a refinement of what is essential to a robust inquiry, building on one or more such unrejectables.[7] All the while, there will be a number of possible pro-cedures whose mastery makes possible a consensus among inde-pendent investigators, concerned with what occurs in particular places or in special circumstances.

3. Systematic Social Inquiry

Objectivity is not precluded because one attends to and speaks of individual human beings, a union of them, or the society produced when the union interplays with an effectively conditioning homeland.

In a society, more evidently than is usually the case in nature, the particulars at a distinctive time and place make an appreciable difference to one another, not duplicated by others in a different time and place. Although the reports of what occurs will be colored by the attitudes, value, and language of the reporters, they can be well-stated and used to ground sound knowledge, and could lead to a desired change in what is confronted.

The appetites, confusions, and ignorance of people make conspicuous the fact that they must change their relations to other realities, both intellectually and practically, if they are to maintain and surely if they are to improve, their situation. When the efforts take an intellectual rather than a practical turn, it is desirable to begin by classifying and observing, alert to what is incidental, accidental, or irrelevant, and to follow this by a formulation of imagined variations on, and of alternatives to what is known; a drawing out of the implications of what is envisaged; and a concluding to what rationally ensures.

Whether one attends to mathematical problems, engages in scientific inquiry, searches for historic causes and processes, or is occupied with making and producing, new ways are to be sought to make possible an advance on what before had blocked understanding, insight, and control. Each discipline focuses on its own kind of objects raises distinctive kinds of questions, and engages in special types of variation on what is initially acknowledged. Social studies are no exception.

Interest in limited positions of a society leads to an occupation with various types of people, their actions, and the outcome of these. Explicitly or implicitly, people will be classified, treated together because of some such shared feature as age, gender, role, or race. The classification will usually reflect a prior categorization, a demarcating that had already been produced in thought or language.

Classification emphasizes the fact that items are being considered together; *categorization* allows only for the designation of them as already together. Pivotal figures present a limiting case. Though singulars, they are faced as representative occupants of distinctive positions which could have been occupied by others. They, too, can be and are to be classified, sometimes in the light of a prior categorization.

Curiosity is ignorance in search of what will dispel it. Let it be supposed that it leads one to attend to the patients in a nursing home.

The home and the patients will be focused on in the course of acts of classification but, in an attempt to overcome hidden biases, one will then have to try to understand those patients in other settings as well, and attend to other kinds of patients in a similar setting. Subdivisions of the initial group will also have to be examined to see if the people there engage in diverse behaviors both under the initial and under different conditions. Classifications of the patients, as old, infirm, and needing care, will have to be supplemented by others which take account of their ages, different kinds of infirmities, and the like.

Initially, classifications have irregular and porous boundaries. Borderline cases await decisions as to whether they are to be excluded or included, with a consequent refinement of the classifications. Further refinements are achieved by attending to subgroups, as well as to the original group in a different setting. A study of the obese must draw a line at some arbitrary point; it should be alert to the differences between males and females, old and young, rich and poor, educated and uneducated, the despised and honored, and be ready to see if they function differently on different occasions, natural or contrived. Each of the subdivisions may be further subdivided for special purposes. The entire group and subdivisions of it need to be attended to at mealtimes and at rest periods, and the behaviors compared with those of others in similar settings.

Although the number of conceivable subdivisions seems to have no necessary end, the various circumstances to which an entire group or different subdivisions are in fact subject are not only limited but depend on whatever nature and social causes happen to be operative. Only by good fortune will other groups be found which fall under the initial modes of classification, or are subject to the same conditions to which the initial group was subject.

Social studies prefer to take people as they are. Psychological investigations of groups will typically differ from the sociological primarily in their prescription of the conditions, circumstances, and tasks in terms of which a designated group is to be examined. To compensate for a possible bias in the selection, controls in the form of other groups answering to the same description but subject to different conditions, need to be and are often introduced. Ideally, the outcomes of sociological and psychological investigations will supplement and correct one another.

Interest in a limited portion of the social world leads to the making of classifications; categorization accepts some people as satisfying various conditions. The first needs explicit help from the second, if it is to become clear and communicable; the second needs help from the first, if it is to be made pertinent to what in fact occurs. Ideally, both will be used together, correcting and checking one another, and promoting a consciousness of what had been implicitly used.

Categorization, because produced antecedently to and independently of what in fact occurs, lends itself readily to imaginative modifications and new ways of grouping. It is more likely, therefore, to become an agency for making new discoveries—and also for the production of trivial groupings. Only in special cases—in factories, offices, hospitals, schools, and the like—are those who are categorized usually close enough together, and subject to well-defined, steady limitations, to warrant their being dealt with as acting under interesting common conditions. As a rule, those to be categorized have to be selected out of important, already classified groups, and then imaginatively joined.

Sometimes it seems as if categorizations did not answer to any fact. They appear to be ideas or words, fixated and authoritatively used, bundling together what in fact is distinct. Also, people often act as individuals, joined with others in adventitious ways. But they are also together, exhibiting some common feature or engaged in related actions. A categorization of them can then answer to what occurs in fact. The categorization will, of course, impose boundaries, separating some items with a selected characteristic from others, and thereby carry out more deliberately and systematically what occurs in daily perceivings, but also possibly distorting what is present.

Perceptions demarcate what is in fact connected with·other items. Unlike categorizations, they need make no reference to anything common within the boundaries they impose, the boundaries serving mainly to promote a focusing on particular items. This will still permit them to remain in accord with what is perceived, as successive perceptions make evident.

Like other actualities, people have boundaries separating them from others. That claim is opposed by idealism. It denies that there are or could be genuine separate realities, "externally related" and, therefore, that anything in fact answers to human finitude or to finite categories. Nothing, it claims, is really bounded off from anything else; the only reality is a single undivided whole. Denying to themselves and others the possibility of having a distinct existence or of uttering a single limited truth, its proponents are inevitably reduced to incoherence, unable to say anything on their own or about anything specific, without self-confessedly committing an error. The assertion that a single whole is real is, even for them, only one assertion among many, made by unique beings about a supposed reality set in opposition to themselves and to everything else.

The fact that categorizations may not match the ways people are together in society is perhaps behind the common view that what is said about social occurrences mainly reflects the nature of an observer's involvement with the observed and, therefore, is able to present little or nothing that is objectively true. But were such an involvement known, the fact that there was an involvement could be stated as an objective truth—and by those in the society—and then held apart from the whole. Were this denied, one would end in the same kind of incoherence to which the idealist was reduced.

Problems still remain: There are arbitrary, inadequate, and defective categorizations, just as there are arbitrary, inadequate, and defective classifications. To use either is to misconstrue what occurs. Still, if the two are independently produced, they can be used to check one another. One can also draw inferences from what one understands and see if the conclusions match what is later or elsewhere observed.

Might not knower and known be inextricably linked from beginning to end? Might not the known always be fitted into a mold provided by the knower? Consider a mirror image. This keeps pace with one's walk and matches every grimace. The correlation between image and object here shows the image to be a function of the object. Might not the occurrences in society similarly be functions of those who attend to them? Yes—if what occurs in society were similar to mirror images, keeping in accord with changes in what is confronted.

Aren't people surprised by what they see in a mirror, just as they are elsewhere? Might not what occurs be due to them at both times? Yes. But there are also other surprising occurrences produced by actual objects occurring despite, and often out of synchronization with, those who face them. Also, some occurrences in society have natures and courses which diverge considerably from those they make possible; some compel people to reply to them; some change people while they themselves remain unchanged; and still others change though there is no appreciable difference made in what confronts them. So far, what occurs in a society is quite unlike a mirror image.

Some images in a mirror, of course, are not due to those who see them, but to chairs and books and walls. But the images of these can be traced back to objects in the same way that a person's mirror image can be traced back to him. Both the objects and the person can be known, and the result expressed primarily as an objective, embedded, or conformal truth.

Observation is needed if we are to distinguish between listening and hearing, looking and seeing, discriminating and touching. It is at the forefront of an attention that is alert to nuances, differences, and variations. Like curiosity, it reaches toward what is to reduce ignorance. Unlike curiosity, observation allows what is confronted to dictate what is to be noted.

To end in good classifications, observations should be backed by categorizations. In the absence of these, classifications would have partial or arbitrary divisions, and some observations would unhelpfully focus on isolated items. If observant, one sooner or later discovers that some categories lead to the making of poor selections, and the introduction of improper emphases. Sometimes, they may prompt needed reclassifications. Unfortunately, observations do not always suffice to let one know what is occurring; they may be too brief, too undisciplined, not well enough conducted to enable one to know what is present.

Close interrogations of witnesses make evident that ordinary observations and reports are not entirely reliable. Not only are the observations not sharply closed off from fears, hopes, and prejudgments; they are quickly overlaid with supposition, details, and untenable beliefs. Even the observations of trained observers may prove to be unreliable. As Peirce remarked, if trained in one kind of laboratory they may fail to observe what others readily note in theirs. Lacking the appropriate categories, unfamiliar with what might exhibit these, they are likely to overlook differences, similarities, anomalies, and pivotal items. Further observation does not help, since they still would not know for what to look. Even within a given field, those who are well-trained and careful may miss what others note. Discoveries are in part dependent on accident and curiosity, and sometimes on the use of new classifications and categories. That still allows people to learn and know truths which hold independently of the limited assumptions and practices characterizing them as members of some limited group.

The exigencies of daily existence prompt painters, as they do the rest of us, to focus on what is of interest in daily life. A painter sometimes tries to be freed from that limitation by looking at the world about, his or her own works, and the works of others in distinctive ways. Some of these acts the rest of us sometimes also carry out, but only occasionally, and then haphazardly and inadequately. A painter may squint, shift position, use mirrors, change the lighting, and turn the painting upside down; perhaps drink, take a drug, or entertain odd suppositions in order to get into a position where nuances, missed by those who assume conventional standpoints and attitudes, are focused on. More important, a painter may attend to the apparently empty spaces between ostensible objects, colors, and shapes which most of us neglect due to our insistent concern with what is obtrusive and useful. Poets, musicians, and other artists also approach what is present in fresh ways, not governed by practical needs or conventional outlooks, in part to make as evident as possible the presence of what is beyond all particulars, and which the work partly captures.[8]

No one avoids classifying some encountered items. Often enough, this is done unreflectingly and unsystematically, under the influence of unquestioned categories. Experiments in new ways of observing make it possible to avoid many of the limitations involved in the ready use that is made of more established categories and familiar classifications. They also provide reasons for limiting, qualifying, and changing classifications already made. The novel, the surprising, the perplexing challenge the usual categories. Often they prompt new classifications. The fact that those who take up unusual positions are already in possession of categories, and that they, too, unreflectingly classify what they find, still allows for their observing what otherwise would not be noted.

Social study is so vast a field and the amount of attention given to it has been so limited that one is tempted to say that what is needed are more and more plain, simple observations, especially in the areas of health, age, race, and gender, rather than variations on observations and particularly on those which are rather detached or specialized. It is also true that such variations help clarify the gross, the common, and the familiar. Unfortunately, much of what is uncovered by taking new approaches also just adds further data, often introduces what is trivial, and throws little light on what is otherwise known.

The merit of the surprising products of novel approaches is not readily seen. A painter's experiments in observation do not offer much that is usable by the rest of society. If the work being considered is relatively well-controlled, one may with little difficulty be able to see what bearing the familiar and unfamiliar there have on one another, but few such limited, well-framed products are widely available. Society, moreover, is too large, and parts of it, despite their independent origins and functioning, are involved with too many others of various types and in different places to allow for many well-bounded ventures requiring no abstractions. It is therefore tempting for a student of society to remain content with making commonplace observations about groups with which all are familiar, but to do this with care. It is so difficult to try to understand what is really occurring and to support remedies for what is amiss, that a serious investigator often has little time for anything else.

Apparently, we all know enough for needed action when we learn that children are abused, that miners suffer from black lung, or that professional athletes have short careers. The fact that the knowledge could be more detailed, and that account should be taken of what is not usually noted, does not seriously compromise the important observations initially made. If we do not know how to fit in the outcomes of novel approaches with what is familiarly known, we may still be able to realize that proposed changes often affect what is conspicuous, as well as its linkages.

It is important to know what is important. We come to know it best when we observe with care, and use what we learn to help us produce an intelligible, coherent, comprehensive account. The observation that abused children usually have parents who had been abused as children does not lose but gains from the knowledge that the abuse was approved by the victims, that it mimicked heroic acts, or reduced anxieties on the part of the perpetrators. Again and again, it is desirable to stop in the course of an advance, to return as close as we can to the initial situation, and to observe it in the light of what had been learned. If novel observations enrich what is normally observed and clarify it as well, the defects in one's approach will become more evident, and will more likely be eliminated. The initial observations and their possible subjective or humanly determined items will not be extinguished; they may even benefit from what is learned later. If one wishes to reduce the likelihood that people might unreflectingly add what was not objectively true, it is necessary to engage in still other observations.

Facts are limited, determinate, articulated units, differing from actual objects or occurrences in being residual and inert. Most of our familiar truths recapture facts in terms appropriate for communication and inference. Since no fact tells anything about its origin, its neighbors, or what might ensue, to try to learn by collecting facts is to try to add together detached items in the vain attempt to arrive at more than an aggregate. *Interpretations* in the form of contexts have to be introduced if meaningful wholes are to be achieved.

An interpretation takes account of what might bound off the already bounded in. Evidently, it provides a kind of classification and categorization, by means of relations joining items already classified and categorized. Its introduction of relations, to connect what was bounded off with what is still to be observed, takes one into new regions, and thereby adds to the difficulties which beset the classification and categorization of items already encountered. The difficulties can be reduced by keeping interpretations firmly grounded in what was already observed and by devising categories supplementing and clarifying those already used. When the results of the different efforts conflict, new observations are needed in order to determine where and how the discrepancies are to be overcome.

Although analysts will insist on their units, and contextualists on their interpretations, sometimes the understanding of separate items has to give way to what is understood of them in relationship—and sometimes the process has to be reversed. In a particular investigation, interpretation will usually prevail, for its generality enables it to apply to many items, making possible a single, comprehensive account of what is observed on different occasions. It will be followed by further observations, and these by interpretations, on and on, as long as one remains curious.

Since the relations which interpretation introduces make what was separate be understood as belonging together, there is always a risk that the original items might thereby be denied their integrity and independence. A risk, though, is not an occurrence; its presence does not mean that a defeat is unavoidable. Relations, introduced by an interpretation, need not deprive the accepted units of their limits, natures, or relations. Roles which intepretations prescribe may be carried out in fact. It is an interpretation that enables us to connect the phases of the moon with the changing tides. We observe and attend to these separately, the interpretation enabling us to provide a good match for what in fact occurs.

Social study builds on what is observed, trying to relate it to what is still to be observed. Inevitably, it is faced with difficulties: If it yields to initially observed items, it may uncritically accept the limits within which previous activities occurred. By referring to what has not yet been observed, it may envisage what may not in fact exist. And by making use of relations of its own contriving, it may introduce trivialities or irrelevancies. The first of these difficulties points up the need to engage in different and perhaps better observations. The other two are more formidable. By moving away from the observed, intepretations may create purely imagined referents or imagine relations answering to nothing; or claiming to be about what in fact exists, they may make only fictional additions to what had already been certified.

Accounts of what is now observed are not jeopardized by using interpretations of it to probe areas not yet observed. If the interpretations do not help, that will not mean that what had already been learned is to be rejected. Instead, the interpretations would then have to be acknowledged to have an unduly narrow scope, to be replaced by others not so limited.

A different and apparently more difficult problem is raised by the fact that an interpretation may include much that is unnecessary. Evidently, one should be prepared to eliminate from an interpretation what is not needed, in order to connect the observed directly with what else is sought. If the elimination made the interpretation have too limited a range, it would of course have to be followed by additions enabling the intepretation to apply over a wider territory. These additions may have to be followed by other eliminations, and these by other additions, until unnecessary factors in the interpretation were excised, while a wider range of occurrences was effectively encompassed. The interpretations can be further checked by seeing how separations, connections, dependencies, and dominations match the relations which had been discovered to hold among observed items. Unfortunately, at no time can one be sure that an intepretation has been able to encompass many observations but did not include the unnecessary.

Interpretation is a categorization, referring in part to what is not yet observed. It is to be used separately and together with other categorizations, and its results subjected to still other operations. There is no theoretically required end to this process. It must, though, be brought to an end if we are to understand what is occurring. Reference has to be made to what has already been acknowledged, perhaps not clearly but usually persistently. Were we to identify someone as weak, that person would be categorized, not just as a distinct being, but interpretatively, as one who is related to a plurality of other occurrences in a plurality of ways. That interpretation could be made more precise, be qualified by some other observations, and be modified when used at particular times and places. At no time, though, is it to be understood to say more than that ordinary tasks are being poorly and slowly performed. Additional observations and interpretations are needed to warrant the supposition that the failure to function well is due to illness or a handicap, and therefore that the person is to be understood and treated differently from one who is overweight, drugged, or recovering from an operation. Each observation and interpretation needs to be carefully made and sharply bounded if the introduction of unsuspected prejudices, hypotheses, and conclusions is to be avoided. A good report of what in fact occurs requires a sharp eye, a disciplined mind, and a controlled pen.

Interpretations seek to relate observed items to one another and to others which might be observed. Since they are produced by people, is it possible to avoid doing more than make what is objectively the case be related in arbitrary, merely imagined ways? The question has already been faced. We can know that what we understand is entirely due to us, only if we know what cannot be so credited—and that means only if we know what is objectively so. Can this be done without introducing questionable interpretations? Perhaps not. But if, even in principle, it cannot be known that whatever is claimed as knowledge is due to us, we are not justified in saying that we did or did not create it. It might, of course, be possible that what was known was (or was not) due to us along lines of which no one was aware. The possibility can be understood in a number of ways. It could be treated as referring to what was just logically possible, free of contradictions; as an occasion for alerting us to the fact that we are always related to realities beyond us, and have only the problem of reporting accurately what everyone more or less discerns; or it could be taken to refer to what was implicated by what we were presently doing and knowing. The last is the best of the views, for even the most sceptical and theoretical thinkers and their theories, doubts, and refutations are inescapably in the present and implicate relevant possibilities. Social study rightly never altogether forgets the daily commonsense world; it is constantly engaged in observing and interpreting what is there encountered. This does not mean that it is timid, naive, but only that it takes place in a world on which it continues to maintain a hold, even when entertaining hypotheses never before considered.

As persons mature, they discover what it is to be individuals with distinctive privacies. By expressing his privacy through a body and thereby interacting with others, each learns what it is to be a good functioning part of a society. The first learning usually follows on the second, and for quite a while, but the order is often enough reversed, particularly when, instead of following the guidance of those who are in authority, one reflects and makes individual assessments. When the two learnings are carried out well and successfully, a series of oscillations takes place, requiring each individual to intersperse personal knowledge with attempts to live in accord with what is socially required. Rather wide to begin with, the swings are gradually shortened under the influence of a steady insistence on an unreflecting commonsense outlook, dictating what it is sensible to affirm and reject, even in the face of what one had rejected or accepted as being proper to do privately or socially.

Commonsense is the base from which inquiry initially begins, whether it be confined to questions in science, philosophy, or the humanities. When overlaid by prejudgments, it is distorted, becoming ill-defined in range and application. Instead of attending to the basic and unavoidable, one then rests with the unexamined, the commonplace. Commonsense acknowledges the commonplace as an initial source of evidence enabling one both to understand, in a steady, coherent, communicable way, what in fact occurs, and to limit the oscillations between inquirer and society. All of us do, must, and should rely on both. But if we do, are we not inevitably caught in humanly relativized results? We would, were the commonsensical and the commonplace other than condensed, humanly oriented, steady, not entirely intelligible mixtures of multiple realities.

Attenuated versions of realities are together in whatever is initially encountered and are more or less unreflectingly accepted as real items in a commonplace world. Because realities are initially so together, it is possible to know them by beginning there, and then isolating what had there been joined.

Social study is often content to remain, not with commonsense objects, but with a version of the commonplace. It then does not free itself from hallowed preconceptions. But once it breaks away from these and clings to the commonsense core that remains behind[9] it will not need a further, more fundamental grounding. Were it to ignore whatever commonsense insists on, it would not be able to avoid mixing the minor and foolish with what is important and needed for social existence. Were it to end with results which go counter to what commonsense accepts, it would fail to understand and properly deal with crucial problems; more likely than not, it would end by making idle claims. Nor may its theoretical accounts conflict with what is otherwise known of ultimate realities. If it did, it would misconstrue the nature of the experienceable world which those realities help constitute.

Rousseau brilliantly, though somewhat sentimentally, made use of the world known by commonsense. Hegel went to the other extreme to concentrate on what he took to be ultimately real. Neither paid sufficient attention to the area that interested the other. Most students of society are aware of both. Rightly avoiding the extremes, they are also too often content to rest with what seems right at a particular time. So far as they do, they remain with the commonplace, unable to tell us what is sound in this, the genuinely commonsensical. No one looks to social study to learn about the ultimate constituents of the world, but no one should look to any other study to tell us what goes on in an area that accords with commonsense deliverances, filled out with what is learned through careful observation, classification, categorization, and intepretation.

Both interpretation and *analysis* ideally take their start with what is daily known. Both interpretation and analysis depart from commonsense by intellectually moving toward what is not present in that form. Analytic philosophy here provides no help, since what this seeks is ultimate units matched by the subdivisions of an ideal, logical language. Stopping with socially significant constituents of observed occurrences, social study is content to know, e.g., that the voting of a group is governed by racial antagonism, fear of loss in the value of property, anxiety about the health and education of children, and the like, without going further. All of these factors, of course, have psychological and physiological conditions to be mastered by the more theoretical enterprises of chemistry, biology, and perhaps even physics. Beginning at the very same occurrences that these do, social study quickly comes to the end of its analyses. Analytic philosophy, instead, continues its conceptual dissections until it arrives at what is conceived to be the ultimate units out of which a complex is supposedly composed. Neither approach offers a good model for the other.

A social analysis may make unimportant distinctions, or entrench on other types of inquiry. Although, by seeing if variations in its analyses accord with differences between one occurrence and another, we can learn if its analyses are pertinent to both those occurrences, we still can not be sure that the analyses have gone as far as and no further than they should. Certainly not before one knows the main constituents of social occurrences, and thus in some sense has already made an analysis before a social analysis begins, could one know that this arrived where it should.

The constituents of social occurrences are analyzed in a rough way in the course of daily living. To begin with, the analyses are partial, though able to be carried out and refined beyond any preassignable point. If what is there is not composed of the units with which the analyses end, the procedure will have to be repeated and perhaps modified. Since the analyses are to take one to irreducible constituents of society, they must be guided by a knowledge of society's indispensable features, confined within the region where common-sense operates.

To avoid trivialities and irrelevancies, social study should be guided by a knowledge of human nature, and the kind of acts in which people usually engage in a particular group. There is no need for it to go beyond that point. At its best it will achieve a systematic formulation of society. Necessarily, it will leave some issues unresolved, and some questions still open. One pursuing such a study can do little more than repeat the different operations, and try to get the different outcomes of its investigations to be in accord, within the compass of a single outlook. This is still a great deal.

The limits within which social study operates are not to be breached—by it. The ways it proceeds are irreplaceable—for it. Other inquiries are not thereby limited.

If people know what realities are present always, and the limited forms these have in experience, they can know if they have come to rest too soon, or gone astray.But, though the knowledge of the nature of those realities helps one learn what can be encountered, it cannot tell one what particulars are present at a particular time, or show that they will be present elsewhere or always. Since social study could not possibly know what it seeks by attending to the outcome of philosophic inquiry, any more than it could just by accepting the claims of the uncritical or by imagining what would result from combinations of known units, it does not wait for someone to provide it with an account of the indispensable factors out of which everything is composed.

Rectifications and refinements in social study are brought to an end somewhat arbitrarily and quite short of what a detached theoretical analysis would tolerate. Similar sudden stops are made in other empirical inquiries. Necessarily left over is the question whether or not the beliefs that remain, the systematic theory which is to range over all the occurrences, and the observed occurrences themselves, have been adequately understood. One will also be faced with the question whether or not references to what is outside society, or to what may independently exist within society, have been socially skewed. Whatever answer is provided, social study will be undisturbed, for its concern is with what it can learn through its controlled use of classifications, observations, interpretations, and analysis. All of these are anchored in what is available to commonsense. When they move away from this, they still continue to be affected by it.

If *explanations* are sought, a social study, while remaining aware of what is confronted and of the results achieved by following its other procedures, has to turn in a new direction. Only then will it be able to produce a general, rational justification for its accepting observations that accord with commonsense. The explanations will have two prongs: a rational and a practical. Peirce dealt with both in his usual original, brilliant, and fragmentary way, the first more often and effectively than the second. By the logical route, we get new ideas, hypotheses, and theories and are thereby in a position to make new discoveries pivoting about original observations, with the practical or pragmatic side coming into play to help determine when the answers are to be abandoned. Peirce called the process an 'abduction'.[10] The most common form of this substitutes a single predicate for a plurality of observed items. That single predicate is the outcome of an inference to a premiss from which the original predicates, and still others having an observable application, can be deduced. It is possible, also, to substitute a plurality of subjects for some one subject. Analysis can be viewed as being occupied with that form of abduction.

What is needed is an explanation with the widest possible range consistent with a reduction in the likelihood of being mistaken or of dealing with irrelevancies. No rules, though, can be laid down in advance to assure the production of what is correct and important. If they could be, we would be able to teach them, and anyone, by thinking along those lines, might be able to make great discoveries.

Peirce thought that there were an incredible number of possible theories that could have been formulated in the past, so that only by sheerest accident could anyone arrive at a theory that was pertinent to what was occurring. He implicitly rejected the idea that someone had once stumbled on a good explanation and that thereafter others did not stray far from it. Apparently he rejected it for the erroneous reason that what had an antecedently low probability could not have occurred. He also thought that there was an affiliation between the human mind and Nature.[11] Since humanity is not altogether alienated from Nature, some kind of affiliation is properly supposed. But the supposition is not needed in order to understand how it is possible for people to discover viable scientific theories, since these are tied to the observed, the boldest and most successful no less than those with more limited ranges, able to be quickly falsified.

Some successful theories refer to entities no one can observe but which are supposed to exist because they provide a smooth connection between what had occurred and what might be subsequently encountered. This still leaves room for an endless number of theories able to explain a particular state of affairs. Those theories are not like so many separate marbles. They are pivotal points in a persistent interchange of guess and experiment, observation and confirmation.

Explanations are the outcome of adventures entered into by those who are at home in a field. There is, of course, no knowing in advance whether or not any particular one will be helpful. It is necessary for experienced investigators to adventure again and again, not afraid to be in error or to appear foolish to contemporaries. The effort plays a role in all attempts to understand, no matter what the topic.

Social study has few broad-ranging theories, does not stray far from what can be observed, and consequently makes few startling discoveries. Physical science's willingness to suppose the existence of entities which no one has or could have observed is one way in which it sets itself in sharp contrast with that study. Although it too begins with commonplace and commonsensical observations and cannot, without giving up all recordings and experiment, ever wholly depart from them, its theories are constructed through the use of part of the great creative freedom enjoyed by poets, novelists, and dramatists.

By expressing its theories in accord with a mathematics having a great number of consequences in different areas, what is entertained by science can be readily questioned again and again in new places and in new ways. Mathematics is not used in that way in social study. This limits itself mainly to the use of statistics, so qualified that the results presumably will accord with what is observed. Using rather elementary branches of the subject, it cannot be expected to illuminate areas far from the familiar.

Some philosophers entertain theories having an unlimited scope within which the world of science is but one province. Most, with social investigators, eschew great departures from what is encountered, and make little use of mathematics, particularly of its more esoteric portions. Unlike both the scientists and students of society, others follow the lead of the evidence that is condensed in the commonplace. Their views often hew closer to daily experience than the scientists', and are bolder and better defended than the social theorists'. Eschewing the bravado of the one and the limited concerns of the other, they deal with what interests anyone who would like to know what can be learned from a controlled examination of what bears on the important dimensions of human existence. To obtain that, they wed a concern with knowing what holds everywhere with a sense of what is important for and revelatory of the nature of humanity and the major complexes of which humans are a part. Only these are true social or political philosophers, rather than commentators reflecting current trends. Like Aristotle, Hobbes, Kant, and Hegel, they too are affected by great and crucial events. None can hope to escape from their times, nor should they try. Yet, with those philosophers, every investigator should also make a great effort to consider the nature and import of what holds always. If this is done, he or she will be able to say what is in accord with what happens at this and at all other times.

Despite differences in interests, the kinds of evidences used, and the nature of the explanations sought, all inquirers are torn between the attempt to avoid error and the attempt to make great discoveries. Their adventures are new, whether they reach far outside the range of present data and produce theories of unusual design, or move more cautiously. If concerned with knowing only finite things, they will engage in creative acts of abduction. Since the best abductions are so bold and far-ranging that they are usually met with scepticism and sometimes with blunt dismissals, those who produce them often need striking successes before they are taken seriously. Such successes are hard to achieve. As Northrop and Popper have remarked, all one can be sure of are failures to deal adquately with some crucial fact. One must agree with the two of them that no number of affirmations can suffice to substantiate a theory—for this is general and of unlimited application. But if one, with them, supposes that science progresses only by the elimination of unsatisfactory views, one will tacitly hold that there are no random occurrences, that no failure is due to aberrational activity, and that the items which do not fit a theory are relevant to it. These suppositions are gratuitous.

A theory can always be saved by rejecting what apparently falsifies it. One might also change it in order to accommodate a recalcitrant occurrence. There could, though, come a time when what is proposed requires a rather large number of rejections or changes. The theory will then be replaced. Sometimes, too, it will be replaced just because people have lost interest in it. Acceptable until then, it will be taken to lack importance, relevance, or truth, and perhaps even use, because the experienced world has changed. That alternative, though not often entertained by scientists, is a constant, live option in a social study and other humanistic enterprises.

It is not wise to suppose the aberrational, random, or irregular occurrences, or large-scaled and shocking exceptions to established views, always mark the start of a new historic epoch. An illustration (foreshadowing the discussion in the next chapter) may make this evident. Although there is nothing amiss in sixes coming up two dozen times in a row, even with good dice thrown as randomly as humans or machines can manage, it is an occurrence not tolerated by gamblers. If the mathematical probabilities are not realized in a few throws, gamblers suppose that there has been trickery—and act accordingly. Randomly thrown dice which are not biased, they believe, inevitably and quickly result in an actual mathematical distribution of probabilities. On a failure to have a warranted mathematical outcome realized in a short time, they look outside the presumably mathematically governed occasion toward what they suppose produced the untoward result. It is not reasonable, they think, to hold that such a deviation from a mathematical statistical result would have been exhibited were there no distortive forces at work.

In the world of practical affairs—and that includes the most theoretical of humanistic inquiries—all think along the lines that gamblers follow. There, too, it is expected that the consequences of a supposed law will be realized in not too remote a time. If there have been a considerable number of occasions when predictions and expectations failed, or if a failure is large and momentous, the theory, law, or formula will sometimes be suddenly abandoned, despite its past successes. Although the failure could be explained by supposing that something external intruded into an otherwise perfect exhibition of mathematical probability and therefore was responsible for the failure, or by supposing that something having a low probability occurred again and again, the failure is instead taken to be due to a change in established ways, making irrelevant an otherwise applicable idea.

Gamblers have a great confidence in mathematical probability theory as well in their belief that there will be a realization of a probability formula in a short time. Since they do not readily give up the supposition that high probabilities have to be exhibited in a finite number of cases, failures are soon taken by them to be due to something wrongly intruded. Students of society, in a similar situation, tend to take customs or the course of the world to have changed and, therefore, to require the use of new hypotheses.[12]

Widespread bankruptcies, revolutions, and mob rule, not only challenge what had been relied on, but require its abondonment. The upheavals usually have such serious reverberations and repercussions that they prompt a search for a new and more reliable outlook. Although much may be carried over from older accounts, something that held on other occasions and had been acknowledged in those older accounts, will then be given up. As a result, one will have to decide whether to attend only to what happens in particular epochs, or to seek a more comprehensive view covering what occurs in a number.

Abduction is a special type of inference.[13] It begins with what has an observational warrant, moves to what would explain this and other observables, and finally replaces what was initially accepted by what is arrived at. Since the other procedures can also be viewed as types of *inference*, it would not be amiss to hold that there was only one method for social study, but that it was to be followed in a multiplicity of distinct, particular ways.

The most familiar inferences operate linearly. Traditionalists say that they should be drawn in accord with the demonstrable, necessary laws of a formal two-valued logic. The suggestion is usually not followed, and there is little reason for following it. Not only are the laws not known to everyone, they need to be used only when one wishes to make sure that the acceptance of some important conclusion is justified—particularly one which is to be formally expressed, is arrived at only after a long inferential effort, and can be dissected and reorganized so that it fits inside an approved formal frame. But inferences can be and have been successfully carried out in the absence of such formal certifications.

Any inference, no matter what the rule, can end with a necessitated conclusion. In considerable accord with Peirce's analysis, we can take a rule to conjoin an antecedent, P, with a consequent, Q. The two may have nothing to do with one another, and may indeed express what is false and even foolish. Let P represent "Elephants are great poets", and Q, "The moon sings beautifully." Joined so as to constitute a rule for inference, we get "If elephants are great poets, then the moon sings beautifully". Were we now to accept as the premiss for our inference "elephants are great poets", the conjunction of it with the rule (P, and If P then Q), will necessarily yield the conclusion, Q, "the moon sings beautifully". The falsehood of that conclusion does not affect the validity of the inference, but it does point up the fact that either the rule or the premiss, or both, are in error. An inference that begins with a true premiss and ends with a false conclusion cannot be certified by a sound rule. A true premiss and a false conclusion reveal the rule, governing an inference from the one to the other, is unreliable. Since a logical law is inviolable, any inference ruled by it but ending with what is not true, must have used what is false as a premiss.

We would like logical inferences to begin and end with what is observed. Strictly speaking, this is impossible. What is said about the observed is turned toward it, but both the premisses and conclusions of inferences are turned toward one another. The truth of an assertion cannot be identified with the premiss of an inference except by being turned at a right angle, thereby enabling it to be used as a premiss in an inference arriving at a true conclusion. Nor is the conclusion of an inference assertible of anything. This, it can be only if it is turned away from the premiss which justified it, toward what exists apart from the inference.

Both rules and inferences have beginnings and endings related to one another. But where a rule has them joined together, an inference deals with them sequentially. It moves beyond what a premiss affirms to get to something other than what had been taken to be a conclusion justified by the use of a sound rule and a true premiss. The truth of the conclusion, obtained by a warranted move from the premiss, is able to become a truth about something only if it is dealt with apart from that premiss and rule—a result achieved by turning it toward what is exterior to it.[14]

Many inferences do not begin with premisses derived from what is known to be or accepted as being certainly true. Quite often they move in a straight forward way from premisses to necessitated conclusions. What is dubious, merely believed or supposed is often accepted, and then followed by movements toward what is tentatively accepted. There may also be backtrackings to qualify what had been originally accepted. The process is sometimes carried out many times, and the rules followed will often be products of careless abductions, making uncritical use of what many happen to accept. Empirical studies start in this way, and never free themselves entirely from the limitations characteristic of that beginning. Our premisses are rarely beyond all questioning, and the rules under which our inferences are drawn are often makeshift, falling radically short of those exhibiting logical formulae. It should not surprise anyone therefore to find that some inferences made in accord with those rules end with what is false, though necessitated by the conjoint use of rule and premiss.

Procedures from observation to inference, that have been touched upon here, are somewhat in the order of greater and greater generality, the last being instanced by all the others, though in no necessary order. The conclusions of each need to be checked by the others. Procedures of one type will usually need to be backed by other types following different rules and having their own distinctive endings. A particular social inquiry will be brought to a close at the point where it seems to most investigators that what is claimed has been sufficiently well-substantiated, and is consistent with what is otherwise known of man, unions, society, and other complexes. That point is often remote from where a logician would say sound reasoning requires one to end.

5. Social Causation

Causality has a number of traits strikingly like those possessed by rules and inferences. It is to be expected, therefore, that there will be those who, with Spinoza, identify causality with the necessities of a logical law; some who take it to be an hypothesis connecting antecedent and consequent in a contingent manner (e.g., Reichenbach); others who view it as having to do with detached items (e.g., Hume); some who allow for only a kind of passage (e.g., Bergson); and still others who take it to combine a theoretical necessity with an actual ongoing (e.g., Kant). The Kantian view finds some room for the others. But because it treats the formal part as involving a necessity without specific terms, and the ongoing part as occurring independently of the other, it fails to do justice to the nature of the indissoluble unity of formality and ongoing that is characteristic of an actual causal process. There are not two separate factors, but just one act of causality in which it is possible to distinguish a formal and a material, an implicative and an active dimension.

The existence of a reality in the present is inseparable from a partial determination and connection with a past and a future. That future is now possible and relevant to the present. A large rock makes a large afternoon shadow possible. This is one of its many pertinent future possibilities, all partly indeterminate and joined. Further determinations, no less than actual separations, will depend on what occurs in the present. Apart from this, the possibilities will have to await actions to demarcate them, add determinations to them, and realize them.

The future is a single indeterminate, at the edge of the present. It is antecedently specifiable there in the form of implicated, predictable, distinguished prospects. These need determinations produced in the course of a process of causation, before they can be actual and present. Were there just present items, cut off from everything whatsoever that could follow on them, they could be followed by a world where such a state of affairs no longer prevails. Were one, therefore, to grant that a Humean analysis was correct at any particular time, one would also have to allow that the world it portrayed could give way to the one we now confront.

A prediction formally follows the route from a present occurrence to a possible, realizable effect. It tells us what will be later, not in its full concreteness, as what in fact occurs at some later present, but only as that which will then have a fully determinate form. If we could make no such predictions, we would have to content ourselves with expectations of what we are accustomed to await, or we would have to be content with living through an experience, never sure of what we were doing or producing, or indeed if we were doing or producing anything.

When a possibility is realized, it is made determinate and present. Determinations articulate and concretionalize the possibility, converting it from an internally, empty delimited portion of a single larger possibility into a located, divisible, dense, present unit—the possible effect enriched and particularized. The possible effect and the initial cause are changed over the course of their interplay, the first becoming concrete and present, facing a future possibility of its own, the second ending as a past fact at the edge of the present.

A cause has the double role of implicator and producer; an effect has the double role of implicated and actualized successor. Since an actualized outcome depends on a contribution, not only from the cause and the process of causation, but from the limiting possible effect as well, causality, even the most routine, must be credited with a teleological component.

Real possibilities are part of a single, indefinite future; they are distinguished and partly specified at the beginning of acts by present actualities, and are thereby enabled to provide these with pertinent, guiding prospects. Those prospects are still indeterminate, but less than what they had been before they were distinguished from one another and, so far, set limits to what present actualities could bring about.

What in fact occurs at the outcome of a process of causation is both necessitated and necessarily new. The necessity and novelty are not just compatible; they are inseparable, for a particular present effect is a singular outcome freshly produced by turning an entailed, real possibility into a new present actuality. Since the conversion is new but occurs within the scope of a necessary connection, it yields what is predictable as general, and unpredictable as particular.

Causality is an ongoing process converting a possible necessitated but general effect into an actual, never fully anticipatable actual effect. The most monotonous of mechanical activities has details then and there produced in the act of converting what must be into what is. For most practical purposes, the novelty in the outcome can be ignored. But interest in the necessary, the gross, and predictable does not make the particularity of an outcome disappear.

This account of the nature of causality[1] is general and universally applicable. Everywhere, a possible, distinguishable, entailed effect plays the role of a limit, and may be used as a guide, imposing some constraint on what is being done to realize it. Since the humanities often take explicit account of the role that a possible effect has on the production of an actual effect, causality there is taken to function in a way not usually acknowledged in the sciences. Nevertheless, causality operates in the same way in the areas that concern the one as it does in the other. The particularities of the effects that interest the humanities, though, are usually more prominent and of greater concern to them than the particularities, confronted by the scientists, are to them.

At no time is there a need to suppose that a possible effect acts on what precedes it. That would make time run backwards. Nothing more has to be affirmed than that a possible effect, implied by and inseparable from a cause, sets limits to the operation of the cause, thereby making this be the production of determinations in that possible effect, and not in some other.

Causation is always teleological in the sense that it involves a limiting of what is occurring by what is future. Because the teleology requires that the causal activity be modified by the possible effect that the cause distinguishes, causation is also partially self-productive, with a not entirely predictable course and outcome. Since a cause is inseparable from a possible effect, alternative determinations of this could have been produced, each of which would have yielded a distinct, realized, specialization of the possible effect. Whatever determinations are in fact produced progressively specialize the effect that ensues. As a consequence, a not altogether predictable, actual, determinate effect in a new present is reached at the end of each process of causation.

If a possibility is of some concern, it will be used to guide and perhaps control the course of its realization. The possibility may have already been partly determined by others; through admonition, training, and education, punishment and reward, we may then be prompted to realize it, and therefore to engage in different acts from those we otherwise would. To overlook the role that such a qualified prospect plays is to make it hard to understand why we acted in ways not suited to the realization of a possibility relevant to independent, free individuals.

Usually admonitions and other promptings are assumed to have produced no more than new beginnings from which desirable outcomes necessarily follow. If these do not follow in fact, it is too often supposed that proper or enough changes had not been made at the beginning. Changes could, though, be produced by introducing successive determinations under the guidance of a desired prospect. Indeed, this is what usually occurs.

Sometimes people are supposed to act on themselves as an animal trainer is supposed to act on animals, and therefore to face a prospect to which they react on cue. It is not often that it would be proper to view them, or even animals, in this way. The satisfaction of hunger, the avoidance of blows, the receiving of desirable rewards, and the like, are guiding objectives for those animals; a human being usually has more conspicuous, and sometimes more effective guiding and controlling objectives than these. Those who would correct and improve themselves or another will do this best if they make themselves or the other more attentive than otherwise to the needed, effective determinants they are to introduce into their activities.

When a rock rolls down the mountainside, and ends in pieces at the bottom, we have no hesitation in taking the entire occurrence to be an instance of the workings of an impersonal, cosmic law. The role of the possible outcome is dismissed as being at best a metaphysical supposition, not helpful in particular investigations. When a living being persistently acts in ways which injure it, such a dismissal is not only less plausible, but prevents one from grasping what is taking place, for the prospective outcome is a requisite and often a great part of the explanation of what occurs. This contention, to be sure, has been frequently denied. Some, following the lead of Descartes, suppose (as he did not) that even humans are just mechanisms. That requires them to ignore the private existence and promptings of pain, pleasure, and appreciation, the guiding role of thought, and the effect of resolutions.

It is not enough to attend to private determinations and the limiting prospects pertinent to these, in order to account for what people do. Although a knowledge of the nature of an action and the prospect it helps realize enable one to understand what is done, more is needed. One must have some knowledge of the point from which a course of action starts, for a guiding prospect is implicated from the very beginning to the very end of an act.

Whatever our view of causation (and truth), it is an irreducible fact that our understanding, of how a society came to be and functions, is achieved while we exist within our own. We can, though, escape from the limitations such a restriction entrains if we recognize that we operate under principles that are specialized by all societies. To avoid inventing fictions, we must recognize that we belong with others in a larger world, under conditions limiting the ways we can act. Objective truths about such conditions are embedded in and conform to us as together, both as individuals and as unit members of a society.

Hegelians clearly see and boldly affirm that social effects require social causes. But they then go on to hold that all the actions of people are to be viewed as delimited versions of those characteristic of society. There are such delimited versions, but there also are causes possible only to individuals—fears, hopes, desires, ambitions, resolutions, thoughts, each with its own characteristic nature and effects.

Nominalists reverse the Hegelian emphasis and take common causes and effects to be collections of others, individually produced. Their move involves a denial not only of the operative role of tradition and ideology, but of the fact that people are sometimes caught up in crowds, mobs, festivals, rituals, celebrations, and contests which have their own beginnings, course, and endings, sweeping them along.

Although a completely neutral examination of things, without prejudgments, evaluations, or a desire to alter, is perhaps not altogether within anyone's power, it is desirable to try to understand what occurs in society in as impersonal and objective a manner as one can manage. The goal is the production of a complete social phenomenology. The more fully that goal is realized, the more will it be possible to reduce the likelihood of distortions stemming from a natural tendency to exaggerate both what people like and what they fear, what is attractive and what is disagreeable. But if society is to be fully understood, and surely if it is to be improved, we cannot rest with this.

Improvement requires that we subdivide what we deal with into two parts, one embracing what should be reduced, destroyed, hemmed in, replaced, or overcome, the other embracing what should be accepted, continued, supported, or strengthened. That requires us to know what people seek and can accomplish. Somewhat similar distinctions and requirements are to be introduced in other enterprises, even where no effort is made to improve anything. One moves away from a physiological to a biological study of mating, e.g., when it is noted that, despite the inconvenience and injuries suffered by individuals, mating has value for the human species. To ignore the role that the species here plays is to be left with the fact that tumescence is not a common state and apparently exhibits a momentary derangement in organic functioning. When we note also that, alongside common human acts appropriate to the continuation or prosperity of the human species, there are others having no such role, we are in a position to engage in a good social study. If we make the move, we will then parallel one that is made to a species when it is found that healthy individuals again and again engage in acts not to their individual advantage. When we recognize that people sometimes oppose what is advantageous to them, and sometimes approve of what is socially undesirable, we will also find a warrant for moving beyond the boundaries of a social study. Refusals to make such moves are sometimes grounded in the supposition that idiosyncratic or aberrational acts are just stimuli and occasions for the achievement of some trans-human good. Such a supposition may allow one to explain why there are social ills, and may lead to the treating of them as normal occurrences. What is amiss will consequently not be rectified, any more than individual aberrations are when these are viewed as though they were just social stimulants.

Social study understands causality—as it does statistics and other agencies—in ways shared by the other humanities, and occasionally by the sciences. It also gives it characteristic qualifications, sharply marking off its use from those pertinent to the others. That is one reason why it cannot be properly brought within their compass, or they treated as special cases of it. The fact, of course, does not preclude cross-disciplinary investigations, or the supplementation of one of them by the rest.

At least four elementary steps must be completed before a controlled and promising investigation of what is occurring in a society, and what should be done to change it, can properly begin. The occurrences there are to be understood to fall into large subdivisions, and together to recapture most or all of what is happening in the society. Efforts also have to be made to control and compensate for the defects of a chosen subdivision, and for the biases involved in its selection and use. An escape from the impurities and imperfections of an actual subdivision will then have to be promoted by attending to the possible effects of what had been chosen. Finally, various occurrences will have to be analyzed into components which, had they been altered or been related to others, would have helped produce different results. Together, those moves make possible the production of other components or combinations of them, and thereby may make it likely that more desirable outcomes will be achieved.

What is to be sought are the causes for a number of primary effects. Those causes and effects should encompass much of what occurs within the society, if their understanding and improvement are to result in, or at least are to contribute to an understanding and improvement of the whole. That is most likely to occur if what are isolated are genuine, distinguishable, separately functioning subdivisions which, while not exhausting the nature or functioning of the society, encompass crucial occurrences there.

Work, play, sex, relations of dominance, taboos, ideals, and conflict characterize quite large areas of societal activity. When we attend to another society, it is tempting to take it to deal with these factors in accord with the values that prevail in our own. Sometimes, it will instead be viewed in terms we think do or should prevail everywhere. Unfortunately, actual societies are too particularized to permit one to be content with either approach.

Subdivisions of society are related to the whole in ways which are both like and unlike those in which individuals are related to the subdivisions—alike in that an aggregation of the subdivisions will not yield the whole, and unlike in that the individuals are not entirely social in nature. When what seems to be the same societal activity exhibits a different rhythm and has quite different consequences at different times, the differences might be due to a change in the prevailing conditions or circumstances. Different effects, of course, also result when a particular type of cause is effective in different ways. What is needed is a control group against which the claims about a chosen one are to be compared, thereby making possible the discovery of unsuspected causes. One or more of those causes may have skewed the observations. And when everything has been done to exclude or to compensate for various biases, it may still be true that some unnoted circumstance had prevented a selected group from having the nature or career it was expected or thought to have. Careful social investigators therefore try to catch themselves off-guard, in the hope that they will then be able to discover if they had misconstrued what was being studied. The difficulty, they know, is not just a function of the fact that they had been studying the activities of humans and what these help constitute. Bias and inadequate groupings, they can see, characterize the work of investigators in other fields as well.

To know what can occur is to know a range of possibilities, one of which may be realized over the course of a process of causation. If we know what might be, we will be able to achieve a better understanding of what is present; this in turn can lead to a better understanding of what might be achieved. A process of moving back and forth from an understanding of the present to an understanding of the future can be continued indefinitely, to be stopped only when no appreciable progress is being made in the knowledge of the cause and the possible effect, and what they could bring about.

Possible effects play a role in all causation, and social study takes explicit account of the fact. When the possible effects are consciously focused on, intention, purpose, dedication, and other distinctively human ways of acting in terms of possible effects, acquire important roles. Although unions and complexes of people are not conscious, and therefore cannot be subject to prospects in the ways in which humans are, the possible effects of the actions of those unions and complexes can be known, and something then done in terms of them. Whether this takes place or not, in addition to being limited by the effects they themselves make possible, people may be guided by effects possible to unions and complexes, and may thereupon turn themselves for a while into agencies by means of which those effects are realized. That is one reason why society lurches and wobbles, with idiosyncracies challenging what is steady and common.

An occurrence contains a number of interrelated factors. These may be real components of it, able to be separated out as distinct units; they could also be distinguished items which had been conceptually approached from a number of different positions. If either is done, what would otherwise be viewed as a single undifferentiated causal activity will be envisaged as having distinguishable factors. An example: The thievery of adolescents could be subdivided into acts due to exuberance, irresponsibility, or lack of discipline, each joined to opportunities to take possssion of that to which they have no right. Alternatively, their crimes could be taken to be the outcome of efforts to merit the endorsement of model groups—older men, the rest of a gang, or imagined successful criminals. If the first approach be taken, the crimes could be imaginatively decomposed, perhaps into the gender of the adolescents and the objects to which those adolescents had no rights. If the second, the crimes could be analyzed as embracing a model group, feelings of admiration and respect by the adolescents, and acts by which the adolescents seek to acquire status.

The crimes are to be made less likely by changing various, crucial factors. The exuberance and irresponsibility might be reduced or deflected, the objects made less readily obtainable, or the adolescents directed toward other ways of obtaining possession than through a violation of the rights of others. The model group might be changed in nature, the adolescents brought to admire others, or the relations between the two groups altered. If changes in these components did not result in changes in the outcome, other modes of decomposition and new efforts at discovery would have to be tried. Whatever was done, the same crime will have been viewed in various ways. It would not be improper to say that distinctions had been made between kinds of thievery committed by the same adolescents, and that different solutions were therefore required.

This account is oversimplified, for nothing has been said about poverty and hatred. The nature and plight of the victims has also been passed over: are these individuals, or are they institutions and shops; have they suffered only financial losses or have they lost both money and status? It does, though, allow one to see that causes can be fruitfully analyzed into independent, alternative subordinates, operative within the compass of a broad-gauged social causation having large social effects.

Occurrences may be in a relation of earlier and later, and have nothing to do with one another, but if the earlier is a cause it is implicatively and effectively related to a possible later effect. In the attempt to show that they are not bundling together various irrelevant occurrences, but are instead dealing with what is causally connected, some students of society justify their claims by appealing to statistics.

Statistics is a strong mathematical discipline. That gives it one sanction. Another is that it makes possible a quantification of results, thereby enabling them to be readily assimilable and manipulatable. Applied to large populations, it makes possible their subdivision into manageable groups, and the determination of the relative standings of these. A third is that it allows for imagined variations, with collateral variations in supposed causes. Its greatest attraction for social study, though, is its apparent effectiveness in the determination of the presence of hidden causes.

Tradition statistical theory and practice is held by some to be too rigid and formal to be of value in a field which should attend to tonalities, contingencies, and values. They would replace it with a Bayesian treatment of probabilities, understanding this to allow a role for new informatiom and changed expectations, thereby enabling one to attend to new data and surmises, and to the changes in emphasis and direction that are being made in a program in the course of its operation.

Investigators who use the traditional, and those who use the Bayesian ways of dealing with statistics usually make the same assumption: if items are chosen at random, they will conform to the mathematically calculated statistics of a random distribution, or indicate the presence of a disruptive cause. If, out of the entire population, smokers are picked at random and the incidence of throat cancer among them is found to be much greater than in the rest of the population, it is concluded by both that smoking must be the cause or contain the cause of the cancer. That conclusion is readily accepted when it is supposed that if a number of occurrences—the number varying with the bearing of the occurrences on human welfare or happiness—deviate considerably from the mathematically calculated statistical results of a random distribution, either the items had been improperly selected, or there is an unknown cause that accounts for the deviance. Were the examined smokers and the cancer victims really selected at random, and instead of a random result a high correlation between the two discovered, it would be concluded that smoking was causally connected with cancer. Yet, as has been already observed, there is no warrant for the supposition that a mathematical distribution of probabilities will be exhibited in any finite set of occurrences, no matter how large this be. Mathematical statistics allows the most improbable of outcomes to occur in any finite run. It, therefore, cannot justify the inference that, if a random distribution is not exhibited in some situation or population, there are distortive causes preventing it from appearing.

Mathematical statistics does not require that the distributions it warrants be realized short of an "indefinitely long" run. Mathematically viewed, six can come up a million times in a row in random throws of an unbiased die. The low mathematical probability of that occurence remains forever the same. It is not an impossibility; the low probability could be exhibited, no matter how many the throws. No die, of course, is perfectly made, and there are habits of throwing a die which preclude complete randomness. Greater and greater care of course can be used when making a die, and a greater and greater approximation to random throws achieved. Even then a die may come up six again, again, and again.

We can, we do, we should demand that a supposed random distribution be manifest in an actual, finite run. This is only to say that we are practical beings, demanding confirmation or discomfirmation of our hypotheses within a limited time. On the failure of a supposed randomized set of occurrences to yield mathematical randomized results, we do and should, sooner or later, suppose that the selections were not actually randomized, or that there was an unknown cause at work. If these suppositions are in error, an established way of making practical judgments has come to an end.

The manner in which populations of smokers and sufferers from throat cancer are chosen, the high correlation that is found, and the conclusion that there is a cause that produces this, cohere with the practices of insurance companies, archaeological investigations, the search for oil—indeed with most of the ways we today deal with a large number of apparently random as well as regularly distributed occurrences. We may be willing to allow that one or the other investigation may have wrongly concluded that some particular cause was at work. What we cannot grant is that most who so draw their conclusions are in error, without our giving up the kind of practical inferences that express the outlook of our society in our time.

The supposition that there is a cause determinative of a failure of a random distribution to be exhibited, falls far short of the discovery of the cause—if there be one. Nor will we find it, if we remain with mathematics, for the cause is outside its reach, occurring at a particular place and time, having its own distinctive prospect, and beginning a causal process that is carried out in a distinctive way. If we conclude that smoking is causally connected with throat cancer, we will not yet know the cause of the cancer, though we will have pointed up areas where it is desirable to search for the cause—in cigarette particles, in throat anomalies or irritations, in various chemicals in the cigarettes, in the immediate environment, and in the body.

Social study differs from practically oriented enterprises in the kinds of causes it considers and the way it uses them, but not in the way it uses statistics to help it ferret out causes. Its concern with various large-scale occurrences, such as crime, poverty, violence, health, customs, leads it to mark out special areas where certain kinds of causes might occur, matching those effects. It is not interested in knowing the cause of cancer. That topic it leaves to physiologists, biologists, and chemists. Instead, concerned with the fact that cancer precedes death in an undesirably large segment of the population, it tries, with the help of statistics, to discover the social causes adequate to produce the deaths, themselves treated as a kind of social occurrence.

The more serious the practical effects, the smaller the number of cases a practical person requires before deciding that there is a cause accounting for a deviance from mathematically calculated results. It is not necessary to collect an enormous number of cases before concluding, from a high correlation of smoking and throat cancer, that smoking, or a concommitant, causes cancer. Were there a similar high correlation found between smoking and the ability to spell, there would be no such readiness to speak of causes and effects. Still, if the high correlations continued to be present when more and more people were considered, eventually it would be supposed that unknown causes were also active there.

Money, time, and patience dictate to practical people the length of the spans in which theoretically justified consequences are to appear. In each enterprise, they come to a moment when they decide that theoretically warranted but unrealized results are blocked by unknown causes. High correlations are then taken to be outcroppings of causal activities, no matter what the statistical theory.

Theoretical accounts are transformed when used. If something is taken to be central to our lives but not realized most of the time, our expectation that it will occur will be revealed to be untrustworthy, and the life we built on it jeopardized. If a number of basic expectations fail, affecting enormously large sums of money or many people, our epoch will have come to an end. Should it turn out that all insurance companies happen to insure all those and only those who die in a given year, our common expectations will be shown to be unreliable. We will not know what to trust, and our present way of living will no longer be possible. We will have come to the end of a particular period of practice. No additional data, no subordinate clauses, no reorganization of our statistics will help us for, at best, these will be brought in too late. We will have to abandon our old ways of inferring, and suppose instead that other kinds will be better satisfied in the new world into which we had been suddenly thrust.

Social study is attentive to what is being contributed both by the investigators and by what is studied. But it cannot provide a complete theoretic justification for what it investigates. Instead, it must proceed in its own disciplined way to lay the ground for the attainment of desirable practical objectives, and be ready to alter its expectations when most of its efforts end in failure.

There are theoretical warrants for what a social study does. After it has finished a task, it may also offer a good theoretical recapitulation of what it did, but this will always fall short of its practice. To take account of that fact, a number of procedures might seem worth following. One is dialectic, particularly in the form Hegel gave it. He thought it was possible to present a rational, systematic set of categories governing all that occurs, by taking dialectic to be at once an ontological, epistemological, and historical process, moving from a basic category to its opposite, together with which it yielded a higher order category having its own opposite. The process was supposed to continue until one inevitably came to an all-inclusive Absolute Idea that both preserved and advanced beyond the categories which led to its understanding and presence. It might be desirable to deal with society as an area where this or some other dialectic was displayed, if categories exhausted what was significant, and if history had a dialectical nature. At best, we would then discover that various large scale features found in most societies, or in societies at a certain period of history, made possible an understanding of any society, but without learning what in fact occurs in them. Yet this is exactly what a social study seeks to discover.

If we could bring a dialectic down to the level of actual social occurrences, and thereby expose a rationale otherwise overlooked, we would of course be alerted to occurrences we would have missed, what was observed being found to have had its nature obscured by irrelevant details and contingencies. Categorizations, though, are all tentative, general, correctable, and themselves need supplements. They cannot be identified with what occurs, without neglecting the particularities of what is observed.

There is a rationale discernible in the movement that begins with a confrontation of a challenge by private beings and ends with the interplay of a union with an insistent societal condition. That does not mean that society has something like the status of an Hegelian Absolute Idea, or of one of its lower forms. What is possible is a succeeding stage, the realization of which involves the addition of determinations, neither predictable nor deducible. The result will have its own relevant prospect to be realized over a similar course, in which determinations are added to make the prospect eventually be realized as a fresh present occurrence. Since the successful arrival at one stage grounds an adventure for achieving another, we can know at what a series will end only if we can correctly envisage a succession of related achievements, each with its characteristic prospect. Where there is intent, purpose, will, or obligation, the situation is altered, for these introduce effective governances of a series of activities by possible outcomes.

The realization of a prospect is a new occurrence, grounding a new adventure productive of a new result. If, therefore, it be supposed that something like a cosmic purpose is at work at each stage, and that it there exhibits the self-same final result in different partial guises, too small a role will be accorded to what is present. Inevitably, there will be a slighting of the novelty of what is produced.

The social studies of Hegelians are more successful when they attend to what had previously occurred, in good part because they use their dialectic to organize what had already been learned from history. So far, the dialectic has only an heuristic role. It could, though, ground good predictions, could it prompt one to attend to genuine prospects.

A dialectic helps one to see that there is something more to consider than what is actually occurring. That surely is desirable. It does not enable one to know the nature of an outcome before it is produced in fact, though its practitioners seem to believe this that is what is does. Making one attentive to the role that a possibility plays in the production of an actual effect,[2] dialectic is not able to discover exactly what occurs. It might, though, lead one to search for defects in what had already been claimed, to imagine what is lacking, and to envisage a union of the two.

An older meaning of dialectic, traceable to Aristotle, brings it ratherclose to an adversarial procedure in which the relative strengths of a number of competing hypotheses are determined by making them face one another's evidences and claims. Each is challenged for not being fully in the direction in which a satisfactory answer lies. The method enables one to accept another hypothesis that in some respect is superior to the various competitors. But that superiority may consist only in the absence of defects present in the others. It may have flaws of its own and could fail to preserve what is good in the alternatives.

A worthwhile dialectic provides for the adoption of all alternatives or, at least, preserves what is of value in each. An adversarial procedure, instead, accepts an alternative solely because the preponderance of evidence is on its side, despite the value of what is present in what is being rejected. Were there a number of plausible alternatives amongst which it were not possible to decide, a dialectic could provide a good way for resolving the issue, if it were confined to the conditioning of each of the contenders in the light of the merits of the others, and if it assessed them in terms of an excellence pertinent to all. It would differ from causality in not benefiting from a control exercised by a merely possible outcome, and in the necessary increase in intelligibility and value that it presumes would thereby be achieved. The dialectic's terms also transcend the area where causal action and contingencies occur. Consequently, the more the necessity of an objective dialectic is insisted on, the more surely will the contingencies of actual occurrences have to be put aside—and the more will these reveal dialectic to be a method of theoretical construction that may not find illustration in the observable world.

A good dialectic combines construction with deduction, novel production with necessitation. Unlike causal processes, the constructions are carried out with the help of mock-ups, diagrams, blueprints, models, taking one beyond the materials available, toward determinate forms of what is possible. Like the implications of a cause, the prospects faced by the dialectic will suffer alteration when they become involved in actual occurrences. The application of the dialectic involves nonformal factors and the production of not altogether anticipatable outcomes. If there is some awareness of the inescapable novelty of the production, it may help one make new discoveries by showing the direction in which a desirable result might be found.

An application of a theory requires that allowance be made for the presence and insistence of what is independent of it. Since the theory must yield to some degree to the material on which it is imposed, from the standpoint of what it is claiming, the result will be a compromise in which the theory is changed to enable it to comport better with that on which it is applied.

Compromise is at the center of all attempts to understand what is occurring. It alters each side in recognition of the fact that each must make provision for what will impinge on it. In effect, it is a method of rectification, providing corrections for what is unsatisfactory. Not claiming to remove the cause of defects, compromise tries to make them innocuous or to compensate for them. Its outcome is always new. The envisagement of that outcome is a means for enabling one to discover a better answer than could be obtained by struggling with oppositional claims.

Dialectic enables apparently exclusive alternatives to be brought within the compass of a more inclusive view. Compromise, too, seeks to accept what is being contended for from different sides. Unlike dialectic, though, it modifies each, as it is apart from the others. In the absence of a compromise, one side might prevail. The outcome might then be better than that which a compromise permits—if no one effectively opposes it. In the absence of a compromise, also, all sides might be harmonized, perhaps only by being made to give way to something else in which none has a distinguishable role.

Compromises are usually brought to a close arbitrarily at a point where it is thought maximum satisfaction is being provided for the competitors, though without yielding full satisfaction to any. Practical acts, they are without predetermined outcomes, carried out without advance knowledge of what must give way and to that extent. From the standpoint of theory or fact, therefore, a compromise points up a regrettable loss. To justify this, it is necessary to take a stand outside the alternatives, or in their interplay.

Intellectual compromise allows some room in a theory for the theories which it excludes, turning them into subordinate clauses, or using them to limit the range of what is accepted. It thereby enables the adopted theory to fit in with what may have some application. Related compromises are involved in the acknowledgment of what is observed, for this is not entirely detached from other occurrences where theory and fact may also be combined.

If a compromise is guided by a knowledge of an end to be realized, it will make possible the achievement of a stage where people can function in socially desirable ways. A practical act, it will have to be carried out by those who, while concerned with knowing what occurs in practice and how this is to be improved, have a good theoretical understanding as well. At its best, it will objectively attend to and evaluate the available alternatives, to make likely the overcoming of antagonisms and conflicts. Discovering what concessions must be made in a world where claims may be urged on behalf of what is taken to have meaning or being apart from anything else, a good compromise gives some satisfaction to opposing sides.

A kind of dialectic carried out step after step in a world of practice, compromise tries to arrive at what is superior to each of the opponents, or to the ways they are together. Whether used to collect data or to enable one to produce a better society, it is a proper adjunct of all practice, allowing one to check results obtained at any one time against the claims of opposite sides, and thereby be in a position to see how greater justice could be done to all. If successful, it achieves a standpoint in terms of which other and better compromises can be sought. Conceivably, it could help one attain a position where it could be replaced by a better agency.

The nobility of truths, the inviolability of religious commands, the absolutivity of ethical requirements, inalienable rights, all seem to be jeopardized by claims which give compromise a central role, since this warrants a modification of any claim, so as to accommodate others opposing it. A compromise need not, though, give equal weight to every side. It demands only that adequate account be taken of the claims of each. Only if there were an absolute evil, no component of which had any positive value, would it make sense to insist on the unqualified rejection of every compromise.

One way in which this conclusion apparently can be avoided is by identifying compromise with accommodation and thereby, in effect, giving it a psychological role. Following the lead of psychoanalytic theory, one might perhaps take an ongoing, desirable interplay of factors to represent a norm, and then go on to take a desirable theory and a desirable state of a people to be analytic components of this. That approach will end with a displacement of the issue; it does not resolve it, for a norm is a prospect, playing a role in what is present but itself still having to be more fully realized. Adopting it leaves one still faced with the need to act on its behalf. Its realization ends with its being filled out, made determinate, and involved with the contingencies of an ongoing world.

Truth is not to be compromised, but allowance should be made for whatever truth there is in accepted errors, and for other truths achieved from other positions. A religion need not make a place within itself for the beliefs and practices of others, but it should be made to recognize that its supposedly universally concerned and available object of worship could be approached in other ways. One's obligations are not to be watered down, but they must be realized in a world where other ethical demands are to be met. People's rights are not to be compromised, but their expressions must be adjusted so that room is made for the expressions of other warranted claims. In these, and in similar situations, compromise does not require a denial or even a qualification of what is claimed, but it does put restrictions in the way of the expression and satisfaction of various claims in order to give others the opportunity to be equally well-expressed and perhaps satisfied. The best of compromises preserves what is good in each contender so far as this permits their joint satisfaction. Neither side may be entirely content with the result, but this may still be better than what either could enjoy in a world where others are also insistent on their distinctive claims and values.

For an alternative to have a role in the world or society, it must accommodate what stands apart from and even opposes it. Self-denial and self-sacrifice are not possible if one takes no account of what is to be overcome, and thus of what one may succeed in hemming in but can never entirely annihilate. Every attempt to free oneself from the supposed evils or obstacles that the world provides involves a recognition, a struggle with, and some accommodation of them. That necessity may entrain the charge that the world or society is imperfect, inextricably involved with what ought not to be, and rightly left behind by anyone concerned with truth, excellence, ethics, or purity. No one, though, can free himself entirely from these splendors. Indeed, the very effort to do so testifies to their presence and depends on their use.

The Golden Rule,[3] the categorical imperative, a social contract, the greatest good for the greatest number, and other ideals, have to be realized by finite humans, in qualifying, limiting circumstances. Since none of these could ever be realized were it not accommodated by what is different from it, compromise requires an adjustment of different contenders both to one another and to the common value they diversely define, urge, or exhibit. The compromise also gives the common value a special, limited form in making it be the value that is actually shared.

Because compromise affects, not only the contenders, but what is used to bring them into accord, it is open to the criticism that it fails to do full justice to the values they are to share. Consequently, some people, insisting on the good that a compromise is to bring about, do not look favorably on any qualification that that good is made to undergo. They treat the modifications, which are made for the sake of harmonizing oppositional sides, to betray a failure to uphold what has a greater justification. Yet, if what is conceived by them is referred to what exists in fact, it would have to be qualified, since it would otherwise not be pertinent to a particular situation, or have an effective role. Of course, it is not necessary that the imposition of a good, dictating modifications to opposing sides, require that that good suffer in the process. On the contrary, since a pure form of what is good is the valuable at its most abstract, it can gain by being filled out—which is what happens in an excellent compromise. There, both the prospective good and the opponents benefit from being well joined. The outcome must be worked out in acts bringing the various components together again and again until the oppositions among them are eliminated or reduced to a minimum. It should then be followed by a rectification, making up for whatever losses the compromise inevitably involves.

A rectification adds, to what is achieved, modifications needed to improve the result. It changes one or more of the factors and the manner of their juncture so as to obtain a better result than a compromise could obtain. It may not only, as a compromise does, require modifications in the contenders; it may also change the degree to which the compromise is insisted on, modify the conditions under which the compromise is carried out, or require an alteration in one or all of the contenders. If rectification is elicited rather than imposed, it will call on hidden reserves and subterranean powers to change what is being done. Teaching is the art of having teacher and student provide such needed rectifications in a common effort to learn. Counterparts of it are to be found in social activities which do not just resolve conflicts, but enable contenders to make concurrent efforts to achieve a desirable common end.

Training, propaganda, and the conveying of information intend an alteration of a recipient's mind, body, or prospective actions. They are rectificatory. They do not exhibit that vital participation that teaching requires. This differs, from training and other ways of changing people, in its use of living discourse, in the ways it interlocks the comparatively knowledgeable and the comparatively ignorant, in its awareness of what has been accomplished, and in its attempt to bring about a better understanding and insight into what is as well as into what ought to be.

The best social practice takes account of a plurality of distinct procedures, imaginatively understands how various components might best come together, and both observes and alters under the guidance of what ought to be achieved. A good society is one that has been made good. This is but to say that a society acts over a region and time somewhat as a mature person does in going about limited, daily affairs—or conversely, that a good practical person does in one way and in the little what an excellent society, carried out by disciplined, knowledgeable people, does in its own way and in the large.

6. PERFECTED SOCIETY

1. SOCIALIZED RIGHTS

Most humans today live in a society and in a state. What they do in the one, may have little to do with what is done in the other. Either could play a major role, not always to its advantage. It might have gained more had it allowed greater free play to the other, or if it had acted in a different way.

Although one has to learn how to live well in both a society and state, even while continuing to exist as a person apart from them, some do not entirely approve of the life that their society or state requires or makes possible. They complain that no adequate provision has been made for them as separate individuals, vitalizing and utilizing their bodies for private ends and that, as a consequence, they suffer, fear, stagnate, or fail to be as creative and well-rounded as they could conceivably be. They reject the long-established view that maintains everyone should endorse and support what enables a number to make use of their common present, past, and future; supplement and support one another's limited achievements; speak a common language; participate in a diversified economy; have common ideals; and prosper.

A right is a valid claim. If it follows from the nature of a being, it deserves satisfaction. Such a right, as privately possessed, is inalienateable, expressing what a being is as apart from all others, living and using a body in unduplicable ways. Each actuality also has an inalienable right to prosper through specializations and the use of this inalienateable right. Though deserving to be satisfied, an inalienable right has its range and satisfaction justifiably limited, just so far as this enables it to be harmonized with the expression of coordinate rights by others.[1]

Whatever rights exist only so far as a society or state assigns them, are bestowed rights. These could conceivably be withdrawn with justification by a society (or state) when they cease to promote the preservation and enhancement of the society (or state). For its own sake, a society (or state) should of course bestow what will help the society (or state) be at its best. Since no actual society (or state) is as excellent as it should be, the rights it bestows, unfortunately, may not be those that should have been bestowed.

For the members, a union's, society's and state's main function is to sustain and make it possible for each person to be perfected. But what perfects a person has its own right to be and to flourish. The instruments used also have rights of their own, setting limits to what can be properly done to them. Everyone gains by being in a society and in a state. Unfortunately, all also lose by being there.

To have one's acts respect the nature of others, one must take account of them and, so far, adjust one's acts so that they are pertinent to the rights of those others to continue, mature, and improve. If this is not done, one will fail to do justice to what the others are and might become. Sometimes, one will derive maximum benefit by radically transforming what is used, but transformations, too, require that account be taken of nature of that on which one acts. A person should gain from being in a society and a state, but the gain will always be accompanied by some loss, for his or her activities must be modified in order to take account of them and of what they can provide, just as they, to accommodate the person in their own way, must take account of what that person is and may do.

The right to live requires people to collaborate with one another so as to meet great challenges. Each must, for a time, neglect acting solely on his or her own behalf. The right to live as a human being also requires an association with others and, so far, that one be turned away from most of the world. The right to prosper requires that attention also be given to those opportunities that society provides, and thereupon perhaps an occupation with items which may be less useful than what ideally could be provided, for as without those items, the right might not be realized, or be realized in a poorer form. Confined to those items, the right would be compelled to accept satisfactions in unduly limited guises.

Whether a right to life is exercised in a prison or a castle, it is loaded down with overspecialized, externally sustained determinations. Living in the castle will, of course, make it possible to continue and to prosper in a way not possible in the prison, but the living, as well as the prospering, will be subject to limitations in the castle as surely as they are in the prison. Whatever the society, what a person is able to obtain from it or through its agency limits, even when it contributes to what must be done and what can be achieved.

The contention, that existence in a society involves both a loss and a gain to people's rights to live and prosper, because a society can provide for their satisfaction only in limited ways, faces two strong objections:

The first holds that were a right not fully satisfied in a society, it would be irrational, innocuous, or meaningless. The objection denies that there are rights awaiting expression or satisfaction. It also implicitly supposes that posterity has no present rights, perhaps because posterity does not have duties toward those now present.[2] Were one to hold that the only rights a person possesses are those that a society does or could satisfy, one could not justifiably object to a society that does not make provision for the satisfaction of a human inalienable right to continue and mature. The objection also supposes that it is possible to have a society in which all rights are sustained or supported, or at least not overconfined. Yet responsibility, thought, and resolution are achieved and maintained on terms that privacy sets. Granting that something external to privacy must be provided, the first objection does not take account of the pirvate satisfactions some rights need and obtain.

The rights people express through the agency of their bodies, the second objection urges, are the only rights which need be considered. Those rights are addressed to others who could conceivably satisfy them. But there is then no assurance that all the rights people privately have could ever be fully satisfied. The objection also supposes that socially expresed and satisfiable rights are detachable from private rights and satisfactions, or it takes private satisfactions of rights to be the inescapable consequences of publicly provided satisfactions.

A person is more than a body, but is also never without one. While remaining private, each possesses and lives a body, and communicates by making use of it. What might satisfy that body as just a body will not yet satisfy the person as a single being who also has a private nature, independently making essential claims. Each person can satisfy some claims only through private acts; it is by such acts that one knows and decides.[3]

Private satisfactions of rights are not consequences of the satisfactions of public rights. Providing quiet, food, and books will not yield a satisfaction of the right to decide what one will do. Preferences require the exercise of a private power, able to accept or reject an alternative. Bodies, unions, and societies provide only qualified, limited means by which rights are satisfied.

If there is nothing that makes possible the satisfaction of the rights to live and prosper, or if these are able to be satisfied only in a limited form, excluding other modes of satisfaction, the inadequacy of what is publicly available is revealed. The right to live requires the presence and use of a body and various items in the world beyond, but it is not a function of what could satisfy it; instead, it assesses whatever it might use as being more or less what it requires. Not only do people not exhaustively express their privacies in and through their bodies while never freeing themselves from an involvement with them; they continue to maintain rights in a form that their bodies, unions, societies, and states are unable to satisfy.

From the standpoint of human privacies and private rights, all bodies, unions, societies, and other complexes are means. It is no less true that, from the standpoint of these others, those privacies, too, are means. There is no more reason to affirm the one than the other. We can therefore no more side with Locke than we can with Hegel. Locke failed to see that people have the task of satisfying the rights of other beings; these, too, have a right to be what they are and a right to be perfected. Hegel made the same mistake in the opposite corner, failing to see that if people are to serve a larger whole, this has the task of taking adequate account of what they are, require, and could become.

To this, it is tempting to reply: "If no body, union, society, or state can fully satisfy an individual's right, the right is just an idle claim. What cannot be satisfied by at least one of these is but a wish for what can never be." This is to suppose that the only satisfaction possible to a private right is to be obtained from what is external to the being possessing the right. That would, of course, require one to ignore satisfactions that could be privately produced. A claim to know is satisfied, not by providing information, but privately, by making use of interpretations and inferences. It is true, of course, that material and occasions for the satisfaction may be provided by what is in the public world. It is no less true that one cannot have a right to be and to prosper there, without also having to yield some to what else is present.

We are justified in insisting on our rights, and in complaining that they have been compromised, just as long as the world has defects that could be removed. Still, since even at its best the world is finite and, since some desirable occurrences are excluded at any given time by what in fact takes place, no one's inalienable rights to be and prosper in a world with others could ever be completely satisfied.

That is one reason why no person can properly be said to live a perfect, full life.

A society introduces requirements which are not absolutely necessary, not simply in the sense that others are possible, but in being dependent on its transient needs and defective nature. Its defects show that it is to be replaced or supplemented by a better society and by other agencies; its inability and the inability of a state and the world to take up all the slack contribute to the inescapable tragic nature of human existence.

A right is respected if it is provided with the opportunity to be satisfied. Not to respect it is to deny its possessor a deserved status and support. The right to exist is respected by the acceptance of a person as having reality; the right to function as an experiential being is respected in the acceptance of one as sensitive; the right to existence as a human is respected in the acceptance of a person as having a distinctive privacy; the right to prosper is respected so far as one is accepted as able to make use of what is needed in order to become perfected. We respect the rights of others by accepting them as persons who have a similar hierarchy of specialized, private powers, some of which are to be expressed apart from their bodies, and others through them.

Respect makes provision for the satisfaction of rights. This is done minimally by allowing for the rights to be satisfied, and maximally by helping people do what must be done so that the rights are satisfied. The respect people actually accord one another is in between these extremes.[4]

Duties, too, have a minimal, maximum, and intermediate form. One of the tasks of society is to determine the limits of these, and to introduce relevant specifications. Usually, it insists on traditionalized prescriptions of the work people are to perform if they are to remain members of it. So far as the society does this, it provides a measure of its respect for the rights of the collaborative and associated people who live under its governance. That right encompasses the private right of each to prosper, qualified by the limitation that this be satisfied when a number together face a common challenge and share a common spirit.

A person's rights receive some recognition when particular expressions of it are given particular satisfactions, various agencies make their satisfaction more likely, and they are dealt with in terms of principles acknowledging their range and warrant. A society can do this. But since it is concerned, not with what people are to have in order to make possible the complete satisfaction of all their rights, or even only those that are publicly expressed, it falls short of doing what must be done if the rights, separately or conjointly maintained, are to be fully satisfied.

From the position of its members, a society is always criticizable, even when it does all that can be done to secure the satisfaction of the determinate, specialized rights expressed there. The criticism will usually be directed at the governing conditions of the society. Although this may be no more accountable for the result than is the union that the people form, the fact is usually overlooked, in good part because a union is the product of unreflective interactions and joinings, while a society's conditions usually require at least a modicum of voluntary acceptance and independent action.

A person continues to be a private being while in a union. Each may there resolutely decide whether or not, as well as on the ways in which he or she will be part of it. No one can, to be sure, wholly escape from being in some union. And though all are affected by the society of which they are members, even when they turn their backs on it, they are able to so function in their union that they may go counter to what the society requires and prescribes. Their value is never fully captured in the duties they peform or in the rights they are able to satisfy in a union, a society, or in some other complex; these are too subject to contingencies to be able to do justice to human promise or to the good which the ideals pertinent to human dimensions specialize.

To make the best use of any means, its nature and course must be taken into account. The use involves the at least implicit acceptance of, and therefore the right of the means to be what it is. Its use should not limit the exercise and satisfaction of the rights it has, but it always does so, at least for a while. Nothing therefore should be treated as a means only.

We live and act by violating the rights of what we use, even when we take great care. An onion's right as a living being is jeopardized just by being seen to be edible; it is an item of food because of the nature it has, and will therefore be apt to have its right to be and continue denied. Because its right has little standing compared to the right of a human, its right to continue is denied with overwhelming warrant. The fact should not be allowed to obscure the truth that there will then be some loss in the value it has as just that one unit being.

2. Reconstructed Societies

Societies interact—they are unities insistently affecting one another. Because each insistency is in part a function of the interplay of a distinctive condition and union, it is always too late to try to avoid conflicts among societies by reducing or deflecting what these severally insist on. Their conditions and unions, and the interplay of these, should have been previously altered, and somewhat different, more harmonious societies produced.

A union and a societal condition are independent of one another. Still, they may arise together and share a common past, present, and future. Sometimes the union and sometimes the condition is dominant, reducing the effect of the other. Together, they constitute a single society that is able to interact with them. That society may at times have to be altered to enable the union and condition to act in greater harmony and with greater strength.

If a number of competing societies are to be properly reconstructed, they must be internally maximized. Each will then be able to be insisted on, even more effectively than it had been. It will surely continue to compete with others, since limited resources will still be separately needed and sought. The competition among the societies need not lead to conflicts; it could be an occasion for determining which one, if any, is to represent, control, or distribute for all. Not until a society is faced with radical deprivations is there warrant for it turning competition into destructive antagonisms. Before that time, there will, of course, be efforts at dominance and preferential use, and oppositions will continue to be fed by lacks and burdensome controls. If accompanied by efforts to make increasing benefits to the disadvantaged societies possible, the likelihood of serious and open conflict will often be greatly reduced. At present, the many steps leading to this result are not evident. An imagined reconstruction of actual societies though, could provide a guide, thereby making it possible to move further toward the desired goal than would occur were one just to vaguely hope that reason, reform, history, or a God will somehow produce what was desired.

From Plato on, it has often been supposed that the correct and perhaps the only way to improve society is by turning people into better social beings. The best of them, at least, it is often held, are to be trained and educated, and are to make themselves into representatives of the rest. Each is to incorporate the society's norms in habits and thoughts, and perhaps add practical wisdom and good will to this. A satisfactory reconstruction of society would, of course, not be possible did some people not act in some such fashion. It is as good role-bearers that they are able both to be joined to a common condition and to interact with the result. Plato was clearer here than Rousseau, explicitly affirming that a society needs some men to carry out specific limited roles.

Were one to succeed in reconstructing a society in an eminently desirable way, with a selected number of perfected individuals leading the rest, one would not yet have produced the best of societies. Such a society not only embraces all people; it recognizes all to be persons and therefore takes them to possess similar rights and to merit similar satisfactions. To achieve it, account would have to be taken of an ideal all actual societies are to realize in consonance. There is, however, little likelihood that that ideal will be realized, unless actual societies are first reconstructed. As they now are, they can separately or together realize only quite limited versions of what they ought to be.

Reconstructions should make societies apt to bring about an ideal society. To do this, the societies must act to realize it. Room must then be provided for people at their separate and joint public best, as well as for communes and communities, by themselves, together, and in relation to the society in which they function. There would have to be concentrations of efforts and the production of limited results, carried out in the light of what else has to be done. The task is enormous. The recognition of its magnitude and difficulty, though, makes it more rather than less desirable to have people try to achieve it. Exclusive emphasis on needed corrections in only a few areas is a major cause for there being so little progress made toward the achievement of an ideal society.

Even societies, each superb, directed at a common ideal, and supportive of one another, are subject to great hazards. Some of these arise from the fact that individual private efforts are sometimes directed at what may have no social import—objects of imagination, cosmological realities, ethical obligations, and the appreciation of the arts. Others arise because societies, no matter how excellent and compatible, interact in contingent ways and in contingent circumstances. If they are not confined within and subject to a state or some other power, they will, sooner or later, get in one another's way.

Sometimes societies exist in the absence of a state. Each can be reconstructed through the help of one, or apart from it. All can focus on the same ideal, work in harmony, and even support one another, without guidance or control. In the absence of a state, there will, though, be no way of assuring their continued harmony. In the absence of a state, too, there will be no clear understanding, protection, and satisfaction of publicly expressed rights, and no explicit formulations of what anyone may and may not do. Habit, memory, expectation, and hope would govern people, while reason and explicit rules would make only incidental and minor contributions.

3. The Best of Societies

All societies are defective. But they can be improved. Nothing in principle is in the way of changing an existent society so that it comes closer and closer to being a society at its best.

The best of societies differs from present societies by not being subject to all the limitations to which those societies happen to be subject. We may never come any closer to achieving it than we already have; the improvements we make might conceivably be inseparable from even greater losses. There is no reason, though, why improvements cannot always be made; no reason why each loss may not be compensated for, and some losses avoided altogether; no reason why the best of societies cannot be established eventually. That, at least, is what we would like to believe. Is the belief justified? We cannot know unti a number of ambiguities, doubts, and objections are overcome. The following italicized statements present some of the difficulties in the way, followed by replies in roman.

There are a number of best societies. One is best from the standpoint of people, another from the standpoint of a union, a third from the standpoint of society itself, and so on.

That is so.

Which one is to be produced?

All of them.

Then one will have many societies, each the best of its kind.

They are to function as components in the production of a single society.

They cannot do this except by being adjusted to one another, and thereby being limited.

The components of what is best need not themselves be at their best.

All the components are not of equal merit. No one would prefer a society that benefits a union at the expense of individuals' rights to live and prosper.

Knowing that, we know that people must play a vital role in the determination of how adjustments should proceed.

Men do not directly interact with the condition essential to the existence of a society.

They determine the constitution of the union that interplays with the condition; they assume positions in terms of which the outcome of the interplay is to be assessed; and they can so act that they make a difference to what is assessed.

Some sacrifice of or limitation in the exercise of rights will be required if people are to join together and the outcome is to be joined with the needed condition.

Human rights are to be satisfied. But their common good also deserves consideration. Each must give way to some extent to allow for the other.

None then will be at its best; the result will therefore have less value than it would otherwise have.

The best of societies is not a perfect society. It is only the best society that can be produced through the conjoint use of components, themselves not perfect.

There is no way to assure the production of the best adjustments. We must proceed by trial and error.

That means we must learn as we go along. We must make trial of many alternatives, and learn from our errors.

There is no evident end to that process.

We cannot now know what is defective in, and what must be done at some remote, later stage. But we can see how the improvements we have already made can provide a base for other improvements. We do not now know what these in fact and in detail must be.

Then we cannot know that they can be made.

We also do not know that they cannot be made.

This still allows for the existence of a defective society that cannot in fact be improved.

What cannot be further improved is the best society that could be produced.

The best of societies could then have serious defects.

Yes. This shows that if the defects are to be removed we must move beyond society.

That requires us to return somewhere near where we began, adopting a standpoint of a constituent of society.

To overcome the defects in society, we do not have to go back to its constituents. Instead, we can and must move beyond the society to the state, and even beyond this.

This is to confess that the best of societies is not achieved by improving actual societies, but by doing something quite different.

No, it is to hold that what is in fact the best possible society may have defects which can be compensated for only by taking a stand at a complex of which the society is a part.

Whatever other position is adopted, it will have to be viewed from the position of individuals.

Not necessarily. One might adopt the position of an imagined state, history, an Absolute, or a God.

Is that what you are maintaining?

Reference is made to these only to make evident that there are various positions from which a society can be assessed. It is not necessary to accept or to attend to them to know the limitations of a society, or how to overcome or compensate for them.

No society is satisfactory if it does not provide for all the rights of all people.

In the best of societies, all the rights will be expressed, and there obtain some satisfaction. These will be greater than what could be provided in other societies. The society, too, will make provision for the presence of a maximum, common good.

The aberrations, obstinacy, greed, fear, selfishness, ignorance, and stupidity of people forever preclude the existence of the best of societies. This is emphatically so, if that society is to be one in which the rights of all are satisfied.

The best of societies encompasses whatever people there are in whatever condition they can achieve. It is not one in which all rights are satisfied.

A society of aberrant or obstinate people is not as good a society as one in which these are not present.

They may be members of a society in the same sense and to the same degree as others are. One society is better than another not because it excludes some individuals but because its members act in mutually supportive ways.

You cannot rightly expect all to be mutually supportive always. No one has perfect self-control; all have vices. You may envisage, but you cannot produce a society where all act and remain in harmony, and still have individual desires, ambition, and energy. All need to be constrained by threat or act.

A society that cannot be improved upon—whether its limitations be due to the failures of people or of some other factor, or to the ways in which these are joined—is the best of societies.

We today do not know how to avoid wars, hatred, poverty, and sickness. This shows that we have not yet found a way to obtain the best of societies.

That does not mean that those defects cannot be overcome.

If we do not now know how to free ourselves from the faults in a present society, will this not be the best of realizable societies?

We do not know what we are unable to remove unless we try. New efforts must be made.

The tyrannical, mean, villainous, overly ambitious, indifferent, and smug will always be with us.

Their likelihood, power, and effect can be reduced.

We have never been able to do it.

In fact, it has been done. Training, discipline, education, admonishment, reward, punishment, counteractions, and safeguards have not been without result. Our society functions in rather steady ways; many of those who did not fit well within it have been gradually enabled to do so. There is no point where one can antecedently put a stop to all possible improvement in character and social activities.

All advice and rules are general, but what is needed are specific acts producing specific results by working over what is now available. No one can know in advance what those specific acts will be, since they exist only when they are produced.

Although training, teaching, and coaching require the vitalization and modification of what is offered in order to be effective, their results are not entirely unpredictable. Sometimes they have been carried out with considerable success.

No matter how adroit the trainer, teacher, or coach, individuals make use of what is offered in unique, unrepeatable, privately determined ways, with results which we cannot fully anticipate.

Success cannot be assured at any particular moment or occasion. All that can be counted on, and what has in fact been achieved again and again, is what is better for most, for the most part, and over a considerable period.

Eastern sages and some Western ones have abandoned the idea that people should or could be made into better social beings.

The claim that it is better to withdraw from society does not require the denial that social existence has value.[5] If people could become better by withdrawing from society, they will also be able to become better beings within it.

This is to make withdrawal a preliminary to a more successful life in society—not what the sages intend.

This is what withdrawal means from the perspective of society. And some sages, the neo-Confucians, for example, do concern themselves with making people better, not only by themselves but in society.

If you know how to produce the best of societies, why not do it?

Understanding the nature of a society is a means to that end.

How could we ever know we had come to that end? Finding that we have not been able to improve on some society, will we not have to conclude that it is the best possible? Yet it may be only what is the best possible for us to attain then.

An account of society which attends to actual people and the ways they can meet their challenges, and also attends to the rights they have, the conditions they meet, their values, and the best ways in which the various factors can be joined, provides a frame within which actual progress can be programmed. We know that we have not come to the end in our efforts to improve society as long as it does not deserve endorsement from the positions of individuals, their unions, and the conditions with which these interplay. Eventually, account will also have to be taken of the state and of the Commonhealth in which all people are encompassed, as well as of the final values in terms of which everything must be judged.

What is to be done now?

Improve our understanding of society, and use this to help us see how actual societies are to be reconstructed.

And then?

Produce the reconstructions, train the young, restrain the deviant, attend to flaws, improve the unions people form, their roles, and the ways the different factors interplay. If we can, we must teach, appreciate, and create, always ready to take account of what had been muted or neglected.

Who is to do this?

You and I, and every other mature human being.

If we do not?

We will need to be helped by those who have advanced beyond the point where we now are, so that we can live in accord with an ideal prospect, within reconstructed societies, themselves guided by what society is at its best.

PART II

Governments
and
States

PROEM

A state is needed *not*

a. In order to enable individuals, each dangerous to the others, to live in some accord. To hold that, is to overlook the fact that people have been and are still together in communities, communes, and societies, functioning well for long periods in the absence of a state, and in considerable independence of any state that might in fact exist.

b. In order to compensate for a supposed incompetence or stupidity of people severally or together. To hold that is to overlook the fact that no one lives long who has not learned from experience what it is wise to expect and desirable to do, both for themselves and for others.

c. In order to overcome the chaos that would occur when groups of people attain a particular size; when they engage in activities involving exchanges of goods; when they want a stable economy; or when they need an impersonal adjudicator to determine exactly what they had agreed upon. To hold that is to neglect the fact that daily affairs and agreements can be well carried out by people with established habits and common expectations.

d. In order that they be properly prepared to overcome dangers from within and without. To hold that is to overlook the fact that societies are stabilized by effective common traditions and ideals, and that their members are intimately and effectively joined to one another in opposition to what is elsewhere.

e. In order to make good a supposed inability of societies to provide the stability, vision, or control people need if they are to live peaceably together. To hold that is to overlook the fact societies often outlast states; that they are governed by steady ideals and common memories; and that together their members effectively limit the actions of each one.

A state *is* needed

a. Because definite formulations are required, stating what may and may not be done in hard, borderline, unusual, rare, or unlikely cases.

b. Because it is desirable to have before people, clearly expressed and stably administered determinants of what they are permitted and forbidden to do, presumably so that all will be benefited.

c. Because it is desirable to have a means for making long-range plans, enabling each person to know what may be required of him or her and of others, then and later, and by their successors as well, in addition to what common traditions and ideals determine and prescribe.

d. Because impersonal, established determinants of justice are necessary, and arbitrary restrictions and denials by others, or by dominant factors in society, are to be avoided.

e. Because account has to be taken of the presence of others with whom it may be desirable to make long-term commitments.

f. Because express account has to be taken of the welfare of the people, and the needs and rights of posterity, beyond the vision or concern of those who attend mainly to their daily affairs.

g. Because people have inalienable rights, the expressions of which need clarification regarding their range and limits, and because impartial ways are needed for amicably determining where, when, and how the rights are to be satisfied.

h. Because each person has individual ambitions, powers, and requirements which come into conflict with those insisted on by others, and impartial effective ways are needed for settling conflicts among them.

A state, though, does not provide a complete or perfect answer to the question of what must be done if people are to be or become fulfilled beings, since

a. It does not take account of what people are privately.

b. It may itself be overwhelmed by the force it needs in order to carry out what it formulates and decrees.

c. It is compelled to take account of the presence of other states with their independent, distinctive needs and demands.

d. It needs a distinct government to formulate, execute, and interpret what is required for the continuation and prosperity of itself and those who are governed.

Neither a state nor its government is the exclusive provenance of people with special virtues, possessions, or inheritance. It needs the help of intermediaries to express what it requires and people deserve; it also needs the backing of force in order to have its decrees be effective in the face of lassitude or opposition, while yielding to Law, a specialized form of justice, to determine what it may do and prescribe. Possessing a distinctive space, time, mode of operation, legitimacy, authority, objectives, and ideal, it will be at its best only when it makes it possible for people to be mature, privately and publicly, and finds a place for itself in a civilized world where people are ethical in intent and in act.

Perhaps even more evidently than in the first part of this work, it is necessary, in order to understand what is here being maintained and to assess its truth and worth, that one join a reasonableness characteristic of mature people in daily life to an understanding of the structures, natures, and relations characteristic of ultimate realities. If this is done, a new, sophisticated reasonableness—"prudence", "judiciousness", "practical wisdom", and "praxis" are alternative terms—will be achieved. This joins a knowledge of specialized forms of controlling final conditions with the good sense used by those who are well adjusted to the course of experience. One is then in a position to know why and how to progress from society to state, and from there to what lies ahead. Its deliverances are to be checked by seeing whether or not it does justice both to what one is able to understand about the nature of space, time, causality, and other specializations of ultimates, and to what people daily know and do.

Once it is determined that what is being said accords both with a specialization of what is ultimately real and what is justified by experience, it will be necessary to understand how they are joined. That knowledge requires a good use of sophisticated reasonableness. This must be used by the reader as well. It differs from the reasonableness carried out by well-functioning members of a state, both rulers and ruled, primarily in being intellectually and privately rather than practically and publicly expressed. It is also more alert to the nature and grounding of controlling conditions, and has a better grasp of what should be than is possible to those engaged in action.

Focal Points

1. People need neither explicit nor tacit agreements in order to be subject to a common governance.

2. A state has a nature, career, tasks, rights, and duties, distinct from those possessed by a union, rulers, and the interplay of rulers and ruled.

3. In a state, people have the status of subjects, governed beings, and citizens.

4. A government is a One for many occupiable positions in it.

5. Givernance needs legitimization; its authority expresses a status; its prospects are possibilities awaiting realization.

6. Positive laws are authoritative, enforceable enactments by a legislature, confined within limits determined by other branches of the government.

7. A government may enact laws which apply to those who rule.

8. Law has a teleological component.

9. Some of the main objectives of a state are presented in the "Preamble" of the United States Constitution, in a descending order.

10. The outcome of an adjustment of government and people is an actual state, engaged in realizing a distinctive objective.

11. Citizens have public rights.

12. A reasonable person takes account of established practices, pertinent objectives, and likely responses.

13. People may assume accountability for what they do; a state ascribes accountability through its distribution of rewards and punishments.

14. A state prescribes what it is right for public beings to do.

15. The Good is an ideal specialized by limited goods, expressing the perfection of distinct entities.

16. Mankind is a constant in every human being.

17. Historic mankind is humanity joined to what is done in time.

18. In the humanized world historic mankind is joined to human achievement.

19. In the evaluated world people assume accountability for occurrences in the humanized world.

20. The Commonhealth is the evaluated world in the form of a state.

21. The demands of ethics are not limited to the Commonhealth or to what it encompasses.

7. The Function of a State

1. Rulers and Ruled

If anything in this shifting world is desirable, some control will have to be exerted to bring it about and to preserve it. If desirable relations are to be instituted or maintained, one or more of the related beings must be in control, or recourse must be had to a power able to dictate to all of them. Were people natively foolish or wicked, they would have to be controlled and redirected for their own good; but even if they were natively good, they would need the help of a neutral power to enable them to remain in that desirable condition indefinitely, and also to give them opportunities to express their supposed goodness when they interact with one another, and what else there be.

Insistent and dominant at one moment, a person may be passive and dominated at another; while in equilibrium with what is here, each may be conflict with others there. Steadily related in some respects, all vary on the ways they are related in others.

A power able to dictate to people will injure as well as benefit, unless they are able to manifest themselves in steady, desirable, dominant ways, in the face of intrusions, as well as in their absence. This is the sound idea behind theories of anarchism and communism—and of democracy as well. All not only remark on the danger of the power that a dominant government is able to exercise, but are also confident that violence, history, or the free expressions of preference, will enable a supposedly latent goodness in man to become persistently dominant. All take account of an obvious part of a great idea: everything should become excellent. But this requires more than overcoming what is in the way of free expression. Creative, productive action is also needed. Whether or not a person is latently good, whether or not any one has a sound grasp of human nature, whether or not that nature would be fully and properly expressed were various blocks removed, it is still correct to maintain that everyone ought to become an excellent, public being. Were one to suppose that people are natively wicked, foolish, or undirected, one could still continue to hold that they ought to be excellent in fact and act. This, fortunately, does not mean that one would have to underwrite the methods or acts of the defenders of such a view.

What ought to be deserves to be realized. That is an objective truth pertinent to cats and trees, indeed to everything. The capacities of each should be realized fully, in harmony, in a world where others have their capacities similarly harmonized. Whatever the being, each is to be as excellent as that kind of being can be. Whatever its nature, its abilities are to be developed and utilized in harmony, in a world where others have their capacities similarly developed.

Difficulties with the idea, that every being ought to be excellent, arise when an attempt is made to state just what capacities each has and should acquire; what must be done in order for the capacities to be present, expressed, and satisfied; and which ones are to be limited, qualified, subordinated, and utilized at a given time and in a particular situation if all are to be benefited maximally. Capacities are potentialities, indeterminate and interinvolved; to express and realize them is to change what is undistinguished, incomplete, merely promissory, into the distinct and determinate, with features and activities not present before.

Since desirable benefits may be achieveable only at the end of an indefinitely long period or, because of untoward circumstances may never be realizable or not be realized except by precluding the realization of others, it is necessary to know which capacity must be neglected at a particular time, and perhaps be left forever unrealized, in order to achieve a result that is better than any other that could be obtained.

There is no knowing in advance what must be done at a particular time in order that maximum realizable good be achieved then or later. The differences which circumstances make cannot be known before they are present and operative. One can anticipate, predict, or prepare for them, but one then does no more than concern oneself with what is general, not yet affected by the obdurate details which occur only in an actual, present stretch of time.

Experience, knowledge, and habit help reduce the surprises which actual occurrences produce; they never succeed in eliminating them altogether. The present is always new. A theoretical science or a logic may ignore or abstract from what in fact occurs, and therefore ignore the difference that so sharply marks off the present from the past and the future, but it would be fatal for social and political theories to do so, for their topic is actual humans in a changing world of goods, opportunities, and difficulties. The use of those theories in practice requires a control and use of the various factors, in consonance with what the theories justify.

Social and political practices depend on the art of determining what must be done if people are to be perfected together to a degree they otherwise could not be. Justifications for the acceptance of the demands to which people are to submit, for their own good and also to benefit that which is required to benefit them, should be provided. Since the agencies by which people are to be enhanced have their own natures and requirements, reference must also be made to human capacity and to possible satisfactions and, therefore, to the time and manner in which demands are to be qualified or denied so that a proper, greater satisfaction can be achieved.

Strictly speaking, ought and should are to be distinguished. "Ought to be" speaks of an excellence measuring whatever occurs. "Should be" speaks of an excellence that could be exhibited. The "ought to be" presents a standard, the "should be" directs. "Should" falls short of the "ought," pointing up the limits within which actualities and actions occur. "Ought" falls short of controlling the "should," thereby pointing up limits to the "ought's" power to determine what occurs.

A statesman brings about what should be to a degree not otherwise likely. A theologian insists on the ought, regardless of what can or does occur. The first dismisses the second as utopian; the second criticizes the first for being content with what is defective. Political action is carried out in between. What should be, for it, is what ought to be. A philosophy of politics goes a step further to consider how the should and ought affect one another. It thereby points people toward an end relevant to but outside the scope of political action.

Like statesmen, political philosophers need to attend to what should be; like theologians, they should take account of the ought. They are interested in a realizable good, and, therefore, both in what can in fact be achieved by people existing together in an excellent state, and in that to which such an excellent state is inescapably attached. That good does not demand the rejection of any state, or the abolition of its good. It assesses all existing states, and makes a difference to their natures, course, and roles. Although the good for this world is superior to that which a state could provide, the presence and realization of that good depends in part on the perfecting of whatever states there are.

What people should be and do is what they politically should be and do, enriched by what else should and ought to be. Each is to be perfected individually and together with others, under common, effective conditions, inseparable from an ideal in the guise of an ought pertinent to all. The best of states, if separated from that ought, would be too neglectful of tradition, insufficiently keyed to the depth of human privacy and its possible perfection, to be able to do justice to what people are, need, and could obtain.

A government is part of a state. It there has a double task: provide an agency by which people are enabled to achieve results not otherwise possible; exhibit a value and nature to be preserved and enhanced. One cannot dispense with it, without losing an invaluable instrument, having a stability, rationale, and power able to maximize the ways people are able to exist together apart from the rest of the world, even while they continue to exist in it. It cannot be reduced to just a means, without destroying a possible embodiment of justice in it, expressed in the form of demands pertinent to those who are being governed. It is also true that no one can remain completely within the confines that a government prescribes without squeezing his or her interests and satisfactions within unduly narrow limits. If there is to be adequate provision made for persons, account must also be taken of their attempt to know, express themselves, act morally and ethically, satisfy their religious concerns, and engage in the arts, sciences, and speculation.

A central problem for politics is that of making the best possible use of whatever enables people to live well together and to be individually benefited to a degree otherwise not possible. Questions of rights and duties, of obedience and service for it refer to what must be acknowledged and supported in order that such outcomes be efficiently and effectively achieved. Although there could come a time when the functions of a state and its government were encompassed within a larger enterprise, there never will be a time when the state and government are rightly eliminated, since there are precious goods which they alone enable one to obtain. Without these, large numbers of people will not live together equitably for more than short periods.

A government is an agency making possible a distinctive kind of satisfaction of the publicly expressed needs of a limited group at a particular time and in a particular place. Like the house in which one lives, it yields a desirable good only so far as its nature is respected and promoted. To function well, it must be sustained and its value promoted. The use of it by people is to be balanced by a use of the people by the government. This makes the people its agents, while they use it to promote their individual and common goods. Both government and people also have their own rights and needs, to be satisfied with the help of the other.

No state is identifiable either with a government or the governed. The product of their interplay has its own nature and career. In it, each side has the role both of a principal and an agent, user and used. Were a state identified with its government, the status of citizens and their public rights would expand and contract in accordance with governmental decrees; were a state identified with the governed, the existence and functioning of the government would await the consent or submission of those who are ruled and, so far, would not lead, not condition, not truly govern. People will not function well together for long unless they are jointly guided and controlled and, therefore, compelled to act in ways they otherwise would not. But there can be no good government except so far as those who are governed have the right and ability to oppose, accept, and modify what is governmentally demanded.

Rulers and ruled are distinct. Each has its own value and being; each both insists on itself against the other and is affected by it. Both are encompassed within the state that they help produce through their interplay. That state's distinctive nature and career is dependent on the ways they affect one another. Somewhat as the meaning of a sentence, while affected by the ways in which its words are ordered, gives the words a new import, a state transforms the very government and governed on whose interplay its very existence depends. There is an ought that applies to it, and there are particular things it should do at different times, depending on what its constituents require; it acts properly only if it helps them flourish in harmony.

People must be governed, for a number of reasons: None are all that they should be. Each is inadequately related to the rest. None exist in perfect consonance with all else, or with reference to what should or is about to be. Only a completely mature person could possibly be perfectly good, since this requires that all desirable potentialities be realized in harmony. Only a completely mature person could be in complete control; but like others, such a person would also have powers which were unexpressed or poorly expressed at some time.

No actual human being could fully exercise all of his or her powers in consonance, in part because past experiences still have an effect, in part because different abilities are expressed with different degrees of urgency at different times, and in part because a full satisfaction of one requirement sometimes demands a withholding of satisfactions from others. Were there someone who had attained perfection, he or she would exist in a world where others were less perfect, unless there were none who were immature, poorly disciplined, lacking restraint, unable to master themselves. Because there are such imperfect beings, others have to do more than be good in themselves and do what that good requires. It is necessary at times for them even to ignore what it is legally expedient to do, in order to be both excellent and well-related to others.

The world is vast and little of it is under human control. No one is perfectly adjusted to its course; all are faced with sudden challenges, unexpected contingencies, and demands on attention and energy, for which they are ill-prepared. One can never do much more than be ready by and large, able to take account of what is familiar, slow-moving, repetitive, and easily controlled. To some degree, the world is always alien. All one can hope to do is to anticipate its course, by and large, and try to avoid or reduce its adverse outcomes.

Contemporaries are independent beings, endangering and satisfying in ways and degrees for which no one is fully prepared. A knowledge of the natures of actualities and the stable course of the world may sometimes enable one to predict what will be, but no prediction will do more than mark out possibilities. The realization of those possibilities involves the introduction of details, obduracies, and compulsions, giving to the possibilities a concreteness and career they would otherwise not have.

The excellence of a person requires both virtue and knowledge. Neither the one nor the other, though, is detailed enough to do full justice to what is needed or to what in fact occurs. People are more complex than other beings, and, since their understanding of one another is sometimes even less reliable than is their knowledge of other kinds of being, they cannot be counted on to have a sure grasp of what any one will do. All mature beings, of course, know something of themselves, and what to expect from others, but no one knows enough. What is known by one will not make possible a sure knowledge of just what any other is and will do.

People live together in some harmony because they have learned to so act that major frictions are reduced and various disagreeable consequences avoided, deflected, or modified. Defects in their virtues and knowledge are partly made good by the pressure of common ways, by the people being disciplined and directed in the course of their development, and by their awareness of the disagreeable consequences which follow on some deviations from acceptable ways.

Part of the governance people need in order to be able to become mature and to function well together becomes available in the course of their unreflective adjustments to the presence, acts, threats, and promises of others. So far, they neither need nor make provision for a state. Tribal ways and social customs, though not enabling people to be perfect in themselves nor assuring their harmony with one another, may still make it possible for them to live passably well together for quite a while.

The question, will there ever be any other governance than that which tradition, ideology, a shared place, and a common spirit provide? has usually been answered in one of three unsatisfactory ways: compensation for the indifference or ignorance, which people have with respect to the needs and welfare of most of those with whom they form some bond, will always be forthcoming; the best of people will make it their duty to control and guide the rest; people will voluntarily submit to some common control in order to protect themselves against aberrational or undue insistencies.

Since few know or care about what most of the others do, most will need the help of those who are able to govern well. A time will come, the first answer claims, when all people will be wise enough to see to it that they are properly ruled, or when the poorly qualified will be fortunate enough to have those who are well-qualified take over the task of governing them. There is, though, no necessity that such governance be forthcoming, or that when it exists it will function as it should. Appropriate and effective at one time, it may not be appropriate or effective later.

The second answer holds that the best people will make it their duty to take over the governance of all, in part because only they both know and are ready to act in the appropriate ways, and in part because they were perfected by having exercised the virtues which are needed in order for a state to function properly. That answer is not much better than the first. The best of people will not always find political life agreeable, particularly since it requires them to give up a concentrated concern with art, science, religion, and speculation.

Plato seemed to deny this, being apparently willing to pay any price to get his ideal state. Aristotle reduced the cost by treating a good state as the locus and occasion for the exercise of a people's primary, practically oriented virtues, but he did not say that this was the best thing humans could do. Nor was he entirely clear about the way to get the desired outcome with less error that would result were the governance in other hands, or were it achieved in other ways.[1]

Like other people, those who rule rarely give up the advantages that accrue from their being able to limit and direct the rest. It is desirable that they be well-disciplined; that they be practically wise to a degree beyond that which others attain; and that they take ruling to be a duty performed for the sake of all. There is, though, no separate set of such humans, who alone have the ability or desire to decide to, and do in fact act well.

The third answer looks to the people themselves, taking them to be wise enough to see that they will avoid needless strife and hurt if they agree to have someone rule over them all. But if they are to do more than form a union, they not only have to be in sufficient consonance with one another to be in harmony, but have to bind themselves and perhaps their posterity to the terms of the agreement. A change in their interests, and the fact that posterity had played no role in the forging of the agreement, would carry little or no weight. A plausible case could perhaps be made out for holding that people unavoidably enter into an agreement with one another and with some ruler—in the shape of a person, an institution, or law—on reaching some stage in their maturation, and that this agreement is revocable when the government fails to act in the ways the people had tacitly supposed it would when they initially agreed to do what it demanded of them. One would then have to suppose that each individual, on reaching the stage of being accountable for actions, joins other equally accountable beings, and that their joint accountability involves a submission to a common power determining the rewards and punishments they are to receive for doing or failing to do what that power demands. Even if it be granted that people's accountability for what is done would be insufficiently determinate were there no such determinant of its range, and of the rewards and punishments that would be relevant, it does not follow that there ever was or could be such a determinant. At best, people would have had to make a tacit agreement with one another as accountable beings who were ready to accept such a determinant. Were they just to wait for this, they might wait in vain. Were they, instead, to agree to produce or to accept some governing power, they might find that it sometimes, or perhaps always, fails to do what was agreed upon. That power may be strong enough to prevent its overthrow. Making provisions for regular elections, petitions for recall, short terms of office, and the like, provide at best only partial assurances that those who are in control will be deprived of their status and power when they fail to do what had been supposedly agreed upon. To become a sadly disillusioned person, nothing is so efficacious as the failure to remember that those in whom public trust has been placed may betray it. Too often these take advantage of their positions to violate with impunity their part in any actual or supposed agreement.

Whether or not there is an implicit or explicit agreement between rulers and ruled, those who rule are required to do certain things just as surely as those who are ruled are required to do others. Each side has its own rights and duties, and should have both the ability to see that the rights of the other are respected, and the power to assure that the other fulfills its duties. It is not the submission of one side to the other that makes for the health of a state, but the support and help which each provides to enable the other to obtain what it needs and deserves. That can be done only when it is known what it is to be ruler and ruled, both in fact and ideally.

Nothing less is needed, if a healthy state is to be possible and enabled to prosper, than a knowledge of a desirable prospect, the tasks the rulers and ruled are to carry out in a common state, and what each must do to support and enhance the other. The achievement of that outcome has to be worked out in a contingent, ongoing process in which each side both functions well and provides maximum accommodation and help for the other. Otherwise it will lose some of what it itself needs in order to be at its best. Neither an absolute sovereign nor the people should be the final arbiter. Each side must not only recognize that it has only limited rights and duties, and should have only a limited power, but should realize that its task is to help the other so that both can be excellent and in harmony, inside a healthy whole encompassing both.

It would be good to have Aristotelian virtuous people in charge; it would help to have a Rousseauean common will determine what the people are to do. It would be better if both ruled and rulers also knew that each depends on the prosperity of the other and saw to it that there were virtuous people who ruled, and who made sure that the people got what they need and deserve. One moves toward that desirable outcome when not only those who rule but those who are ruled are good, concerned with promoting the excellence of others as well as of themselves. Rulers need to be attuned to the rights of people, and the ruled need to be concerned with the enhancement of what they wish to have benefit them. So far as either side fails to do what helps it and the other be perfected, it falls short of being and doing all it should.

Tradition, ideals, common practice, rituals, and moral codes keep most people in stable and tolerable relations to one another. Often sufficient when aberrational behavior is infrequent or minor, and the rest of the world keeps more or less within familiar grooves, the restraints do not enable one to know what to do in borderline cases, in crises, and when subject to great challenges. If these limitations are to be overcome, people must have the intelligence, power, and virtue to act so as to benefit both themselves and others.

These three answers incidentally show that one needs a governance other than what established ways provide; they should supplement one another. More will be needed. No matter how wise and will-intentioned, how well-trained and concerned rulers may be, they not only have moments when they are incompetent and yield to unwarranted and regrettable impulses, but they need help from those they rule—and conversely.

To make it possible to plan for and protect against conceivable, but not precisely predictable deviations from usual desirable behavior, clear formulations of what is permitted and forbidden are needed. They will most likely be produced if some people devote themselves to the task of stating and enforcing conditions to which all should submit, and make provision for both minimizing untoward effects and compensating for losses. Since no formulation, no matter how precise, could provide for all details and contingencies, were one to try to take account of all possible occurrences, one would end with an intolerably complex program, and still fall short of what in fact occurs.

What is formally or linguistically expressed never does and never could duplicate an actual occurrence. Not only do actualities have a dynamism not caught in any formalism or language, but they are subject to forces operating outside these. Practical wisdom, therefore, moves beyond the generalities with which such expressions stop, to attend to what in fact occurs. As a consequence, it inevitably alters the import of what is formally or linguistically presented.

Formalists take details to be incidental qualifications of what is essential, constant, and important. Their laws and codes seek to capture the essence of what occurs, so specified as to enable one to determine when, where, and how the essence is present. Personal involvements lead others to take certain situations to be unique, and therefore to require unduplicable treatments. Where the one finds justice embodied in laws, the other finds equity exhibited in the way in which unique occurrences are treated. Neither is able to deal well with what must be done in a state. Here pragmatism makes its most defensible stand. Taking a position between the other two, it allows for both general formulations and the difference that actual occurrences produce.

Makers of laws need to be pragmatists, modifying the meaning of what they formulate by an understanding of how established law functions. If they are good law-makers, they will fit their formulations in with others which have withstood the test of time, presumably because they have been sanctioned by a grasp of what people are and need, what they do, and what is to be expected of them.

People need to be governed, because they would otherwise not be able to know how to act well for an extended time, except so far as the course of the world, as well as their tradition and ideals, remained fairly constant. What is formulated must be carefully applied, and recognized to be altered on being brought to bear on actual occurrences. Laws will help, since they make possible a clarity, range, and use not assured by custom, virtue, or good intent. Without these, though, the laws people need in order to be well-governed will not likely be enacted or be successfully applied.

A law must take account of existent people and prevailing circumstances, and have its meaning transformed in the course of being carried out. To provide intelligible guidance, it should be well-formulated and well-applied, pertinent to people as they in fact are. Those who are subject to it must, on their side, be receptive to it, while insistent on expressing themselves and obtaining what they require. As a result, a law will be triply transformed—by being brought into the body of established law; by being made pertinent to actual people and circumstances; and by being altered by the people's acceptance of it.

Laws are intelligible and imposed; behavior is both habituated and more or less unpredictable. Laws are vitalized by the people on whom they are applied; people have their public behavior stabilized by laws. Together, they constitute a single complex where that people is subjected to prescribed, intelligible, inherited, stabilized conditions and demands; all the while, as so many individuals, with their own minds, wills, interests, and powers, they will make a difference to themselves as public beings together in a union under a common governance.

Laws must have their meaning and range modified if they are to be in accord with the union people form, and the circumstances that then prevail. The laws will still continue to have a status apart from their application. Also, no matter how receptive, obedient, and submissive people are, they will, in their privacies, and as quickened and sustained by those privacies, continue to maintain a status apart from their common governance and the laws. Even when a union of the people and governing conditions are well joined, each member will continue to be a private insistent being, able to assess what is done, as well as that to which all are publicly subject.

From the standpoint of those who are being governed, the governance to which they are subjected needs a warrant. That warrant has a three-fold form. One is grounded in the past, providing it with legitimacy. A second is grounded in the present, expressing its authority. The third is obtained from the future, defining its desirable projects. Of course, from the standpoint of a governance, the behavior of people, to which the laws inevitably more or less yield, is itself in need of a warrant.

People are to act in accord with what is governmentally permitted and required, and thus are to be obedient—which is to say, law-abiding in ways which almost always respect past practices. By giving power and direction to what governs them, they help maximize the degree to which their governance will be preserved and enhanced and they, incidentally, revealed to be well ruled. So far as they are occupied with and act to sustain the powers that restrain them, they become people of practical wisdom, acting in consonance, to produce a single public world where they live in a steady and designed accord.

These requirements are subject to qualifications by a state. Although this is only a product, it has a nature and prospects of its own. Once brought into being through an actual interplay, it sets limits to the interplays that can thereafter occur within its confines—ideally, in such a way that it will continue, be stabilized, move toward being as excellent as a state could be, and be able to interact with other states in ways neither its government nor its people, or these together, could wholly determine.

It is tempting to deny that a state has any reality, when one approaches it from within, since all that there ostensibly occurs is the interplay of what governs and those who are governed. The temptation must be resisted. States are unities, bounded off from one another in a larger world. There, wars are fought, treaties and alliances made and broken, and a common world-history forged. Once that fact is acknowledged, it is possible to return to the state as self-enclosed, and to recognize that, in addition to the interplay of its constituent government and people, there is an ideal prospect that can be used as a guide by it as well as by the government and the people. A state deals with this directly, but without deliberation or consciousness. Its government deals with it incidentally as it pursues its own objectives. The people may concern themselves with it in either of these two ways, but they may also deal with it deliberately, so as to help produce a state in which they can be at peace and prosper.

The constituents of a state, and the state itself, need grounding in the past, help in realizing what they should, and an opportunity to be adequately expressed in the present. Any one of these requirements may be met at a particular time, but nothing less than the satisfaction of all will yield a state where rulers and ruled come to full expression, aiding and sustaining one another, and the state itself is renewed constantly in a progressively better form. What actually happens is usually less than this, for every act, no matter how well-prepared for by people well-trained, has its elements of novelty, requiring a creative adventure, rarely well and fully carried out by rulers or ruled, separately or together.

One can formulate the primary conditions that a good interplay of rulers and ruled should meet, and still not encompass all that in fact occurs, for it is not possible to do more in advance of an actual effort, with its not entirely predictable course and outcome, than to limit the likelihood of radical deviations. The greatest of artists, despite their unusual control, skill, and intent sometimes blunder. It is not to be expected that even great statesmen, alert to the ideal their states are to realize and maintain in opposition to others will, with their more recalcitrant and unfamiliar material, have a greater degree of success or a greater number of successes than great artists achieve with better training, techniques, insight, and discipline, using more controllable and better known instruments.

The knowledge of what is required in order that excellence be attained, though eminently desirable and perhaps indispensable, never suffices to guarantee that result. To bring about what should be, one must call upon fresh, free efforts of creativity. But those very efforts contain within them the risk that they will prevent or reduce a success otherwise possible. Politics, like art, is an adventure. No one can predict what will be achieved in either, except in outline, by and large, and in the absence of untoward contingencies, failures of insight, loss of control, misjudgements, and the like. There is always room for even the well-planned to be side-tracked, radically altered, or precluded.

Governances and governed need help from one another in order to function at their best. There are eminently desirable ways in which each side is to act. Tradition must be continued, ideals given an effective role, and both supplemented by the interplay of rulers and ruled. It is necessary, too, if a state is to become as excellent as it can be, for its continuance and well-being to the concern of both those who govern and those who are governed.

2. THE TASKS OF A STATE

A society offers people a greater degree of guidance, protection, and success than they themselves separately, or as just together, could provide. Were it not that it has no well-focused or well-controlled power or boundaries, and no stated, intelligible, stable rules and regulations, there would usually be little need to go beyond it to find other ways to help and protect people who collaborate and associate, sometimes quite well for a time. The help and protection are provided by a state.

A state imposes articulated, enforceable demands on people who are together in a society. It may forbid the actions that the society prescribes or allows, thereby revealing the society, itself, or both to be defective. Defective or not, a state has the necessary function of providing a governance that could benefit people in a way and to a degree not otherwise possible. Inevitably, it credits the people with a different value and gives them a different status from what they had or could have in society.

To this it may be objected: a state is no more than a fragment of a society, distorted and controlled by a powerful segment of this; it yields whatever is desirable and possible for people to have, their private or social status having no power or reality; or it can provide all that people require.

It is a Marxian, or at least an Engelsian, claim that a state is the result of an usurpation of power on the part of the socially privileged, whose status is the result of an economic exploitation of others. Once that usurpation is overcome, it is thought, the state will "wither away", and people will live together properly. That such usurpations have occurred, that evidences of them can be found everywhere, it would be foolish to deny. Perhaps they can never be eliminated. Even millionaires compete with one another, denying one another opportunities and rights, and assuming for themselves, while denying to others, the status of members of a superior class. But there is no reason why discrepancies in power and income may not be denied importance or radically reduced without eliminating the state, or even the situations where such usurpations occurred. They surely do not show that a state is undesirable or unnecessary.

To suppose that after a state has "withered away", there would be no need to reestablish some other, is to suppose that it is possible for people to function together splendidly over a considerable period without explicit rules and the enforcing of these, and thus without an authorized government determining what others and perhaps itself as well are permitted and forbidden to do. It is also to hold that warranted rules and enforcements merely make explicit what is implicit in a supposed excellent society. But it is naive to think that people are natively good, and are corrupted only by an economy in which some inescapably exploit others. No matter what the society, some people most of the time, and others some of the time, insist on themselves to the disadvantage of others. An absolutely unselfish person who does only what is good to others is a fiction. At best, all have to be occasionally redirected by those who rule, and helped to maintain a position where they know how to and will act with benefit, or at least without serious loss to others.

Marxian thought diverges from the Hegelian, with which it is related in vital ways. Hegel thought more highly of the state than Marxists do; he also had less interest in individual men. There is warrant in Hegel for an Hegelianism of the right which takes people to be truly human only in a state, and to be envisageable as distinguished from this only as inverted, condensed versions of it. On such a view, whatever a state provides is both all that could be expected and eminently desirable. One's rights will here never be violated if one does what the state demands. But a state reaches only to the limits of people as publicly together; it entrenches on but does not govern private beings. Were there no such beings, there would be nothing beyond the limits of a state, and therefore nothing which could independently assess, contribute to, or intend to act within it. There would be no one to decide to carry out the state's demands, or who could privately enjoy what it provided; no one to ask if the state was functioning properly; and no one to determine whether or not, in fact or in principle, the state could be improved.

Disobedience, for an Hegelian, is either a mystery or marks a deficiency of being. If so, it is not possible to see how any person could oppose his state. No being, deriving all its existence and power from a state, could have power enough to oppose it. Let a state be grander, more real, and more persistent than any person could possibly be. It may still be ignored and sometimes opposed and may even be overthrown.

Legal and political positivisms start and end with an actual state, while conceding that men exist in contradistinction to it as so many public beings. What that state requires and does, on this view, is observable, articulatable, and verifiable. Claims about people's privacies or inalienable rights are dismissed for referring to what no one presumably could know or make intelligible. Since, on this view, only the state has rights, nothing from its position is to be deemed inviolable. Violations of its decrees are forbidden and are to be prevented, supplemented perhaps by new opportunities offered and sustained. This much, it is thought, could be guaranteed; this alone is to be affirmed. Whatever a state does will then, once again, be beyond all criticism. Yet a state sometimes imposes requirements which work to its own detriment. And it can surely be biased, unfair, inconsistent, and arbitrary.

If rights are credited only to people or to governing law, the claims of the other, to be or to do what it requires in order to function, need not be acknowledged. And we would have to suppose that the laws or the people were just brute or imaginary occurrences, able to have defensible or intelligible roles only so far as they had been lifted up or vivified by the other. Laws would be a naked force verbally disguised, or individual private beings would be fantasies mistakenly thought to be real. Yet laws place restraints on force, and people sometimes act deliberately.

Since a public person is continuous with a private, and since public adventures make a difference to what can be privately realized, what a state does, to protect and promote public people and rights, will make a difference to the viability, and therefore to the expressions of privately maintained rights. A person will continue to have privately grounded rights as long as he or she lives but, depending on what is publicly allowed without penalty and one is publicly helped to maintain, those rights will have to be expressed in different degrees and ways at different times.

Whatever rights a person privately has are inalienateable, unable to be taken away, though their public exercise may be limited, qualified, and even precluded. The rights possessed by a public person are those inalienateable rights given a bodily role, and thereby the status of inalienable rights, which is to say, rights that could but should not be denied. In addition, a state may bestow various rights at different times; with the same authority and with the same justification or lack of it, it may also take away those rights. To suppose that all rights originate with a state or with whatever governs or controls, therefore, is to allow for those rights to be withdrawn or limited when this so decides. Nor would there, on the hypothesis, be anything amiss if some rights were allowed to some and denied to others.

People have inalienateable and inalienable rights, and continue to have them even when their public expression is unduly hobbled or denied. A constitutional right to speech or assembly refers to what a state permits them to do in public without penalty. If those rights or any others be recognized to have private grounds, they will have a different form and meaning, as private, from what they have as public. Privately, they will be one with an inalienateable insistence of the person, or some epitomization of this, to be and continue; publicly, they will be inseparable from an inalienable demand for protection or support by a state.

Privately, the right to speech or assembly is the inalienateable right to frame expressions for oneself or to decide to come together with others. Publicly, the right to speech or assembly is the inalienable right to say or do things in public which do not adversely affect the persons and activities of others. A state has the task of giving the right a protected expression.

Well-formulated, enforceable laws clearly express the public rights that may be exercised. No consideration so far is given to the question whether or not these have private forms or grounds. The reference of the Ninth Amendment to the United States Constitution to rights reserved by the people is a reference, not to inalienateable private rights—these are outside its purview—but to the inalienable rights men possess.[2] Unfortunately, the Amendment does not indicate what these are.

Positivistic theories of law rightly insist on the fact that public rights are what a state determines. When the theories go on to maintain that there are no other rights, they deny not only that there are rights which people privately possess, but also that these have inalienable rights held in reserve or in opposition to the state. A somewhat similar denial has led some theologians to take a state to owe all its powers and privileges to God. Evidently, positivism and theology are not as radically opposed to one another as they suppose themselves to be.

By crediting people with rights, and taking the state to be just an agent for seeing that those rights are satisfied, one does not obtain the opposite of what a positivistic theory of the state affirms. Credited rights are not rights privately possessed. A genuine opposite of a positivistic theory would be a personalism that takes all rights to be wholly private. The acknowledgment that there are inalienateable as well as inalienable rights, never reducible to one another, stands in between positivism and personalism, with their respective denials of private and public rights.

A right not exercised in public is outside the reach of the state. So far as a right is carried out in public, it limits and is limited by rights allowed to others. Exercised in opposition to various realities and their rights, it is open to control, definition, modification, or denial by whatever powers govern public existence and activity. The private form of the right will thereby be affected, for it is continuous with the public, while still maintaining an independent nature and way of functioning.

A public person, alone or together with others, has a distinctive nature, power, and career. Each faces various opportunities and challenges, and can be controlled in ways that are not possible to anyone as just private. Although a state may be able to offer support for whatever is publicly expressed, it is never able to deal with private inalienateable rights. At best, it will take account of these when they are exercised against the expressed rights, demands, and acts of others. Necessarily, what it does on behalf of any of a person's publicly expressed rights, whether inalienable or credited, will never be adequate to the claims made by that person as just a private being.

A publicly expressed right may have unwanted effects, and for that reason a state may demand that its expression be modified. A state also has requirements of its own. It cannot allow any expression whatsoever to be a proper public form in which a right is publicly exhibited. The most that one can ask of a state is that it impose the fewest possible restraints on activities, and then only so far as those restraints are consistent with both the people's and the state's demands to continue and to prosper.

No state is a person; what it requires of people is expressed through the agency of a government and in the way this defines citizenship. When its rights are urged against its own citizens, or against the claims of other states, some people within it will act as if they had expressed what the state rightly needs and demands. Hitler was properly called a "leader", for this marked him off from all officialdom, and pointed up the fact that he claimed to do more than govern. As a leader he made demands on all the people, both governing and governed, and did so as a sovereign presumably acting on behalf of the state directed toward the achievement of a particular objective. A related role is sometimes assumed in non-fascistic states by those who act as their statesmen, a fact somewhat obscured by their also being members of a government. That there is a difference between these and a true sovereign[3] becomes obscured in crises, when the citizens for a while are treated as just subjects.

From the people's standpoint, a state is to be used to promote their continuance and perfecting, enabling them to be together in mutually enhancing ways, and thereby better able to function as mature beings. From the standpoint of the state, the people are its agents, to be used to promote its perfection. Neither, though, should be used without regard for what it is, needs, and could become. A state and people are likely to be most effective and yet beneficial to one another when the natures and powers of each, as well as the government's, are understood, respected, and sustained.

A so-called right of disobedience is expressed when people refuse to obey what they take to be bad laws, or when they question the warrant for holding that some decree is a true law. To lay proper claim to such a "right"—strictly speaking a privilege—people must act to benefit others, and deliberately place themselves in a position where they can be dealt with in accord with established legal procedures. They will then differ from criminals, not only in acting on behalf of all, but in inviting apprehension and trial, and accepting as proper whatever decisions, favorable or unfavorable, are reached through the use of established legal agencies. No one has an inalienateable right to disobedience against the state as such, since they could have this only if states always coexisted with people. They could, though, be said to have an inalienable right to resist and oppose whatever precluded the full satisfaction of an inalienateable right to continue and prosper.

That inalienable right is the inalienateable right viewed from the position of what might limit, qualify, or ignore it.

If there were no neutral way for determining whether a decree is just or unjust in requiring that some acts and not others entrain penalty, acts of disobedience which would be criminal when viewed from the side of the state might be desirable when viewed from that of the perpetrators. Someone might be asked by both sides to determine which should prevail. That person would have to make, not an arbitrary decision, but an objective judgment about the competing claims, requiring a reference to a standard outside both.

The fact that either people or the state can raise relevant questions about the acts of the other, points up the governing presence of Law[4]—a distinctive kind of general condition—independent of both, instantiating a primal justice. A state, though standing apart from and comprehending both governing laws and governed people, still remains under that Law. More or less embodied in expressly formulated laws, the Law prescribes equitable requirements and procedure, to be appealed to as independently assessing the acts of both rulers and ruled, and the state that encompasses these.

To know whether or not and to what extent the people in a state, the government to which they are subject, and the state itself, may be rightly opposed, one must know what each would be like at its best, and what makes such excellence possible. That means one must know what Law requires of them, and therefore what is to be considered if they are to be at their maximum and in harmony.

Just as people privately exist apart from the state, and the state has an existence apart from them and the government, so Law has a reality apart from the people, government, and state. Pertinent to the essential natures and functionings of people, government, and state, it provides a basis for determining what should be done if these are to work well together, and to receive what they deserve. Appeal to it is sometimes rejected because it is not formulated, and seems to have no other meaning than that of an imagined admonition that justice is to be done. It is, of course, not specific, but neither are references to due process or reasonableness. The criteria which enactments must meet in order to be good, sound, genuine laws cannot be formulated, without being unduly narrowed—and they would then depend for their full warrant on a still unformulated Law. The neglect of that fact has led many to suppose that Congress makes laws.

When it is said in the First Amendment to the United States Constitution that "Congress shall make no law . . ." what is evidently meant is not that Congress is forbidden to pass—and is threatened with punishment should it do so—whatever enactment it does, following its usual procedures, but that the other branch of the government, the Executive (and later also, the Supreme Court), is expected to deny the status of genuine law to any enactment that establishes a religion, etc.[5] If this is not done, the United States of America, as defined by the Constitution and the Amendments, is at an end. The Amendment would have been more precise had it read "There shall be no law respecting an establishment of religion, or prohibiting the free exercise thereof", and if an appeal were made to Law, specialized in the requirement that the branches of the government are to agree on what is an actual law.

Each branch of the government is to act in terms of Law; it is not to put irrelevant obstacles in the way of the other branches. The appeal here, as always, is not to Law as apart from all specific laws, but to it as a condition able to be present in every law, a universal to which every law adds details and specifications, a constant prescribing the limits within which every law is to be confined.

Law is inseparable from itself as grounded in a less specific conditioning form. Although Law is not formulatable in terms appropriate to specific laws, it is not unknowable, and surely not unknown or always ignored. Knowledge of it—like the knowledge of a person's privacy and the nature of a state as determinative of the roles that persons and laws will have within it—is to be obtained, not by turning away from what occurs and trying to imagine something else instead, but by using actual laws as evidence, somewhat along the lines followed in learning about ultimates, privacies, and the functioning of actual states.[6] Like these, laws provide evidences of what conditions and expresses itself in an observable area.

To know what Law is, one must move through particular accepted laws toward their common condition. New terms will then be needed to express what is being evidenced. Both those who practice civil disobedience and those who determine the validity of their claims, appeal to that Law. Disagreements regarding the validity of laws requires an independent determination of the nature of Law, and of the limits put on its instantiations. Beginning with any enactment, challenged or not, one must look for its warrant first in legal procedures, and then in the legitimacy and authority of the laws' sources and interpretations, to end finally with what preserves a tradition of accepted decisions and the prospect of a peaceful coexistence of fulfilled men in a well-functioning state.

Law does not embody an absolute ethical principle. Nor is it a command that needs to be sanctioned by a religion, or by being universally accepted. We know it because it is partly embodied in the history of civilized humanity and in the established frame within which generations have lived, and expect others to continue to live. Since civilized humanity is precisely that segment of the past that is known to have lived in some accord with Law, the claim appears to be circular. It is not actually so. The nature of civilization is learned in part through historical study, while the nature of Law can be discovered through the use of evidence provided by accepted laws.

Since a state is independent of people, both in its nature and requirements it is conceivable that the promotion of its interests might interfere with theirs. The use that people rightly make of a state may conflict with the use this rightly makes of them. It is not correct, therefore, to hold that a people's primary task is to serve a state, or that a state is to do nothing more than promote a people's good. Each, to become better, we see once more, must strengthen the other, and use it so that both benefit.

Able to enter into relations with others of a similar nature, a state requires its rulers and ruled to interplay in special ways. That it is distinct from both of them, it sometimes makes evident by demanding sacrifices from both. In crises, it will demand the sacrifice of power by the one, and of leisure and the pursuit of noble ends by the other—and sometimes of their lives as well. Those demands need justification. This is not completely done by showing that a greater number is saved or enriched than is ignored or diminished, for the good that it would then provide would not be an unmitigated blessing; instead, it would make evident in another way that this is a world in which desirable instruments and achievements are brought at the price of regrettable losses.

Ideally, the private rights of people are to be provided with occasions to be satisfied, and are to have their public expressions both harmonized and satisfied. Sometimes a state is where this is best done. Because it has its own nature and needs, and can act in only some ways at a particular times, a state will also require what is regrettable from the standpoint of people, their unions, and the conditions with which these interplay. If something better is to be brought about, one must perfect the state—and then pass beyond it.

8. GOVERNMENT

1. GOVERNMENTAL POSITIONS

The members of a government fill out positions there and may there be subject to the very rules they promulgate and enforce. A dictator, or other sovereign, who makes a government do what he or she wishes, is still distinct from this, not only as a master is distinct from a servant or slave, but as one who has no governmental position. Such sovereigns have subjects, humans who are subject to them, shifting in status and privilege as those sovereigns decree. The truly governed are, instead, people together, keeping in some accord with what is impersonally demanded of them by a government through the agency of laws, formulated, interpreted, and backed by those who fill various governmental positions.

Were just one person a ruler, he or she would be lawmaker, judge, and executive in one, interplaying with independently existing people. The governments of actual states, though, are so complex that they must be carried out by a number engaged in performing different tasks. Some people might change the conditions under which other roles are carried out, add or subtract power from them, and the like, but they would not be able to take over all those roles without having to be in many places at the same time. No one person could ever be an absolute ruler without having to preclude the functioning of indispensable parts of a government.

Being dictated to is often so disagreeable that one does not care whether this is done by the members of a government, by a sovereign who acts independently of any government, or by one who uses this solely as a channel for decrees. Nevertheless, there is a great difference between a subordination to an interlocked set of people carrying out fairly well-defined roles who not only affect one another but together interplay with those who are ruled, and a sovereign to whom others are subject and who interact with that sovereign only by complying or resisting. The interplay of ruled people with a ruling government is an interplay of parts which need one another; the interaction of subjects with a sovereign has each maintaining itself as well as it can, over against the other.

A government maintains a number of positions where distinctive

179

work is to be done. Some tasks may be more important or carry more prestige than others. Sometimes a government outlasts a dominant figure; sometimes it does not last as long. The two evidently cannot be identified. Even if a government pivoted about the decisions of some one person, it need not change with that person's passing, since he or she may there have acted in a position linked with others and, with other people, helped constitute a persistent legitimate rule.

A government includes all the rulers in a state, no matter how they reached their positions, and regardless of the nature of their status or power. If subject to parliamentary control, a monarch is part of the government. If the monarch is set apart, perhaps with special privileges but with little or no power, the sovereignty is in name only, not in act. The sovereign might then not be able to make contact with subjects except through the mediation of them as governed or as citizens. If so, those people would not be directly subjected to the sovereign; their functioning, as governed or as citizens, would be in the way. The sovereign would be privileged to stand apart from, but would not rule them.

Those elected by ballot become part of a ruling government as surely, but no more surely than do those who are appointed, meet civil service requirements, or usurp power. Some laws may expressly apply to them, just as others may apply only to those who are governed. Despite the claims of a Nixon—"If a President does it, it is legal"—to be above all laws, he too is subject to them, as Nixon eventually learned. Were no laws to apply to him, he would not be part of a state, but at best only a sovereign for it.

A government embraces a number of positions in various relations to one another. If those relations are antecedently laid out, or abstracted from a functioning government and then formally stated, it should be possible to draw a diagram indicating how the different positions are related to one another, and to show whether they are ordered hierarchically or coordinatively. A constitution, so far as it specifies the ways in which primary powers and duties are distributed, is in effect such a diagram. There, positions and relations of the main subdivisions are marked out and perhaps segregated into a number of groups—executive and legislative; legislative and administrative or, as in the United States of America, executive, legislative, and judiciary. Other groupings are surely possible and may at times be desirable. In the United States, the judiciary achieved its present standing as often at the top of a hierarchy of itself, the executive, and the legislature, largely through self-definition. But the other two also occasionally take themselves to be more than they were designed to be. Each, fortunately, has been held somewhat in check by the others, and by its own sense of the need to function in some consonance with them.

Although in principle subject to the orders issued by a superior, some of those in subordinate positions in a government enjoy a good deal of autonomy. The armed forces may be under a president, their commander-in-chief, but they more or less go their own way. They also use funds, for which they are theoretically beholden to the legislature, with astonishing independence. And though the legislature is the designated source of enactments, multiple regulations and rules are promulgated and enforced by regulatory agencies and other bodies about which it knows little and does nothing.

A legislature is hemmed in by an executive; the interpretation of what it does is within the provenance of the courts. A judiciary, in turn, can have its decisions blunted (in the United States) by amendments to the Constitution and by legislation; it also recognizes that the executive has special privileges, not within the power of the courts to curtail. An executive—particularly in such a state as ours—while under the law can, through veto power, pass judgment on it and, through the command of the armed forces, defeat or deflect what was legally prescribed. Like the other two branches of the government, this too is but one part, with a distinctive position related to the others in a single interrelated whole, readily positioned on a diagram.

A diagram is empty. Its positions are not filled; instead, they are related by what are no more than notions for actual connections. Its import and functioning depend, not only on what is outside its control, but on those who fill the positions and vitalize the relations. The people who are part of a government will, of course, actually be together in ways the diagram can do no more than outline. The shifts in power which inevitably occur in the course of the daily conduct of a government makes evident that a diagram can be accurate only on a high order of generality, and to the degree that struggles among officials and departments for dominance are muted, postions are properly filled, and relations among these are maintained.

In a schema, the lines between positions on a diagram are changed into arrows, some going in one direction, but most going in both. Those arrows point up the fact that what is done in one position has bearings on what is done in others. In one case, they represent a transmission of information; in another, commands; in a third, reports of compliance or achievements; in a fourth, requests. Some arrows end at what is nearby; others pass beyond these to what is remote. The order of importance, dignity, or graduated steps that an initial diagram may present are thereby transformed into a multiplicity of attachments.

Hierarchically ordered positions are of various types—principals and agents; complements; regions and subregions. These may be mixed in different ways in actual governments, with one becoming dominant for a while and then giving way to others. Knowledge of their pure forms makes possible a better understanding of the mixtures that usually occur.

When there is a strict chain of command, those at the top of a hierarchy issue orders which those below are expected to carry out, usually by acting in sequence, each performing part of what was initially commanded. Although the subordinates are supposed to enjoy some independence, they so far function primarily as agents. Many of the problems raised by their status have been spelled out in a long history of legal decisions dealing with masters and their servants or slaves, employers and employees, generals and subordinate officers, officers and privates, husbands and wives, and parents and children. While a hierarchy of rulers in a chain of command does not match any of these exactly, many of the rights and duties are quite similar. Principals are accountable for some of the acts of their agents, just as masters are accountable for some of the acts of their servants. The principals determine the kinds of lives their agents will lead, not as much but still somewhat as the owners of slaves do. Employers appoint, promote, and dismiss; their commands have to be obeyed just as surely as the commands of generals, although the cost of refusal or delay is usually not as great. Unquestioned acceptance of directives may be required of agents, just as they are of noncommissioned officers and privates. And the principals may be held accountable for acts they explicitly forbid their agents, somewhat as parents are sometimes held accountable for what their heedless children do.

The relationships connecting occupied positions have been largely determined by constant readjustments over the course of a slowly modified, unexamined series of practices. Sometimes, they are suddenly produced at times of crisis. Their exact nature is then not easy to determine, with borderline cases inevitably breeding inconsistencies and promoting confusions. Ideally, a hierarchy has the different parts of a central task antecedently prescribed as having to be carried out in distinctive positions by people able to do what is required. To form such a hierarchy, it is necessary to distinguish what is essential from what is accidental to the functioning of the whole, identify its essential joints, and effectively order the various parts in relation to one another. This is rarely done. The divisions of labor that prevail in governments, as they do in factories, railroads, and other organizations, are often adventitously produced, and may be retained long after the passing of the need that prompted them. Sometimes subordinate positions are occupied by those who function without explicit instructions, or in considerable independence of what is being done elsewhere. This is to be expected whether the positions are filled by experts or by incompetents. Commands and orders may be quite simple and clear, but require action by a number of more or less independent agents. Sometimes it is difficult, and even impossible, to mark out in advance where and how different parts of a complex enterprise are to be carried out.

A government moves with elephantine grace and speed. The attribution of its faults to a bureaucracy, where impersonal, indifferent, minor officials waste time and money, tends to hide the fact that the bureaucrats operate mainly as agents for others who are themselves subject to still others of higher rank, none with a sure, definite understanding of what may or may not be done. Orders are given, tasks assigned, evaluations instituted, but these often fall short of determining just what in fact is needed, is to be permitted, or is to be done.

Those in lower positions do not always just follow orders. Often enough, they also work together with and against principals, reassessing, modifying, and sometimes redirecting and correcting what they are asked to do. They, and their acknowledged superiors, more or less complement one another, somewhat as the members of a family do. When the contributions of subordinates are equal to or greater than those of their superiors, they still continue to remain subordinate. The information, advice, reports, and activities that they provide add to what their superiors already have and use; these, in turn, may complement the work of their subordinates by extending advice, guidance, and training, and modifying what is presented. The complementation can be codified. Express times and ways may be provided, specifying when and how all are to work together. Conferences, briefings, and general discussions, too, may promote complementary activities without disturbing the established order.

Complementary positions in a hierarchy require reciprocal activities, somewhat similar to those carried out by naval officers on shipboard. The hierarchy is preserved, at the same time that the activities, in which the different officers engage, serve to support one another instead of fitting into a possibly prescribed, unilateral order. Mutual support may become so dominant in fact that a hierarchy may become hardly more than an order of precedence on minor issues, or a matter of honors and privileges of little practical importance. The establishment of a hierarchy, through the provision of titles, privileges, or even power, may then prove to be mainly a means by which complementary activities are hidden from public view. Just as nonacademics think that presidents, deans, and chairmen of departments are more knowledgeable than the faculty, those outside a government mistakenly think that high ranking officials are more knowledgeable than those at lower ranks.

Were a single movement downward alone permitted in a hierarchy, agents would do no more than introduce modifications into what was being demanded by principals or their intermediaries. If, instead, people, principals, and agents complement one another, they can make possible the production of a body of conjoint rulers. There, transmission upwards as well as downwards occurs, and a common result obtained. A hierarchy in which such complementary action takes place is not properly identifiable with a group of cooperative people. The latter presupposes some equality; the former does not.

Contributions by agents in a hierarchy are always open to unilateral review, rejection, or modification by principals. Since complementary activity occurs within the compass of a continuing hierarchical ordering of positions, it is perhaps inevitable that those at the top of a hierarchy will not be strongly complemented. Not only will their status contribute to that result, but the other members of the hierarchy will tend to take them to be a source of decisions, and not their objects. That is one reason why principals rarely receive the frank, uncensored advice they should get. They need to be guided by those who have learned what the commands in practice mean. To get that, the principals have to be complemented, not simply obeyed.

An ideal complementary ordering of positions adds, to a well-ordered hierarchy, a subordinated reverse hierarchy where agents guide their principals. It can be achieved when subordinate positions have the secondary status of being at higher ranks in some respects with reference to those which are higher in a primary hierarchy. The positions and ranking in the reverse hierarchy may not coincide with those in the primary. Yet what is to be done will be partly determined

at positions in the reverse hierarchy. There, suggestions, emenda-
tions, and the like will be made and transmitted. This is what is
mainly done when the highest position is the source of a command, or
of a primary, indispensable element in what is to be achieved.

In a bureaucracy, where commands are muted, there will rarely be a
well-segmented task carried out in a well-defined sequence. Instead,
passive resistance and neglect will modify what is being demanded,
thereby giving the reverse hierarchy considerable effectiveness. The
whole will function best if both hierarchies are explicitly acknowledged. Channels for complaints and redress of grievances, and a common means by which positions in the reverse hierarchy are connected,
are vital to the functioning of an effective, well-ordered government.

A diagram may reveal a government to have a well-articulated
structure. The different positions marked out in this will have distinctive relations to one another and, with these, provide an articulation
of the whole. In the light of this, cabinet posts may be abolished or
added to; departments may be merged or subdivided; postions in one
part of a hierarchy may be moved to others. None of these changes
need affect the ways in which different kinds of components are
interrelated to constitute a single, intelligible government, though, of
course, the elimination or addition of a position will affect the articulation of the whole. Just as a sentence may maintain a constant meaning while an adjective, adverb, or phrase is added or subtracted here
or there, so a government may remain constant, despite changes
made in and to various positions. Each position can be distinctly
defined, with its special tasks and limitations specified. If it is, the
rationale of a government, where various positions are occupied by
those who rule, will be spelled out mainly in the relationships which
intelligibly connect those positions with one another.

Positions considered apart from their occupants form an abstracted
set of termini for an abstract rationale. This is to be distinguished from
the rationale connecting positions in a diagram or schema. In these,
positions are so many place-holders, enabling the whole to be intelligibly presented. Detached positions of principals and agents, or of
complementaries, are the product of abstractions from a functioning
hierarchy; positions in a diagram or schema are connected by means
of formalized relations. The nature of the one depends on what occupants do at different positions; that of the other depends
on what a hierarchy of positions—which may not be occupied—require. Were one to start with occupied positions, the positions would

be primary, and the relations connecting them secondary. Were there just a hierarchy of positions, there would then be no more than vacant places, formally joined. Political analysis attends to the abstracted positions and relations; constitutional conventions attend to diagrams and schema. The one tries to report a fact where the other tries to attend to structures.

A government is to be distinguished from actual people. Like them, it also exists through time, occupies space, and carries out various activities. That it is temporal, will perhaps be readily granted, for were a government not in time, it would have no place for activities. It must be spatial and dynamic as well for there would otherwise be no way in which it could be brought to bear on separated individuals and, like an empty promise, would never issue in act.

A government embraces an ordered set of positions. In that guise, apart from all the occupants of its positions, it has a unitary temporal, spatial, and dynamic distension, somewhat similar to that possessed by private persons.[1] Like them, a government sets boundary conditions for a limited number of occurrences within it, in relation to one another.

A government stretches over the entire region that a state effectively controls, though on a different plane from this as well as from that occupied by those who rule or who are ruled. Not until a government interplays with a people is there a single active state with its own distinctive occupation of an extended spatial, temporal, and dynamic region. Then the government is related to individuals in somewhat the way in which these are related to the subordinate bodies which exist within the individuals' boundaries.

What is lower in a hierarchy of principals and agents, or of complements, may extend over larger extensions than those in positions which are higher in other hierarchies. And, since it would not be amiss to take the position of an executive or of a number of rulers to stretch over an entire government, it would not be improper to add that their positions achieve a greater extension than others do. If subordinates are viewed distributively, of course, each will usually fall within the range of the extensions of those on a higher level.

There is no necessity that a hierarchy of positions coincide at every point with one determined in other ways. A larger region of space may have a different contour from a smaller; a longer period of time may have a different rhythm from a shorter; a process of causation on one level may have more remote effects than one occurring on another.

A government whose offices are located in a particular city is, so far, an aggregate of occupied positions. As pertinent to the entire area in which the people it rules exist, it is a set of interrelated positions. The nature of its rule determines the reach of the government, a government being no more confined to the places its offices or officeholders are than an earthquake is confined to the place where its tremors originate.

A government cannot be exhaustively subdivided into separated smaller parts. Its occupied extensions in space, time, and causality are undivided and indivisible; the positions marked out and connected there, are not separable from it.[2] When occupied by actual people, those positions will, of course, be separated out from the whole, without compromising their continued joint presence or their own extensional regions.

To deal with a government properly, we must act in accord with its contours, keep abreast of its rhythms, and reply to its insistent rule. In order to extend its rule, it need not always be provided with further space, given a longer life, or enabled to have a greater influence; it may be necessary only to increase the number over whom it rules. This will be desirable, of course, only so far as these are thereby benefited.

The claim that the less government the better the government, the people, the state, or all three together, has warrant so far as it refers to unnecessary regulations and an exhibition of an excessive degree of governmental independence. The main task of a government is to contribute to the flourishing of an excellent state, a result that cannot be separated from its enabling people to live a good life together. No less valid at times may be the claim that the best government governs, not less but more, for this may then be the best way to achieve the required result. What is to be feared is not government, but the kind that does not respect the nature, promise, and rights of those who are ruled, and what must be done to enable their state to be perfected.

There are at least two distinct, valuational hierarchies worth distinguishing. In the one, more and more positions are harmonized; in the other, the harmony is more and more effective, involving the positions with one another in greater and greater degrees. There seems to be no way of assessing the two types of hierarchy in relation to one another except in terms of an objective demanding that a maximum number of positions be splendidly joined. Although something can be said for a small staff that is well-integrated, there is little warrant for holding that it is always superior to one that is larger and more loosely connected, particularly since the two may be engaged in non-interchangeable tasks. Sometimes, the first is to be sacrificed so as to promote the second; sometimes the second is to be sacrificed to promote the first. A maximal, effective combination of both is needed, conceivably in any one of a number of forms.

No matter what the virtue, power, or dignity of principals, they will not do sufficient good if they do not enable those below them to be at maximum strength, to work effectively together, and to be able to benefit those principals as well as themselves. A harmony of wide range can be bland, lax; one that was effective might awaken antagonisms and disruptions. A principal may have to emphasize one form for a while, but sooner or later an equilibrium point should be found where all can act as they ideally should.

2. OCCUPIED POSITIONS

When positions are occupied, their natures and those of the people who occupy them are affected. By occupying the positions, each enters into special relations with the occupants of other positions within the same unitary government. Although when occupied, the positions are related to one another in ways they were not when empty, often enough the difference is not great, and one could take empty and occupied positions to be not worth distinguishing. One will then be inclined to speak as though there were people who fit snugly into their positions, just adding tonalities to them. People, though, are alive, and positions, while without content, have definite relations to one another. Each makes a difference, but in a different way, the one providing concreteness, focus and energy, the other terms for relations to other terms.

Despite their lack of content, unoccupied positions may be differentiated sharply on different levels, and recognized to require different kinds of occupants. Interrelated in a government, they are affiliated, and this in a number of ways. The different positions, which are to be occupied by legislators, an executive, and the judiciary, may there fit well together, oppose one another, or exhibit both features. The consonance is expressed in the United States in references to the relations holding among the branches of the government; the opposition is expressed in references to their independence. The combination of the consonance and opposition is expressed in the bearing the branches have on one another.

Branches of a government relate limited numbers of governmental positions. They are unities intended to divide the main work of the government in essential ways. Their independence from one another should, therefore, be so limited that the formation of separate, antagonistic subgovernments is avoided. The determination of the ways in which they are to act will require some self-limitation. If the branches cannot or do not limit themselves, they will make evident that they are so far not able to constitute a final rule. They would then have to await determination by a sovereign distinct from them all, possessing power enough to be able to make them function in a prescribed order and manner. Such a sovereign, able to regulate and control all the branches effectively is, of course, not part of a government, or subject to the particular laws under which this, its branches, or the occupants of particular positions operate.

Wherever final decisions rest, self-restraint has to be exercised. A division of a government into branches, instead of avoiding this necessity, provides a number of places where such self-restraint is to be exercised. The more branches there are, the more likely it is that one or more will fail to exhibit a necessary restraint—but, also, the more likely it is that they will be effectively restrained by the rest.

To determine the ideal number of branches, one must know what a government's essential tasks are, and the likelihood that one or more branches will insist on themselves to the detriment of the others. Statecraft is needed for the one; an acknowledgment of a common government for the other. Nothing can be guaranteed. If a people is appealed to, it will be to it as a supposed sovereign or as representing the state, without any assurance that it will then decide wisely or well, or act effectively.

It is not possible to assure political success by any antecedently formulated principle. A government functions well only as long as each branch respects the roles that the others are to carry out, and can be persuaded or forced by those others to confine itself to its required functions. Constitutions provide diagrams or schema, not guarantees that something will in fact be done.

When reference is made to a government as a "we", what is intended is usually the government as a single whole of affiliated positions. The affiliations can promote a coherence to a degree other kinds of connection do not. When the members of a government say "we", what is intended is the government in the form of a single condition bearing on all. When those who are being governed refer to the government as "we", they instead attend to it as a whole in which there are affiliated positions occupied by representatives. Somewhat as lawyers do when they draw up contracts in which "we" is used to refer to people other than themselves, those who are governed refer here to a government of which they are not an actual part. Unlike the lawyers, though, they will be conditioned by that to which they refer.

"We" may be used to refer to a government by those who are part of it, as well as by those who are ruled by it. Neither usually distinguishes the government's characteristic relations, or notes what kind is dominant. Were either rulers or ruled more legally-minded, they would take only an equitable government to be a conditioning "we".

A government, from the standpoint of its subjects, is a single unit, embracing an interlocked number of affiliated positions. Those employed by the government, instead, usually take the subdivision they occupy to be the object of their "we".

A people is a conditioning "we", if it prescribes to the people constituting it; it is a factual "we" so far as it is made up of units which together are subject to the same conditions. Conceivably, there could be a conditioning "we" without a factual, and a factual without a conditioning "we".

The United States Constitution's "We, the people" evidently intended to refer, not just to those who drew up the document or signed it, the states which had sent them to the convention, or the states which accepted the result, but also to those who were to be subject to its rule. When initially stated, the "we" though could refer only to the former; only after the Constitution was "ordained and established" did it refer to the latter. At both times, it excluded some of the population—slaves, indentured servants, Indians and, apparently, women. A complex "we" is produced through the interplay of the other two.[3] If "We, the people" refers to this, it has the further, derivative meaning of a referent to the outcome of the interplay of ruler and ruled.

When it is said "Ours is a good form of government", though no one may have in mind any of the many ways in which bare or filled positions are there interrelated, reference is incidentally being made to a condition pertinent to the governmental employees (and occasionally to them as joined with those who are being ruled) as having power enough to enable them to rule well.

The better the ideal affiliations among branches or the particular positions in a government are understood, and their realization sought, the better organized a government is likely to be. The realization is promoted if account is taken of what subdivisions of a government are needed if it is to function not only effectively but with an expectation that the positions in it will be respected, backed by an understanding of how they are best affiliated.

A hope grounded in despair leads to the postulation of a native wisdom in the people, planners, or history. What is in fact needed is a knowledge of the nature of the best possible government, and a willingness to engage in an endless series of adjustments directed toward its achievement. There is, though, a long tradition, continued down to today, that takes a government to be needed solely or primarily to assure that people will receive their due. Justice, it is thought, is what in particular is to be promoted. Some truth is here certainly being expressed. Were there not a dominant, equitable, and effective control exercised impersonally along established lines, it is not likely that various recurrent conflicts would be prevented, reduced, or redressed.

People tend to look more favorably on their own personal causes and wants than on those of others; each is surely more directly and constantly aware of what is personally required and desired than of the requirements and desires of others. Seeing themselves to be together with others, but still apart from all else, most think they are deserving of available goods as much as or perhaps more than any other person. If, therefore, they obtain less than or just as much as some of the others do, they are confident that they have not been properly dealt with. Justice, they believe, since it requires that there be some common treatment of all, would allot them a better share, more than they are getting. In fact, what justice requires is only that they be treated objectively, even-handedly, impersonally, with some regard for their singular merits and (as they tend to forget) for the singular merits of others as well.

Justice demands equal treatment for all people as persons, with account being taken of their distinctive needs and deserts. The requirements need the backing of a sound understanding of what people are as publicly together, and what they should have if they are to be fulfilled. Both have distributive and rectificatory forms—to speak with Aristotle[4]—referring to what they deserve and what will overcome inequities.

Special forms of justice are pertinent to a government's treatment of the positions in it, of those who seek to occupy those positions, and of those who are ruled from there. The first is usually neglected, the second confined to questions of fairness in hiring practices, and the third to a rectification of wrongs. But the first is central to an examination of what is to be done in different branches and occupied positions in a government, while the latter two are involved in studies of the range and task of laws.

Were positions to form a mere aggregate of places to be occupied, they would have the same status. The positions in a government form no such aggregate; they are either analytically determined within a whole, or are abstractions from occupied positions. In either way, they are diversely suited to the tasks of government. To place all on a level is to identify them apart from a government, and thereby to enhance some unwarrantedly and diminish the importance of others.

Objections to a government for exaggerating the rights of rulers or minimizing those who are ruled, are properly made from the perspective of an ideal justice. Because people have natures and beings apart from that government, a problem of justice also arises in connection with the ways in which actual positions are open for occupation by anyone qualified to fill them, and how what is done at those positions deals with the natures and rights of people. As part of the government, there is nothing to be said of the positions except that they are positions there, appropriate or inappropriate, well or poorly related, and this whether or not they are just marked out or are abstracted from those already occupied.

References to the justice possible in a state take account of an ideal form of government, the people who are to occupy specified positions in the government, and those who will be affected by what is done at various governmental positions. If this is not done, one must be content with determining whether or not procedures are being carried out in established ways and without regard for personal differences. Justice will so far have to do, not so much with what should prevail, but with what should be avoided. It therefore will serve primarily to curb or remove what is amiss, not promote what ought to be. It will be confined to reducing inequities in an accepted ongoing state, and not with replacing this with one more closely approximating what a state ideally should be. The removal and avoidance of injustices, of course, are desirable, but they do not transform a state into one where desirable goods are always pursued and preserved. Making room for what had been neglected, they do not necessarily provide what is needed.

In order to lay out positions equitably, a government should initially treat them as independent of one another. It must surely avoid having them so joined that the people in them will most likely get in one another's way. This is best done by dealing with a number of positions in terms of the tasks that are to be performed, sometimes elsewhere. Here, too, justice requires that what is being considered be well understood and respected.

When justice is requested of insensitive or corrupt governments, unless they are being vainly asked to give up their control, an appeal is being made to them to restrain themselves in a way they could have, but have not yet done. In effect, they are being asked to so act that they also truly benefit themselves. Full justice is done to persons only if their natures and functionings are enhanced. If governed, they should be so improved that they are able to contribute maximally to the success of the government and thereby to themselves, the governed.

Like people who treat their cattle so badly that these are unable to produce what is wanted, poor governments cripple the very means that would enable them to flourish. There is a point where they would benefit more were they to demand less than they do. Good governments master the art of self-restraint; they make provision for what is to be separately performed in different positions and branches, and see to it that those in the various positions and branches make room for one another. As a whole and in its parts a government is to govern less only if its governing more would deny what is needed in order for all to function well.

Apart from its bearing on those who are being governed, "we, the government" has two meanings—a collective, referring to the government as a single unity, and a distributive, referring to a plurality of positions. The two are inverses of one another, the plurality exhibited by the second spelling out the nature of the first through the use of distinct elements.

The positions laid out in a diagram need to be occupied, if they are to become positions where governmental tasks are carried out at distanced places, and there able to affect one another. As having positions which could be occupied, the diagram is like a map of a projected city, with its streets and houses given various designations, and their relative distances and locations indicated. An actual government should so use it that the designated positions and relations are dealt with as relevant to prospective occupiers of the positions.

A good map of a city offers a miniaturized version of it. Kept to two dimensions, and forced to ignore the curvature of the earth and small details which might nevertheless loom large in the lives of people, it inevitably distorts what it is intended to recapture. What is being mapped, as existing apart, has an actual magnitude, concreteness, and complexity which the map, instead of re-presenting, can only indicate. Still, a diagram of related positions, resembling such a map in being abstracted from positions actually occupied and distanced from one another, may offer a not too misleading mirror of what they are like in a functioning government.

Observations somewhat similar to those made about spatially related governmental positions are to be made about temporal and causal ones, as portrayed in a diagram or schema, and occupied by and relating actual people. To do this, it is necessary first to overcome a common way of speaking of time as though it were a line, or was adequately represented by one. A line connects nothing more than points or shorter lines, and cannot therefore offer an appropriate representation of a time in which a multiplicity of copresent items enter into the next moment together. Nor can it take account of the fact that the length of a present moment is determined by the unitary occurrence that occupies all of it.

What occurs in a government occurs within an indivisible present moment. As distinct, the occurrences have their own indivisible presents, measurable as shorter or longer than one another by what is distinct from both. Were the government bypassed, and the state as controlling both rulers and ruled focused on, presents of both the people and the government would have to be viewed as being no more than conceptualized segments of the state's indivisible presents. The move would be similar to one that took a clock to exhibit objective presents, and treated smaller portions of those presents as fictions.

Positions in a governmental diagram or schema have no being apart from it. Occupied, the positions have another status, each with its own unity and distinctive present. When the positions are treated as simply occupiable, and thus as having a form not wholly determined by the government, they will be only conceivable subdivisions in a larger, indivisible, governmental present. Occupiable positions thus stand midway between a unitary goverment and occupied positions, having no distinctive temporal boundaries as in the one, and having their own presents when transformed into the other. As long as the positions continue to be occupied, a government can do little more than dictate their order of precedence, or help determine how their temporal spans are to coincide with its own, in whole or in part.

A government has occupiable positions. On being occupied, the government becomes a unity of related, activated positions. People there function in relation to one another without necessary reference to the government as a single, undivided whole. While its activities, and what occurs in the various positions, provide causally effective accompaniments of itself and the positions as just spatial and temporal, the positions as just in a diagram will remain not only empty but inert. They will continue to be so, even when what is to be done in each occupied position and how the positions are then to be related, is there described.

So far as they are in a schematized government, positions are places, marking out terminal points for formalized, causally connected beginnings and endings. A government orders them in causal links, but it is the people there who initiate acts. In a chain of command, the relations are pointed mainly in one direction. A set of concurrent positions instead could allow for beginnings at any position and for effects at any others, without necessarily giving any position a special status.

We tend to speak of what has a higher rank as being more effective, in the role of a cause, and of what has a lower rank as passive, in the role of an effect. If this be allowed it is still necessary to note that there is a considerable difference between an effect that is suffered, and another that is absorbed or utilized. Effects are sometimes enriched by being attained in special contexts. More work is often done on lower than on higher levels of a hierarchy. But whatever is done is done in occupied positions, carried out by their occupants. Apart from these no transactions occur. Evidently, the art of government can be carried out properly neither by those who are exclusively interested in government as a single unit, nor by those who take it to be just an aggregate of positions or branches. There must be a constantly maintained concern for both. At the very least, it is necessary to have the singularity of a government well-joined to a multiplicity of occupied positions, so as to constitute an ongoing, desirable, ruling governance.

3. Coalescence

In a schema, positions are connected by arrows, serving to mark out the directions and ways in which the positions, as occupied and occupiable, are to bear on one another. There is nothing in such a schema that shows a government to be distinct from the interrelated positions, able to act on and through them. But if a government were just related positions, it would not have a singular unity. A government makes the positions be its positions, and thereby turns them into a single, related set. An identification of a government with its positions (or its branches) will lose what makes them all be part of one government.

At the same time that a government is provided with a plurality of occupied positions in interrelationship, the government stands apart from any and all of them. So far as it does, it is able to continue unaltered even when the interrelated positions change in number and nature. The occupation of the positions in a government is one with the distinguishing of the government, as a single unity, from all of those positions and their occupants. The distinguishing is not a separating. In being distinguished from the interrelated positions, the government, while standing apart, continues to make the positions refer to one another. This would not be possible had the government no nature insisted on, no matter what the related positions.

Recourse need not be made to some power outside a government to enable this to be distinct from and to limit the positions and relations into which it is analyzable, any more than account need be taken of an exterior power in order to have an assertion maintain a single meaning while it is being expressed through the agency of related terms. The same meaning is conveyed by "John loves Mary", "John is in love with Mary", "Mary is beloved by John", and "The two, John and Mary, are in a relation of lover to loved", because the different expressions are carved out within the compass of the same meaning. Just as the meaning of an assertion does not float over the interrelated terms, but instead keeps them together and thereby makes them provide conduits for it, so the unitary nature of a government keeps interrelated positions together while they provide it with opportunities for making contact with what is outside it. It has a quite different kind of status from that of a state or a sovereign. Because they too have realities of their own, they are able to act on and thereby dictate how a government and occupied positions are to be related.

If one marks out positions in a government as distinct from and related to one another one will, at the same time, distinguish the unity of a government from these. The government will thereby be coalesced into a single nature, distinct from but pertinent to every position and relation. As a unity, a government is conditioned by occupied positions, and those positions are conditioned by the government. Each limits the other, but without exerting any force. At the same time, the self-restraint required of the occupants of the positions needs to be supplemented by one exercised by the common, governmental, controlling unity. Both restraints are needed if there is to be a functioning government.

Nominalists reject such contentions. They acknowledge only particulars, individuals, a plurality of units, taking the nature of the groupings of these to be the products of a language having no counterpart in fact. Individual people, occupied positions, unit acts, are affirmed, at the same time that it is denied that there are governing unities for these, distinct from and able to limit them. If the view were persistently maintained, it would require the denial that the items, with which the nominalists begin and seek to end, have controlled parts. It would also be impossible to hold that organic beings were irreducibly real. Despite the nominalists' own desires, allowance would be made only for the irreducible reality of atomic units. But then there would be no one who would be able to acknowledge those units. In any case, if there were a plurality of units, these would have to be together. To be together, they would have to be connected with one another; but for that to be possible, there must be a unity distinct from and able to be a unity for all of them.

Were one to assume a nominalistic position when dealing with a state, or government, and not elsewhere, one would still be faced with the fact that the various positions (and branches) of a government are distinct from one another. Were they not subject to a unitary government, they would not be subject to a common unity; their consonance and disagreements would just follow one another, no one more required than any other.

A government's unity is not another unit alongside the positions, branches, and relations for which it provides a common condition, enabling them to be together. If it were, there would have to be another unity that enabled the government to be together with the interrelated positions, and so on and on. Still, a government and interrelated positions are distinct. Both, moreover, are units, themselves interrelated in a single Many, subject to the One of a state.

Those who provide for a government in a constitution may have only a unitary government in mind when they begin to set down the main positions and branches, and their interrelationships. In the United States Constitution the fact is expressed in the so-called "Preamble", where a unitary government is characterized mainly in terms of the objectives it is designed to realize. The framers of that Constitution, to be sure, might have had a unitary government, as involved with many positions and functions, in mind when they began, and then gradually distinguished the unitary government and the interrelated positions as the Constitution took form for them. If they did, they would have provided a partial, mental duplicate of what occurs when a government arises in the course of history out of the not well-defined relations that the heads of a society had to one another. At both times, a governmental unity, as it emerges into clarity, coalesces into a unity, while its various positions are bounded off, and related to one another. In either way a government that is at once singular and diversified is produced.

Hierarchical and related positions in a government are primarily oriented toward one another. In effect, they allow many types of activity for the rulers to perform together. Little attention may then be paid to the needs or demands of the governed; too much time may be devoted to making the government operate smoothly. It is possible, therefore, to have a government in which positions are filled by unusually qualified and cooperative people, without much attention being given to the problem of how to govern well. Ideally, a government and occupied positions will be joined under the controlling guidance of a state. Lacking that, the government and the occupants will just limit one another, without being subject to any compulsion to find a position where they can function well together.

Cutting across the hierarchical and concurrent divisions of a government are others which divide positions in terms of common tasks to be performed, perhaps on behalf of the governed. The result is a number of combinations of positions to be occupied by people who not only work together with others alongside or on a different rank of a hierarchy of positions, but who may work with them to achieve a single outcome.

A number of positions of different ranks—those in the United States Senate and House, for example, or those occupied by the Supreme Court and those by judges in the lower courts—can be considered together. One could then distinguish types of tasks a government is to perform, preparatory to an examination of the ways in which those who engage in each of them are ordered hierarchically or coordinately. This is the usual practice—but not the only one possible.

Political theorists typically start with the idea that a state is to protect or promote peace, security, and justice for existing people: They then go on to deal with the branches of government where these are to be carried out. Within the branches, positions are so specified and related that required work could presumably be done efficiently and effectively. The government's reference to those who are subject to it is emphasized, usually with a corresponding neglect of the government as apart from those who are governed. One consequence is a slighting of the fact that the government and its positions have natures of their own. The tasks of a government should be determined apart from a consideration of the ways in which positions there are specified and interrelated, but in such a way that the reality of an actual government with its interrelated positions is not obscured.

Its positions filled, a government functions together with the governed to constitute a single complex. The result is subject to a state or a sovereign. Each makes demands on the others. Its right to do this and insist on it, raises the issue of its legitimacy and authority.

9. LEGITIMACY

1. INHERENT AND DERIVED LEGITIMACY

From the first moment of existence, each person is subject to constraints and, soon enough, to more explicit demands. Movements are limited by the womb, and then by the arms of the mother, the crib, steps, buildings, roads, and other obdurate realities. Each person is kept within the confines of common usages, common speech, utensils, dress, practices, taboos and commands. Most of these are readily yielded to, and often with benefit.

An enormous number of limitations are accepted without reflection, largely because they do not evidently stand in the way of the pursuit and enjoyment of desirable goods. Some, though, do force a change in course, blocking an occupation with what seems important; others seem to invite punishment for those who do not yield and act as required. Many are traceable to the prevailing government which, with the state and sovereign, makes demands on people. These demands, because they impose restrictions on what might otherwise be attempted, need justification.

It is good to protect one's offspring from hardship, but one must pay taxes and pay off debts, thereby precluding the doing of all that need be done for those in one's charge. It is good to see that a loved one is not unduly exposed to danger, but a young man is made to go to war. It is good to enjoy the protection of a sovereign, but one needs and wants to have opportunities to function as more than a subject. These sometimes onerous requirements prompt the questions: Which demands, whether implicitly or explicitly made, are to be satisfied? What is their justification?

The first question requires one to know whether or not a demand is idle; the second, whether or not it is right to make the demand. Is it reasonable to do what is being required? Is the demand made by what has a warrant for doing so? Although the first of these pairs is usually to the fore and is readily settled by indications that one has overwhelming force or other persuasive power behind it, it depends on at least a tacit answer to the second.

Those who have considerable power often enough take this to be its own warrant, and frequently hold that what they thereupon effectively demand is legitimate as well. Those who believe that they have a genuine right to rule, often believe that their demands have authority. Both may be mistaken. What has legitimacy is backed by a reason why it should be acknowledged to have the position it does; an authority requires that what it insists on be privileged. The two are independent—but they can be combined.

A satisfactory defense of the source of demands made on people must show that it is legitimate; a satisfactory defense of an insistence on the demands must show that they are authorized. When the demands are viewed from the position of a sovereign, state, or society, justifications are also needed for what any two of these, and men as well, require of the third. Legitimations of them provide reasons, warranting the acceptance of someone or something, as having a particular status. An authority's demands may be backed by what is legitimate; if it is not, it must have some other ground than that which an intrinsic or acquired reason could provide. A bogus doctor may act with authority; a legitimate ruler may act in ways for which no authority has been given. An injunction may lack legitimacy, but having the backing of an appropriate official it must be obeyed. If properly elected representatives command no one's respect, they will so far lack authority, at the same time that the positions they legitimately occupy will endow some of their decrees with authority.

Governments and states need legitimation and must have authority. They may be given these by a sovereign who claims to have both legitimacy and the authority to make a government and state act in certain ways. In turn, a sovereign looks to a state to give it an effective role, perhaps even a place in history, and to a government to give it a means for controlling people. Both may question its legitimacy and its authority. Deprived of legitimacy, a sovereign would be at most a claimant; deprived of authority, a sovereign would be only a figurehead.

Whatever the warrant, a sovereign stands over against both state and government, and from that position faces people as subjects. Only some of those who are governmentally ruled belong to the state; these are its citizens. A government rules over aliens and foreigners, as well as citizens; a sovereign takes slaves and children, as well as those who are ruled and those who are citizens, to be its subjects. People are justifiably and effectively required to act in certain ways only by governments, states, and sovereigns which are both legitimate and authoritative.

To legitimize is to provide an adequate reason for having a particular status, or for engaging in a particular type of action. That reason may be inherent or acquired. Each mode of legitimation has a number of forms, the acquired eventually depending on the inherent.

A long-established reason offered for a sovereign being justified in having that position is that a God had so decreed. Monarchs have often maintained that they have a divine right to be and to act as they do. That claim they never did or could substantiate. No God ever confirmed the claim that this or that sovereign was legitimate.

An appeal to a God is a special form of an appeal to what has the right to determine who is a legitimate sovereign. A Hobbesean contract theory takes agreeing people to bestow on some accepted individual a legitimacy which, like a sovereign chosen by a God, is then possessed forever, either by that legitimacy being automatically renewed in successors or by being legitimately passed on to them. While some who look to a God suppose that he legitimizes each sovereign, those who follow Hobbes tacitly suppose that the office of sovereignty has been so established by the contract that those who occupy it are thereby legitimized.

A God could, of course, be supposed to give legitimacy to the office of sovereign; a contract could be taken to justify a particular individual assuming the status of a sovereign. But designations of a sovereign office, or of some individual as a legitimate sovereign, need not be traced to a supposed God or contract. Voting or acclaim by the people, a governmental decision, or a state's constitution might yield all that was needed.

Today, a people, more evidently than the others, seem to many to be able to provide a sufficient reason for the existence of government, state, and sovereign. Locke is here one with Hobbes. Both look to the people for legitimation. They differ mainly in Locke's holding that a legitimacy is perpetually possessed by the people, and only lent to a sovereign and perhaps others. It can, he thinks, therefore be rightly retracted when a sovereign neglects duties or misuses power.

Locke and Hobbes not only take it for granted that a people is a source of a sovereign's legitimacy; they suppose that those who are immature or foolish enough to live disorderly lives are nevertheless wise enough to establish or endorse a sovereign to whom they and their posterity will be subject. If people could do this, the sovereign they sanctioned would then have to legitimize a government and a state, or separate warrants would have to be found for these as well.

Granted that a people is a proper source of the legitimation of a sovereign—and/or a government, state, or combinations of these—it is still necessary to choose between the views of a Hobbes and a Locke. Since what has an intrinsic reason has this always and can, therefore, exercise it again and again and in different ways, Locke's position is evidently stronger than Hobbes'. But one is still left with the question of whether or not a people is the source of all legitimate control over itself. How could it be so, if it can get in its own way, turn into a self-destructive mob, and is sometimes so poorly focused that whatever wisdom it might natively have is not well-expressed or used?

To this question it might be replied that a legitimizing source is not necessarily intelligent and perhaps may not act voluntarily. Just as an infant, unable to take care of itself, it might be said, tacitly legitimizes an adult to make decisions on its behalf, so a people's incoherence and self-destructiveness could be taken to legitimize a sovereign to act on its behalf. This answer, of course, supposes that a sovereign, like an adult, has the ability and the right to act on behalf of what cannot act properly on its own. The analogy begs a question. A people, unlike an infant, does not depend on others to get whatever it needs.

A reason for a sovereign could be an ingredient of it. One would, so far, not have to look to a God, the people, or anything else to justify its existence or functioning. The incapacity of people to act properly, unless subject to it, would sanction their subjection to it—provided that it had a right to be such a sovereign.

The legitimacy of a sovereign is intrinsic, or there is something that had it intrinsically and transferred it to that sovereign, directly or through intermediaries. Were there such a sovereign, it would still be necessary to take account of possible, independent legitimacies possessed by the people, the government, and the state.

History is sometimes taken to provide a reason warranting the position of whatever is in ascendancy. This is to suppose that history is intrinsically rational, governed perhaps by a dialectic[1] or some inescapable objective, or that the final reason is to be found in things interacting as they do.

The idea that history is all-encompassing and justifying, not only goes counter to the fact that people, at least, have privacies not yet caught within history, but to the fact that history contains contingencies which need not be, and that its course can be modified by what people, governments, states, and sovereigns decide. If there is no other source of legitimation than whatever happened to be, all expressed objections, resistances, and criticisms would be as valid as their opposites. In effect, everything and therefore nothing would be legitimized. Implicit but operative in this view is the supposition that what occurs in the historic present is legitimized because it is the latest in a possibly improving course. The isolation and acceptance of this idea has the virtue of permitting one to recognize defects in what is present, while enabling one to defend it as the best possible situation at the moment. Whatever occurred would be legitimized— but only for that time. It also identifies or confounds a kind of practical reasonableness with reasons. The latter, not the former, legitimizes. If there are occasions when reasonableness should be allowed to prevail, it should be because it has passed a test provided by reason.[2]

The acceptance of the *status quo*, in part or whole, here or there, needs legitimization. This is but to say that no occurrence, whether it be all or the best that history provides, is legitimized, unless it can be shown that its place in history contains a sufficient reason for its being what it is and does. The supposition is implicitly made, but not defended when it is held that what occurs in history is what reason endorses. Some past occurrences, though, are regrettable; some past decisions foolish; and some long-held practices and views barbaric.

A related idea assumes that there once was a sovereign, government, or state that had legitimacy, and that this was passed on to what follows or continues some phases. This is related to the idea that a people once had a right to decide what will control it, and this right was properly transferred to a sovereign, a government, or a state. Both views accept some past moment as a point where some intrinsic legitimacy existed, and from which a sequence of transfers began. Once again the issue is pushed back into a past where there was a supposed legitimate rule, followed by a supposed sequence of proper transfers. Once again, we are referred to what is assumed to contain the needed reason, and are asked to suppose that this was passed on to successors with warrant. It is, though, never shown that the initial event and the transfers ever did occur—or even could have taken place.

All temporalized accounts must come to rest with some supposedly inherent justification. Were this not now present, we would be driven back and back to some other present, or would be unable to find the needed justification. A satisfactory warrant cannot be provided if one does not acknowledge that there is or was something inherently justified, and able to legitimate others.

If presents that had once been are like that now occurring, either this will have its own intrinsic legitimacy, or neither will have one. Were it supposed, instead, that some nontemporal power, acting independently of anything that in fact exists, bestowed legitimacy on what is now past, it will be necessary to explain why similar bestowals are not made on what comes later.

Account should be taken of the justification that follows from the nature of a being, and is either capable of being persistently maintained or could be transferred with warrant. Three efforts stand out: an Hegelian location of justification in a rationale, supposedly intrinsic to a state; a classical location of it in the virtues of people; and a constitution's location of it in a government.

For Hegel, an actual state is a localized, historic form of an Absolute. This, the supposed source of all reasons, provides an intrinsic reason for the existence and activities of the state. Since a state, like everything else that is real for Hegel, is the outcome of the Absolute's internal arrival at some crucial point, Hegel should also have held that his Absolute has a congealed form in individual men, as surely as it has in a state, since people too are real. If individuals were not his Absolute in a limited, genuine oppositional form, they would not be able to act in opposition to or interact with a state, lacking, as they then would, any being or power. In fact, they are unities who not only control subordinated pluralities but effectively exist apart from, oppose and interact with their state.

Hegel's Absolute would have to be invoked only if no legitimate acts could have originated with the people, or if the acts acquired legitimacy only when fitted within a final whole. Those who always look to law, government, state, or sovereign, to determine whether or not this or that act is legitimate, embrace a form of the latter alternative; people, they think, act in ways which have no intrinsic merit, and they should, therefore, do what is officially prescribed. It is then tacitly supposed that law, one of the others, or some combination of them, has or once had intrinsic legitimacy. One would in effect then have Hegel's Absolute in a miniaturized form.

Plato's ideal state, as the very incarnation of the virtue of justice, was self-legitimizing. One could interpret his *Laws* as re-presenting that ideal state in a form that was able to be in this world, and thus to have the self-legitimizing character of the ideal so modified that it could be realized. To suppose, though, that people have no other merit than that which is obtained from a state, is to tolerate any use this might make of them, consistent with its nature. Carried out relentlessly, such a view allows for the abolition of families, the denial of private property, the rejection of the practice of altruism—some of which were seen and even urged by Plato—and allows no other role to people than that of serving the state, in the face of their right to perfect themselves, and to help determine the nature and career of the kind of state in which they live.

The opposite of such accounts is not an individualism or anarchism. These have no place for government or state, except in the guise of an irrational, brute, unintelligible force, incapable of providing or sustaining a reason. The opposite is the Aristotelian view that takes legitimacy to be grounded, not in a state but in a number of individuals. A state, or more exactly, a government, is taken by him to be legitimized if carried out by people jointly exercising basic virtues. Apparently such a state remains legitimate even when it does little or no good to those who are always ruled and never govern. Aristotle thought that if a state were well-ruled, these would prosper, but that would be true only if they were incompetents with the status of wards or less, and the rulers were all they could and should be. That would be possible only if the rulers were themselves not part of a union, making its own legitimate demands on the very government of which they were a part.

Aristotle's state granted citizenship only to some, and took these to legitimize what is done by a government. His own definition of humanity should instead have led him to see that other people not only might be virtuous, but that, whether they were so or not, they make legitimate demands which a government is to heed. Ancestry, gender, and nationality should not have been taken by him to preclude any one from having rights deserving satisfaction. This is only to say that those who are ruled legitimately require something to be done for them.

Not everything individuals do or demand is legitimate; they might assume that they had privileges they do not in fact have. Nor is everything that people jointly decide and do together legitimate; they could make mistakes about their common and individual public rights. If a people has legitimacy because of what it intrinsically is, it will be because it is composed of and expresses persons who possess the right to be and prosper together and, therefore, to act in various ways if this is how they can best promote their continuance and prosperity, without undue injury to others. If they alone had rights, they would, of course, be justified in acting to the detriment of anything else, if this enabled them to be thereby benefited. Not only do other beings have rights; a government also has rights, and may properly restrain people if this is the way to promote justice and protect prosperity. A state, too, has its own objectives, as well as relations to other states, though no one, except its representatives, need take account of the latter.

Where Plato and Hegel would trace all legitimacy back to a state, and Aristotle would trace it back to a segment of the people, some legal scholars trace it back to a document defining and legitimizing a government. That effort immediately raises the question of the legitimacy of those who produced that document. They might not have had the needed legitimacy.

Before there was a United States of America, a convention was called to modify the Articles of the Confederation that were then operative. The delegates who were sent to the convention usurped a power when they decided instead to produce a constitution for a new government. That constitution was intended to legitimize that government, but those who produced the constitution could not provide the requisite legitimization, even if only preliminary to their presenting a constitution for acceptance by the several states.

A constitution can legitimize a government, but if the constitution itself has to find a justification in an acceptance by separated, sovereign states, these must themselves be able to bestow a legitimacy on what was able to limit them. The several states before 1789 did not have the right to do this. Crediting a legitimacy to themselves as a consequence of their successful overthrow of what had denied them an intrinsic, limited legitimacy, they nevertheless owed part of their legitimacy to their rejected sovereign. That sovereign gave the original colonies some modicum of legitimacy. But this he could not have done unless he had a legitimacy of his own, or had somehow obtained it.

A sovereign might claim legitimacy because of a supposed singular virtue or because it was part of an unbroken line of special beings who had been legitimate sovereigns. One would then have to show that those credentials were in fact possessed, and that in this particular case, these sufficed to give it the status of one able to legitimize a government. This, so far, would not have a legitimacy of its own. But since that government had a distinctive nature which a sovereign should respect, this could have warrantedly made the government function on its terms only if it took account of what this was, and thus of what it legitimately does. The colonies which finally revolted charged the British sovereign with flagrant violations of the sovereignties that had supposedly been granted them.

Those who identify a state with a sovereign hold that neither a government nor a people could have any other legitimacy than that which a state bestows. Those who make a people sovereign hold that both government and state derive their legitimacy from it. If, instead, a government alone is taken to be sovereign, both a state and a people would have no more than a derived legitimacy. None of them could legitimately assume the status of sovereign without being backed by an adequate reason: The best of reasons is one that expresses a right natively possessed. This, all three have. If a government or state came to exist through the acts of people, that would not mean that the government's or state's rights were all obtained from them. Some of their rights follow from their natures, whether or not those natures were produced by the actions of other beings. People, too, are effects of causes, but that does not stand in the way of their having their own rights.

A primary difference between a monarchy and a democracy, or other ways in which states are traditionally distinguished, has to do with the question of where the warrant for sovereign status is located. This is not an issue central to the functioning of a state or a government, or to the promise of a good life for people together. It becomes blurred when 'monarchy' and 'democracy' or other classifications are used to refer to the locus of a final decision. As Great Britain makes evident it is possible to have a monarchy that is also a democracy; as Marcos in the Phillipines has shown, it is possible to have a democracy that in effect is a monarchy.

What is intrinsic cannot be given away. Could a sovereign or a people give up an intrinsic legitimacy, it would in that act cease to be what it had been. But either could extend its legitimacy to whatever promotes its interests and, in that sense, continues it. The recipient would then have a legitimacy additional to what it intrinsically had.

There have been people who, having been acclaimed sovereigns, took themselves not only to be set apart from their subjects, but to be beyond the reach of any warranted judgment regarding merit, justice, or achievement. It is no less true that the lives and economy of millions depend on the ways in which states are able to coexist in some consonance. But inside a state what is of central importance is the nature and interplay of government and governed.

People wish to know not so much how and to what extent they are being ruled, but how to get rulers to be more benign and beneficial. Almost as important for them is the knowledge of how they could obtain the opportunities and privileges of full citizenship, and be protected against harm. If they are governed well, and are allowed to enjoy the status of citizens in a well-functioning, steady, strong, peaceful state, it usually makes little difference to them whether or not they are subject to an illegitimate sovereign, having no adequate warrant for acting as it does. When required to do what is onerous and has no clear warrant, though, they quickly raise the question of the legitimacy of their sovereign, government, or state. Occasionally, it will also be necessary for them to determine the legitimacy of their own acts, for these sometimes spoil the roles of the sovereign, government, or state.

Just as a sovereign, government, or state may ignore what people need and deserve, so a people may be blind to what these must have in order to function well. Each has not only to be understood to have some legitimacy of its own, but to join with others so as to constitute a complex in which each part expresses itself legitimately in consonance with the rest.

It is no more correct to say that a chicken is only an egg's way of making another egg than it is to say that an egg is only a chicken's way of making another chicken. They have these roles because they are chicken and egg, each with its own nature and, therefore, with a right to be and function well. To take subjects or a sovereign to have no other status than that of mere instruments without legitimacy is but to substitute them for the chicken and egg in the initial observation, and to put 'being related to' in place of 'making'. Similar substitutions are made when government or state, and people in the guise of citizens, are spoken of instead. Government, state, sovereign, and people all have some legitimacy, precluding the reduction of any of them to the status of a mere agent for one or more of the others.

2. SELF-CONSTITUTED LEGITIMACIES

The present is not free from influences from the future and the past. The future, just so far as it is able to make the present be part of itself, possesses the past as at the other limit of that present. The future does not here act as a cause, working backwards in time, but as a because, an enabler. It stretches through the present to terminate at the limit of this, where the past has the shape of settled facts. By holding on to the past it makes the present be the locus of that past.

Nothing that has happened is lost; it remains forever in the form of fact. Nothing, though, that has happened continues to act. Nor is the future able to act; it is too indeterminate to be able to do more than limit and guide. Only what is now actual is at once sufficiently indeterminate to be able to undergo change, and sufficiently determinate to be able to act. Only what is now actual is at once sufficiently determinate to be more than a mere possibility, and sufficiently indeterminate not to be a fact.

The recognition of the role that the past has in the present, because of the future, makes it possible to avoid Bergson's supposition that the past is completely preserved in the present, without also being forced to suppose that it vanishes altogether as distinct, finished, determinate, and inert. The past is present as a plurality of future-sustained facts at the limit of the present.

People use the future in the form of a prospective outcome, or of an expected result deserving to be realized, while accepting their past in the form of determinate customs. As operative in present persons, the customs assume the role of the customary, and the expected becomes the anticipated. What is effectively present in each person is the customary tinged with anticipation, the counterpart of the enriched present that conditions them together in a union.

Made specific, filled out, approached with emotion, the future may function as a measure of what is more or less desirable. Occasionally, it is expressed in a fabulous story, a myth. Emotionally toned, this expresses values to be cherished or disowned, guiding the people and affecting what they inherit. Shorn of its bearing on the present, a myth turns into a mythology. There, the meanings expressed in the myth are preserved, but without an affect on what is occurring, and therefore without necessarily making a difference to those who are present.

The counterpart of a myth is a common heritage affecting the ways of people; the counterpart of a mythology is a shared belief or conceit. Together, myth and heritage qualify the tradition that is making a difference to the way people live together.

Although what is past or future cannot act, the customary built up in the one, and the anticipated qualifying the other, are operative in the present. While actual people are wholly in the present, and not the slightest in the past or future, they are therefore able to make use of these. Nothing here is deliberately done; no actions are carried out; no force is exerted. The past and future are conditions, effective in and sustained by the present. When their roles are exaggerated, the present is taken to be just a channel through which people are subjected to what is no longer and to what is not yet. Were their roles minimized, past and future, as operative in the present, would be at once innocuous and mysterious, while still making evident that there had been a present that had passed away and a possible present still to come; memory and plans would then have no referents, but would at best be qualifications of what is present.

Ruins are more than rocks strewn about; they are those rocks qualified by residua of the past in the form of facts that cannot be reduced to what it is sustaining them in the present. The foundation of a building is more than a hole in the ground; it is that hole qualified by the presence of a retained past as well as of the future in the form of a controlling guide. An old man is as fully present as a young. Even if he does not remember his past, and envisions only a short future, these still qualify him as present. An ambitious young woman is as fully present as a lazy one; even when she is not thinking of her past or possible future, her present is affected by them. In all present realities, past and future make a difference, while maintaining their integrity as facts and guides.

Custom turns a present common condition into a preserving locus of what people had done together. Sometimes it so enriches the present that it makes this conform to the prevailing myth. At other times, the myth so acts on the present as to make this just a locus of custom. The former mode of enrichment is more common, both because custom is more insistently operative, and because a myth reestablishes, at least partly, what had been or was supposed to have occurred.[3]

Freed from a reference to the prevailing myth, tradition reduces to fashion; freed from a reference to a common heritage, it reduces to remembrances; freed from the present, it reduces to lore. Fashion, remembrances, and lore may occur together, but are not then joined. They are kept alive by being perpetually revived in new experiments, new formulations, and new retellings. Myth and heritage, instead, persist because they are sustained by a relevant present that maintains a hold both on what might be and what had been.

The past, when inherited by the present, effectively conditions what occurs. That past is not simply accumulated. Just as a new born infant today is as innocent and ignorant as its siblings had been, starting life afresh just as they had, so each present moment is as new as every other. As sustaining the future and past, though, it makes it possible for people and the other factors in an actual complex to benefit from what had been and what may be, the one in the form of added determinations, and the other in the form of a directive agency. So far as anything is involved in such a present, it is able to acquire a legitimacy from the past, and thereby be in a position to legitimize some beings who are able to act apart from it.

If the social contract is a fiction, and the relentless march of history another; if complexes are not produced or empowered from above or by some Absolute; if we are not to invent a hidden hand pulling people toward a good life; if we are not to suppose that people are initially entitled to get and to hold on to what they can; if we are not to suppose that complexes of people, sovereign, state, and government are the result of accidental junctures, or are reducible to aggregations of these, we can not leave unanswered the question of the legitimacy of each factor, and of their combination. If we also accept the fact that all are temporal, we can come to see that they turn an enriched present into an integral part of themselves, and may so far achieve legitimacy. Each can do this, by so using the available, enriched present that this contributes to justifiable activity by itself and others. So far as a people, sovereign, state, or government does not use such a present to enable it to have that status, each is properly characterizable as weak, corrupt, or distorted. Everything that occurs, it can therefore properly be said, is legitimate, being illegitimate only so far as it does not make proper use of what had been legitimate before, or has not fully succeeded in incorporating the conditions which would endow its status or activities with legitimacy. Everything should make inherited or present legitimizing conditions integral to itself. If it does not, it will be as single and as full-bodied as any other present reality, but will not qualify its acts by legitimizing factors.

A usurper, though no less real and often enough more energetic and surely more effective than a legitimate heir, is illegitimate because the position claimed is part of a past that had not yet been made integral to the claimed position. That need not prevent the usurper from then and there engaging in legitimate acts.

To be without legitimacy in one respect need not jeopardize the possession of legitimacy in others, but only in the latter cases will the needed reasons for an act be integral parts of it. Usurpers may take their positions to be legitimate because they have assumed them. For that assumption of the positions to be legitimate, they and the positions would have to be rationally connected.

3. LEGITIMATE GOVERNMENT

In the United States, it is commonly believed that when a government fails to represent the people—a fact manifested in its failure to take full account of the rights they natively have or which are expressly stated to be theirs in the Constitution—the people will in fact and by right raise up against it or compel it to make needed changes. There is no surety that this will be done, even through the agency of voting. Governments elsewhere, in any case, continue despite their failure to benefit their people. Some sovereigns have not only abolished the government, but have successfully forbidden people to do what had been long practiced with considerable benefit. Others have destroyed great works of art or crushed cherished forms of worship without arousing successful opposition. Still, none ever fully extirpates all people's memories, habits, expectations, their customary practices, or moral attitudes and temper. Whatever success a revolutionary government might have in the beginning is subtly and inexorably modified by practices and attitudes continued within the newly imposed forms.

It is possible to modify ways of acting radically and even to get rid of some altogether. The process is usually excruciatingly slow. The legal abolition of slavery left debasing, serious descriminations in place for a long time; the achievement of equal rights for minorities and women has been found to be a long drawn-out process in which almost every achievement sets a new problem. Also, the portion of the past that is worth maintaining may not be what bears directly on individuals; it may benefit only a union of them, society, government, or state.

Whatever is done is inseparable from a possibility that limits what is done, and is in the process of being realized in the course of present activities. Possibilities are inescapable part of every act, no matter what their nature or by whom performed.[4] If human beings are to walk, they must not only be able to fall forward alternatively right and left and stop the falls by forward alternative movements of their legs; there must be a possible place they will be able to occupy as a consequence of their acts. That place is a demarcatable part of a larger space; it will become a place where they are in fact, at the outcome of their walking.

The fact that the future is an inseparable factor in determining what is to be done, has a distinctive import in a legal system, in addition to that which it enjoys as maintaining the past at the limit of the present, and adding a tonality to that present.[5] As a controlling objective or guide, it is operative in the process by which it is realized. Purposive beings, which humans surely are, give the future a role in the present it otherwise would not have, just as their memories enable the past to make a difference to what they do, additional to that which that past provides by being sustained at the limit of and affecting the present.[6]

The United States Constitution says that it is being ordained and established "in order to . . . secure the Blessings of Liberty to ourselves and our posterity".[7] Nothing was said about establishing justice, insuring domestic Tranquility, providing for the common defence, or promoting the general Welfare for posterity, but this apparently was also intended.

"Posterity" could be taken to refer to those mature successors of present mature people, who will be in the majority at some later time, and to the similar replacements of these, and so on and on into the indefinite future. That meaning is too limited, for posterity also properly includes those noncitizens who, by a change in law, may achieve the status of citizens. Whether this be done or not, posterity is to be considered when determining what is to be done by the government. Even governmental acts, directed toward the preservation and reinstatement of the past, are carried out for posterity as well as for those now existing. In addition to providing for those who are not yet existent, or to whom the provisions are not yet applicable, those who govern must also keep in mind that circumstances in the future may be quite different from those pertinent today. Nor are their efforts to be limited to securing only the blessings of liberty.

Inevitably, present activities produce both constraints and opportunities, with which those who follow must grapple. We must try to limit the one and increase the other by now seeing to it that posterity is not prevented from using its inheritance with at least the same degree of self-determination that is presently enjoyed.

Ideally, every decision made today will take into account the affect it will have on those who follow. Efforts now directed at the conservation of natural resources, the building of roads and bridges, the course of education, and the support of museums and philanthropies, will attend to the rights and needs of posterity more evidently than other decisions do, but there is none that can be said to have its effects confined wholly to the present. No one lives in a time in which present moments and occurrences are completely detached from a future limiting and enriching the present, able to be realized as a succeeding present, and given the status of a context in which later acts are to fit; nor does any one live completely detached from the past, as limiting and enriching the present, able to be distinguished as settled at the edge of that present, and given the status of a context related to what is occurring.

Like everything else in the present, a government faces a relevant, future, indeterminate possibility. Despite its indeterminacy, that possibility is distinguishable, though not separated from the rest of the future in which other possibilities, relevant to other present entities, also are. The realization of its possibility is one with making it determinate, detailed, and present. That possibility does and can be explicitly, and with various degrees of emphasis, be brought to bear on what is being presently done, thereby affecting its course, and the nature of what is achieved. At a minimum, it will provide a limit within which present activity introduces determinations; at a maximum, it will guide and control what is happening. The minimum inevitably occurs. A greater role is played by the future when the government distinguishes and orders present positions, to make them appropriate to what the government will subsequently do and face.

A government uses its own relevant possibility to make certain positions, and certain relations among them, be germane to what will be at a later time. It is also occupied with some of the possibilities faced by the state. Just as a walk, not only makes a possible place become determinate by being occupied, but also requires that the place be denied to others, so a government, in realizing its own pertinent possibilities, qualifies the possibilities which are open to the state. It is also true that a state, in realizing pertinent possibilities, inevitably limits the nature of the possibilities available to the government. Here, as elsewhere, a number of possibilities are realized together, to produce a plurality of actual, interrelated, present occurrences. These may have been anticipated, and sometimes even be predicted, but one must await their occurrence to know what they are in their full concreteness. Every present item is a relevant possibility realized through actions carried out then and there.

When a number of actions affect one another, the different possibilities they are realizing receive further determinations, for a realization of a plurality of possibilities is inseparable from a single possibility encompassing them. The realization of that possibility imposes limitations on the determinations that the subordinate possibilities receive. Consequently, the most thorough knowledge of what men and a government are now doing is confronted with inexplicable occurrences, due to the state and to the interplay of the people and the government, which that knowledge does not embrace. To know what will occur in a state, one must know not only what people and their government will do, but how they affect one another at the same time that they are separately and jointly affected by the state. Political commentators, nevertheless, attend primarily and sometimes exclusively to the first, political scientists to the second, and historians to the third. The last know more than the others do, but only after the fact. The first are like those who think they can understand why an arm moved, by studying muscles and tendons; the second are like those who think it enough to know the nature of an arm; while the third consider the ways people had used their arms in the past. All attend to what should be considered; together they do no more, though, than provide a pattern, vivified then and there in ways no one could fully know in advance of its occurring.[8]

A state is a locus of a power expressed in and through a government, and by governmental agents who deal with other governments. That power is subject to governmental conditions and prescriptions. What a state is and can do, therefore, cannot be understood unless account is taken of what is done by a government, but it would be paradoxical to take the state to be identical with or to be a part of that government. Governments do not carry on wars, make treaties, form alliances, have a place in world history; they are turned inward toward those who are to be ruled. States, in contrast, are directed both inwardly and outwardly, affecting their governments and people, and distinguishing themselves from other states while interplaying with them.

Justice can be done to the nature of a state, as distinct from a government and as a part of a functioning complex with its various components in interplay, if it be recognized that a government prepares positions and their relations for occupation and use by people who are concerned with the state as a locus of power, able to act independently of the government. That power will be modified, accommodated, and transmitted by the government. Were a state's power exercised outside the limits a government imposes, its actions would be brute, unchecked, neglectful of, or go counter to other proper demands. The limits are set when a government determines the positions which are to be occupied by people utilizing the power of the state to rule on behalf of the ruled, the government, and the state as well.

A state is not the creature of a government; its power is not subjugated by the government's. Nor is a government just a mediator of state power. A government makes state power pass through separately determined and related governmental positions, at the same time that the state acts on the government. As just a locus of power, a state is only a part of a functioning whole. There, its power limits and is limited by people, a government, and a sovereign, the latter two being able to be carried out by the very people who represent the state in its dealings with other states.

If governmental positions are to be readily occupied, they must be made attractive and appropriate to the possible occupants' natures and abilities. Money, the trappings of power, prestige, and in fewer cases, virtue, friendship, or a desire to serve, will be sufficient to lure some to accept the opportunity to be part of the government. The observation is likely to be misconstrued as cynical or mean-spirited because it goes counter to some well-entrenched and honored views. It also raises some vexatious problems.

Aristotle thought it was a privilege and duty to be part of a government, and that only the best of people were worthy of the double honor. Its legitimacy, it was thought, was a function of the excellence of the rulers, and was inevitably acquired by a government whose work is carried out by good people. It does not follow, or course, that if people are virtuous, even in the sense of having just those habits that are required for governing excellently, that they will mesh well together. A high degree of reasonableness, deep public concern, a generosity of spirit, a sense of what people need and ought to have, offer better grounds for crediting some with the status of legitimate rulers.

Today, many would take being a significant part of a government to be the privilege and duty of anyone who had reached maturity.

Few would agree with Aristotle's way of determining who are most qualified to be part of a government, since it excluded those of low birth, workers, women, merchants, and those born in other lands. One can still maintain that it would be best to have people of wisdom, good will, and sound habits occupy positions in the government, while denying that they provide the only warrant that a legitimate government might have. The provision of stability and protection will support whatever legitimacy is possessed by those in power; the need to maintain continuity will lead to the legitimation of heirs; a need to have a government rule will support the legitimacy of those in it who inspire respect and obedience. Ideally, what is to be provided is a government that rules equitably and firmly, backed by a state and people, who have the right to demand that it act on their behalf.

No matter how important ruling be, it does not justify the abandonment of all other pursuits by mature, good men. Other enterprises also require good people, and people have other things they can and ought to do. Artists, scientists, philosophers, religious leaders, and educators do more good by living up to the ideals of their enterprises than they would were they to abandon these in order to help rule.

A government does not have an overriding claim on the time and thought of all people, regardless of their gifts or their capacity to contribute in other ways to human welfare, and eventually to the excellence of all. Only those who are not qualified to contribute to those nonpolitical activities which contribute to the production of not otherwise obtainable goods for all, could possibly have an obligation to take up governmental work. A legitimate government would then be one carried out by those who would not do as well at other tasks, and will govern better than others could or would.

To this it may be replied that, precisely because governmental work involves a sacrifice, the best of people will seek, or at the very least, will accept positions in the government. Do not those who engage in other tasks also have to make sacrifices to attend to these properly? Is it not appropriate to remark that those who write treatises on the overwhelming importance of participating in governmental work, take time away from such work to think through and write about the supposed duties of people to become part of the government? Do they not do less than they should if actual governing is as important as they say it is?

All that can be properly demanded of people is that they do what they are most qualified to do. Each should so function that desirable activities, carried out by others equally qualified, are also promoted. The principle has universal application, and is relevant no more to politics than it is to art, religion, philosophy, science, or any other enterprise that contributes to the production of a civilized world of human beings who are excellent, privately and publicly. Good government is usually a precondition for all the others. It is no less true that education, free inquiry, maturation, creative expression, insight, and vision are preconditions for good government. It would seem, though, that one might be able to dispense at least with art, philosophy, and religion, or bring these under strict governmental control, and still provide for a good government. If so, government might be a precondition for what is not a precondition for it. Such a government would inevitably be run by people who are less civilized than they need be, and what they do will surely lack nuance, breadth, and depth. The directing and conduct of the government will surely presuppose knowledge and presumably free inquiry and intellectual adventure; if it did not make use of these it would be unable to do little more than provide a conduit for state power.

People have the duty to support and enhance government and state, directly or indirectly. They carry out that duty indirectly when they contribute to other areas where they, other people, the government, and the state as well, can acquire needed support and deserved enhancement. All are to make possible the achievement of the great goods which enable civilized mankind to continue and to be enriched.

Place political demands above all others, and it immediately follows that censorship and control of what people do may not only be taken to be legitimized but will be carried out with a consequent impoverishment of the state and its people. Still, since a government and a state have rights of their own and may promote the good of people, one must accept whatever they do in principle, even while trying to change this or that particular, just as one, who credits art or inquiry with rights of their own and recognizes their value in promoting the good of people, must accept the fact that their pursuit and use will be spoiled by blunders, failures, and false starts. The legitimacy of neither art nor inquiry is determined by those who occupy governing positions or who represent the state.

A legitimate government governs well; a legitimate state is a product of such a government and a well-functioning union of people. Both the government and the state vary in their abilities and value over time. Did they not also have legitimacy, one would have a right to replace them.

A legitimate government is a properly instituted, functioning government. Were none of its positions filled, it would not be a government at all, legitimate or illegitimate. It could compel certain people to fill various positions, but that act would require it to have some of its positions already filled. The compelled people, moreover, would more likely than not be drudges, incompetents, lax, or over-submissive.

With the help of a state, a government could make people submit to whatever it did, but they would then be subdued in spirit as well as in fact, where they were not provoked to rebellion. A government needs to make its positions attractive in order to have them properly filled, and it must have what is done in them take account of what the rest of the people need and want, if it is to have its rule be effective and itself strengthened. Not until then will it be one whose rule is legitimate.

Positions and interrelationships, even when they pluralize a governmental unity splendidly, must be altered if they are to become appropriate to the nature of those who occupy the positions and what those occupants might do. It will then be found that when individuals occupy the positions, they modify what was antecedently prescribed, and that, in the course of their activities, they inevitably give additional distinctive meanings to those positions. The fact that positions, when abstracted from themselves as actually filled, deviate considerably from occupiable positions antecedently defined, might of course be anticipated by a government. If its anticipations are expressed in determinations of positions and their interrelations, what the government anticipatorily does will, though, still be subject to modification when the positions are in fact occupied.

All that a government can do to make its rule legitimate is to have its positions occupied by those who will do what good governing requires. There is, unfortunately, no known way to anticipate how people will occupy governmental positions and act there. Those who fit snugly into them tend to become bureaucrats; those who fit badly are misfits. The best one can do is to avoid these extremes by having people constantly modify their ways, and therefore the positions they occupy, so that the outcome of their work is good ruling together.[9]

A government has as one of its tasks the provision of opportunities for some people to be part of it. If it did no more, there would be no reason why any but those who wish to be such parts, who might otherwise suffer, or who stand to gain by the act, should be concerned with the government. It is not a kind of minaturized Absolute giving meaning and value to those who share in it. People exist apart from it, as so many individuals, as members of societies, and in other nonpolitical ways. Though they may then limit and be limited by the government, they will also continue to be outside its reach, with distinctive irreducible privacies.

It is not necessary to deny that loyalty is a virtue, political participation desirable, and public life inescapable in order to warrantedly affirm that a government should so determine its positions and their relations that the people it rules will not only be helped to be and act harmoniously, but enabled to be enhanced as private beings. It should do for people, as having privacies, what it must do for itself and for the state—make possible excellent functioning then and later, and the enrichment of what is done. The age-old controversies as to whether or not people have an obligation to obey the government, and whether or not the government has to satisfy their rights and needs, are two sides of one issue, improperly presented as oppositional.

So far as a government makes provision for excellent governing, it is legitimate in and of itself as just a government; so far as its positions are filled by able, mutually supportive people who benefit those who are ruled while keeping the government functioning well, it is a legitimate functioning government. It is also legitimate if, through the help of tradition, ideals, and other agencies, it continues a legitimacy previously established. It always acts more or less well; when it moves toward a limit where the less is indistinguishable from very badly, or not at all, its legitimacy will be questioned. Whether it is then found to be legitimate or not, whether its legitimacy is inherent or derived, it may still have acted with authority, and have had people do what it demands of them.

A human being who acts inhumanly is still a person. A government, state, and sovereign though, are products which exist only so far as they satisfy certain conditions. When they fail to meet those conditions, they cease to be. If this be true, must it not be said that a tyrannical state, a brutal government, or a cruel sovereign are no longer a government, state, or sovereign? To say this is to go directly counter to established usage. Putting aside the fact that they all may have inherited legitimacies, if positions are maintained and related in them, and if there are established channels through which their decrees and force are carried out, they will have some legitimacy. Those who insist on preserving the government, state, or sovereign cling to them; those who would overthrow all control, attend to the rulers' failure to function in consonance with what people deserve and require. The hard task is to get in between the two. While allowing for an established, legitimized conditioning of people, one should see if what is done is in accord with what ought to be done by and to them.

A government should not trespass on the right of people to express themselves conjointly in public. It should therefore respect the unions they form. And they, in turn, should respect its right to rule them. Failures to act properly, either through excess or defect, may be both unanticipatable and unavoidable. But one can specify in advance the limits within which government and people are to function, and make provision for ways to alter acts which tend to go beyond those limits. Unless the limits are arbitrarily set, they will take account of what each is and can give to the other, without minimizing itself.

It is desirable for a government to limit its activities so that people may become better, and they thereby incidentally helped to sustain and benefit the government to a degree or in a manner they could not before. Altruism, charity, sympathy, and other acts beyond the call of duty are not precluded. All may be permitted, and may even be encouraged, provided that they respect the limits within which rulers and ruled should act. Generosity, of course, is not expressed when what is sought is to have the benefactor benefited—that would equate generosity with shrewd selfishness. Generous acts should be carried out with a respect for the value of what is being sacrificed, and allowance made for the recovery or replacement of its value; a sacrifice on behalf of others is most noble when made by one acting freely in such a way as to promote a better life for all. Where a life is being sacrificed, there is, to be sure, no recovery or replacement possible. This is only to say that the act is tragic and regrettable, without compromising the fact that it may be noble and even enviable, an act, one hopes, that will be carried out only when nothing less will serve.

The disadvantaged—the handicapped, diseased, awkward, alien, uneducated, helpless—are to yield to others if the gap between themselves and those others will thereby be shortened. This is the evident warrant for their being confined or placed under the control or direction of institutions, people more mature, doctors, and the like. It is more difficult to determine what the advantaged—those accidentally benefited, favored by chance or circumstance, the naturally gifted—should do. There is something amiss if they are deprived of what they happened to possess or had acquired without effort, particularly if there was no injury done to others. It does not appear to be right to deprive them of advantages when they did nothing wrong to get them, and made no one suffer by their possession or use. There is, though, something wrong in allowing them to retain whatever benefits happen to accrue to them, thereby distancing them from all the rest, for no good reason. An answer, somewhat along the lines explored by Rawls, can be found by holding that a person at any one moment, with all the advantages then possessed, is to yield to others, so far as this promotes the continuance and improvement of both. Advantages must, for a while, be given up in order to be able to so to narrow the distance between them. The situation can be readily pictured when the advantages and disadvantages are quantifiable in terms of money, numbers of similar items, and the like. When they are not, and the contenders have different native abilities and opportunities, one must be content to hold that the advantaged are to so act that they make it possible for others to benefit according to their natures and needs. The adjustments at both times are to be governed by the principles that equality is a desirable objective; that what is superior is not to be sacrificed for the sake of what is inferior; and that what is advantaged, if it has been adventiously favored, has no right to insist on itself against the need to cooperate or to promote equality.

When one moves from a consideration of the adjustments which are to be made by people in relation to one another, to the consideration of the adjustments that are to be made by each in order to obtain the best way to be at once a private and public being, similar conclusions are to be drawn. The most desirable outcome is where a privacy so acts that both it and its body are benefited according to their natures, and therefore their rights. The most desirable conditions are those which maximally promote and sustain that result.

Conditions bearing on unions are assessed by private beings who are related to those conditions through the mediation of the unions. The unions make desirable those conditions which indirectly enable each person to be perfected by having a splendidly adjusted privacy and body, i.e., to become genuinely healthy.[10] It is individuals who are to decide what is to be done, but the decisions are to be made in terms of conditions dictating what these and others are to do.

A merely political animal is still an animal; a merely private spirit is only a spirit. People are private beings existing in public. It is no more true that they are fulfilled only if they live public lives than it is that they are fulfilled only if they perfect themselves privately. If they are at their public best, they will do all that they can in such a way that they promote the public and private beings of themselves and others, as well as the government and the state.

Each person is a public being with a privacy. What is done privately only that individual can do, while what is done publicly, because it impinges on what others do and need, can never be done solely on individual terms. To make sure that what is done is appropriate to those who are publicly together, common guidance and control are needed. A government can provide this. Through it, the legitimate power of a state can be so expressed that laws are effectively and properly applied. Public positions and their interrelationships are to be so determined there, that those who rule benefit the ruled, the government, the state, and themselves. Before people can gain from the workings of such a government, however, this must determine positions through which its rule is carried out well, and then find those who can properly fill them.

A government relates positions where acts are legitimately performed on behalf of those it rules. It can be conveniently divided into subdivisions concerned with such matters as education, trade, defense, justice, liberty, and welfare. Keeping these and other functions within a single governance devoted to the task of having people function well together, makes it possible to see how necessary it is to distinguish branches and pivotal positions in a government, fill and relate them properly, and rule through them. To decide what should be marked out, and in what relationship, reference has to be made to the nature of the government and what it can do; to the nature of the state whose power is to be channelled; and, most important, to the nature, proclivities, rights, and wants of the people, both those who are to fill the positions and those who are to be ruled from them.

The interplay of positions with those who fill them is a large and neglected issue. Civil service, salary scales, and conditions for promotion all play a role. The outcome may reinstate the governmental conditions quite well. Or, at the other extreme, it may reflect the ways in which a governmental work force is constituted. At its best, it will unite governmental conditions and workers in a single excellent functioning whole.

A government, carried out by a revolutionary group or the military, may act better and may do more good than the one it replaced. If the rule of the new government had been usurped, the government would be without a requisite legitimacy. It might, though, obtain this eventually, by becoming transformed into a properly functioning government.

Even when benign, and able to provide great benefits, so far as a despot had moved into a position for which no better justification could be offered than a power to crush, or at best an ability to prevent or reduce chaos, a needed legitimacy would still be lacking. It could, though, be achieved were the despot to change into a good sovereign, one who respects the government and works on behalf of the governed. Similarly, were a revolution to end with the creation of a state, that state would not thereby become legitimate, since a legitimate state is more than one that replaces another. Nevertheless, though legitimacy will not be obtained simply by replacing a state that had legitimacy or by supplanting one that lacked legitimacy, a new state could acquire legitimacy on being converted into a properly functioning one.

Neither a despot nor a freshly created state is without some modicum of legitimacy, the one having the native rights that any man has, the other the minimal rights of a complex constituted by a government and people. The rights in both cases, though, fall short of what is needed in order to warrant their determining what others are to do. If there is to be a legitimate determination of those who are dealt with, account must be taken of their natures, needs, desires, hopes, and promises. When it is said that this or that person or group has the virtue, power, intelligence, or vision to dictate what others are to do, the two ideas are conflated.

What is without an appropriate legitimacy may do what is required, while what acts poorly may have legitimacy. These contentions are rejected by both historicists and idealists, the one taking whatever happens to occur to have legitimacy, the other taking whatever is true to itself to act unerringly. The first tolerates usurpations, or at least all those which people prefer over what is replaced; the second allows for any acts if they are deducible from the nature of the performer. The legitimacy that characterizes the acts endorsed by historicists seems not to be better grounded than the legitimacy that the idealists take to characterize a different set of acts.

Legitimacy may be inherited; it is always grounded in the natures of beings. The inheritance is never perfect or unqualified, while the natures never wholly account for the acts performed. Since those who inherit are not just duplicates of their predecessors, their difference from these will not yet be legitimated. And since every action is partly worked out as it occurs, no nature will wholly account for it. Legitimacy is part of a sovereign, government, or state so far as this provides a condition enabling a people to live well together in such a way that each can become enhanced as a public and private person. It can be only partly justified by what once had been, and can only partly justify what is now done.

10. AUTHORITY

Authority expresses a status warranting the acceptance of what it presents. What is authorized represents an authority. The authoritative re-presents it. Authorization begins with one of these and stretches over a region to make a difference to what occurs there.

Legitimacy and authority are distinct ideas. The first is backed by a reason. The second characterizes a distinctive status. It has at least a dozen distinct forms, all of which must be acknowledged if a full justification of a state and its laws is to be provided.

1. *Legitimized Authority:* A legitimized authority demands acceptance for various claims and acts it is justified in making. So far as the demands are backed by and keep in accord with what is legitimate, they are authoritative. What might otherwise be only an authoritative statement of an official's opinion becomes an authoritative statement of justified governmental demands if expressed by a genuine representative of the government.

Just as deceptions by what has legitimacy may be authorized, so demands originating with what lacks legitimacy may be warranted. It is possible, also, to act as an agent for what lacks the appropriate authority. Such an agent (and principal) may be authorized, and may even be treated as an authority by those whom the agent directs, subjugates, or even injures.

Each person can authoritatively report what feelings, memories, hopes, and other occurrences were privately undergone. Only that one who has these knows if what is said about them is true.[1] Were some being, that acted and spoke as a human, not accepted as one, he, she, or it might still be able to speak authoritatively about what was being privately undergone.

Were a person known to be calculating, to use common language carelessly or poorly, or to tend to exaggerate or falsify, we would hesitate to accept his or her report about what had been undergone and, so far, would not take what was said to be authoritative. It might nevertheless be authorized, and in this or that case might be authoritative, reporting what in fact occurred.

Poor, careless, exaggerated, or falsified statements can be authorized as surely as good, careful, precise, and truthful ones. Where the first tells us only about their source, the second allows us to offer the statements to others as not only having been authorized but as possessing authority because they express truths. The fact that people are authorities about their private activities, of course, does not mean that they present what deserves acceptance in the form presented, but if we allow authority to none of their statements, we would have to say that they never say anything that is true—and for that we never have sufficient evidence.

People can be compelled by a despot. His commands may be presented and carried out by those whom the despot authorizes. These may rightly say that they are acting on authority, because they accept the despot as the source of what they are demanding or doing. Were they or the others to yield out of fear, and affirm that the demands are justifiable, it would still be true that the despot does not have the right to make those demands. The despot is an authority about some things, may speak authoritatively, and may authorize various expressions and acts. But none of these may have legitimacy. While it may be possible to know what was being authorized, and learn from this what was intended, it may still not be possible to find an adequate warrant for it.

Every expression re-presents what is privately done and, so far, attains the status of a legitimized, authoritative presentation of it. This does not mean that what it demands is legitimate. What a legitimate sovereign or other source demands is legitimate only if it follows from a legitimized position, since only so far is it backed by an adequate reason. Agents, who are both legitimized and authorized, may insist that those demands be met, their fear of punishment, if nothing else, prompting them, it is hoped, to keep within the boundaries their principal legitimizes and authorizes.

A demand, like a statement, usually expresses what is intended. It could fail to do this. The demand would then not be authoritative. Not the demand, but an intended expression of this, is like an authoritative statement for, like the statement, it re-presents its source. Repetitions of a true statement by others continue an authority; repetitions of a demand by others may lack it. Truth is transitive, attaching to replications of it; a demand is intransitive, needing the help of an authorized agent to reinstate it so that it properly bears on those who are subject to it.

Legitimacy expresses a reason; authority justifies an acceptance. The one is inseparable from a ground, the other from a relation that means by which what is intended is conveyed. If they have authority, they deserve a demanded acceptance.

A legitimate government that fails to take account of the natures and activities of those who are ruled, will not act with an appropriate authority. Reciprocally, too, if those who are governed, while acting legitimately, fail to take proper account of the nature and activity of their government, they will not act with appropriate authority in relation to it.

All persons are legitimate sources and authorities for their expressions. They provide a warrant for the expression's occurrence, but do not necessarily warrant what the expressions demand. Despots may be legitimate sources of and authorities about the nature of their private desires, motives, plans, and the like, but that will not justify whatever is despotically demanded of others, for the despot does not have the required legitimacy.

2. *The Authority of the Superior:* At the root of all authority is the expression of a superiority in some respect and, therefore, of a grounded claim to have what it presents be accepted by those who are in a relatively inferior position. Conceivably, the superior position could have been unjustly achieved; the source of what is being presented might not be known. What is superior may not have had a readier or more complete access than others to what is being presented; it may not have been a cause of it, not understood it, or not be able to insist on it to a degree others can. It will not thereby cease to be an authority for what it expresses. Authorities make claims others are justified in accepting; those claims have a warrant that avoidance or denials by others are unable to diminish.

When a government is superior in dignity, power, right, etc., to those whom it governs, whatever it does will, so far, have authority. The fact was recognized by Plato when he took his ideal government to have the right to censor, to control the time of intercourse, and to banish dramatists and poets. Since people, even when properly subject to governmental control, have rights apart from it, a government, despite Plato, is not the only or a final authority.

People enjoy a superiority over their government in a number of respects. They are able to understand what they are doing, can assume responsibility, may privately initiate acts of their own, and jointly determine what is moral. These limit the authority that a government could have. Neither the people nor the government has an absolute right to reduce the other, and any tendency to do this is an acceptance completes. When there is legitimacy without authority—e.g., the careless remarks of a legitimate ruler—the legitimacy is not expressed appropriately; when there is authority expressed by what is without legitimacy—e.g., a bogus doctor telling nurses what to do—acceptance is being demanded for what does not have a warrant for being accepted. What is not legitimate nor an authority is neither well-grounded nor properly demands acceptance; what is both legitimate and authoritative deserves and demands to be accepted.

What is legitimate authoritatively demands, says, or acts so far as these re-present it. Since it authorizes only what continues it, it alone is the final referent of inquiries as to whether or not something has been authorized by it, but not necessarily an authority about the truth or worth of what it claims. Nor is its authority, or any other, necessarily lost because external causes contribute to what occurs. When it is said that someone was provoked beyond endurance, one must still ask whether or not this was the act of another using him as a carrier.

Threatened with death, a person betrays a comrade or kills another. From the standpoint of the victim, the action was carried out by that person. We, looking at the entire situation, see the reason for the act to be part of a larger, and therefore may excuse the perpetrator, but without thereby cancelling his or her status as the responsible origin of the action. Picked up suddenly by a storm, a man is brought down suddenly, causing the death of a stranger. Unless we can find some reason in him, such as carelessness, an unnecessary placing of himself in a vulnerable position, and the like, we will not only excuse him, but will deny that he accounts for what occurred. Were he overweight, some of the reason for the death of another might be traced to him as a partial cause of the occurrence. It would not be right, of course, to say that he authorized his share in the tragedy, though, it would be correct to say that he contributed to the result and, so far, provided an authorization for what he did. In order to provide an authorization, it is not necessary to be active or explicit. A policeman or a parent may do so simply by not interfering. The uniform of the one and the status of the other give a backing to what occurs within the scope of their warranted control, even when what is done is not what they would prefer or would endorse.

In the realm of politics, a government has legitimacy so far as it has in itself the reason for what it does. Expressions of that legitimacy are authoritative. If the expressions are also authorized, they will be natures never wholly account for the acts performed. Since those who inherit are not just duplicates of their predecessors, their difference from these will not yet be legitimated. And since every action is partly worked out as it occurs, no nature will wholly account for it. Legitimacy is part of a sovereign, government, or state so far as this provides a condition enabling a people to live well together in such a way that each can become enhanced as a public and private person. It can be only partly justified by what once had been, and can only partly justify what is now done.

justifiably opposed. The superiority of either, like the superiority of anything else, is relative, a superiority in this or that respect, and does not extend beyond the expressions of this. It is, to be sure, easy to assume that a superiority enjoyed in one area carries over into others. Advertising and propaganda build on the fact; outstanding figures in entertainment, sport, business, war, and politics, are taken by others, and often by themselves, to be knowledgable about what should be bought, consumed, and done in fields outside their competence.

3. *The Authority of Rank:* A superiority may be due, not to the possession of some feature, but to an occupation of a position in a hierarchy, or to its representing what is higher in some respect to what is acted on. Those who rank whatever exists in a hierarchy, placing a God, Being, or Unity, or whatever, at the top, and people, things, or a sheer matter at the bottom, provide a schema in which one can express how authority may be transmitted from one end to the other, like the command of a general of a well-organized army. A hierarchy though, need not embrace every item. There are hierarchies which rank just a few, but whether it be large or small, items on a lower rank may acquire authority from what is relatively higher.

Rankings involve the use of determinations relevant to the items, justifying their being related as higher or lower because of the degree or manner in which they exhibit those determinations. Consequently, for the authority of a government to be a result of its superior ranking, relative to the people who are ruled, there would have to be some feature allowing the two to be so ordered. If the government has its authority because of an acquisition from what is higher in some hierarchy, these two must also share some ordering feature.

Since a hierarchy of government and people may be constituted in a different way from the hierarchy in which that government is ranked relative to some superior condition, it is possible for a government to have certain features which are related to the ones people possess, and different ones related to those possessed by a state. That government may not have any feature pertinent to both. When sovereigns take themselves to have a divine status, they build on that idea, supposing that they have nothing in common with those they subject.

A government is not human; humans are not a government. The two can, though, be ordered relative to one another as contributing more or less to the existence and functioning of an actual state. The order can be read in two ways: The government could have a superior position so far as it beneficially ruled, or the people could have a superior position as living possessors of rights. Similarly, a government could be taken to be superior to a state and a sovereign, because it was an intelligible, articulated locus of effective governance, at the same time that it was ranked as inferior to them because it was relatively incomplete and weaker. The isolation of one of these orderings, accompanied by a dismissal or neglect of others, lies behind the attempt to trace all government back to the people, a state, or a sovereign.

Different orderings may themselves be ranked. That could make one or some of them have a superior status relative to others. In theories defending democracy, such a superior status is sometimes credited exclusively to those who are ruled, but this is justifiable only if the value, range, power, historical position, persistence, and control of the other factors were due to their being inferior in relevant respects.

The right to rule effectively is not cancelled because people refuse to obey, any more than the right to be ruled well is cancelled because a government rules badly. In a well-functioning complex, the authority of each side is acceptable to the other. Taking that as an objective, it will be necessary for both to be carried out in the light of the need to have the authority each has, by virtue of its superiority in some respect, to be accepted by what is so far inferior to it. The recognition that an ordering in one direction has an equally warranted reciprocal in another, allows for a government's right to require people to act differently from the way they do, as well as the people's right to require that the government change its ways.

4. *De Facto Authority:* Simply by being accepted, what is offered acquires a *de facto* authority. So far, though, one would not distinguish what was being required of the ruled from what was not, the sole factor taken to be relevant being their submission to their rulers. But an authority could be taken to establish a precedent, thereby warranting subsequent governmental demands to which men are to yield. Obeying voluntarily to begin with, by that act a people would have made it possible for the government to have an authority it might otherwise not have.

When, with Aristotle, it is said that one ought to obey bad laws in order to maintain the habit of obeying laws, the principle that there be a governance through laws and that the government be obeyed is upheld. Violators of actual laws, no less than those who obey, are subject to a legitimate government's intrinsic right to demand that justice prevail.

What is weakened by a disobedience of this or that law, however, is not the habit of obedience but the habit of obeying without reflection. In some types of situation unreflecting obedience may actually be eminently desirable. Traffic and crises are best controlled by people unreflectively obeying what is in a familiar position of authority, or by following some established signal indicating what is to be done, and when and how. Unreflecting obedience is of course inappropriate when one is asked to go counter to what is moral. While submitting to laws and legitimate government, a person should function well in a union, society, and state, and thereby make it possible for better laws to be produced and made effective.

The Aristotelian principle could be understood to underscore the fact that Law, a primary demand that justice be done, has an inextinguishable authority. If so, it ought not be said that people should obey bad laws in order to respect the habit of obeying laws but, instead, that there is a majesty to Law that makes disobedience always in the wrong, just so far as it questions that Law. The acceptance of that Law is consistent with a rejection of particular laws. Since such rejections so far deny the right of a government to rule, a government's acceptance of Law is not to be equated with the right of a government to rule, but only with that government's right to rule justly. Every law produced in accord with authorized procedures has authority, the obedience it requires being derived from the government as a locus or producer of laws in accord with Law.

It is surely wise to require obedience when minor bad laws, mere irritants of little moment, are being considered, but when people's rights are denied, what does this loses justification. If there is an appeal made to the courts, they are being asked to decide if proper account had been taken of the rights of people and if people had respected the limits within which they must act under that government.

A supposed right to disobey is a request made to the courts for a determination of the authoritativeness of a particular law in that state. Whatever violation the request must exhibit, before the courts will deal with the issue, is itself governmentally determined. A challenge to laws, expressed in the form of a violation, can do no more than assert a people's authority to act in various ways under Law. So far as the government and people are at cross-purposes, their opposition is to be resolved by adjustments on both sides; by the successful insistence by one side to have its claims prevail over the other's; or by some neutral power effectively assessing their relative claims. Laws are to be obeyed by and large within limits which vary with circumstances. The testing of them through violations is justified only as a tentative, limited effort at determining what a legitimate government authorizes.

Men grant a *de facto* authority to a government through their acts of obedience; a government grants a *de facto* authority to people through its toleration of their acts. Violations of laws on religious grounds, because of the urgings of conscience, a yielding to ethical demands, a respect for life, the preservation of the family, and the like, cannot be justified except on the supposition that these have an intrinsic right to prevail in a conflict with the government. A neutral resolution of the conflicting claims requires the adoption of a position distinct from those held by the different condenders. This can be nothing less than the prospect of both being perfected together.

Disobedience denies to a law the status of a *de facto* authority, but does not cancel whatever authoritative status the law has as an expression of governmental rule. On its side, the disobedience expresses the independence of people, either as they exist apart, or as representing an ideal assessor of the contenders. In either way, people are evidently not wholly subject to a government, no matter how splendid and benign this be.

Although no one has a native or bestowed right to disobey, each has a right to become mature and perfected together with others, and to express this in act. That right, if warranted only by the nature people have, makes them beings who urge their good against opposing claims. To know what is justified in the face of opposing claims, acts must be assessed in terms which are neutral to them and that with which they contend. A refusal to obey is rightly subject to penalty, except so far as one's limits and the government's are properly set at other places—a matter to be determined only by knowing what each rightly demands, not only because of what it is and can become, but because of what must occur in a state where other demands are also authoritatively expressed.

The ideal good is not very good. The fact that this final determinant of the proper scope of rulers and ruled is also possessed of little power is evidenced by the conflicts that in fact occur. That does not diminish its ability to determine the limits within which different contenders are to operate. Being no more than a remote possibility, more likely than not, it will never be fully realized, but it still should effectively guide what is done. To the degree that it succeeds in guiding actions, to that degree authority is acquired from it.

People discover what they have the authority to do when subject to governmental rule, by learning what they can do without penalty. An attempt to discover through disobedience how far governmental rule actually extends is a kind of experiment to determine what it means to be subject to that government. Like a physical experiment which failed to elicit from nature the results desired, a punished violation would then be an act that failed to obtain a governmental acknowledgment that it was acceptable. The fact that intentions may be noble and that there is nothing to be gained from a violation, does not make it less a violation than if it had been deliberately produced for selfish ends. In either case, it lacks a *de facto* authority, an authority possessed just by being acceptable to a government.

There are laws which perpetuate long-standing iniquities, particularly those which discriminate against some because they do not have the ancestry, gender, color, wealth, property, or other appurtenances of the dominant or more powerful who control governmental actions. To allow for only minor violations of such laws is to allow for injustices to continue for an indefinitely long time; to insist on a right to disobey, no matter what the law, is to invent a supposed neglected or abused right, to be maintained no matter what the nature and need of a government or state.

There can be no legal right to disobey. To suppose there is, is to suppose a right to rebel. So far as a government is concerned, there is no such right or, if there is, the government does not and cannot recognize it. No government can coherently sanction what would weaken or overthrow it. Still, people have rights that a government ought to respect. Short of a revolution that seeks to install such a government, there is nothing to be done except to look to what can authoritatively determine the relations a government and people are to have to one another. This, most immediately, is the state. It could so function, of course, only if it had some being of its own. Yet a state lacks the substantiality that people and governmental officials possess. It does, though, have something like the unity of a living being which, without deliberation, affects subordinate parts and maintains itself by interacting with other similar realities. The fact is recognized when the state deals with other states and is seen to have a place in history.[2] It then is acknowledged to have its own boundaries and ways of making some people function as the primary means through which its various parts are regulated in relation to one another.

So far as those over whom a state has control are under a government, some people must take on the role of adjusting rulers and ruled to one another. Although a state is not an organism, the Absolute writ small, or people writ large, it does have a nature, and affects what is within its confines in ways which are like those exhibited by a bodily health operating through a regulatory heart, lung, and liver.[3]

5. *Accreted Authority:* An ideal certifies that some acts are warranted because they promote its realization. As a mere prospect, it is not superior to the people who accept it. It is not even superior to those who reject it or who act in ways which make its realization unlikely or impossible. Indeterminate, without power or ability to act, it controls what occurs only in the sense that it sets limits within which the actions to realize it are to occur.

The highest of ideals is still only an ideal. The worst of people are superior to it, precisely because they are able to realize it to some degree. They have a concreteness, power, and effectiveness nothing merely prospective could ever equal. It is therefore a terrible blunder to sacrifice people in order to make it possible for an ideal prospect to be realized. Realized, the outcome might be thought to be better than what now is; conceivably, it might embrace people and a government far superior to any now existing. No one, though, should be sacrificed to make room for these. Granted that it is ever right to make sacrifices, it is still one thing to do this by giving up possessions in order that a better state of affairs prevail, and another to injure or kill people in order to realize that prospect.

Sometimes justifications for deaths due to a war are offered on the grounds that a better, more equitable, peaceful world, with inevitably benefited people, will thereupon ensue. Let that dubious belief be accepted. It is still not right to sacrifice any human being for the good of another, or even for the good of all the others. A war is always a tragic occurence. Nothing can justify maiming or destroying people to achieve goods not equal to the worth of any one of them. Both the victors and the defeated in a war necessarily lose what is irreplaceably precious.

Let it be supposed that a war is begun by a state to obtain territory, wealth, control, or even to exterminate the citizens of another. Evidently the aggressor must be stopped. And there may in fact be no way to do this except by taking up arms against it, with an inevitable destruction of innocents on both sides. That situation is a function of a failure to have attained the position where all people ought to be. Since there is no making good the losses that ensue, one must try to keep the carnage to a minimum and thereafter see to it that further aggressions do not occur. Those who lost their lives, presumably in order to prevent an aggressor from destroying them and others as well, were sacrificed for the sake of those who remain. That sacrifice cannot be justified by showing that the number hurt and destroyed is smaller than the number preserved, since the value of a single life is incomparable.

The only conceivable justification there is for the sacrifice of people is that it is an inescapable means by which further destructions are limited or eliminated. The justification cannot be understood to warrant the destruction of some people now so that others may not be destroyed later; that would be to advocate killing. It must be understood to demand that losses in value be limited, and to hold that this today may require the commission of regrettable acts. Although there is no justifiable quantifying of people, it might still be thought necessary and desirable to sacrifice some in order to prevent the destruction of more. That loss is not justified, even if one does not know in advance just which people will pay the price. There is no way of resolving the issue, as long as humanity is not fully civilized, for to be civilized is, among other things, not to have a world where aggressors flourish. This is no more utopian than is the decision to have an undefended border between the United States and Canada. Until we achieve such a civilization, we will commit unjustifiable wrongs.

Whatever contributes to the nature or capacities of people to realize what is ideal, adds to the authority of what so contributes. In addition to the authority they may have on their own, the wise, the good, the reflective, and the perceptive, therefore, have authority because of the ideals to which they are attached. Actual governments may be guided by and may more or less realize those ideals. So far as they do, they add to the authority they already have.

States and people, when they help a government be better related to an ideal, are incidentally authorized by it. Conversely, when a government helps them be better related to it, the authority it already has is increased. Every functioning government receives such additions to its authority, and makes additions to the other factors, for all are interlocked in a single ongoing where each, while maintaining itself apart, more or less gives to and receives from the others.

Separate examinations of people, governments, states, and sovereigns pass over the contributions each obtains from the others. Usually, the importance of a government or the people who are ruled is emphasized, with everything else taken to have a possible instrumental role. While it may then be recognized that a government is valuable for what it does on behalf of the governed (and conversely, that those under a government are commendable because they sustain or contribute to an excellent governing) the authority that the government has to perfect those it rules (and the authority that people have to promote good government) will be neglected.

The more surely a government is an integral part of a single complex where it supports and acts to enhance people, the more surely does it have an authority greater than that which follows from its nature. While its legitimacy will continue to reflect what it is, its authority will reflect the fact that it is also a contributor to a single ongoing of mutual supportive factors.

6. *Evidenced Authority:* An articulation has authority to the extent that it is authoritative, accurately re-presenting something, and thereby justifying its acceptance as a proper substitute for the original. Although a belief has no authority, an articulation of it has authority so far as it offers a re-presentation of it in another guise. What is true of belief is true of decisions, hopes, and thoughts.

When authority is conveyed in an articulation, one is able to examine, utilize, and deal with what was privately begun. Language is the main agency by which this is done. To credit it wholly to a community is to suppose that people never rightly use it in novel creative ways, or that what they say has no authority, individually and privately provided. When the common language is used to articulate what is individually produced, any authority that the production possesses is carried over into what re-presents it.[4]

A government can be articulated in at least two ways: One is in a diagram or schema in which its various positions are laid out; a second is in laws and regulations expressing what is permitted and forbidden, what the limits of permissible action are, and the penalties that are to be suffered by violators. The first does not need to be explicitly laid out; a diagram or schema may even be abstracted from the positions and branches that are in fact occupied by those engaged in governmental activities. The second is articulated, not as the first is, to make possible the carrying out of governmental functions in relation to one another, but to express what those who are ruled are to do. The first has the authority of the authoritative, since it represents; the second has the authority of the authorized, since it represents. Laws are authoritative so far as they express the government in a communicable form; when they fail to do this, they still provide authorized indications of the fact that there is a government of laws.

7. *Idealized Authority:* Confucians hold that those who have wisdom should be accepted as authorities on how one is to act toward others. Those authorities are as they ought to be, or, at the very least, know what it is like to be so, and what must be done if one is to become wise. Unfortuntely, they provide little that is especially pertinent to a government. Usually, they give advice only to a sovereign, while the government is assumed to be carried on by functionaries faithfully keeping in traditional grooves. Although the final concern of the Confucian is for every human, he is particularly concerned with those who, as members of families, join others in living stable, civilized, social lives, well-aware of their traditions, occupied with the meticulous performance of established rituals, and concerned with respecting the dignity that is appropriate to different stations and their relevant duties. There is a tendency also to favor the outlook of an agricultural economy and the kind of culture that were in the background of Confucius' own thinking, in order to take advantage of his insight that traditionalized wisdom lends authority to what is thought, taught, and practiced in accord with it. But different forms of wisdom have their own seasons.

A wise person sometimes knows what abilities must be acquired, and how they are to be exercised so that one can be fulfilled together with others. The knowledge is not alway expressible in clear affirmations, advice, admonitions, and corrections; some of it is conveyed through demeanor. Practical and humanistic, it cannot be caught in formulae, injunctions, or even laws. To benefit those who possess it as well as those who allow themselves to be guided by it, it must be expressed in actions enabling people to be at peace with themselves and one another. So far, Confucianism provides an excellent guide for conduct. Authority is here a consequence of a superiority in doing what is needed in order to enjoy a humane life with others. It is an authority that does not have to be insisted on in order to be effective, since its effectiveness flows from the excellence that it expresses. The view has strong affiliations with the Greek idea that virtue is a habit determining what one is to do. It differs from this in progressing without pause or slip, from where one does what should be done in a family or in a small group, to what must be done when in command of multitudes. The road is rockier than the Confucians seem to admit. One big boulder in the way is the fact that a society and a state differ considerably in origin, nature, achievement, and functioning from one another, as well as from persons, each with an unduplicable privacy.

Those who govern, if they follow the Confucian lead, are presumed to be people of virtue, or are to follow the guidance of others who possess it. There is a paradox lurking here. The Confucian insists that people should understand what they are doing, and that they have well-established habits for acting well—which is what virtue is—but he does not want anything formally presented or set down as a rule to be understood, and then freely obeyed. Instead, he wants people to be both guided by wisdom and to act wisely, expressing what it is to be persons, and not to subject themselves to some abstract principle or rationally-defended demand. This, though, is precisely what must be done if people are to live under law, and thereby under the rule of a well-functioning, articulated government.

Wisdom will help one decide where the limits of an act are to be drawn; virtue will help one prevent self-interest and conceit from getting in the way of what is to be done. Both are needed if people are to forge good laws, and are to live in accord with these. Those laws should be explicitly formulated; at their best, they will satisfy a rational reflection on what is to be demanded if people and government are to prosper together. Although wisdom cannot replace, it could add to the authority such laws possess. These already have some authority of their own. Those laws should make room for the possible, differently exercised wisdom that might be possessed by those who are to obey.

8. *Acquired Authority:* Authority gives what it presents a status this does not of itself possess. A child can say, as well as an adult, "Do this, or I will hurt you." Rarely can a child say this with sufficient authority, able to follow a refusal with the threatened, punitive acts. The child's threat may authoritatively express its intent, but this, unlike the adult's, will normally be confined to a wish and have no bearing on an outcome that can be authoritatively assured.

An acquired authority is its source in another guise. That source may be an intent, idea, belief, or some other private occurrence. It could reflect the character, temper, indeed any aspect of a privacy, giving the expression a dignity, and warranting its acceptance as a public and usable translation. Were the expression distortive, misleading, or incoherent, it might reflect the presence of private confusions or of determinations to deceive. If the former, it would warrant the characterization of an individual as being at fault; if the latter, it would lack authority, just so far as it did not have the presumed source. Those who deny that there are private sources of what is publicly expressed, privately permit no distinguishing of what is private from what is publicly available. They are surely mistaken. It is not easy, though, to determine when we have a genuine expression re-presenting in public what occurred in private, rather than just a presentation of it as a consequence of the addition of another element. A liar expresses himself through public forms purporting to re-present an intent to speak truthfully, when in fact he has combined an intent to express with a perhaps undetectable intent to deceive.

Expressions have in insistency requiring others to accept them because of the authority behind them, and which they presumably incorporate. That insistency, though not physical, may nevertheless be effective, leading to its acceptance as a fit communicable form of what is privately determined. The distinction between it and physical power is partly preserved when it is termed a "persuasiveness", able to make a difference to others who are receptive to it.[5] However it be designated, it is authoritative since it re-presents in public what is privately intended.

Despite the fact that men have been persuaded, sometimes against their strong desires and beliefs, by what is presented authoritatively, the fact has not been to the fore in most discussions of the nature of knowledge or communication, any more than it is in discussions of the nature of government. Yet, when no place is allowed for privacy and the warrant it provides, one of a person's public expressions may have no more justification than another. Good articulations in a public language might tell us about an ability to use this well, but would not necessarily report what was intended.

A lie may be well-articulated by a liar and communicate what is authorized by him. To be effective, it would have to be placed in a context of ordinary communication, where it will readily be taken to authorize the acceptance of what is said. When poor arguments, propaganda, pomp, and rhetoric are persuasive, they function somewhat like lies, leading others to misconstrue what in fact is being expressed.[6]

That is related to the reason why, when a poor argument fails to be persuasive, those who do not accept it are sometimes made subject to such pejoratives as "irrational", "stupid", or "obstinate".

What is freely made available is authorized but it may not be authoritative and, so far, will lack authority. An authority will be behind what is presented, but that authority will not be expressed in what is being conveyed. Recognizing that authority, and the fact that what is being expressed is authorized by it, people may suppose that what is being conveyed deserves to be accepted at its face value. But they are not always fooled. At the time of the Great Depression, J.P. Morgan, the financier, made widely reported statements in which he said that the stock market was in good condition. He persuaded no more than a few. For most, he was not an authority about the health of the economy or, if he was, he was seen to be saying what he really did not believe, but instead was trying to 'canute' an irresistible movement.

Those who resist authoritative governmental decrees are criticizable for failing to be accommodative of that to which they should submit. More likely than not they will be receptive of a bad rule, ready to accept this without requiring alteration, in somewhat the way poor thinkers are prepared to accept poor arguments and to reject what strong thinkers accept as good.

A government's authority is expressed primarily through laws, each authoritative, and authorized to demand that people act in consonance with what is being decreed. Ruling here is not an imposition of brute force, the converse of a passive acceptance but, instead, an insistence on demands deserving to be accepted. Those who are receptive of them presumably want and need to be ruled, while others will have to be restrained and redirected until they become no less receptive.

If they are good public beings, people are receptive of a good rule; if they are not, they open the way to a bad. If the first, they would have to be transformed in order to be receptive of a bad rule, just as the second would have to be transformed in order to be receptive of a good. Good and bad, applied to the people, here refers to them as acting in accord with a legitimate government's rule. Applied to a government, it refers to what it authoritatively decrees. The good in either defies and is defied by what is so far comparatively bad in the other.

9. *Credited Authority:* What accepts an authority may not be quali-

fied to do so. Those who accept what scientists report may not have the right to do this because they do not have the ability to assess it, judge it, make it their own in any other sense than that of being able to repeat what was said. It is, of course, true that those who are ignorant should accept what is maintained by those who know. If they are not able to understand what they are accepting, they will act somewhat as a child does when it goes where a parent goes, even though this is not where neither it nor the parent should be. The fact that people usually accept what others say as being truths, makes evident that they belong in a common complex where what is said is accepted on its face value; the fact that they are not qualified to accept or reject what scientists affirm is not due simply to their being outside the scientific commune or community.

It is not necessary for people to know what a government is or ought to be in order to credit it with the authority to rule them, and for them to be ruled by what it authorizes. To say this is to come strikingly close to the root of contract theories which hold that people agree to submit to control by a sovereign, for although people do not credit a government with an absolute right over them and their posterity, as such theories sometimes maintain, they also do not make it into a mere tool and, so far, deny to it a separate nature and mode of functioning.[7] The acceptance of a governmental rule, at its best, is concurrent with its acceptance of people as deserving respect.

Submission carries an aura of cravenness in the West that it does not in the East, where it is treated as a moment in a rhythmic, nuanced process of functioning extremely well. A government that operates along the latter lines accepts the authority of other factors, and submits to their guidance and control, alternatively with or as qualifying an insistence on itself. It would obtain less than it needs were it to persistently insist on itself without regard for what people are, desire, and deserve.

Both government and people should act with authority on behalf of whatever legitimacy they have. Each is to yield to the other so far as this authoritatively acts so as to promote its own and the other's proper functioning, and the achievement of other desirable objectives. Ruler and ruled must not only mesh; each is to yield to the other in order that it be helped to obtain what it requires.

Good government is more than a multiplicity of different agents somehow fitting together. It involves both ruler and ruled, each separate, authoritative, cooperative, subordinating and subordinated, constantly adjusting to the other so as to constitute what is more than the two added together. Carried out blindly, the outcome of their interplay will as often be chaos and conflict as peace and supplementation. Both, though, could act so as together promote the realization of an excellent state.

10. *Empowered Authority:* The stupidity and brutality resulting from the use of sheer power makes it fearful, needing to be hemmed in and perhaps even radically reduced, where it cannot be abolished or kept latent. It has no known limits and usually no other result but reduction or destruction. It could, though, be harnessed, channellized, brought under control, and used so as to make possible the achievement of what is desirable. Technology offers a splendid way for doing this. By itself, as just an effective sluiced power, it has no authority in a state except so far as it has been credited with this. Without authority, it is merely a smoother, harnessed form of brute force, understanding nothing, allowing no opposition, lacking modulation or direction. It can and deserves to be authorized and authoritatively used; it needs to be restrained, channelled, and expressed with nuance.

Power can enable what would otherwise be incompetent or merely formal to make a desirable difference. It could help some authority be more effective. Since it could not become completely subservient to anything without ceasing to be, all that could be properly required of it is that it add effectiveness to what has authority of its own, function authoritatively, and authorize only what promotes the good of itself and people. If it does not, there is warrant for the use of a counteracting power. Reciprocally, what it affects could give authority to it. If this is not done, it may be necessary to make use of more power.

Stalin's dismissal of the Pope, with the question of how may troops the Pope had at his disposal, contains a bitter truth. Stalin saw that he could, through the use of an available force, compel submission to his demands.[8] His power, though, did not legitimize his repressions and destructions. What he crushed had its own legitimacy and authority. For a good state to exist, both rulers and ruled, the powerful and the powerless, must be credited with making legitimate and authoritative claims.

Were a government to derive power from a state or sovereign, or even from those it rules, that power would, on being brought within its scope, be its own. The government would then not just formulate laws but would warrantedly and might effectively insist that people live in consonance with them. To compel obedience when the appropriate functioning of people is not forthcoming, it would have to depend on the availability of further power. Were it backed by no power it would at best be only a bureaucracy in which papers are passed from desk to desk.

While constitutions may be written by utopians, and rule by law may be promised by dictators, governments must govern and therefore be in a position to compel what resists their rule. Were a government to depend for its governing solely on an acceptance of its rule, as Locke seems to hold, it would depend on what could be withdrawn at will, for any reason, or for no reason. A government must have at least enough power to persuade people to live in ways it prescribes, and should be able to call on more to transform the recalcitrant into the receptive.

The authority that a government has because of its legitimacy is increased by power lent or given to it by the people, state, or sovereign. It needs the added power to enable it to be persuasive enough to make people become sufficiently obedient. Since, as has been observed, the threat of or actual use of power often makes people become obedient—or more accurately, submissive—it is tempting to hold that power could be reduced to persuasiveness. The threat of the use of power, even if this is achieved just by displaying the means by which it will be used, can be persuasive, and thereupon met by an accommodation by those who will be subject to it, but we speak ironically when we say that someone has been persuaded to conform by the immanence of a compulsion.

The power that is available in the limited political world where men exist within narrower and more specialized limits than those that nature provides, is present and used by every factor there, making the course of the state as much a series of adjustments of powers as it is of claims and counter-claims. The total amount of power available and divided among various factors depends on what they have been able to produce from within themselves, or to obtain from the world about. The resulting complex is nestled inside a larger world, some of whose power the complex has made its own, and used in various ways and degrees. The strengthening of one factor at the expense of others will eventually reduce the stability and value of the whole and add to the contribution each must make if the government is to function well, and people are to benefit by their so turning away from the rest of the world that they are effectively together under a common government. At one moment, the power of government, and at another, the power of the people is to be increased, depending on how their interplay can make for their most desirable combination. To assure that result, we must learn how power should be distributed, and then see to it that the knowledge is used. If the result is not to be merely something hoped for, the effort must be subject to a control over what is occurring. In the absence of this, little more can be done than to go through a series of modifications of the different activities, in the attempt to achieve a better distribution of the power than had prevailed before. Otherwise there would be just an acceptance of whatever occurs, despite the fact that the legitimacy and authority of others might be effectively denied.

11. *Traditionalized Authority:* On birth, a person enters a limited world, where authority has been and continues to be constantly exercised. Immediately, and most effectively, the authority of parents and family becomes apparent. It will not be long before that authority gives way before greater and greater authoritative demands by union, society, and state. These compel all to find places for themselves in what is not altogether prepared to receive them.

An infant may be welcome and loved; parents may be ready to make great sacrifices on its behalf. It surely has native rights and, in a civilized state, will be credited with publicly viable ones. Recognized to have the legitimacy and authority characteristic of a person, the infant will still lack the legitimacy and authority of one who is a functioning member of a union able to interplay with a common needed governance. At most, it could be properly said to have the right to belong to a union, society, or state, not the right to be or to be treated as a contributor to one. It does not and cannot have the legitimacy or authority possible to those who are mature. Since it is not yet able to assume roles in relation to the roles of others, and has not yet come under the direct control of anything that it is in a position to acknowledge, it could have no more legitimacy and authority than belongs to it by virtue of its being a person.

The authority of a common governance has to be accepted before one is in a position to act well in a world with others. There is no deciding that this be done, any more than there is a creation of something which is thereupon yielded to. The fact lies behind one of the problems that adolescents face; they have to be transformed by what is authoritative if they are to reach the position where they have the authority of an adult. Still, they have native rights, and rightly demand that their public expressions be both supported and protected against denials or confinements, even by those who have more rights, and surely against those who have more power. None will ever reach the stage where all actions are adequately backed solely by an individual's authority; even the freest, wisest, noblest, and most advanced person, when functioning in public, makes use of a tradition and ideals, as already having authority. The influence of these can never be reduced to nought, though use may be made of them to a degree and in a manner that cannot be fully foretold.

It is not easy to determine if people together do or could have an authority greater than a government's. In place of that knowledge, voting, referendum, resistance, and sometimes rebellion decide the issue. Since the authorities of government and people are independent, and diverse in nature and scope, no correct determination along this route seems to be possible, even in principle. Disobedience can, of course, be contrasted with demands for obedience; demands on behalf of rights can be set against those who give or deny them. Since all have their distinctive natures, and the kind and degree of legitimacy and authority that those natures ground, in the end one is forced to acknowledge a plurality of authorities unable to be scaled in relation to one another. If so, no matter how mature a person may be, he or she must, like a child, find a place under an authority maintained independently, and which may not always fully respect that person's authority.

Each person exists apart from every government and state; each person has a distinctive legitimacy and authority. Confronting the claim that people enter a world where there are long-established authorities to which they are to submit, therefore, is the no less valid claim that a government (and a state and sovereign, as well as a union and society) is produced in a world where people have already established some legitimacy and authority for themselves, with the accompanying right to challenge opposing and limiting claims.

The claims of government and people are irreducible. Often they are incomparable. Once again, therefore, recourse must be had to a series of *ad hoc* adjustments, or to an ideal able to guide what is being done, so as to make possible a harmony in which each side expresses an authority to act as it does, adding to and also limiting the other's. The best government neither governs most nor least; it does what it must in order that those who are ruled be able to express their natures and needs as fully as it expresses its own. The two together must achieve an accord with the state, for this, too, deserves to have its expressions respected.[9]

12. *Symbolized Authority:* There is an honorific component in the

idea of authority, justifying submission to what possesses it, as that which rightly determines what is to be done, affirmed, or sought. The authority need not know what it is doing and may have achieved its status in one of a number of ways, but it will, as present, still have its own status and value. Were the nature of its authority misconstrued, or if it operated to the detriment of others, it would still rightly demand consideration. Since the authority in these cases is actually present, it is not identifiable with something mistakenly taken to be an authority.

An agent who goes beyond an assignment, so far, has no authority. Nevertheless the agent gives the principal's authority a place and role. Wrongly claiming to have a particular authority, the agent is still authorized, and may authoritatively make certain demands. The claim opens the agent to the charge of wrongful possession; the demands, to a possible error of judgment. If there is no authority for what is done the actions, instead of being performed by an agent, will be carried out by someone wrongly claiming the authority that an agent possesses.

A person, we say, speaks "with authority". What we then mean is only that the person acts in such a way as to make others alert to the weight of what is being said or done. A father's deep voice, a mother's attentiveness, a judge's robes and higher seat, a nurse's confident moves, and official seals are among many symbols of authority, preparing the way for what will then be presented as having authority of its own. Such symbols need not make one attend to what will exercise another and usually more momentous authority. Still, they sometimes do, at the same time that they authoritatively make one be more receptive to what will thereupon be done. They are intermediaries which make one attend, not to themselves, but to their sources. They could therefore be said to open the way to the acceptance of their sources, somewhat as a grimace or an expletive does. There are some, of course, who confound the trappings of office with the office itself, just as there are those who readily identify what is being said with what is intended. Both are literalists, misconstruing the nature of a symbolized authority, an authority presented in a guise intended to make others act in some particular way.

Conceivably, a government could function efficiently and well if its officials were casually dressed, had tiny offices, and spoke a plain language. They might have all the authority they need to make a good law. But if they are not preceded or accompanied by symbols representing authority, others will not be as ready to obey as they might otherwise be. Symbols help make people ready to accept a governance. By being receptive to a symbol of its authority, they are prepared to accede to what their government demands of them.

It has sometimes been supposed that a government is itself a symbol of a state, and sometimes even of a God. Sometimes it has been supposed that those who are governed symbolize hidden virtues. It is hard to find a warrant for these suppositions. The idea has more plausibility when a government is taken to be a symbol of supposed inescapable conditions to which people are subjected by a God or the world, and public persons are taken to be symbols of themselves as private. One then brings into sharp focus the symbolic role of the constituents of a state and thereby allows for a passage into what is beyond them.

Were there nothing behind what usually functions as a symbol, this would play the role of a disguise, serve as a pretense, or be part of a masquerade. A police or soldier's uniform is intended to make one alert to somebody who has been authorized to act in a particular way. Those who have no right to wear it will, in ordinary circumstances, make its wearing a kind of lie, a way of presenting to others what is readily accepted as marking out one who deserves to be recognized as having a number of distinct functions for which those others are to allow.

The better the ways in which symbols interplay, the less need there is to have those behind the symbols engage in action, with all the energy, danger, and time that this involves. What is here true of the ruled and ruler in relation to one another is true of these in relation to the state, and this in relation to them. Both save time and energy by interposing symbols of themselves. The interaction of the symbols yields a world in which both officials and people live, as they go about their daily tasks, the one mainly by making its symbols evident, the other by exhibiting such symbols of obedience as remaining quiet or not forming large and threatening assemblies.

Conceivably, this account of authority could be expanded to include more than the forms here focused on. Nor would there apparently be anything seriously wrong—and in some sense, it would be eminently right—if some of those here distinguished were combined. It is necessary, though, to realize that there are times when only one of them is operative—and surely times when only one of them is conspicuously present—and that it is possible for one component of a state to have one kind of authority, and another component to have a different kind. No harm is usually done by concentrating on a few forms, provided only that the others are kept in mind and brought forward when needed. A state, government, and a union of people are distinct authorities, to be respected by the others, even when it is necessary to qualify what each authoritatively does.

What cannot be denied ultimacy cannot properly be denied authority. Each person privately establishes an authority nothing else can effectively challenge, a fact that is made most evident in the course of living and dying. The occasions and conditions for these may be set by others. Although a life may be suddenly snatched from someone, the dying will be undergone alone, effectively establishing that person as an authority whose exercise allows for no denying. That truth is glimpsed by suicides. They are acutely aware that all authorities are defied by theirs. It is sad that it is not also seen that one gains by continuing to express oneself in public, and thereby helps constitute a complex of interlocked authorities, each of which has something to contribute to the others.

The authority of people in a state extends no further than to where they publicly are together under laws. For them, law presents the conditions under which they are to act if they are to obtain desirable outcomes not otherwise realizable, and if they are to avoid undesirable penalties to which they otherwise would be subject. Laws authoritatively formulate the conditions under which and the limits within which people together are to live and act. To keep them there, reference has to be made sometimes to one and sometimes to another of the laws' various types of authority.

So far as a state and its government are concerned, an important, and arguably the most important part of their functioning is encapsulated in the laws they formulate, insist on, and use to adjudicate what people do. An adequate consideration of the nature of those laws would require a work larger than this. Fortunately, the present study requires only an understanding of their essential features. They have a distinctive authority, resulting from the fact that they exhibit specialized forms of various types of authority here distinguished. The fact that laws are authoritative in a plurality of ways will not, though, necessarily make them superior to what is authoritative in only one, since the latter may exhibit its authority to a degree and with an effectiveness not possible to the former.

11. Positive Law

"Law" is used in many different ways.[1] Today, two are common—one referring to the governing structures of natural occurrences, and the other to enforceable, formulated prescriptions imposed on people and their institutions by an authorized instrument of the state. The empirical temper and the linguistic concerns of philosophers of science over the last decades have led to the comparative neglect of the first sense of law, leaving only the second with a genuine objective referent. Despite attacks by legal realists,[2] who sought to understand law as dissolvable into accounts of the decisions made by judges, and despite the great differences that separate the different schools of legal thought, it is still true that there are positive laws in the form of authoritative demands made and carried out by the organs of a legitimate government.

If there are laws of Nature, they relate possible, realizable, cosmic occurrences as antecedents to entailed and realizable consequents. If there are no laws of Nature, there will of course be no application of that idea. The laws of a state, "positive laws" are all intended to have an application. The result of human decision, they are publicly stated and backed by an available force that could be used to promote the production of prescribed outcomes.

A positive law says that if such and such is done, then such and such will be done to assure that a governmentally prescribed outcome ensues. The consequent is what is to be achieved, with privileges, restraints, rewards, penalties, and punishments promised so as to encourage its production. The additions could be provided for at the beginning in the form of restraints and privileges; over the course of action in the form of directions, admonitions, pressure, and explanations; or at the end, by means of rectifications converting the achieved outcome into what is required. Circumstances will be different at different times, making possible differences in the nature of the consequents that are in fact brought about, and therefore requiring variations in the degree and manner in which the additions are made. The fact that desired consequences guide and control what serves to realize them, reveals positive laws to be purposive, dictating to and partly compelling antecedents, activities, or outcomes to take on required forms.

Associated people live together in some consonance. Cooperative ones act in mutually supportive ways to bring about a common product. When the former are viewed in the light of the support they give to positive law, and when the latter keep within the limits the law prescribes, the people could be said to be subject to a "living law",[3] a stable, regulative, unreflectively followed, unformulated determination of what they are to do. Governments must take account of it, or risk a persistent resistance that could reduce them to mere sources of recommendations, or to regrettable users of brute force. Positive laws go further, providing means for a government to make the "living law" articulate and effective. Authoritative and explicitly formulated, the positive laws express decisions about the way people are to be ruled.[4]

Usually, laws are the product of interrelated activities of different parts of a government. There is no necessity that those parts be marked off as different branches. As long as judiciary decisions and express commands are enforced as surely and as well as enactments of legislative bodies are, those required to conform will usually find little point in distinguishing the enactments from the decisions and commands. Distinguishing the three, though, keeps one attentive to the complex nature of positive law.

A government is both a principal and agent. As a principal, it enacts laws applicable to those who are to be ruled. As an agent, it functions on behalf of a people, state, or sovereign. As both principal and agent, it provides laws under which it itself operates.

The comparatively little power that a government has relative to a sovereign or a state inclines one to view it as just an agent for them. More likely than not, one will then neglect its status as an authoritative source of requirements which limit the activities of those others. In modern states, a sovereign has its tasks and powers defined by law, though this does not prevent it from treating its people as though they did not have the rights which the government might acknowledge, and which other sovereigns and states explicitly acknowledge to be possessed by their people. Lincoln in wartime assumed the position of a sovereign and suspended the Writ of *Habeas Corpus;* indeed that suspension was provided for in Article 1, section 9 of the Constitution. "The Privilege of the Writ of Habeas Corpus shall not be suspended, unless when in Cases of Rebellion or Invasion the public Safety may require it." The privilege, expressed in the Constitution as a condition not to be denied except in exceptional times, makes room for a sovereign suspension of some of the usual practices by the government. The Constitution, designed to define the powers of a government, here permits a part of the government, an executive, to function as a sovereign. The sovereign is, so far, not required to stay entirely within the limits where, as part of the government, or as a representative of the state, he or she will usually and properly function.

Approached from the side of a sovereign, laws are primarily ways in which a government expresses and insists on what the sovereign requires of its subjects; approached from the side of a state, laws are enforceable, articulated demands, which citizens are to obey; approached from the side of a people, laws are enforceable demands which a government expresses on behalf of them, itself, the sovereign, or the state. The laws here articulate what some other principal requires. Since a government, through the agency of its laws, not only acts on behalf of a people, but of a state, a sovereign, and the government itself as well, the common view, that laws are means by which people rule themselves, evidently deals with them from only one side. Those who defend the view usually claim that the state, sovereign, and government are just agents which people set up for their own benefit. Although there is no historic, and apparently no adequate theoretic reason for supposing that this is so, granting it still leaves one faced with the fact that once in existence those supposed agents have distinctive natures and engage in distinctive activities. Each may be legitimate and have authority, and so far deserves to have its nature and requirements sustained and satisfied. Laws, whatever their origin and justification, have this as one of their tasks.

Some positive laws are primarily avenues through which power is expressed. Others attend primarily to objectives controlling what is done. In modern states, various combinations of the two are common, with the latter expressing what most would like to have dominate. To this are added explicit or implicit affirmations that there will be compulsions introduced to make sure that the consequent ensues, should it not otherwise be realized. Positive laws, consequently, are to be taken to assert: "In such and such circumstances, these acts are to be performed, or such and such governmental actions will be carried out, to make justice, peace, etc. prevail, to help the state continue, or to help it realize its objectives."

A legislature may provide enactments under which it will formulate others. Some of those enactments concern procedures; others express accepted standards for coming to reasonable decisions. A government, such as that of the United States, has branches serving as checks on one another, each with an authority to assess and limit what the others do. All may look to the Constitution, history, custom, or power for their legitimacy. The fact that other governments are subdivided in different ways and are legitimized differently, usually expresses a difference not in principle but in particulars, pertinent to local practices and circumstances.

Positive laws have authority both for those in the present and for those who come later, because they are enacted by an authoritative government operating within the compass of a continuing, legitimizing state. There, people together in a homeland act in some accord with what the governmental actions require. Those who govern may or may not accept that homeland in the same way, or grant it the same importance as do those who are being ruled. Still, they must take some account of it, or risk an unarticulated but effective rejection of what they demand, despite a threat of penalty if their demands are not honored.

In the United States, the state is the primary authority, whose essential parts and functions are stated in its Constitution. Each of the branches into which its government is divided has an authoritative role to play in determining the operative meaning of the governing laws. Each branch imposes some limitation on what the others may do, and enjoys a status the others must respect; otherwise one risks a dissolution of the state defined by that Constitution. A legislature may produce enactments governing the activities of the president and the courts. These in turn may limit one another's activities as well as the legislature's. Other branches could have been provided, and any one of the three might not have been instituted.

No matter how many branches a government may have, no matter how they are constituted, or what they do, they fail to exhaust the authority of a state. This not only has distinctive relations to its citizens, who look to it to direct the government to respect their rights, but has its own ways of functioning in relation to other states. A government can restrict needed funds and may lay down various conditions to which a state should adhere, but it cannot control how the state in fact will deal with other states, in part because the acts of each state are partly dependent on what the others do and, in part, because each acts as a single unit in a world of unit states.

Since there is no way to enforce so-called "international law" this can at best play only a minor role in what a state does. Great powers brush it aside when they find that it gets in their way. There may, though, well come a time when all states are under an effective international law. At that time, what international law today endorses but cannot implement, could serve as a precedent.

If a law were formulated and enforced by some overarching state, a large-scale tyranny would become likely, unless its power could be countered by the powers of the several subordinated states, and by the people acting through these or directly against the offender. Each of the subordinate states would have to take account of the roles, and would have to respect the needs of the overarching state, and conversely. If they did not, nothing would stand in the way of conflict and confusion.

By helping constitute a state through their interplay with common governing conditions, people became citizens with an authority able to help determine in what form their rights are to be made publicly viable. To hold that they are the source of all authority, and that governments and states are no more than their agents, is to suppose that what has only a limited, short-spanned existence and authority is a source of more powerful ones of indefinite duration. It is to suppose, too, that those who are to be ruled legitimize what governs them, for good or ill. Although governments and states depend for their existence on the acts of people, their legitimacy follows, not from the people, but from their own natures and what they inherited from their predecessors. They also have an objectivity grounded in conditions sustained in an objective space and time, and the authority of independent powers able to express, in the form of enforceable laws, what they require their people to do.

A state has a status, power, and tasks of its now. Authoritative, able to endow its agents with authority of limited range, it gives a government authority to govern. It can also give people authority both to function together and to change the government. Did it deny people that authority, their status as citizens would become indistinguishable from their status as subjects of a sovereign; did it deny authority to a government, this would become indistinguishable from a bureaucracy doing what it is told to do.

Subjects do as they must; a bureaucracy is engaged in governmental work. Subjects may rebel; but they do not have an accredited independent status. A bureaucracy may call on force to have its decisions carried out but, like subjects, it is required to do what a sovereign demands. Were a state to act only through people who were part of a government, it would reduce its citizens to public units required to obey; were it instead to act only in response to its citizens, it would assign to the government the position of an intermediary. A state exists so far as both government and people have authority, subject to modification and limitation, not only by one another, but by the state that they together partly articulate.

Governmental rule inevitably meets some resistance, since it is imposed on what has needs, rhythms, and demands of its own. Even if what it decreed were gladly accepted, it would inescapably have to take account of what people are, can do, and how they will most likely react to what it decrees. Because it it imposed on those who have some authority to determine how and to what extent they are to obey, it is also rightly resisted by them to some degree, despite the fact that it has the authority to formulate those laws and to insist on them. Its authority may itself be stated in laws, to be carried out in accord with procedures not always explicitly noted. When those procedures are noted, the fact is referred to as involving a not clearly demarcated or understood "due process", "reasonableness", or "justice."

Authoritative governments demand acceptance. Since the demand is imposed on people who have the authority to help determine how they are to be governed, the government and its demand are also rightly limited by the people. The result would be an unresolved conflict of authorities, were there no state with an authority of its own, requiring ruler and ruled to be in better accord.

If we subtract the people who make up a government and the people who are ruled, a state would no longer remain. But were it denied that there was anything more to the state than a government and the people, they would not be able to function as legitimized authorities rightly acting on one another. A state has a past and a future. Constituted by a union of people interplaying with a common government, it also has a nature and authority of its own, of which the government and people take some account in different ways. Conflicts between a government and the people, as a consequence, do not have to be settled by force, nor does one or the other have to be credited with the right to be in absolute control. Their state can, and often does, determine the role each should play in relation to the other. It does this by conditioning both, confining them within a distinctive present with its own inherited past and prospective future.

Were one to yield to the common complaint that laws are to be made intelligible to the layman, one would have to give up many of the distinctions that are needed in order to convey exactly what is being required. Laws are expressly stated in a technical language in the effort to make precise what is being demanded by an authoritative government. They should be made the concern of a number, qualified both to formulate and interpret them.

Laws contrast with the provisions laid out in a constitution. This constitutes a state's formal nature, and defines the limits and powers of a government and the people who are to be governed. If produced by those who live under a different type of rule, a constitution will have to acquire authority. This obviously could not be obtained from the state that is still to be instituted, nor from the citizens who will thereafter be under that constitution. Those who forge such a constitution have taken it upon themselves to do so, or have been assigned the task either by a people or by some other authority. If the former, they do no more than offer a suggestion. If, instead, they are given the authority to produce it, that authority will obviously not extend beyond what they were authorized to do. Since a constitution, such as that of the United States, credits it with an authority greater than that possessed by any of the delegates' sovereign states, at least in dealing with taxation, the army and navy, and the establishment of courts with national jurisdiction, the delegates, at the very least, would have had to pool their limited authorizations in order to create a single state which had the right to subordinate the sources of the delegates' authority.

The delegates to a constitutional convention do not enact laws. Such laws are possible only after a state and its government are in existence. Nor do the delegates have the authority to institute a new sovereign state. They could, of course, have been given the authority to combine their limited ascribed authorities, to transfer the result to the new one overarching State, and to await endorsement of their acts by their different sovereigns; but were these not to accept the outcome of the delegates' decisions, the constitution that these produced and endorsed would have no authority. There is no evidence that the delegates to the convention, where the Constitution of the United States was accepted, had the authority to combine their several authorities. And since they were sent, not to produce a new State, but to patch up the old Confederation, the delegates to the convention that drafted the United States Constitution so far acted without authority.

What the delegates to a constitutional convention establish is different from what could be accomplished in an ongoing State. At the convention they are able to do what is both more or less than what can be done in a State—more because what is decided in the convention has application to the State and to multiple, subsequently enacted laws, and less because the delegates produce, not a State, but a recommendation that their separate sovereigns subject themselves to the new constitution and to the new single sovereign power that the constitution defines.

The United States Constitution provides for a sovereign able to compel acceptance by various subordinated sovereign of what that sovereign requires in order to be a One for their Many. There would be no such single sovereign if the various sovereign refused to accept what their delegates had agreed upon. It is here possible to make reference to something like a social contract among the states, since the new State awaits acceptance by the several states of what their delegates had agreed upon. Not until the new State is in existence, of course, will laws be enacted in conformity to the demands of its constitution. In States where there is no constitution, the people, and the government with which that people jointly interplays, must still take account of what those States require so as to be able to function in a larger world of States.

When governments are divided into such branches as the legislature, executive, and judiciary, there is no law, except so far as what is enacted by the legislature is tacitly or explicitly endorsed by the others. Were there no such branches, what is done at various positions in the government would have to be designated as required to do what is prescribed at the others. Whatever divisions, a law (in contrast with a proposal) will express the demands of a government as a single whole. It will therefore require that what is done by one part of the government be in accord with what it is the task of other parts to insist on.

What was intended by "Congress shall make no law," was not well-expressed. Congress makes no laws. It can do no more than produce enactments in the expectation that these will not be vetoed by the executive, that such a veto will be overridden, that the enactments will not be rejected or reinterpreted by a court, and that they will be properly enforced. If the legislature passed an enactment that established a religion, abridged the freedom of speech or the press, or went against any other provision of the First Amendment, the result would be no more and no less a law than any other. The President could conceivably sign it, and the Supreme Court could conceivably endorse it. There is nothing in the way of such enacting, signing, or endorsement. If the other two branches allow such an enactment to stand, of course, the United States would be radically changed from what it was supposed to be and had been for about two hundred years. The statement "Congress shall make no law . . ." is a warning to the other branches, telling them what the limits are beyond which Congress should not have its actions sanctioned.

Nothing prevents a government from enacting any "law" whatsoever. If it endorsed the establishment of a State religion, no member of Congress would be punished. The President would not be prevented from withholding a veto. Nor would the Supreme Court be compelled to declare it invalid. Each branch functions autonomously, making its own decisions. These may or may not concur with those made by the others.

No law is invalid just because it says what is apparently the opposite of what the Constitution specifies. The determination of its invalidity awaits the independent decisions of the other branches of the government. If they concur, the result is a law, but one that might in fact so change the character of the State that this in effect will have been replaced. The import of the original Constitution, of course, is constantly undergoing change. Moves by any and all parts of the government into new regions, if only to keep abreast with new situations created by changes in technology, common habits, and cherished values, make a difference. When it is expressly said that "Congress shall make no law . . ." attention is being called to the fact that an attempt to do what is apparently being expressly forbidden makes for a change so great that it would justify the claim that a new State had been allowed to replace the old. "Congress shall make no law . . ." means that there are conditions which legislative enactments must meet, or fail to be laws because they pass beyond the limits that the other branches of the government will presumably tolerate.

A legislative body may be intimidated at various times. Sometimes an executive is cowed. Courts sometimes yield to the pressure of public opinion. Conceivably, all three may be made to give way by an army whose officers are ready to take over. Although it might be convenient to suppose that the branches continue to exist even when prevented from functioning, and particularly when merely threatened, they would, in those circumstances, not constitute an authoritative body following its own stable procedure for converting bills into enactments, enactments into laws, and laws into precedents. They would therefore, no longer exist as independent, essential parts of a single constitutional government. Nevertheless, one might credit them all with a continuous existence in order to provide a basis for a criticism of whatever stood in the way of their functioning. This is a desirable, practical move, for it permits one to recognize the rights possessed by different branches, and allows one to avoid supposing that what is being effectively suppressed is not to be defended in fact or in principle against what is crushing it. Although the integrity of the branches may have been compromised, and they perhaps made impotent, the claim that they continue to exist may provide a desirable reminder that they should be reinstated in their original form.

If there is to be law, a government must have the authority to determine how people are to be ruled through the agency of enacted, enforceable demands. Limited by the state and the people, the government demands will still be formulatable and be able to be insisted on independently of both, tacitly requesting them to accept and support what it does, and to make possible its better functioning.

Intended to hold without regard for the distinctive natures of different persons, laws have a three-fold generality: Expressed in words, they exhibit a general meaning; designed to apply to a number of people, many unknown and some perhaps yet to be born, they have the generality of unspecified application; applied in particular cases, where they meet modifying resistances, they are maintained as having their applicability elsewhere unaffected. The first takes one back to the government; the third to an area where law is applied; the second to a position in between these.

The laws enacted by a government are inseparable from a connection with actual people, applying to them, as it were, before they are effectively applied. This means that there are no completely idle laws, laws which never were applied or never could be applied. It also requires the admission that a law may have multiple references.

Each application of a law adds qualifications to the meaning that the law has apart from that use. The fact is to the fore in recent discussions. These take every expression, even of fictions and errors, to be tied to the world where terms are made to undergo modifications until they become one with the very features of their referents, and are thereby able to be possessed by these.

Since laws are formulated with an eye on their application, they are inescapably "pragmatized" when enacted. Like personal pronouns they are able to bring one toward that which is able to accept them.[5] On its face, a law is a tissue of general terms. But, on its face, it is also not a true law. It is a law only so far as it is applicable, not simply in the sense that it can be enforced, but in its acting like a personal pronoun. Because it has reference to actual people through the use of a tacit "You", reaching to those who are subject to it, it is to be understood to occur within a context encompassing actual people. Sometimes special places, individuals, or occasions are signalized, but it is the intent of a law to take these to be instances of something more general. Its application, though directed at what occurs, extends to whatever may have a position and features like these.

The city which is to be given special funds because it is in distress is one whose distress, were it suffered to the same degree by another city, would entitle this to the same treatment. Though the degree will never be exactly the same, the treatment may be. Approximations, not exactitude, is what practice demands. A person signalized as deserving honor is marked out because of a trait or achievement whose semblance elsewhere deserves the same kind of acknowledgment. The deserts will be roughly compared, the honors duplicated. A proper name may be used to fixate the object of the honor, but the honor will be tied to a public occurrence conceivably similar to those for which others had warrantedly received theirs.

It is law in its generality that is enacted. Initially, its applicability will refer to people as having duplicable traits, or as forming a single union that is to be so subdivided that the law bears equally on a number of its members. The generality of a law here, as in other situations, can be exhibited in the form of a conjoint disjunct—an *a*-or-*b*-or-*c* . . . in which none of the terms is separated from the rest but is still distinguishable as one whose realization would exclude the realization of the others. The conjoint disjunct is dissolved, in the course of an application of a law, into the disjunct, *a* or *b* or *c*, with the realization and therefore isolation of one of these, on its being involved with encouragements or restraints, rewards or punishments.

Those who are subject to a law, whether viewed as a single body or dealt with distributively, exist apart from it, able to make a difference to it when it impinges on them. Limiting the range and specific meaning of the law, people deny to it the full generality that it has apart from any application. Since the law retains its general meaning, it is not bound by the fact that just such and such persons are subject to it in a particular situation.

Starting from a law, one never gets to individuals as radically different from one another, or from it. Starting from a people, one never succeeds in getting to a law as able to do full justice to what the people need or can do. An applied law is the outcome of the meeting of the two, each of which makes a difference to the other and contributes to the nature of the result. The concreteness and uniqueness of people is countered by the abstractness and indefinite applicability of the law, thereby making them legally designatable beings, and the law an operative condition assessing the acceptability of what is proposed or done. The people thereby acquire a new status while the law is limited in range. Although individuals are dealt with together, the law applies to them as public units; because the law's range is thereby restricted, its universality is qualified.

The legislature of the United States, well before the Supreme Court has ruled on what is has done, may be backed by an effective force. If what the legislature produced is not granted the status of a law, that force would have been illegitimately used. There is no sure way to preclude this. The United States Supreme Court will not deal with issues which are purely hypothetical; it awaits apparent violations of what the legislature and executive endorsed; should it decide that what the legislature enacted is not a genuine law, any force used to make people obey this, will be said not to have a needed authority behind it. It is, of course, not necessary to compel obedience in every single instance. Many laws are obeyed without any coercion being explicity used or threatened.

The right of a government to rule is minimally expressed in enactments backed by a force sufficient to assure that those who do not obey will be subject to penalties. The penalties may take various forms—fines, prohibitions, imprisonment—all putting a limit on the exercise of liberties. An enactment that is so strongly resisted or so widely ignored that there is no sense in trying to have people obey it, will at best express an intent. Lacking adequte backing, remaining within the domain of the government without bearing on the people who interplay with this, it will be quite different from an unenforced law. It may nevertheless be enforceable and, so far, be a law in principle though not in practice. Ideally, every law formally expresses a relation connecting ruler and ruled, and effectively stands between them with authority. So-called "blue laws", still on the books, restricting activities on Sundays, are still enforceable. Because no effort is made to enforce them, those who should request enforcement, and those who should engage in such enforcing, strictly speaking, are so far chargeable with negligence or contempt. Since such a charge will not be legally made until a violation of the law is contested, a failure by the government to see to it, that what is in fact enforceable is enforced, exhibits a disregard by that government for what it is required to do. This is one with its failure to act with authority, and thus one with a limitation, self-imposed. It may be practically wise to do this, but it also means that the government is not doing all it had taken upon itself to do. If a law is silly, it should be repealed.

A legislature requires the help of independently existing agents to make its laws effective. Those agents are implicitly taken to be subject to it; whatever authority is transferred to them is properly used only so far as it backs an enforcement of what is enacted. A legislature, while depending on those agents to apply its laws, implicitly demands that the agents not go beyond or act counter to the authority it credits to them, for though not necessarily exercised outside the scope of laws, enforcements may be carried out without regard for what the legislature intended.

Use of force may be legislatively prescribed and limited. If the prescriptions are not followed or the limits not respected, other powers will have to be invoked to see to it that the required actions are performed. The military is one force to which a legislature might look; another is a segment of the people able to intimidate others. An appeal to the courts or an executive offers still another, though more round-about way in which force could be called upon. All invite a hobbling or a rejection of laws, and a suppression of the people. Once the power of the military, or some other organization enjoying autonomy in the use of force is invoked, it is not unusual to find other parts of a state limited to doing little more than ineffectually approving or condemning what is being done.

Whatever authority laws possess is derived from the state, either directly or via the government.[6] As the one, the authority is a continuation of the state's authority; as the other, it is partly dependent on the authority that the government possesses. The claim to authority on either ground would be ineffective, were there no force available able to compel obedience. Since the force that a government invokes is as much outside its laws as are the people who are to come under the government's rule, the government has to depend on the force yielding to its authority, and thereby making the laws be properly operative. The degree and kind of force to be invoked evidently should be proportionate to the discrepancy likely to be exhibited between what is legally demanded and what is begun, being done, or will likely be produced by those to whom the demands apply.

A state grants authority to what is able to enforce laws. That force adds a wild card to the deck; it may not do what it is invoked to do. The danger lurking here is only partly limited by the fact that individual users of the force may be subjected to other forces, since these may not be used, or may themselves need restraint. The danger is reduced by dividing the available force among various independently functioning agencies, each of which is required to back certain types of law in limited areas at particular times, and to be able to block others when these go astray. There would still, of course, be no protection against the possibility that all of them might unite to form a single force brooking no opposition; that the strongest might not tolerate any limitation imposed on its use; or that any one might fail to set proper, desirable limits to the others. No state is completely protected against the tyranny of force. What a state needs and can use may cripple it and anything else that might stand in the way.

An enforcement invoked on behalf of laws—even dictating their nature, range, and mode of application—has, as its function, the assuring that laws are obeyed, without other laws being violated or rights denied. Necessarily, it adds to what is enacted. That on which it is imposed inevitably resists it, but whatever the degree of that resistance, the laws will still have their authority. Enforced vigorously, they will sometimes have a considerably different practical import from what they have when enforced minimally.

To know what the laws of a state are is not yet to know the laws as they are actually operative there, for the same force expressed in different places encounters different kinds and degrees of resistance and, thereupon, yields different results. As long as force is available it plays some role, and since the application of laws makes a difference to their import, the laws in a state, where force is readily and effectively invoked, will always have a different meaning from what they have on their face.

The enforcement of a law modifies, and thereby helps determine its operative meaning. Since an effectively enforced law is a law obeyed, with equal propriety it can also be said that the meaning of a law is altered according to the degree and manner in which it is obeyed. Only the existence of wholly passive people, completely plastic, indifferently sustaining what has been decreed, would allow laws to be carried out with no or only a minimal change.

The change that an applied law undergoes is usually less than it could conceivably undergo, since people are partly accommodative of what legally governs them. Laws can, therefore, be viewed as though they were hypotheses whose meanings are given new determinations on being related to what may or may not support them. This will add multiple details, while involving the laws in multiple contingencies, and giving them new neighbors. If adequate provision is to be provided for the meanings that laws have, account must be taken of their natures, not only as enacted, but as subject to possible disobedience, as enforceable, and as enforced.

Enforceable laws are directed at people existing independently, and are to be conceived as envisaging both a possible disobedience and supplementation by sufficient force to overcome this. So far, they are inferior to prescriptions addressed to those who are ready to do what is being demanded. Still, while such prescriptions may make demands which have a greater range and may sometimes be carried out more completely than enforceable laws, these are usually accompanied by some assurance that what is demanded will be persistently and effectively insisted on. To be sure, the prospect of a force, that could be invoked on behalf of a law, may fail to make people obey. One then has to look to them to do what is required. If they are not responsive, additional force may have to be invoked to make them do what was to be done without it.

Laws, of course, are not just formulations awaiting the backing of force. They are themselves prescriptive, differing from other prescriptions primarily in their being supportable by a force when their demands are not met. Logical or medical prescriptions, no less than legal ones, may be disregarded at considerable risk, but the sources of these prescriptions are not often able to impose effective penalties when the prescriptions are neglected or defied.

Laws for a state are avenues through which some of its authority is expressed, an authority to be respected by both the government and citizens. More than disguised and incipient ways of transmitting or invoking force, they are also more than a set of abstract requests appealing to a people's sense of duty. Each is authoritative, usually enforceable, and sometimes needed.

Were one to take laws to be just authoritative prescriptions of what the mature and reasonable are to do, one would also have to hold that force is little more than a regrettable device to be employed to make good a people's failures. Were one to allow for only the enforceable side of laws, the authoritative character of laws would be slighted and their prescriptiveness would be a truncated way of stating what people must do in order to avoid restraints and penalties. Were no forces considered people would have to be viewed as having habits which were the products of a series of responses to what should be realized, or as being the products of a series of reactions to circumstance. Both approaches are needed. Both, the prescriptions and the authoritativeness, are teleological, the one because it places a prospect in control, the other because it functions on behalf of a prospect. When the two are joined, those who are law-abiding will act as they should.

The acknowledgment of real prospects, and surely of prospects controlling what is being done in the course of realizing them, goes counter to the positivistic temper still evident here and there, mainly in the law, but also elsewhere. To conform to that temper, one would not only have to avoid references to prescriptions, but would have to reject the claim that laws are to be obeyed because they enable people to achieve desirable outcomes. Instead, laws would have to be taken to be no more than arbitrary enactments, backed by force. They would be less than rules of the road, where it is largely a matter of arbitrary decision whether all are to drive on the right rather than the left, or are to travel at fifty rather than sixty miles an hour, for such rules are authoritative ways of relating drivers to the prospect of preserving order and increasing safety.

Were one to avoid all reference to guiding prospects, it would be necessary to take laws to be just brute commands, to be enforced perhaps for no other reason than that they express the decisions of those who rule. Even the preservation of the people who make and enforce the rules might play no role. Once it is seen that there are better and worse prospects and that, at the very least, a prospect, supporting or enhancing what is related to it, is to be preferred to one that promises no such benefits, an acknowledgement of the prescriptive character of authoritative laws is not only desirable, but unavoidable as well. There will still be a need for a power able to enforce the laws, or for people who can be counted on to do what is prescribed. The latter, though, is not likely. Even with the best of intentions and the most excellent habits, people act in unwanted ways, sometimes for extended periods. Often enough, they lack the knowledge and control that would enable their bodies to function excellently; rarely do they know what would fully satisfy their minds, desires, and other epitomizations of their privacies.

Because people do not often order their public actions so as to enable them to live well together, they are inevitably dependent on laws which provide that ordering. These prescribe by controlling what the people do, by what should be realized. That control, when read by beginning with what is prescribed and ending at the people, has the character of an "ought".[7]

Prescriptions may have authoritative and effective dimensions of their own. An authority is a source of the one; the other reflects the ability of someone to promote an obligating end. If a prescription preserves a desirable past, it will add to a present authority what may have been previously endorsed and successfully carried out. Such prescriptions should be part of the laws that are brought to bear on a people.

Although laws may be formulated, enacted, enforced, and obeyed as distinct units, they are not neatly bounded off from all else or from one another. One of many products of a more or less persistent government, they usually incorporate past meanings and a future prospect, have a reference to people, and express the needs of a state. The neglect of any of these seriously qualifies the laws. Inevitably, each will be embedded in a context where it is related to others. Isolating one of them will separate it from that context, and thereby change its import, perhaps slightly, but sometimes in great measure.

No law holds regardless of all others; each makes a difference at least to some. Since the claims of one law may get in the way of another, courts are needed to provide a special context in which the claims can be so harmonized that rights are protected and promoted. There, the laws obtain a new meaning, modifying what they are as just enacted, enforceable, or enforced.

A good understanding of the meaning and applicability of laws enables people to function peaceably together. Those laws are related in a plurality of ways, functioning in each more or less in consonance. In every context, the meaning of a law is modified by the meanings of the others. It would not be wise, of course, to require one who sought to understand a particular law to try to take account of all the others in all the different contexts in order to discover how these affect it, but it is not foolish to take account of a number, bearing on the same subject matter or as involving the same people, and then adjusting the understanding of the import of each in light of the need to have it operate compatibly with the others.

Legislative intent is exhibited both in what is said regarding a particular law and in the attitude assumed by a legislature toward all laws. Since a legislature is but one of a number of branches of a government, each contributing to the existence of an actual law, reference also has to be made to each, as well as to all of them as functioning together. Practical wisdom, though, requires an initial concentration mainly on what appears to be express statements, leaving it to judges to determine the range of any one law in the light of competing claims by others.

A particular law is a focused item within a totality of laws, many limiting its range and modifying its meaning. Since the needs of practice require a restriction of attention to what is conspicuously important, various laws, and nuances in some, will inevitably be neglected. As a consequence, the meaning that a law has in a context of laws will be necessarily, and sometimes regrettably, minimized and sometimes not even considered.

The Anglo-American system of legal concepts, procedures, and applications is only partly expressed in the form of enacted laws. In good part, they are also subject to an inherited set of principles extractable from the decisions made by the courts over the centuries. A present law is but one in a long line of others, with its meaning affected by them as surely as it is affected by other present enactments. But new decisions are always required, both because past decisions are not all consistent with one another, and because long-established laws are brought to bear on new situations, and may have to be radically altered if they are to be appropriate. Indeed, if any law is to remain pertinent for a while to what people are and can in fact do, fresh determinations will have to be added to it, again and again.

Reference is made to the past when one appeals to common law. That past is already partly embodied in the present practices of the government, determinations of the status of the law, the habits and customs of people, and the reasonableness used in the formulation and administration of enacted laws. By treating past decisions and practices as precedents, one turns them into present operative conditions helping determine what the laws now mean. A legislature, absorbed in current problems, slights that fact, thereby requiring the courts to be alert to it, ready to add interpretations of which the legislature may have been unaware.

Even courts, which are most receptive to the common law tradition, have only a fragmentary grasp of what it requires, in part because their derivations from it follow no well-defined method. Each court, too, inevitably provides its own determinations of what it takes to be in consonance with the spirit of the law as it had been understood by trained legal minds over the centuries. When it does this, it brings its own past, as well as those of the state and the people to bear on what is being decided. Because this is usually done unreflectingly, the outcome varies from judge to judge, and from court to court, to make an often unnoticed difference in the import of what was accepted.

The past, of course, is gone, never to be recovered. What once happened is now only a fact, a determinate distillate of what had been. Inert, it would be left behind, were there nothing able to incorporate it and thereby enable it to make a difference to what is happening. The past of laws, like the past of anything else, though, is preserved in and enriches the present through the help of the future. This occurs apart from all reference to precedents. The future, pertinent to laws, because it guides and controls what is done to realize it, also is part of them, acting as a leaven in what is to eventuate in it.

Because deliberate intending adds authority to what is being expressed, judicial bodies inquire about the intentions of legislators. Unfortunately, what these are recorded as having said, though it may be all that is available to the courts, inevitably falls short of what was intended, before special interests and belated reflections played a role.

Although nothing seems so obvious or so difficult to focus on as the spirit, outlook, the temper of the day, in part because it is all-pervasive, we do succeed at times in obtaining a good enough grasp of it to enable us to see that a multiplicity of occurrences are qualified by it. Despite many cross-currents and quite independent movements, it does make sense, e.g., to speak of a German romantic period. And as we look back into the history of our own country, it is painfully clear that the Supreme Court, on the eve of the Civil War, had a strong, anti-black bias, and that the entire country was deeply affected by the opposition between Northern and Southern values, economics, traditions, and expectations. There is a different spirit today, affecting the meaning of the laws, but not in complete separation from what they had previously meant.

It is also important to attend to the bearing laws have on both present and future people. Just as an assertion is addressed to one from whom a response is to be expected, and who accepts, rejects, or qualifies what is being claimed, so a law refers to people who are to obey it, in part on their own terms. Even when these are the very people who were present when the law was enacted, the reference will inevitably be to them as existing later.

Legislation is always directed at people existing at a time later than when it is enacted. Since some of these may not even exist at the time of the enactment, laws should be forged with an awareness of the rights of those who could not, at the time the laws are enacted, have the appropriate duties, be able to obey, or be in a position to have or exercise a right.

A legislature is one part of a state. Not only are there other governmental branches, but those who are ruled are also part of the state. Although it is common in democracies to say that its laws are made by and for the people—and there surely is a sense in which this is true—they are also made by a government and on behalf of the state, whose continuance and prosperity they should promote. Restraints and penalties are instituted, not just to enable well-behaved people to continue undisturbed by limiting the adverse activities of others, but also to allow the government and state to carry out such tasks as protecting institutions, making alliances, providing for the common defense, and preserving great achievements.

It is an error to suppose that a legislature, when it acts on people on behalf of the state, thereby enables the state to act directly on the people. A causal determination is confined to its effect; it does not determine the effect of that effect. If a causes b, and b causes c, it does not follow that a causes c. The effect of a's causation is a b, having its own nature, power, and mode of action, itself able to be a cause of c in a way that a could not be. Conceivably, one might assimilate b within the causal process which ends with c, but that assimilation would have to take account of the fact that b, as an actual occurrence, is no less causal than a, and that the outcome, c, is the result of the activity of b, while b is the result of the activity of a. The often told sequence, "For want of a nail, the shoe was lost, for want of the shoe, the horse was lost, for want of the horse the message was lost, for want of the message the battle was lost, therefore the battle was lost because of a missing nail", erroneously takes causation to be a transitive activity, instead of recognizing that it has to be renewed again and again.

Legislation is primarily directed at people. Prescribing to them, it needs a backing able to assure that what is enacted will be carried out. Legislation may also be designed to promote the interests of the state; but if it does not also take account of people, and particularly the expressions of their inalienable rights, it will deny to them the opportunities they need, if only to act properly in that limited portion of the public world. To take account of people's publicly expressible rights, laws should be so formulated that action, in consonance with the rights, will enable these to be satisfied. The rights will then not just have been allowed expression; they will have been publicly prepared for, supported, given room, and exercised, to be insisted on.

An actuality, just by existing, has rights, justifiably claiming protection, help, and support for its essential dimensions. Humans differ from all others in making more, other, and superior claims, and in being able to decide what is to be done to assure, that what should be, is achieved. Were their rights bestowed by a state, whatever account the legislature took of those rights would supplement an initial acknowledgment and thereby provide a desirable support. Such rights would be acknowledged so far as the legislature served as an agent for the bestowing state. Since what is bestowed could possibly, and might at times even justifiably be withdrawn by the same power that bestowed the rights, rights so granted would exist only so far as and in whatever shape the state and legislature determined.

The right to vote is a bestowed right that becomes adherent.[8] The right to peaceably assemble is another; the right to petition for a redress of grievances is a third. All supplement the inalienateable and inalienable rights people have, rights which follow from the primary divisions of human privacy and take account of the ways people must be together if they are to prosper.

At the very least, justice requires that people be given what they deserve to have because of what they are, as well as because of what they do, what they might become, and what is required of them. Because no person is a state in small print, justice requires that each be dealt with as quite distinct from it. Each is a public person to be governed in accord with precedent and established procedures, and thereby enabled to mature and function as an enriched private being. Only then will he be given his due. To assure this, what is due to each as a public being in a state should be covered by laws, and what is due to each as a private being should be made available in the form of opportunities to develop, as well as to epitomize and to express a mature privacy.

Every law, so far as it is characterizable as just, is designed to give a person's public acts a deserved impartial treatment in accord with their relevant merits. Since references to the transcendent status of justice[9] take one away from laws, and since these specialize a just Law which is ingredient in and an evaluator of every law, a refusal to consider the demands of justice necessarily ends with an inability to distinguish good from bad laws, and true but defective laws from what are not laws at all. However, in order to make use of the connection between justice and laws, it is not necessary to attend to the transcendent status of justice, or even to it in the form of Law, justice as pertinent to governed public people. References to justice, as a transcendent or as present in Law, are needed only if one wishes to explain how it is possible for laws to be just, apart from applications.

An understanding of the rights people have in a state requires a reference to what justice demands be done in a limited world where individuals impinge on one another. The operative laws there do not preclude the private satisfaction of the rights that individuals privately possess, for those rights are beyond the reach of any such law.

The exercise of rights is promoted by providing opportunities for people to live apart from, as well as in and through their bodies, in consonance with their fellows. One will still not have an adequate knowledge of what form the laws should take, for this requires a knowledge of inalienable rights, and the forms these must assume if they are to be well-expressed and able to be satisfied. Because people once did not have that knowledge, it was not difficult for judicious, civilized people to pass laws supporting slavery, child labor, peonage, and discrimination against those of a particular color, gender, or age. Nor is there any surety that all that a legislature should know about people's privately grounded rights is now possessed. That assurance would be possible only if it knew all that people intrinsically were and could become.

Justice requires that all persons be dealt with in terms of claims that they rightly make by virtue of their private and public natures. As pertinent to a state, it demands that they be dealt with through the impartial application of the laws. Those laws constitute a single domain, able to become integral to the people as publicly together. When the laws unite with the people, there should be a merging of the two with the demands of justice; but before this can occur, the laws themselves must be so formulated and carried out that they are in consonance with what Law requires, and people must so act that they enable this to be well exemplified.

Formulated, laws are to make equitable demands; carried out, they are to be insisted on with magisterial impartiality. If this is done, justice will enable the laws to be pertinent to people as so many equal units in a common, public world.

Were justice completely confined within laws, it would not be amiss to take it to be only a qualification of the intelligibility that Law introduces into the joint activities of people. It is more than this, with a nature of its own. The fact is tacitly acknowledged in the idea of "due process", the requirement that laws be enacted, enforced, and adjudicated in accord with established procedures for making impartial decisions, while bringing all the relevant material to bear.

Justice demands that different sides in a dispute be dealt with as equal bearers of different claims. Sustained by laws, it governs procedure. To enable it to get a better foothold, reference is sometimes made to "substantive due process". Unlike the due process, referred to in the Fifth and Fourteenth Amendments to the United States Constitution, this is intended to bring justice to bear, not only on the maintenance of established ways of administering and interpreting laws, but also on the relation that enforcement agencies have toward the people. Instead of permitting compulsion and obedience to be related in any way whatsoever, with one or the other able to be minimized almost to the vanishing point, substantive due process insists on a more balanced relation between the two.

An insistence on either form of due process is unable to make rulers act properly. To assure this, it is necessary to have due process apply to the carrying out of laws, and thereby promote the use of force by reasonable people in ways and to the degree others also take to be reasonable.

Force may have been invoked on behalf of the law, and for the sake of having its objectives realized. Although these objectives may be accepted as eminently desirable on all sides, justice will still demand that the force stop short of a compulsion, if this overrides what people really are and need. In crises, the range of the force may be extended, but here, too, there are just limits to its use, defined by the nature and extent of the crises.

John Stuart Mill in his essay on liberty thought that people should not be compelled beyond the point where they are prevented from harming others. He immediately introduced qualifications, holding that "There are also many positive acts for the benefit of others, which he may be rightfully be compelled to perform, such as to give evidence in a court of justice, to bear his fair share in the common defence, or in any other joint work necessary to the interest of society of which he enjoys the protection; and to perform certain acts of individual beneficence, such as saving a fellow-creature's life, or interposing to protect the defenceless against ill-usage. . . . A person may cause evil to others not only by his actions but by his inaction, and in either case he is justly accountable to them for the injury." These qualifications make his view differ from the accepted only in the range of compulsions it says that a state may justly impose; like other states, his is allowed to compel beyond the point where one makes sure that a person does not harm another. Since a state is supposed by Mill to be an agent by means of which some of a people's demands are enacted and enforced, allowance has also to be made for the state to function and, therefore, for the requirement that people, contrary to Mill, be compelled to act to sustain and enhance it. And once it is allowed that the state is to assure the "defenceless against ill-usage" there would seem to be no reason why it should not be acknowledged to have the right to compel the moneyed to pay large taxes to help the poor.

Anarchists are bolder than Mill. So are the utopian Marxists. Both take the proper role of the state to require no more than the exercise of minimal police power. People, they suppose, will do what they should for their own benefit and for the achievement and continuance of an ideal way of being together, once they are freed from onerous, biased, and unwarranted controls. Both take most people to be natively good and pure, but to have been corrupted by a few who use the state's power to further their own interests. Those who do this, the anarchists think, are wicked; the Marxists take them, instead, to form a class that has taken advantage of economic conditions and usurped the power this provides. But people are not noble always; there has to be some governance of them, if only to enable others to get what they require. And it is naive to suppose that all that is needed could be provided by good management, centralized planning, or an abolition of competing economic classes. Were these suppositions granted, moreover, it would still have to be admitted that different planners need to have their decisions coordinated, and that some of their roles would have to be prescribed, preserved, promoted, or implemented. Above all, the ways in which decisions were carried out would have to be subjected to controls, if the desired state of public existence is to be achieved. Were no limits set on what planners may demand and are permitted to insist on, the rest would live under the tyranny of a bureaucracy. The impersonality and remoteness of this will sometimes prove more intolerable and unjust than would a regime governed by selfish people, occupied with preserving their dominance over the rest, since these sometimes find it expedient to make concessions and exercise self-restraint. Anonymity not only encourages callousness, indifference, and unchecked stupidity; it prevents one from learning about and perhaps stopping those who are making important decisions which seriously affect what others may do.

At the other extreme from anarchists and Marxists are those who set state's rights above those of the people. Here, too, concessions have to be made if the state is to prosper. To get people to be of most service to it, provision has to be made for their health, growth, and self-respect. Were this not done, much of what could be contributed to the prosperity of the state would not be forthcoming. People are to be enriched by their state, if for no other reason than that the state will be likely to benefit from the result, since they will then be able to work on its behalf in better and more effective ways.

An oppressive state invokes a force that does not respect people's rights. Where it does not breed indifference, it may provoke rebellion or revolution. A state that bears down hard on people usually discovers that humans are surprisingly resilient, and that if its use of force does not yield to the demands of justice, it will, more likely than not, awaken a counter-force.

Justice specializes a final condition in terms of which everyone, no matter what his grandeur and powers, is faced as a person on a footing with every other. That condition insists on itself, thereby making justice not only present but sometimes able to modify whatever improper limits have been put on what people do.[10] It may also require a renewed use of force. Rarely, though, is there an occasion to encourage this. Both in principle, and in practice, justice requires that force be used only to produce a needed obedience that would otherwise not be forthcoming. Laws are to be enforced up to the point where they are to be obeyed—but no further.

The justice that the judiciary is expected to insist on is embodied in its awareness of a discrepancy between what is done and what reasonableness requires. Its sense of justice is the means by which it faces and assesses what occurs. Instead of making justice an object of reflection, though, the judiciary directs its sense of justice at what has been done, thereby measuring this. It would be more reasonable, were it to take a stand between actual injustices and an absolute justice, using the latter as a guide for correcting the former.

Legal justice takes account of the merits of what is relevant in a well-functioning state. It decrees that government and people be paired, with each side made into an agent for the other, at the same time that each is recognized to have a nature and rights of its own. Operating on behalf of the interests of the state, it is primarily rectificatory and restrictive, emphasizing the kind of relation that should hold between enforcing agencies and the people who are to obey. For it to be a strong component in every decision and act of every part of a state, and to enable all to be in consonance, every part must be occupied with making justice prevail. The warranted claims of ruler and ruled, persons in relation to persons, people in relation to things, as well as those of the past, present and future, have to be met. So far as a state is needed to make such justice prevail, it has the authority of what is unimpeachably legitimate, because it embodies within itself the best of reasons, both for its being, and for its encompassment of a government and a governed people.

No matter how desirable it is, justice does not and cannot stop force from being exercised how and where someone in control of it may decide. At best, those using force, or who are being compelled by it, will be guided by the idea of justice, and do no more than help people do what should be done. To assure this, it is desirable to provide stable ways in which justice can be carried out. The establishment of justice is therefore properly stated at the beginning of the United States Constitution to be one of the main reasons the Constitution is being adopted. Some of the other stated reasons are presupposed by, and some presuppose the establishment of justice. By making provision for all of them, a rather clear and comprehensive justification for the Constitution of the United States emerges. If justice and the other provisions set down at the beginning of the Constitution are essential objectives, not only for that Constitution to promote, but for any state, whether or not it has a constitution, account should be taken of them in all political theory and practice. That they are such objectives will, I think, become apparent if one examines them, one by one, guided by their explicit formulation at the beginning of the United States Constitution.

12. Political Objectives

1. A More Perfect[ed] Union

A task has two main components: an objective to be achieved, and the means for achieving it. Without the first, there could be activity and even desirable outcomes, but nothing could be prepared for, no guidance or directions provided. Without the second, there could be splendid prospects, but nothing could be done in order to achieve them. An objective is a prospect, sometimes an ideal, warranting what promotes its realization.

One would be helped in understanding an existing state if one attended to the nature of an ideal state and its main subdivisions before one tried to determine what the actual state in fact does. If there could be an agreement on the essential dimensions of the ideal, and on how this is to be promoted and at least partially realized, one could profitably concentrate one's efforts on the determination and implementation of the most promising methods for obtaining desired results in a reasonable time. The use of those methods, of course, will involve a good deal of trial and error, since contingencies, mistakes, resistance, and failures in insight and leadership will surely crop up, and preclude undeviating and steady progress. Reflection on past experience and history, supported by honest and vigorous discussion, will, though, not only reduce the difficulties, but will help clarify the nature of the objectives to be realized. A quicker, and a better way to do this, would be to read the so-called "Preamble" of the United States Constitution carefully. (Because there is no such term as "Preamble" used in the document, it needs quotation marks. The term was introduced at a later time to justify the courts' neglect of what they took to be "not substantive". Yet that "Preamble" sets out the main objectives that the new United States was to attempt to realize, apparently in a hierarchy of descending importance.)[1]

The"Preamble" presents a list of reasons why the Constitution is being "ordained and established". That it has such reasons, it shows immediately by following "We the people of the United States" with "in order to". What is placed after the latter is a statement of objectives the Constitution is intended to promote.

The first—and presumably the most important—of the objectives, was not justice or liberty, or the other favored goods of political theorists; it was "to form a more perfect[ed] Union". The framers were wise to do this, for in the absence of such a Union, there would be little hope that the other objectives would be achieved at all, or in any other than a limited and impermanent form.

To speak of forming "a more perfect[ed] Union" is to tacitly acknowledge the existence of a not entirely satisfactory Union. This was the Confederation of states that the thirteen separate colonies formed, and which was to be replaced by a new State whose main tasks and limits were to be spelled out in the document. ("State" will be capitalized when it is desirable to contrast an overarching One and a plurality of subordinate states). The members of the Confederation levied import duties on one another's goods, had their own armies, and insisted on their own sovereignties. As a consequence, they in effect were together only in an alliance, maintained for a while by a memory of a short, shared, glorious past, a fear of common enemies, and a common isolation from the rest of the civilized world.

The members of the Confederation were somewhat like the members of a later United Nations. Like the members of that feeble body, the different states acted in some accord with the rest—when they so wished. A more perfect[ed] Union would have to subordinate some of the separate and competing interests of the several states to a power greater than theirs, without necessarily making them lose all their legitimacy and authority as separate sovereignties.

Each state had already provided a model for such a more perfect[ed] Union, for each tolerated limited sovereignties within its boundaries, maintained by subordinate parts. Each overrode the sovereignties of cities, townships, and counties in somewhat the ways in which a more perfect[ed] Union was intended to override the states that once were separate colonies and then were confederated.

It is not clear whether or not the framers of the Constitution thought that by their ordaining and establishing a more perfect[ed] Union they thereby did in fact establish it, or whether, instead, such a Union was supposed to be an objective to be realized later. The desired Union might conceivably have been thought by some to have been achieved with the signing of the document, by its acceptance by the legislatures of the various states, by decree, or in some other way. The framers surely had decided to form a better Union than the one that was then in existence, and took the Constitution to make it possible. It would be reasonable to hold—and therefore likely that it was held—that the more perfect[ed] Union they sought to realize was to be approximated over a series of stages in which closer and closer approximations to it were achieved. If so, what was sought was less than a perfect State, then or later.

The founding fathers were not utopians; they had urgent practical work to do. Nor were they legalists or pure contractualists. If they had been, they would have supposed that they could form a perfect Union by fiat. In any event, subsequent generations had to live through struggles in fact and thought before realizing that what was required was the recognition of the supremacy of a single sovereign State over the more limited sovereignties of the several states. *The Federalist* is clear in its insistence that such a State was needed. That collection also left some crucial questions undecided. It was with these that subsequent events and decisions had to, and will have to answer. Two stand out, a factual and a legal:

The claims of some of the states to be able to withdraw from the Union was settled by the Civil War, to describe it from the side of the dominant sovereign, (or by the War Between the States, to describe it from the side of the various separating, dissenting states.) By force of arms it was demonstrated that the sovereignty of the United States was superior to that of any one state or of a number of them. A governing Union of all was thus factually shown to be "more perfect[ed]" than a combination resting on agreements from which some of the members could withdraw if they so chose. The demonstration by force of arms was effective. But it came over seventy years later and provided no reasons. There should be no surprise, therefore, in finding that the war and its aftermath produced a number of anomalies.

One anomaly was that the federal government denied that the Southern states ever had seceded; yet Lincoln, in his Emancipation Proclamation, explicitly freed the slaves only in those states, and not those in Maryland and Kentucky. Another anomaly was that the rebelling states were compelled to accept the Fourteenth and Fifteenth Amendments, and, therefore, unlike the other states, were denied the privilege of ratifying or not ratifying it. (It had been expressly stated in article V of the U. S. Constitution that "no state, without its Consent, shall be deprived of its equal Suffrage in the Senate" and presumably, therefore, from being able to be part of the "two-thirds of both Houses" which proposes amendments, and which had to be counted as making up the necessary three-fourths of the several states then needed to ratify an amendment. These requirements were ignored.)

The second great event on the way to the achievement of a more perfect[ed] Union through the acceptance of the dominance of a single sovereign, was the Supreme Court's "doctrine of selective incorporation". This brought some of the first ten amendments of the so-called "Bill of Rights" into the Fourteenth. As Justice Cardozo stated in Palko v. Conn. (1937), ". . . the due process clause of the Fourteenth Amendment may make it unlawful for a state to abridge by its statutes the freedom of speech which the First Amendment safeguards . . . freedom of the press . . . free exercise of religion . . . right of peaceable assembly . . . right of one accused of crime to the benefit of counsel . . . [I]mmunities that are valid against the federal government by force of the specific pledges of particular amendments have been found to be implicit in the concept of ordered liberty, and thus, through the Fourteenth Amendment, become valid as against the states." (Justice Cardozo, somewhat arbitrarily, excepted the right to trial by jury, immunity from prosecution, and double jeopardy). Justice Black went further. In a dissenting opinion in Adamson v. California (1947) he held that the Fourteenth Amendment fully incorporates all the first ten. "I would follow what I believe was the original purpose of the Fourteenth Amendment—to extend to all the people of the nation the complete protection of the Bill of Rights." His position is most persuasive, if one ignores both the "Preamble", with its reference to a "more perfected [ed] Union" [of states], and the Tenth Amendment with its explicit reference to "powers . . . reserved to the states respectively . . ." These require the acknowledgment of the sovereignty of the subordinate states and, presumably, their power to determine whether or not certain rights adhere to the people within their jurisdiction. Accepting Justice Black's position would require one to suppose that the application of the Amendments to the people, regardless and in the face of what states decreed, should have been but was not always recognized; that a distinctive Amendment had to be added solely to underscore what had been affirmed in the previous century; and that most of the justices of the Supreme Court had failed and continue to fail to understand the reach of those Amendments.

The Amendments were evidently designed to spell out rights people had against the Federal government, and presumably against any subordinate government. Were they understood not to allow for any claims of the separate states to sovereignty and thus to their retention of some powers against the claims of the United States, the reference to the powers that the states have in reserve would be innocuous. Legitimate power has its rights and always determines the rights of those within its provenance. It is another question whether such determination by subordinate states should be permitted to override determinations which the one United States provides. If the states are correctly credited with powers, they are also surely credited with sufficient independence to impose some conditions on what is within their jurisdiction.

The people have no right to prevent the President from granting commissions; nor do they have the right to stand in the way of the vesting of judicial decisions in a Supreme Court. These are matters within the provenance of the State, just as the determination of states' schools, police, and taxes are within those of the separate states. The State properly overrides states' decisions when these conflict with its determination of what the citizens of the State may or may not do, but that still leaves a large area within the jurisdiction of the several states.

Whether the Fourteenth Amendment be taken to supersede all the first ten, only some of them, or all or some of the provisions in them, or not to have in principle been needed, the fact remains that the jurisdiction of the United States has in fact and theory limited the jurisdictions of the several states, thought by some to be inviolable. No matter how strongly the fact is emphasized, it still remains true that the states continue to have jurisdictions of their own. It could not be otherwise, without depriving them of all sovereignty. The failure to face that truth points up a serious omission in Justice Black's contention. His way of speaking seems to allow for the kind of absolute sovereignty that directly ruled from one position, allowing for no intermediaries, with their own distinctive autonomies, rights, powers, and some determination of the rights possessed by those they govern.

There will always be some opposition between the one sovereign State and the various states. Even those states which were most obedient could not but exercise independent judgment and power over particular matters within their provenance, and thereby reveal the sovereignty of the United States to be limited in fact as well as in principle. Conceivably, Justice Black took the people of the United States to have inalienable rights, and all state governments to have only designated or assumed functions. Whether this be granted or not, it is still necessary to recognize that the various states have some sovereignty. Multiple issues are dealt with by them not only independently of but in tensional opposition to the demands of the United States. Since every regulation has some bearing on men's rights, the most that could be warrantedly claimed is that the United States has unquestionable jurisdiction over various common pivotal questions, leaving it to the several states to exercise their sovereignties on the rest. Anything less would replace a "United" States with a single state having a plurality of subordinate auxiliaries, to which it granted partial and perhaps only temporary privileges.

Either there are no subordinate states, or they have some sovereignty, with a power to make various decisions which may come in conflict with those made by the One State. This cannot, even in principle, claim to determine the merit of every decision made by the various states, without denying them their status as limited, but still distinctive sovereignties.

Every One opposes and is opposed by, supports, and is supported by a Many.[2] If the One is a single State with subordinated states, the Many will be made up of states. If the One is a union of people, the Many will be made up of people. In either case, the Many will and must exist in contradistinction to the One, since otherwise, the One would have nothing to be a One for. Since the Many exists in contradistinction to the One, it necessarily limits it. Were a perfect[ed] Union required to embrace a plurality that did not oppose it in any way, it would therefore be required to do the impossible. A sovereign One needs an independent Many. It may dominate this, keep it confined within limits, but must still allow it to function, as that which independently maintains itself against it, and perhaps others.

A more perfect[ed] Union embraces a distinct, forceful One State and distinct, forceful, Many, states. This, apparently, is what Hamilton had in mind when, in No. 9 of *The Federalist*, he held that "the proposed Constitution, so far from implying an abolition of State governments makes them constituent parts of the national sovereignty. . . ."

In No. 33, he went on to remark that "acts of the larger society which are *not pursuant* to its constitutional powers, but which are invasions of the residuary authorities of the smaller societies . . . will be merely acts of usurpation, and will deserve to be treated as such. . . . the clause which declares [The] supremacy of the laws of the Union

. . . *[E]xpressly* confines this supremacy to laws made *pursuant to the Constitution* . . . [T]he individual States would . . . retain an independent and uncontrollable authority. . . ."

Answers to objections, indications of dangers that would be avoided, and a listing of advantages that the new sovereign would bring, do not, of course, make evident either its nature or its intrinsic merits. It should have been more clearly shown that a more perfect[ed] Union was a precondition for the attainment of the other objectives. This it could be only if it avoided even inclinations toward an anarchy by the Many or a tyranny by the One. The civil war blocked the one, but Cardozo and Black opened a way to the other.

Most of the arguments advanced on behalf of a more perfect[ed] Union were framed in terms of supposed benefits which would be quickly obtained. Jay, Madison, and Hamilton devoted most of their energies, as was to be expected, to trying to quiet the fears of those who feared that a new, cruel power was to be set over the several states. The revolutionary war, in their opinion, had been fought to free the colonies from a hated king. They feared that he might be replaced by another tyrant, whose evils would not be much mitigated by having its work divided among different branches, or by having its status as sovereign given to it by "the people". Attempts were made in The *Federalist*, not only to quiet those fears, but to show that the new sovereign One had various needed features. Jay (in no. 3). maintained that the "first" (i.e., the best) of reasons for having a sovereign state was that it provided *"safety* . . . [T]he preservation of peace and tranquility, as well as against dangers from *foreign arms and influence*, as from dangers of the *like kind* arising from domestic causes". He added that it would also be in a better position to prevent, punish, and avoid injustice within its borders, while Madison (in no. 10) emphasized "its tendency to break and control the violence of faction."

Four different types of excellent Unions are to be distinguished: an *organic*, where a One and a Many are subordinate to a greater One, or where the One determines how the combination of it and the Many will act; a *powerful*, where they are distinguished and mutually dependent; a *self-maintained*, where they are both distinguished and mutually supportive; and a *realizable ideal*, where they act steadily on behalf of one another. The *Federalist* emphasized the second, and it is this which has been to the fore over the years. All depend on the expression of an attitude that allows each side some independence;

a procedure that maintains them in tension; and an interplay of the sides in such a way that other goods of the State are thereby made possible. The history of the United States shows that no one of the four has always been in focus. Fortunately, other goods, such as the protection of the environment, have been promoted through an occasional good interplay of the One and the Many states.

If the United States is to become an ideal Union, not only must it allow for and even protect the states' powers, but those states must allow for and serve the superior sovereignty of the United States. The One State and the Many states could be part of such a Union only so far as they strengthened and enriched one another. If one were to take all the ten Amendments to be fully incorporated into the Fourteenth, thereby making their provisions override the several states' determinations, those states would somehow still have to be able to express a sovereignty of their own, or be unable to be part of a single "United" States.

A sovereign "United" States needs subordinated states to provide for the particular needs of the residents of their limited regions. The several states in turn need a single sovereign over them, to protect them from one another and from foreign powers. Each, on its side, should help the other to be strong and to flourish. Provisions were explicitly made to have the first occur. The states had to give up their armies and were to be served by a single effective defense force. They were to yield to the federal legislature, executive, and judiciary in important areas—particularly, the all-important right to tax. ". . . there must be interwoven, in the frame of the government, a general power of taxation . . . A complete power . . . to procure a regular and adequate supply of [money] . . . may be regarded as an indispensable ingredient in every constitution. . . . [E]ither the people must be subjected to continual plunder, . . . or the government must sink into a fatal atrophy, and, in a short course of time, perish." (Hamilton, in no. 30). Those states were also said to have powers in reserve, and to have some autonomy, presumably so as to benefit their own people and, together, to benefit all the people of the United States. The benefits that the states were able to provide (apart from diversity and limits put on federal powers) were not, however, focused on, apparently because it was thought to be obvious, and therefore to require affirmation but not explication. The new One that the Constitution endorsed made a workable Union more likely than the Confederation did or could, but only when the Constitution was adopted was it possible for the One State and the Many states to so act on one another that both could be enhanced.

2. ESTABLISHED JUSTICE

The second, and presumably, the next important objective it was intended to have the Constitution realize was to "establish Justice". The "Preamble" did not say that justice would be done, or that it would be promoted, but only that it was to be established, apparently by the institution of federal courts. Exactly what was intended is not clear, and there is very little in *The Federalist* that helps clarify it. The most extended discussion is in Hamilton's no. 78, which was primarily occupied with the establishment of courts of justice. Justice was to be achieved by having the courts deal with constitutional matters, enjoy "complete independence" and have the duty "to declare all acts contrary to the manifest tenor of the Constitution void . . . The interpretation of the laws is the proper and peculiar province of the courts." Such a federal establishment of justice can make provision for only highly general principles exemplified in those issues which are covered by constitutional law.

Hamilton (in no. 17) claimed that "There is one transcendent advantage belonging to the province of the State governments . . . the ordinary administration of criminal and civil justice . . . [T]he most powerful, most universal, and most attractive source of popular obedience and attachment." It is the independence of their courts, he thought, which insures the states "so decided an empire over their respective citizens as to render them at all times a complete counterpoise . . . to the power of the Union."[3]

The nature of justice is not referred to either in the "Preamble" or in *The Federalist*, perhaps because it was thought to be obvious. Even little children seem to know when specialized forms of it are or are not present in matters which concern them intimately, and sometimes at other times as well. For everyone, it demands that one assume an attitude of impartiality while attending to all the evidence, and to require a procedure which sees to it that whatever is relevant is given due weight. If justice is to be promoted by a court, this will have to be blind to differences in persons and, therefore, ready to consider evidence impartially, follow due process, consider only what is relevant, and render grounded decisions serving to give men what is rightly theirs. Or, as Daniel Webster put it in Dartmouth College v. Woodward, it will be a court that "hears before it condemns, which proceeds upon inquiry, and renders judgment only after trial."

Justice requires that nothing be prejudged, relevant factors be weighed, and decisions be consequences of what had been shown. These consequences, it is assumed, are what ought to be reached. If this is to be assured, courts must be able to count on a force that is able to back their decisions.

The most impressive, extensive study of the nature of justice in recent years was presented by John Rawls in his *A Theory of Justice*. He takes his "concept of justice" to encompass "characteristic set of principles for assigning basic rights and duties and for determining . . . the proper distribution of the benefits and burdens of social cooperation . . . [W]hen no arbitrary distinctions are made between persons in the assigning of basic rights and duties and when the rules determine a proper balance between competing claims to the advantages of social life." (p. 5) As he goes on to say, he is concerned only with "social justice" (p. 7) whose "primary subject . . . is the basic structure of society, or more exactly, the way in which the major social institutions distribute fundamental rights and duties and determine the division of advantages from social cooperation. By major institutions I understand the political constitution, and the principal economic and social arrangements . . ." (p. 7). He is "concerned with a special case of the problem of justice . . . [T]he principles of justice that would regulate a well-ordered society." (p. 7, 8).

Since Rawls' view is tied in with a fictional social contract theory— "Eventually", Wallace Stevens said, "an imaginary world is entirely without interest"—it is rather difficult to make much use of his careful examination in a study concerned with states as they are and could become. Were his idea restricted to the determination of how fundamental rights and duties are to be distributed, it would be more useful, but would yet not take adequate account of the kind of justice possible and needed in actual states. Supposing him, though, to be concerned with the principles by which actual states might in fact be guided, one could go on to suppose that he is referring to an ideal every state could and should realize in a world where diverse claims, distributions, adjustments, conflicts, rewards and punishments are unavoidable. It is doubtful, though, that the "justice" of which he speaks is realizable by any state. If so, his "justice" would have to do with a desirable equality that was perhaps only logically possible.

The age-long controversy, whether justice is the outcome of the expression of power greater than others, or instead is identifiable with some ultimate virtue or standard, is carried on within a view shared by both sides. Each turns away from a consideration of justice as a transcendent condition to attend to the more limited demand that men receive their due. The two sides differ mainly on the question of what is due and why. In contexts where might is accepted as the decisive factor, the stronger and weaker receive their due when they obtain what they can. A problem arises, though, when the claims of might come into conflict with those of virtue, prior possession, need, and other claimants. To adjudicate such questions some would have us move back to ask what is due to man *qua* man. The answers might interest philosophers; conceivably, it could be attended to by legislators. The courts, though, are concerned with more particular questions, having to do mainly with the ways goods are distributed among competing claimants, and therefore also how rewards and punishments are to be assigned. Governments, too, are just and unjust, depending on whether or not they are impartial in their formulations and applications of laws, and in their determination of what is to be done to satisfy people's rights and their corresponding duties.

What is legally just is produced in accord with established rules and practices. The resulting laws might deny people their due. What was legally just would then end in the commission of injustices. The problem was faced in an acute form by the judges in Nazi Germany, and is now being faced by those in South Africa. Every state, in fact, no matter how benign, has to face it, since two ideas of justice are inevitably involved in the formulation and application of laws on one side and, on the other, with the determination of how the laws are to be carried out. The question points up the fact that justice has an ethical, no less than a political dimension, and that a state and a government are able to be ethically just or unjust whether or not they properly express and apply their laws.

If ethics be recognized to take account of what people intrinsically are, requiring them to act toward all else so that these receive what is due to them, the justice possible in a state, and thus one pertinent to people as public beings, can be grounded in an ethics. No persons and no collections of them, though, give everyone all that is deserved. Rulers lack the knowledge, the power, and even the interest to do so—a fact that reveals their ethical imperfection. They do not do all they ought.

Politics falls within the compass of ethics, as does everything else, at the same time that it has its own tasks. Restricted to the limited sphere of politics, ethics applies to the claims to justice made by people living under a common government. Respecting the limits of a state's possible achievements, it provides a measure in terms of which one can assess the degree to which the state realizes what it ought and could.[4] Both the state and people are to be given their due, account being taken of their merits, and of their obligations to one another.

A state can be judged on the basis of its ability to enhance people in such a way that their privacies are enriched as well; from that standpoint, the people are to be judged according to the contributions they make to the enhancement of the state. Each person, and the state as well, can be ethically assessed, on the basis of the degree to which contributions are made by each to the perfecting of both.[5]

Each person, people together, and the state should be just toward one another. Each should also be just to itself. It is no less unjust for anything to reduce or exaggerate itself than it is to reduce or exaggerate others. The acts of people should benefit people; a state is to so act that it is strengthened.

Justice does not ask for self-sacrifice, generosity, self-denial, or humility. These are, of course, desirable, a fact making evident that justice does not always have an overriding claim. Because it is an essential concern of a state to see that justice be done, it must also be true that what it seeks is so far less than what ought to be sought, and that sometimes what it demands may have to be minimized or ignored in order that other goods be realized.

Politically guaranteed justice is, and must be left in charge of those who carry out the work of the state. The success of that work is prepared for by establishing effective means for preserving and obtaining justice in steady, reliable ways, and therefore through the presence and independent functioning of a well-organized system of courts.

A constitution cannot guarantee just acts. All it can do is to establish justice by seeing to it that the requisite agencies for its production are in place. And that is what the Constitution of the United States does, leaving to those who rule by means of it to act in accord with what it requires.

3. Insured Tranquility

It is hard to find a detailed discussion anywhere of the next provision listed in the "Preamble", "to insure domestic Tranquility". And that is most unfortunate, for today it is difficult to understand what was intended by "insure", "domestic", and "tranquility". "Insure" might mean either a guarantee or an assurance; "domestic" might refer to the members of families, to all the people who are then within the borders of the State, or to what has no bearing on international activities. "Tranquility" might mean being at peace or being undisturbed. I think what was intended is best conveyed by translating the expression as "assure an undisturbed public life of the people" and as serving to bring the first two provisions—a better Union and an establishment of justice—together, since the likelihood of eruptions, riots, revolts, even dissatisfactions and irritations, is reduced by providing for a well-ordered State and for establishments which exemplify and promote justice. There is no way, though, to constitutionally guarantee that the One and Many sovereigns will in fact be properly related, or that the makers, enforcers, or interpreters of the laws will decide or act as justice requires. So far as this is true, there can be no assurance that the people will be tranquil.[6]

Implicit in the idea of this third objective is the notion that people are reasonable, and therefore that an articulate, intelligible statement of what they are or are not may make them be content with their public life, in a well-structured state where the practice of justice is well-established. Made explicit, the objective could be expressed as "assuring satisfaction to a reasonable people". Since possible eruptions by them, suddenly in the grip of passions or pursuing diverse objectives without regard for one another's interests or rights, cannot be foreseen, all that one could do in advance is to minimize the likelihood of such eruptions; try to control them when they occur; reduce the possibility of their recurrence; and counterbalance the losses they produce. The reductions in the likelihood and the control of the disturbances depend on the ability of the State to use whatever force is needed; on the legislature's reduction of the possibility of recurrence; and on the courts' provision for a just redress of wrongs and compensation for losses.

A partial confirmation of this interpretation is given by Jay (in no. 3). He not only saw the need for a "security for the preservation of peace and tranquility, as well as against dangers from *foreign arms and influence*, as from dangers of the *like kind* arising from domestic causes," but the need for a "cordial Union, under an efficient national government." Here "Union" refers to the One State, whose "administration, the political counsels, and the judicial decisions . . . will be more wise, systematical, and judicious than those of the individual

[s]tates and . . . more *safe* with respect to us". He thought that the tranquility of the people was a function of the power of the State to attract the best people in the country and that "The wisdom of the convention, in committing such questions to the jurisdiction and judg-ment of courts appointed by and responsible only to one national government, cannot be too much commended." The importance of the One State and the role of the courts is here recognized, but the role of the separate states minimized. Hamilton (in no. 29) does more justice to the problem. He held that the various states reserved *"the appointment of the officers, and the authority of training the militia according to the discipline prescribed by Congress."*

When the One State is protected against foreign enemies, and sup-ports and satisfies the just claims of particular subordinate states, the likelihood that undue disturbances will occur is reduced. But there is still a need to insure that the people will be tranquil. This, though, will require one to go further than the authors of *The Federalist* did, and perhaps wished. Their primary aim was to make evident the desirability of setting a new One State over the former confederated states, while allaying the fears of those who thought that these would thereupon be unduly submerged or annihilated, and that the people would be denied their rights. One would also have to establish justice, for if injustice were the rule, the people would not be tranquil for long. They might be quieted, subdued, or regimented by threat or the force of arms, but they would not be peaceably together. What is wanted is the kind of government that not only does not compel people to conform, but so acts that they conform voluntarily, unhes-itatingly, and properly.

No state can insure tranquility by threat or force. An insurance of tranquility requires the recognition by the people that they are in a "more perfect[ed] Union", with well-established ways of seeing that justice will be done. People need to know that they will be allowed to live peaceably together, and not be compelled to keep quiet about what they take to be amiss. Provision for their tranquility could be viewed as a combination of the previous provisions, joined to a rec-ognition of what mature persons require. It would be better to take the three provisions to be ordered in a descending hierarchy of ob-jectives, coming closer and closer to the lives of people. Further prog-ress in that direction could then be seen to be intended in subsequent references to the common defense, to the general welfare, and, finally, to the blessings of liberty to be enjoyed then and later.

Tranquility refers to an objective, not to a means, to something sought for its own sake and not for some other end. In this respect, it is unlike defense—unless this be taken, somewhat in accord with Hamilton's account—to provide the State with an externally and internally determined limit, the one setting it over against external powers, the other strengthening it against possible assault from within.

Since a people's tranquility depends at least in part on its lack of fear of foreign invasion or the possibility of war with other States, it might be taken to be just a consequence of the successful avoidance of these. Tranquility would then be thought to be promoted by offering protections against what is exterior to the State, rather than by providing for a strong Union where justice is well-established and regard is shown for what is needed if people are not to live in fear, tensed against threats to their dignity and prosperity. An examination of the next stated objective, to "provide for the common defence" should help show that tranquility is primarily a precondition for, and not just a consequence of this.

4. THE COMMON DEFENSE

The common defense is sometimes held to express the primary and even the only objective a state is to realize. It is not unusual to hear military people say something like this. Defense, they seem to think, perfects a state, fixating and making its nature and extent distinctive and invulnerable. Serious threats to the state are taken to jeopardize it; they make it necessary, it is thought, for the state to be in a position where it can effectively reduce or avoid their consequences. Only after such a defense is achieved, it is apparently believed, could all the other and truly subordinate objectives be achieved. If this position were tenable, the "Preamble" would have to be said to have been poorly constructed.

Defense is needed, but it is not the only objective, or a precondition for all others. A good defense will help preserve the Union and its institutions, including those involved in establishing and dispensing justice, and the quieting of fears. But it comes into its own only after a more perfect[ed] Union, an established justice, and tranquility are attained, for these provide defense with the material it is to defend and perhaps enrich through its effective maintenance of the State.

Viewed from the perspective of other objectives, defense could be taken to be a means for protecting these, particularly by training and preparing people so that they are technically proficient, more courageous, and readied to risk life and limb. It could increase confidence in some. Had it no other functions, it is likely that it would also awaken fear in those it is supposed to protect, tempt the use of untested power and equipment, and sometimes prompt other states to attack in anticipation of what is taken by them to be the beginning of an attack by it. Defense also adds to the people's tax burdens, to the possibility of a military take-over of the government, and to the danger of having weapons, explosives, and an army close at hand, blindly ready to follow the commands of a limited number, not always judicious or wise. Evidently, it is a means for good as well as for ill. So far, it is both necessary and regrettable, revealing a state and the people in it to be in that primitive condition of spiritual poverty that Hobbes, in *Leviathan*, part 1, chapter 13, took to be the normal life of savages, "solitary, poore, nasty, brutish, and short".

A perfect[ed] Union, an establishment of justice, and an insured tranquility are also means. Defense presupposes all of them. Without a strong Union, the several subordinated states would be a prey to separate and conflicting authorities, making it more likely that they will be attacked, while leaving them unable to answer adequately. The establishment of justice stands in the way of defense offering an excuse for using force to decide issues, and to the military's temptation to limit the liberties and threaten the lives of the people. If there is domestic tranquility, defense will allow the people and the State to be better able to attend to unwarranted intrusions. All three, as we have seen, are also genuine objectives. Defense should help preserve and promote them.

The authors of *The Federalist* thought of defense mainly as a means for protecting the sovereign One from those foreign powers likely to try to cripple or destroy it, and thereby the Many states as well. Hamilton (in no. 24): "If we should not be willing to be exposed in a naked and defenceless condition, to their [Britain's and Spain's] insults and encroachments, we should find it expedient to increase our frontier garrisons in some ratio to the force by which our Western settlements might be annoyed. . . . If we mean to be a commercial people, or even to be secure on our Atlantic side, we must endeavor, as soon as possible, to have a navy. To this purpose there must be dockyards and arsenals; and for the defence of these, fortifications, and probably garrisons." And (in no. 25) "The danger . . . is . . . common. And the means of guarding against it ought, in like manner, be the objects of common councils, and of a common treasury." ". . . State governments will too naturally be prone to a rivalship with that of the Union, the foundation of which will be the love of power; and that in any contest between the federal head and one of its members the people will be most apt to unite with their local government. . . . If . . . the ambition of the members should be stimulated by the separate and independent possession of military forces, it would afford too strong a temptation and too great a facility to them to make enterprises upon, and finally to subvert, the constitutional authority of the Union. . . . As far as an army may be considered as a dangerous weapon of power, it had better be in those hands of which the people are most likely to be jealous. . . . [T]he people are always most in danger when the means of injuring their rights are in the possession of those to whom they entertain the least suspicion. The framers of the existing Confederation, fully aware of the danger to the Union from the separate possession of military forces by the States, have, in express terms, prohibited them from having either ships or troops, unless with the consent of Congress. . . . If . . . it should be resolved to extend the prohibition to the *raising* of armies in time of peace, the United States would then exhibit the most extraordinary spectacle which the world has yet seen,—that of a nation incapacitated by its Constitution to prepare for defence, before it was actually invaded. . . . We must receive the blow, before we could even prepare to return it. All that kind of policy by which nations anticipate distant danger and meet the gathering storm, must be abstained from, as contrary to the genuine maxims of a free government. We must expose our property and liberty to the mercy of foreign invaders and invite them by our weakness to seize the naked and defenceless prey, because we are afraid that rulers, created by our choice, dependent on our will, might endanger that liberty, by an abuse of the means necessary to its preservation." And Madison (in no. 41): "Security against foreign danger is one of the primitive objects of civil society. It is an avowed and essential object of the American Union. The powers requisite for attaining it must be effectually confided to the federal councils. . . . With what color of propriety could the force necessary for defence be limited by those who cannot limit the force of offence? If a federal Constitution could chain the ambition or set bounds to the exertions of all other nations, then indeed might it prudently chain the discretion of its own government, and set bounds to exertions for its own safety. How could a readiness for war in time of peace be safely prohibited, unless we could prohibit, in like manner, the preparations and establishments of every hostile nation? . . . If one nation maintains constantly a disciplined army, ready for the service of ambition or revenge, it obliges the most pacific nations . . . to take corresponding precautions. . . . Every man who loves peace . . . his country . . . liberty, ought to have it ever before his eyes, that he may cherish . . . a due attachment to the Union of America, and be able to set a due value on the means of preserving it."

The Union that *The Federalist* and the Constitution sought was to be achieved in a world where there were States armed for attack and conquest. From that time until today, as was true throughout previous recorded time, States take themselves to be faced with possible or actual enemies. It is inevitable, therefore, that defense was and still is understood to be primarily for the sake of preserving the State against attacks from without. In turbulent times, it is inevitable, too, that part of the defense forces will be directed against possible or actual insurgents within.

Whether it be viewed from without or from within, defense sets a limit to attempts to interfere with the State's authority, possessions, or people. If no State had offensive weapons, defense would not have to be prepared against any; if other States had offensive weapons, defense against these would provide a means for countering them, or be part of an offense, supposedly anticipating and forestalling attacks.

No State of any magnitude allows itself to be in a condition where it can do no more than fend off others. All prepare against possible attack. Since some of the preparations are made by those who think they will succeed in a likely conflict, they also tempt preemptive strikes, particularly if these seem to give them a great initial advantage. In the absence of a single, overarching, strong State, and therefore at the risk of being subject to a world-wide tyranny or an indifferent bureaucracy it must be regretfully concluded war is not likely to vanish as a means for settling differences among States in the form they have today.

Were there a perfect[ed] Union, an established justice, and an insured Tranquility, and no actual or imagined external threats, defense would have a purely precautionary role. It then could be effectively used against Nature, since this both perpetually challenges all the people, and yields much of what they need in order to live well. Defense would then be directed, not solely at possible enemies but at the conservation and use of resources, the conquest of the elements, the obtaining of necessities, the support of scientific studies, and the encouragement of technological innovations, conservation, and exploration. Defense would thereby enable a State to become more than a tenant precariously existing in a world that is indifferent to and sometimes hostile to its presence or needs; it would, instead, enable the State to be maintained in such a way that avoidable natural dangers were anticipated and countered. So far as defense enables a State to be such a master of Nature, it will not only help perfect the State apart from any anticipation of or engagement in war, but will help it to extend its provenance beyond subordinated states or a border, to a world which goes its way indifferent to human needs and desires.[7]

Defense, most compendiously, is an objective that a State is to realize, so as to become self-contained and, so far, to have in its control at least a part of the very Nature within which it had carved out a place. If defense be understood in this way, it will be possible to reverse the usual way of dealing with it, and see the preparation for war, whether against foreign powers or possible disturbances from within, to be a special case of the State's continued effort to maintain itself. Viewed in this way, the "defence" listed in the Constitution, will be taken to refer to the desirable objective of becoming self-sufficient. This is a good to be added to the good of a Union, Justice, and Tranquility. Not only does it not require these to be subordinate or even coordinate with it; it awaits their achievement before its nature and need can be fully understood.

Were some State self-sufficient, it might now perhaps be said, it would have no need to concern itself with other goods, since these would inevitably ensue. The supposition is overly optimistic. It is possible for a State to be self-sufficient and yet be internally self-discrepant, with its One and Many getting in each other's way. It is possible for it to be unjust toward itself, and toward its several parts. It could govern a discontented people. What is to be sought is a State in which the objectives of Union, Justice, and Tranquility ground and are supplemented by an ability to maintain itself against possible political and natural threats to its identity and persistence.

5. General Welfare

The intent of the next provision in the "Preamble" is not immediately evident, for it is not altogether clear just what is meant by a promotion of the general Welfare. No extended discussions are recorded,
and *The Federalist* is silent on the issue. We do not, therefore, know
just what the founders thought should be brought under that heading. From what was elsewhere said in the United States Constitution,
general Welfare apparently was not intended to extend to slaves,
Indians, indentured servants, and perhaps was not intended to encompass women, aliens, or the impoverished. It surely does not coincide with welfare as it was later understood. Today it includes a
concern for the health and safety of all the people, and for whatever is
needed in order that all be able to grow and function, with no unnecessary limitations placed in their way.

The major question that a reference to general Welfare raises is,
what must the government do in order for it to be promoted? Is every
problem involving a segment of the people to be dealt with by the
State because this alone has the finances, the reach, the power, and
the impersonality that makes adequate action possible? Are prejudice, moral standards, education, religious beliefs and practices, and
art the proper objects of the State's effort and control? At one extreme
are those who claim these and a host of other activities—sport, dress,
the meeting of boys and girls—are a state's proper concern. At the
opposite extreme are those who claim that government activity is too
cold, bureaucratically governed, monolithic, or remote to be permitted more than a very limited role. Both hold that natural disasters,
particularly if they affect large numbers or severely cripple a region,
are proper objects for state action. They agree, too, that there are
spheres of (what lawyers call) "privacy" into which the state should
not intrude, even though what occurs there is stupid, depressing, and
self-defeating. There is also wide and strong disagreement in each
faction about what is to be done, and how one is to deal with occurrences in between these extremes.

It is reasonable to hold that a State should concern itself with the
general welfare of the people, but not interfere with their individual
styles of living, and that the people, instead of waiting passively for
it to do what they can do for themselves, are to contribute to the
success of the State. Each side presents a danger for the other, as

surely as it offers an aid and, with some warrant, both fears what the other might do to injure it, and looks to this to help it prosper.

Those who want the State to do as little as possible include many who, successful in their lives and work, wrongly infer that what they could do and had the opportunity to do, is possible to all the rest. Those, instead, who want the State to take up every slack and make good every deficiency include many who have been unable to reach even a minimal standard of decent well-being, pleasure, ease, happiness, or independence, and believe the rest have just had good fortune and established privilege on their side. Neither seems to consider the good of the State to be a relevant issue. The controversy between these contenders will never be resolved if one asks only about what is good for people, any more than it will if one asks only about what is good for the State. When the needs of either side are ignored, it will be granted no more than an instrumental role. To deal properly with the problem, it is necessary to begin at a neutral position, and there ask what the people and the State are, can be, and ought to do for themselves and for one another. What each can do for itself, and surely what each can do for itself better than the other could do for it, is not only appropriate for it to do, but should be done by it.

What arouses passions is the fear that promoting the general Welfare will jeopardize the realization or presence of other important goods, or that its benefits will be primarily enjoyed by others who may not really deserve them. Nevertheless, general Welfare is a proper objective for a State. It should, therefore, act both on behalf of all the people and for its own good—at the same time people act on behalf of it, as well as of themselves.

General Welfare resupposes a strong Union, the establishment of Justice, an insurance of Tranquility, and self-maintenance. Once that series is recognized to list objectives as more and more directly involved with people, the promotion of general Welfare will be seen to be that objective which, more than any of the others listed before it, is occupied with the good of those who are governed.

The "Preamble" not only lays out the various purposes which the new Union is to realize; it is also concerned with what the people need. The Welfare of the people of which it speaks is an objective for it, but one which is to promote the good of one of its constituents, the people. The State could not do this, were it to exist as an independent reality, so functioning in contradistinction to the people that it was neglectful of their needs. The promotion of the general Welfare is an objective whose realization should bring government and governed in closer accord.

Once it subordinated while respecting the sovereignties of the various states, established justice for a tranquil people, and provided protections against challenges from an alien world, the United States would be positioned to and should concern itself with the common welfare in a way it otherwise could not. This is only to say that one of its essential commitments, as standing in contrast with the people, is to achieve a great good for them, and that it therefore should incorporate in its principles the statement that this will be promoted.

The overcoming of discriminations, the imposition of quotas in hiring, or in admissions to professional schools, and similar determinations of how the general welfare of the people might be promoted, await a determination of whether or not these, if they promote the welfare of the people, also contribute to the continuance and strengthening of the State. The issues are to be dealt with together with others which are raised when it is asked whether or not what people do on behalf of the State also contributes to their welfare.

The fact that the provision of a good for a people is inseparable from the good of a State, makes it impossible to do justice to the question of general welfare without paying attention to what is done by and to both it and the people. The limits of what should be done are determined by what each requires for itself, as well as by what they are thereby enabled to do for the other. What is demanded, under the heading of the promotion of general welfare, therefore, has the double form: an extension of help to the people in such a way that they become better citizens together, and the enabling of the people to act on behalf of the State so that this will continue and improve. Were one to ask a State to contribute to the present welfare of the people, at the risk of their destroying themselves or jeopardizing their continuance, one would ask it to endanger itself, just as surely as it is true that were one to ask a people to act on behalf of a State, but in such a way that they effectively crippled it, one would ask them to act to their own detriment.

A constitution presents conditions under which general welfare should be achieved within the sphere where other goods of the state have been instituted. Those discriminated against, whether for color, gender, race, religion, or any other feature differentially exhibited throughout the people without evidence that those discriminated against were unable to function as full members of a single people—are to be given preferential treatment. This must be done, not because one should counterbalance wrongs previously done or to provide special opportunities, but because and so far as the general welfare will thereby be promoted. A State should overcome what reduced the general welfare below a proper level, and should remedy the situation by particular acts directed at particular abuses, but only because and so far as what it does promotes the welfare of all. Just what the particular acts are by means of which the general welfare is promoted, is, though, a practical question whose answer can be found only by trial and error.

A true democracy gives everyone an opportunity to become skilled and to practice in whatever area he or she is able to function, as long as others are not thereby injured. Denying minorities opportunities to learn what they could master as well as others can, or discriminating against their employment at positions they are qualified to fill, violates principles of justice. Such denials and discriminations also reduce the general welfare by stratifying work, goods, and lives on irrelevant grounds. But to require that those who have been discriminated against be given educational opportunities, training, or jobs for which they have been unable to demonstrate competence in the same way and to the same degree others must, is to lower the general standards and the quality of the people. That is not a good way to promote the general welfare.

It is one thing to use tests to determine the likelihood that a person is qualified to do advanced work, and quite another to deny entrance into professional schools, or the opportunity to exercise acquired skills because the applicants have or lack some feature not germane to these. The requirement that decisions should be minority-blind does not, of course, mean that the lifting of the level of life for the underprivileged is not part of the task of promoting the general welfare; but if justice is not to be compromised, what is done must be justified by principles which apply to all the people.

There is something seriously amiss when children are segregated in schools according to color. If the segregation is the result of housing patterns, and therefore of a concentration in various areas and neighboring schools, the situation adversely affects the general welfare. It is doubtful that the proper remedy requires the transportation of children to distant areas. To have children from different neighborhoods sit together in the same classrooms is not yet to integrate them, or even to assure that they will be better educated than before, either with reference to one another's qualities or with respect to traditional subjects. If black, hispanic, or asiatic children in this country are poorly educated, there should be better teachers assigned and greater opportunities offered. If the children need to know about contemporaries with different backgrounds, and therefore about those who are white, richer, differently disciplined, or with quite different backgrounds and interests, they should be taught about these and given opportunities to benefit from that knowledge. There could be times when transporting children with some advantage or disadvantage— and that cannot be determined solely on the basis of color, religion, or the financial status of the parents—will benefit both the children who have been transported and those whom they join, but there is no reason to believe that it is the best or only remedy, or that it is always appropriate. A wide-spread evil is not necessarily overcome by applying the same correction everywhere.

These observations and their denials are pertinent, not to the constitutional provision for general welfare, but to the particular ways in which this is promoted. The United States must, of course, content itself with providing those protections and opportunities which can be formulated in universally applicable laws, and can be carried out by effective institutions. These are presumably inplicitly provided for in the body of the Constitution; many are guaranteed in the constitutions of the various states, themselves already assured the status of distinct sovereigns, operating within the scope and under limitations set by a single, sovereign State.

Looked at as turned toward the people, a State is to act on its behalf, at the same time that it demands that the people so act that it can continue and prosper. The people, should benefit the State, at the same time that this acts to benefit them. Together, they are to articulate the general welfare as a single desirable good. This will most likely be realized only if both sides act independently; each works on behalf of the other; and each uses the other as an agent, able to provide it with what otherwise could not be obtained.

6. The Blessings of Liberty

The last listed objective in the "Preamble" is to "secure the Blessings of Liberty to ourselves and our posterity". Distinguished from free-

dom—an independent exercise of privacy—Liberty is here opposed
to servitude and undue restraint. This objective is so important that
one is tempted to treat it as the primary objective of the State, and to
suppose that its primacy is further assured when account is taken of
men's fear of tyranny, their insistence on their rights, and the idea that
a State exists for the sake of the people. The formation of a more
perfect[ed] Union, establishment of Justice, insurance of domestic
Tranquility, provisions for the common defence, and promotion of the
general Welfare would all then be subordinate to it, or just be agencies
serving to produce or protect it. This would, I think, be an error, for
what is sought is a protected Liberty, a Liberty which is secured for
themselves and those who come later. The other objectives are to
ground it—and it is to enrich them. They can exist in its absence, but
it cannot exist if these have not been achieved. The other objectives
are presupposed by Liberty, not conversely.

To have Liberty is to have the right to make public use of one's
powers, and to engage in whatever activity one desires as long as the
acts are in accord with prevailing laws. Because some of the framers of
the Constitution feared tyranny above all other dangers, Liberty
stood out for them as the greatest of goods, which all the other goods
were to serve. Yet, despite its great value, and its enshrinement in the
Declaration of Independence with its claim that it was "self-evident,
that all men are created equal, that they are endowed by their Creator
with certain unalienable Rights, that among these are Life, Liberty,
and the pursuit of Happiness. That to secure these rights, Governments are instituted . . . " Liberty was denied to slaves and others.
This, of course, did not make it less precious to them.

Were Liberty to have a range greater than the other objectives,
these would have to specialize and limit it until it was germane to the
people. The theory that people have a natural right to liberty, but that
this is subject to the conditions essential to the operation of a State
(and therefore also when the idea is so qualified, as it apparently is in
the Declaration of Independence and the Constitution, that it is applicable only to certain people) backs that idea. Liberty is a good existing
apart from any State, but exercised within the compass of one, and
subject to its conditions. It therefore has a practical meaning only after
a particular State has been formed, and various essential objectives
established, stabilized, and realized.

Conceivably, the framers of the United States Constitution may
have thought that Liberty was the primary good that the State had to
secure, and that this had an initial ground in a natural right and

perhaps in God. The "Preamble" does not give support to that supposition. Nor does it say that Liberty is to be secured only for a selected
number of people. What was there listed were a number of primary
objectives, one of which was the securing of the Blessings of Liberty—
not Liberty—in such a way that these would be available to later
generations as well.

"Blessings" is an unusual term. Initially, it was religious in import,
referring back to the days when altars were concecrated by sprinkling
them with blood. Rarely thereafter was it altogether freed from a
reference to divine favor. To make it refer only to what makes one
happy or fortunate, to treat it as a kind of delightful and perhaps
even undeserved bounty, an unexpected addition to what one has
achieved, is to extend its use considerably. Whether freed from all
religious connotations or not, references to "Blessings of Liberty" are
to something already provided for. The "Preamble" tells us what these
are. The realization of the other objectives lays the ground for our
and our posterity's benefiting from the Liberty achieved.

It is possible for men to have Liberty and to have it secured, without
anything more being considered. But the "Preamble" was concerned
with more—the Blessings. (I am not, I hope, here making too much
of the wording of the "Preamble"; I am surely not taking it to provide
a perfect statement of the objectives of a state. I have not forgotten
that it was written under the pressure of time and circumstance by
fallible men, and that the discussions of the day focused not on it but
on the provisions contained in the Constitution. It does, though, offer
a splendid guide, and provides an excellent occasion for asking fundamental questions, and indicating what a systematic account should
consider.) The Blessings are what Liberty sustained and made possible; it was these that were to be secured. Concerned as the framers
of the Constitution were about Liberty, it is not likely that they in-
advertently failed to focus on it, and carelessly referred instead to
something else—"Blessings . . . and our Posterity".

Those who have achieved Liberty are able to be and do what had
not been possible in its absence. Not subject to tyranny, and able to
live and act without being improperly restrained or threatened, they
can show what they are capable of thereupon becoming and doing.
How could the Blessings of such Liberty be secured? Could they be
secured for later generations as well?

To insure the Blessings of Liberty is to make provision for Liberty;
to secure the Blessings is to provide agencies which will protect them.

The first requires that the likelihood of tyranny be overcome; the second, that people be able to express themselves fearlessly as mature beings in a State where specific agencies for securing those Blessings are instituted. Because a perfect[ed] Union—and most emphatically, if other objectives are also realized—suffices to provide for Liberty, there is no need to take this to be a distinct objective needing listing in the "Preamble". But, though the "Preamble" rightly ignores the question of Liberty, since this has already been provided for, it still has to secure its Blessings. People must be sure that they will be able to do what is beneficial to themselves and others by exercising their Liberty, without fear of being punished.

The securing of the Blessings of Liberty is partly provided for by producing a strong Union, establishing Justice, insuring Tranquility, achieving self-maintenance, and enabling men to live decently.[8] The Blessings are further secured by providing for amendment to the Constitution; giving the legislature the power to formulate laws; and making it possible for the people to express their judgments about those who govern, through a periodic use of secret ballots. And, as Madison remarked (in no. 51), by multiplying perspectives: "In a free government the security for civil rights must be the same as that for religious rights. It consists in the one case in the multiplicity of interests, and in the other in the multiplicity of sects. The degree of security in both cases will depend on the number of interests and sects." . . . When either the State or the people is endangered, a previous securing of the Blessings of Liberty in these various ways increases the likelihood that the requisite remedies will be available.

A State should enable people to enjoy the fruits of the liberty that the satisfaction of other provisions make possible. It should take people to have rights that it protects, and other rights—held in reserve, not yet exercised—which the people are to be permitted to exercise, consistent with the avoidance of harm to others. Not only should all people be able to count on being justly treated, not only are they to be allowed to act in as yet unknown ways; those in the government are themselves to be subject to the laws they enact. Madison (in No. 57) "The House of Representatives . . . can make no law which will not have its full operation on themselves and their friends, as well as on the great mass of the society."

It has already been remarked, that "posterity" cannot be restricted to the actual descendants of those who were taken to be under the Constitution at the time it was ordained and established. And though slavery was not abolished, and other denials of equal standing were left untouched, there was a faint indication in the Constitution that slavery might some day come to an end. The first clause of the ninth section of the first article states that "The Migration or Importation of such Persons [*sic!*] as any of the States now existing shall think proper to admit, shall not be prohibited by the Congress prior to the Year one thousand eight hundred and eight. . . ." Allowance was thereby made for a conceivably minimal Blessing of Liberty to be acquired by Posterity in the form of a possible restriction in the number of those who will not enjoy liberty after 1808.

There is little that can be done to provide for people in the remote future, even as confined within a continuing State. They undoubtedly will have interests and needs no one anticipated. It is possible, though, to prepare for that future somewhat, by producing a strong State with flexibility enough to deal well with new problems. To secure such flexibility, provision was made for it in the Constitution. Making allowance for new expressions, through Amendments by the people for whom the Blessings of Liberty had been secured, was the main way it did this.

The reference to "Posterity" (and perhaps also to such other provisions as the "general Welfare" and to the "establish[ment of] Justice") also points up the fact that a State must not only provide people with the opportunity to be together under a good common rule, but requires that they are now to so act that something later will occur or could be done. Were this all it did, a State could take those in the present to be in training for some later, prescribed performance. This might, as in an Aristotelean state, be similar to that in which they then engaged, or as in a Spartan-like state, be a new activity to be carried out in a war, or as in a communistic state, be what a classless society requires. A State should also take account of the fact that people are unit persons, with distinctive privacies, and that there is to be a civilization of which they are to be freely acting, contributing parts. If it did, the State would make provision for well-ruled people to be in a position to produce new and better ways of functioning together, with the State playing a needed but still limited role.[9] Now, States enable people to function like a single orchestra or team, without preparing them to engage in just this or that way of acting, or to produce this or that work. None clearly demands that people later engage in certain kinds of activities. Instead, at best, present States enable people to take advantage of what they can obtain from their

State, in order to become people who act and are together in better ways than they do today.

The Posterity of which account should be taken is one that apparently will enjoy the same Blessings of Liberty that their predecessors did—and possibly others as well—but will do so in its own way, within political confines which continue those that prevailed. By becoming harmoniously functioning beings, promoting such an objective, it is possible to form a single unified people whose successors are able to benefit from what this does and promotes. Posterity, by having various achieved Blessings of Liberty secured, should thereupon be able to realize and enjoy greater goods than are now possible in even the best existing States.

The "Preamble" ends with the declaration that the People of the United States "do ordain and establish this Constitution for the United States of America." The people, of course, did not do this and, until the Constitution was signed by the representatives from the required number of states, it surely was not established. The ordaining was achieved through the decision of the delegates to accept the Constitution as the primary condition under which the Many states were to be joined to the One State and all people were to live in both, while the establishing had to wait for the Constitution to be ratified by the conventions of at least nine states. As a consequence, the written document of 1787 had to wait two more years before it in fact became the Constitution of the United States of America.

7. Other Objectives

Are there other objectives of a State which should have been listed in the "Preamble"? To obtain the answer to that question we must, of course, attend to goods not considered in the "Preamble" or even *The Federalist*, but which the United States could and perhaps should have pledged itself to achieve and support.

To know if there are goods which the United States should achieve, in addition to those listed in the "Preamble", it is necessary to know what else a State should realize if it is to be as good as a State can be. An answer is possible if one can get a clear understanding of the nature of an ideal State, and see what features of it are not present in the envisaged United States. A good deal of the discussion that follows will help answer that question. Most would prefer to take the question to be asking what goods a people should have, and what and how the State could promote or provide for them. That question might be taken to have been already answered in the securing of the Blessings of Liberty then and later, since the additional goods could be thought to accrue from the exercise of a well-established and protected Liberty. And then one might put a stop to further discussion by remarking that the Blessings had no determinate nature until the Liberty was exercised. Such a view faces serious difficulties. Not every potentiality which liberty permits should be actualized. Some, such as defamation, should not be permitted. Nor is every potentiality to be actualized as long as no injury is being done to others. That would permit self-mutilation. Some would allow for this. There are libertarians who hold that whatever one does to oneself is outside the sphere of the State, and requires no permission from it. Their case has an initial plausibility when the private and public sides of people are identified. The plausibility immediately vanishes with the realization that private people only partly express themselves, and can do so only in modified ways, because of the contributions and demands made by their bodies and by other people. All can be properly required to so exist and act that they at least do not fall below the level at which mature people can live well together, and presumably where a State both enables and requires them to be and act.

There are at least two additional primary objectives that the United States should realize on behalf of itself and its people, in addition to those listed in the "Preamble" of the United States' Constitution: the advancement of peace, and the promotion and support of civilized life.

It would be possible to take the advancement of peace to be a subordinate part of a provision for the general Welfare or defence, were such peace advanced by a successful protection against, or an overcoming of what internally endangers the State. Since peace is not only to be pursued when there is no rebellion, or threat of one—or the possibility that there ever would be one—it requires that account be taken of what other States ought to have, and that the United States act accordingly. The advancement of peace could also be taken to be one of the Blessings of Liberty, but only so far as those Blessings embraced the attainments, creative powers, and achievements of other States and other people.

To advance peace, apart from the supposed protections that a proper attention to Welfare, defence, and Liberty might be thought to provide, the United States must allow for a power over it and the other States, able to compel them to adjudicate their differences. Today, faint moves are made on behalf of this objective, through participations in the United Nations, alliances, world banks, international trade, joint peace-keeping forces, world courts, and the like. More could be done. At the very least, there should be a willingness to submit all cases of serious disagreement with other States to a neutral agency, able to have its decisions backed by a force effective enough to compel compliance with its decisions. It would be good for all sovereignties to affirm that this is an objective which they seek to realize. Each, and therefore the United States, should make this an objective whose realization is to be more and more approximated over the course of years, helped by a multiplicity of friendly and cooperative acts. The prospect of such a gradual achievement distinguishes a true objective from a utopian proposal. Unfortunately, it does not assure peace, even in the distant future. This does not mean that peace is not a proper or realizable political objective. If it did, no State would have to make efforts to achieve it. With all the others, it would at best have to await the arrival of a World-State, perhaps as a result of a decision on the part of a State far more powerful than all the rest, able to elicit their cooperation. Will this ever occur? No one knows.

Although the achievement of a universal peace is not possible unless all those involved cooperate, its desirability can be kept before each, to prompt it to do what it can to elicit that cooperation. If the advancement of universal peace were made an objective for the United States, this would be required to so act that the peace would be promoted. In the end, that outcome requires the support of other States.

The promotion of the good of any State requires some support from others, at least in the form of cooperative activities against common dangers, which it would be wise to prepare for in mutual pledges and common preparations. A universal peace carries that idea to its limit. It also seems to compromise the sovereignties of the various States, apparently making the paradoxical demand that they exercise their sovereignties to make themselves be limited in range and power. This, though, they do all the time. Whenever a State accepts international agreements, treaties, or the decisions of international boards and courts, it sets a limit on how it will act.

To hold that the United States could not properly yield to some sovereign superior to it and other States, requires one to retrospectively deny that the members of the Confederation of the original colonies could affirm in their constitutions that they would submit to the Constitution of the United States of America, or to deny that they were able to accept the decisions of their delegates to replace the Confederation. The United States of America can agree to abide by international agreements, without going counter to the meaning of its Constitution, or having to deny that it is a legitimate State.[10]

The second primary objective that could be added to the other objectives listed in the "Preamble" requires the United States of America to attend to the fact that its people should be helped to benefit from great achievements. At the very least, it should preserve these and make still others possible. That objective can be promoted by it independently of the efforts it makes to realize other objectives.

For a people to live as civilized beings, not only the understanding of the nature of their governments and what it is actually doing, but great achievements in the arts, sciences, thought, invention, and discovery need to be supported and promoted. Some consideration is given to these tasks today, but in a desultory, unsystematic fashion. A free press, educational institutions, the preservation of landmarks, museums, archives, support for creative endeavors, and a concern for what will ground a more civilized future need more explicit formal recognition than they have received. They are worthy of special attention; the civilized life of its people is a good a State should seek to preserve and enrich. Through legislation and by means of judiciary decisions, those objectives could be set before the United States of America as of primary importance, and could have been stated in the "Preamble".

A State neglectful of its inheritance, slighting its creative people and their products, and making no provision for further fresh productions, would have to start anew every day. That kind of daily renewal occurs nowhere. People refuse to let go of their pasts, and their States unavoidably and properly take account of what is clung to. Many protect educational institutions and museums. Some provide stipends for artists and explorers. Patent and copyright laws show that some thought was given by some to making creative and inventive lives more profitable. If such matters are left to occasional legislative or other governmental acts, there will be times when what should be done may be forgotten, or treated as undesirable or unnecessary. There is, of course, no guarantee that if civilized living is made an express objective, efforts will in fact be made to realize it. But this is the kind of difficulty that besets every statement of purposes. Each focuses on objectives in the possibly defeated expectation that it will then be more likely that something will be done to realize them.

A people tends to stress its own limited past, present, and future. It will not live a truly civilized life, though, if the achievements of other people are not also acknowledged and accommodated. An expanded "Preamble" properly includes a reference to the objective of promoting a civilized life for its people. Better still, would be a reference to the objective of benefiting from the achievements of other people as well. Best of all, would be a reference to a desirable sustaining and promotion of a civilized life for all people, from the base of an achievement of a civilized life for its own. The current practice of promoting cultural exchanges, giving grants, holding international forums, and the like, offers a partial indication of what might have been anticipated and provided for in the Constitution. Whatever greatness has been achieved deserves preservation; great achievements everywhere should be encouraged by every State.

"Bread and circuses" was a tyrant's contemptuous acknowledgment of the fact that men are passionately concerned with more than the glory of the State. Communist countries encourage the arts and speculations that seem to undergird their political aims and practices. Neither recognizes that what is needed is independent, politically neutral encouragements and supports for what men can accomplish and appreciate. Narrowness of vision, insensitivity to what genuine creativity requires and how appreciation is properly nurtured, have kept even the most benign and benevolent of states from benefiting its people, and incidentally itself, to the degree it could and should.

Other important common goods, besides those which are pertinent to a State or a people, are also possible. A community has a characteristic good. So does a society. A state may tolerate these, modify them, or try to replace them. Those goods and others are sometimes supported by men's passionate concerns to a degree they do not extend to the State, except perhaps in crises. It is a wise State that knows how to take advantage of that fact and get its people, while conforming to the demands and meeting the needs of the State, to occupy themselves with the production and appreciation of such nonpolitical goods.

Subordinate groups, of course, present problems for a State. Communes join people together with an intimacy not otherwise possible, and sometimes oppose what a State requires of them. Societies build on practices and values carried out in families, and expressed in the course of daily living, independently of political institutions. Since these turn people's attention, and often their loyalties, energies, and activities in directions other than, and sometimes in opposition to those a State demands, this is forced to attend to them. It may permit them to realize and enjoy some or all of their goods; it may support and control them; it may require modifications in their actions, and may forbid some of them. It will, though, do what it should only if it allows them some free play. A State cannot grant them full autonomy without risking its own destruction; but, also, it cannot deny them all autonomy, without losing what they can provide when allowed to function apart from political influence.

Strong States have wiped out religions widely practiced and firmly adopted. Others have made societies yield before political demands. Sooner or later, though, new communities, separately functioning economies, and self-maintained societies began to make their presence felt. Still, because no State can safely allow for the unsupervised pursuit, possession, and enjoyment of all goods without endangering itself, it has no other recourse but to allow for only a partial realization and enjoyment of some goods by subordinate groups.

Religious communes often face a State with a recalcitrant issue. Their members may converge on objects treated as having been ennobled by powers greater, more permanent, more imperious, or more rewarding than a State's. Even when a State adopts a religion and governs the ways in which its activities are conducted, people continue to act as private beings joined in spirit, no matter what they may be prevented from doing in public. Artists, scientists, and creative thinkers also fasten on privately pertinent goods, and do so with a concentration no State elicits. And almost every person, at some time, is faced with ethical questions which have to be settled, regardless of, and sometimes in opposition to what a State might endorse. In none of these cases, though, do we have the kind of commune that religions promote.

A State might adopt a religion and regulate all its public forms. It might also sharply set itself in opposition to every religious commune. Neither procedure is altogether successful. private determinations inevitably erupt into the public domain, and sooner or later challenge a secular State. Nor are religions ever long content to allow many dimensions of human life to remain outside their scope; sooner or later, they intrude into the public domain, claiming privileges and insistently demanding acceptance of their decrees.

For its own sake, a State must make some provision for the participation of men in communal goods. For its own sake, it must take some of these to be worthy of its respect, and perhaps to deserve public expression and support. For its own sake, it must also set limits to what they can do.

Economies impinge on the lives of people, dictating whether or not and where they work, and on what. They help determine what a people will consume, demand, and forego, and how well they will be housed, protected against insufficiencies, and helped to obtain desired goods. States therefore cannot, without unduly limiting their own power and range, permit economies to function as though they were completely closed-off systems. None in fact allows production and distribution to be determined solely by the play of the market; all pull purely economic goods within the orbit of the general welfare, the running of the government, and the demands of defense. Sooner or later, money supply, deficits, interest rates, trade, duties, regulations governing ban ks, corporations, cartels, and trusts, are made the object of its governing acts. The nature of the economy—and whatever good this embodies—is thereby altered.

The economies of modern States are partly under political control. That control is directed at different places at different times, as the several States stumble now this way and then that in their attempts to limit inflation, avoid depressions, increase the standard of living, help industries flourish, further international trade, determine money supply, avoid deficits, reduce the unemployment rate, and see that basic necessities are provided.

A State should put before itself the main competing economic demands, and face itself with the task of enabling them to be maximally realized together. Stated clearly, it would then provide itself with a guide pointing the way it should deal with economic matters. In the absence of this, there is little one can expect of it beyond delayed efforts to meet undesirable trends and outcomes in one area by attempted counteractive moves in another.

Corporations, operating within a State, act in considerable independence of it. Even while conforming to the laws of the State, they add requirements of their own, and so specify the State's demands that these become pertinent to the corporations' problems and objectives. The fact is partly acknowledged when corporations are taken to be quasi-persons—a status they juridically achieved before women were able to get a clear acknowledgment that they were persons enough to be permitted to vote or to have other public rights already enjoyed by men.

A Marxist takes corporations to use a capitalist State as a means for formulating laws and using power for their own ends. Advocates of deregulation take corporations to be centers of economic health and opportunities where people exhibit their abilities for the eventual benefit of all. The regulations to which corporations are subject stand in the way of the contentions of the one; the existence of cartels, monopolies, and control of the market stand in the way of the other. A modern State, while keeping corporations under its control, does and should allow them some free play, so that they are able to benefit from their distinctive concentrated efforts, and thereby be in a position to do what is not possible to individuals, a union of people, or a society. The corporations in turn can give a State an economic position in a world of States, thereby enabling it to acquire goods not obtainable within its own borders.

Since people continue to live in a society even while they live in a State, they are conditioned in two ways, one largely unformulated, well-established, and answering to their practices, attitudes, mores, and habits, the other articulated, backed by well-distinguished authorities and able to use a possible force to achieve specific results.

A State might replace the governance of a society with its own. This is properly done when it takes account of the needs of the society, and then goes on to give them express formulations in laws backed by a force to be expressed only where and to the degree it need be in order to make those laws effective. People will then be able to live together socially as they had before, but under a system of laws. Instead of submitting to insistent and persistent social demands, sensed and experienced rather than known, the people will then be able to understand what it is they are to do, and will thereby be in a position to make deliberate efforts to promote desirable prescriptions and to eliminate or alter undesirable ones.

A State rightly governs a desirable society. Its endorsement of a community, economy, and organizations are steps in that direction. The incorporation of the demands of a society in the laws of a State, while usually extending them beyond the limits which concern the society, may benefit it. In addition, then, to the other objectives which a State should realize, because these enable it to govern supportive and fulfilled people in such a way that it is itself enhanced, there is the objective of doing justice to the requirements of other groupings, and particularly of a society where its people function well together.

A State has to adjust itself again and again in order to benefit from the obedience, loyalty, and support of its citizens. If too lax, its laws will be flouted and its continuance jeopardized. If too severe, it will be defied and its continuance jeopardized in another way. At both times, its concern will be primarily with a union of people rather than with them individually.

A statement of a State's objectives does not assure that they will be attended to or realized. But it is not foolish to hope that it will contribute to their realization, and that a good realization of a number of them will make evident unsuspected others that the State could and should realize. Even if that did not occur, a great advance would be made were the more obvious but eminently desirable objectives attended to and their realization urged to a degree not yet attempted. A knowledge and acceptance of the "Preamble" lends considerable support to that venture.

13. PEOPLE TOGETHER

1. PUBLIC UNITS

On birth, every person becomes part of a society. Well before that time, each is affected by its patternings, conditions, limits, and constraints. One may already have been defined as "illegitimate", given a status, and be prejudged as belonging to a particular despised or preferred class because of a likely color, gender, state of health, or physical fitness. At birth, and thereafter, various conditions will be imposed, some of which may have an effect throughout life. Today, most live within limits set by states and governments, some as full citizens, others as semicitizens, and others as not citizens at all. As a consequence, when functioning in their society, inextricably involved with its conditions, they are also governed by others, independently determined, and pertinent to them as unit beings in a common, limited part of the public world. There they are subject to constraints and laws, some of which have been long established and of which they may know nothing.

By means of laws, persuasion, suggestion, force, and threat, a state makes people attend or yield to its demands, even when they are concerned with other matters. So far as it does this, people have the status of public units who, while together, remain continuous with themselves as individual private beings who are able to assume accountability[1] for what they do and do not do. Apart from all relationship to a government and state, they have relations to one another and are able to modify these; as a result, they are able both to interplay with the government and to respond in a plurality of ways to the state's constraints and demands.

As was seen in the first part of this work, people are joined in collaborations and associations. These wax and wane in intensity, and allow for the formation of subgroups. At their strongest, they force a submergence of the individual interests and other ways in which people express themselves publicly in relation to one another; at their weakest, they allow people to be publicly joined in superficial ways. When the associations or collaborations differ in nature and effectiveness in different places, they tend also to promote factions, special interest groups, and sometimes centers of rebellion. In a state, one or more of these may be made the object of special legislation, or the members of different groups may be dealt with in similar ways. In either event, a number will be faced as together.

It would be an error to take people as together to be an abstraction from an aggregation of individuals or from a number of groups. Yet that is what is done when they are viewed as so many separate beings, or as essentially members of different economic classes, races, or genders. This is to at least tacitly allow that public life is an arena of necessary or likely conflict.

The same reasons that lead some to take different groups to be marked off from one another should lead to a subdividing of these into smaller ones with more special emphases. These could be further divided, until one arrived at the point where there were at most only separate families or individuals. People, of course, compete with one another, and pursue interests shared by only a limited number of others, but there is no necessity that the competition be due to, or that it result in antagonisms and violence. All could be under a common, harmonizing governance.

Some of the main ways in which people are ostensibly associated with one another, have been focused on over a centuries-old Confucian tradition.[2] While explicitly affirming that people have duties to society and to humankind, the Confucian emphasizes the obligations individuals have to parents, spouse, siblings, neighbors, and the like. As has been remarked, the view offers little help to one concerned with overcoming conflicts among large numbers of people, or between people and a sovereign, state, or government, beyond the recommendation that people should take the advice of sages, sanctioned by long tradition, and make this part of themselves through practice.

It is necessary to go beyond where the Confucian stops, and prepare for new circumstances, an unpredictable future, and the demands made by an actual state. One must also master the distinctive art of understanding how actual states are to realize an ideal state. To say this, of course, is not to deny that there would be considerable gain were people to function in consonance with what Confucian wisdom recommends.

The recognition of the rights that a government should respect, the need to deal with a large body of people neither closely associated nor directly collaborative, and the desirability of having clear enforceable controls, lead to the acknowledgment of a state. Only this prepares stable, intelligible, effective, and just ways for overcoming conflicts among insistent smaller groups or among individuals. Only it makes possible the successful completion of tasks requiring considerable preparation, the precise specification of mutually supporting roles, the controlled interlocking of diverse activities answering to the needs of all, and the formulation of impartial, enforceable laws, promoting not only its own interests, but those of subgroups and individuals as well. Only it establishes justice; only it makes provision for the presence of Law in a multiplicity of different enactments.

The facts, it has sometimes been maintained do not allow for such contentions. People are said to be together primarily as economic or hedonic units, and to fall necessarily into one or the other of competing groups. The state, it is held, acts as a front for a dominant group, with the consequence that when the state concerns itself with the demands of other groups it finds that it is not desirable, convenient, or even possible to do what it should.

There is little doubt that members of dominant groups receive preferential treatment. This is wrong from an ethical, and should be from a legal point of view. Marx was acutely aware of the ethical injustice, but it is hard to see how the justice an ethics sanctions could be reconciled with his doctrine of economic determinism and his supposition that people, as we know them, are inescapably clustered in radically opposed classes. It surely is a dubious theory that holds all significant public action to be a function of economics, or that this does or should always have a primary role.

Different punishments and recompenses are allotted to different people for similar acts; a hierarchy of honors are given by the military; income tax rates vary in some accord with income. All the recipients are nevertheless supposedly being dealt with in the same impersonal way. Different impartial treatments should also be accorded different groups, so far as the treatments are relevant to what they do. Always, there should be a differential but impersonal and impartial consideration given to pertinent factors. During the process by which governmental demands are interlocked with associated, collaborative people, the differences that various groups introduce are to be compensated for by a differential application of what is required of all. Indicating in advance where the different emphases will be placed, makes it easier to assure proper treatment. That an equitable result is difficult to obtain is due in part to the fact that different people are affected by and resist common impositions in unpredictable ways and degrees. When the differences are very great, a different kind of attempt to produce an equitable result will often be required, but what is needed cannot be fully known until one sees the kind of response the previous efforts in fact provoke.

References to what people are entitled to, because of their special gifts or contributions—and presumably references to what they are to be denied because of their failures to reach a particular level—anticipate how they are to be interrelated. In order to preserve initial differences by acts attuned to them, account must be taken of the ways they fit together in a union. A failure to do this will surely lead to a neglect of what is needed if they are to be under a common governance where special acknowledgments are properly formulated, attended to, and preserved.

People are together in a union as both collaborative and associative units, in one of two ways: they are there primarily as related and secondarily as bounded, distinguishable, unit beings; or they are primarily separate as units and secondarily related. The first way presupposes the second. Because they have privacies they are necessarily distinct; because they are also public beings they can be together in a union. While they are in a union they continue to be distinct unit beings alongside others, able to act in a state, because they insist on themselves through the agency of their bodies.

When references are made to special types of work, gender, or age, account is still taken of unit beings, though as in particular subgroups, and therefore as able to be acknowledged through the use of general terms. Were they not also seen to have sustaining individual privacies, there would be nothing amiss in having laws apply to them in ways which preclude or deny that they are also private persons. They would then be acknowledged as being at best equal, and perhaps also, to be interchangeable, public units. Laws, of course, stop at people as public beings, but their public existence is not torn away from their privacies. No person is explicitly supposed, even by lawyers, to be divided in two, one part functioning as a unit in a public world, where it and others are subject to common conditions, the other part independently functioning as a privacy beyond all public interest or influence. Although some theories of law and economics seem to allow no place for privacies and even ignore the fact that people are associated in ways no formalism adequately exhibits, all at least tacitly acknowledge private and independent expressions, enabling each person to become a public unit under a common governance.

Every human not only has a palpable body, but has the status of a person in a public world with others, because his or her distinctive privacy is expressed there. Were this not so, people could be properly said to be just public units, without minds, wills, or feelings of their own. Although all that the laws could know of a person is what can be inferred from public reactions to what publicly occurs, perhaps pieced out with acceptable reports of what was privately done, and although what else might be true of a privacy remains outside the limits of legal interests or control, a person's privacy is still accepted as the initial source of some of the important things that he or she does. Only if all those who failed to live in accord with the laws were taken to be simply malfunctioning bodies, would it make sense to stop short with their bodies as so many public units interacting with one another.

Both the strength and weakness of a state lie in the fact that it deals with persons who exist in unions. The strength is in its ability to control them; its weakness in its inability to reach them as privacies, able to think and to make decisions. When, in criminal cases, references are made to intent, responsibility, knowledge, memory, or past activities, an often unnoted transition is made to the people as more than public units. Their public side is then tacitly acknowledged to be affected by their privacies, but no account is taken of this except so far as the privacies have been expressed in legally pertinent ways.

People are wont to deal with one another sympathetically or antagonistically, moving beyond what they are as publicly together, toward one another as separate, and then to them as private individuals. Their passage from what is publicly evident toward the privacies of others is usually immediate and unreflective. In a society, one often reaches more deeply into another's privacy then one does or perhaps could as just a member of a state. A society also is usually more concerned than a state is with what people are and do apart from their expressions in and through their bodies, and more readily passes from them as publicly conditioned to what they independently initiate.

Failure to allow that people are both unit public, and individual private persons, is characteristic of contextualism. Some forms of this are idealistic, others materialistic, linguistic, or legalistic. All take people to be knots, junctures, or delimited portions of single wholes, and therefore unable to express themselves as separate privacies. No adequate provision is then made for dealing with those who deliberately deviate from what they are supposed to be publicly, or for those who also willingly enter into other contexts, for no knots, junctures, or delimitations of wholes could either possess anything or act. If others were treated as though they were nothing more than such knots, etc., they would be taken to be of a lower order, and to be incapable not only of making judgments, but of assuming account- ability for some of the public things they do.

The fact that what is done is affected by preparations or publicly expressed commands, or is a consequence of something else that occurs in public, does not mean that the acts are not independently initiated and at least partly determined internally. Instead, such pri- vate occurrences are presupposed. Persons are able to be together in public because they are able to express themselves from privacies, and thereby able to form unions. Even a census, treating each as a unit who sustains various statistically relevant factors, depends for its accuracy on a privately initiated honesty and a willingness to co- operate. Each will be counted, even when not trying to be of help. A census taker will, though, try to report what is elicited from a human being and, therefore, from one who is functioning as more than a public unit.

So far as people are public units, they are equals. That, though, is not the only or primary equality people emphasize when they ask for justice. At best, it is an abstraction from this. Not only is the justice sought a justice to be provided by the state: it is to be appropriate to the people as public persons, and thus as more than public units. A state refers to them as equals, if only tacitly, by making general de- mands and paying no attention to them as specific individuals. Yet the obedience often needed and demanded by it is not conformity, but an expression of privacies issuing in required actions.

Mere conformity provides little room for private assessments, re- sistances, supplements, reflections, and plans. Conformal acts do, and are therefore preferred by a state and, often enough, supposed to have occurred. Were one, with some analysts and philosophers of language, to deny that there were private occurrences or that one can know anything about them, one would not only overlook what even tyrants know, but would do this in privacy, and intend this in what was being publicly expressed.

Nothing could be done to what were just public units, but to modify their public powers and to change the relations they have to one another. Each could be made to be publicly different and compelled to be related in different ways to the rest, and that is all. Were public units not continuous with privacies, nothing more, therefore, could be done than to change those units or make them be present in new situations. Instead of speaking of people being penalized, it would then be more correct to remark on when, where, and how various units were changed and redistributed, with the state dictating the nature of the changes and distributions to be brought about at different times.

The privacies of people entrench on their bodies as in a public world. They are thereby made into public persons who are loci of accountability, and agencies through which a privately assumed accountability and a responsibility are expressed. Because they never cease to be persons, are more or less moral and reasonable, they can also not only make themselves be together as units, acting in directed ways, but can interact with common conditions, opposing and accommodating the actions of both government and state.

Despite the fact that people are more than public units, and that some account is taken by a state of the fact that they are also privately grounded public persons, there is something gained when they are dealt with as just public beings together. Not only can large numbers then be approached in similar ways, not only can each be granted a position alongside others, no matter what the individual nature, character, gifts, ancestry, desires or achievements, but all will then be able to be referred to by using wider-ranging, general terms.

Although relatively contententless in comparison with what they are as privacies, all persons are bearers of publicly expressed inalienable rights. Those rights are valid claims made against one another. The presence of those rights underscores the fact that each of the units in a state is always more than a recipient of a public benefit or loss. The rights that a state endows, in contrast with those that are inalienable, are ascribed to public units, but they would be of little worth were none of them pertinent to privacies making use of their bodies. Although the rights to vote and to assemble refer to public units, their acknowledgment and protection are desirable in part because they enable individuals to become richer private, and therefore richer public persons.

Did one ignore the fact that people are private as well as public persons,[3] a detached determination of what is legally permissible would alone be needed to determine who is at fault. It is because we know that a person is at once private and public, each having an affect on the other, that we require lawyers not only to represent the state but to defend their clients to the best of their abilities. It is their task to see that what is decided does justice, not only to what people are and do publicly, but to them so far as they are inseparable from freely used privacies, able to envisage and act in a world where they are rewarded and punished, depending on what they thereupon and publicly do.

2. CITIZENS

Whatever its type, a state deals with people as citizens. These have inalienable and bestowed rights maintained against one another, and the state as well. Were it denied that people had such rights against one another, there would be no injustice in allowing some to do to the others whatever they wished. None would be chargeable with murder or cruelty, and any could be slaughtered, eaten, or beaten without reason. Were it, instead, denied that the people had such rights against the state, the state would be just a sovereign, with them as subjects, to be dealt with as it would. A state always has people existing over against it, each a locus of rights that the state should protect and help them satisfy.

States differ in the conditions they demand that people must meet before they are granted the status of citizens. Usually, these must have a particular kind of parentage, be born in a designated region and, often enough, have property, and a specified age and gender. Further conditions could be added. All depends on what the state determines, usually through the agency of a government, and preferably without provoking opposition within its borders or outside them. If it were to view people, who live under other jurisdictions, as its citizens because they meet its criteria, its claim would be viable only so far as the other states accepted its determinations as binding on them. If they did not, its claim, that the people in the areas controlled by other states, are its citizens, would express little more than a hope, awaiting the pleasure of those other states.

A citizen is a functioning unit in a state, with distinctive publicly sustained rights, usually legally defined. A subject, in contrast, has only those rights and privileges which a sovereign grants or concedes. Although in fact a person, a subject may not be acknowledged to be one, and will then have only the degree and kind of liberty that the sovereign grants. A citizen, instead, is an acknowledged person with the liberty to function within assigned limits. In contrast with both are aliens, the protected, and the enslaved. The first have the temporary status of special subjects; the second, the more or less permanent status of privileged subjects; and the third, the status of subjects who are also property, legally defined to be mainly means, and usually able to be bought and sold.

The people in a society are to be dealt with by a state as distinct, interrelated citizens, or as both citizens and subjects. When a state is said to govern by the consent of the people, "people" is understood to refer to what is at once more and less than a multitude of citizens—more, because they make the state their instrument and do not, as citizens do, presuppose the state and its government as determinants of their legal status; less, because they have not yet been given the role of units by the state, with various public rights and duties.

Each state has its own nature and history. Those who are not citizens of one may or may not be recognized to be full persons. Even its citizens may not be taken to be full public persons and, therefore, not recognized to have all the rights such persons have. Whether they are so viewed or not, those citizens are the direct concern of the state, to be treated as equal members of it, and, ideally, of a union and a society as well.

Because the laws, regulations, and procedures of a state are expressed in general terms, they refer indifferently to any person. Different groups of citizens may still be accorded special allowances and have various rights protected, while the rest are subjected to constraints. The units in the preferred groups will, so far, be distinguished from others, as having some distinctive, desirable features, roles, or ways of acting. These do not have to be native, acquired through effort, or be a consequence of the performance of noteworthy or meritorious acts. A state sometimes endorses and condemns without making any necessary reference to what warrants the distinctive treatments.

The difference between inherited monarchies and states with elected rulers is of little importance if they classify people and administer laws in similar ways. In both, there can be an insistence on the impartiality of laws, due process, fairness, and justice. What is to be met is the apparently paradoxical requirement that persons are to be treated "without regard for their persons". The paradox vanishes at once with the recognition that what is intended by the phrase is an exclusion of references to features or positions not relevant to what is at issue.

On achieving the status of a citizen, a person acquires various roles, rights, and duties, whose functions are defined by the state. Whatever social or individual aspects that were not then incorporated in the definition of the person as a citizen are abstracted from, though they, of course, will continue to be connected with, and be both affected by and affect what the person as a citizen is required and permitted to do.

This conclusion appears to be at odds with the views of Aristotle and a number of other distinguished political theorists. They hold that a fulfilled person need be no more than a good citizen. The position has considerable plausibility if we overlook the importance of theoretical studies, art, and individual decisions and control. Rightly maintaining that it is eminently desirable for people to be fine citizens of a well-ordered state, these theorists fail to remark that all humans also have private lives where they may achieve what has little or no bodily, social, or political value.

Not to live as a good citizen within a well-ordered state is not to be in a position to benefit from a peaceful settlement of conflicts, a resolution of hard and ambiguous situations, impartiality, a sense of common interest, protection against unexpected and great organized assaults, long-ranged plans, and an enhancement, protection, and guidance of cooperative activities. These benefits make possible an easier and fuller expression of privacy and the likelihood that it will be developed and properly exercised in some independence of what must be publicly done. If all that Aristotle and the others intended to maintain was that a complete, fulfilled human being is also a good citizen of a good state, they would presumably accept such a prospect. Those who, perhaps on behalf of a supposed exclusive demand by a God, or on behalf of some final all-encompassing reality, find no merit in a bodily, social, or political life do not, of course, agree. They sometimes also hold that nothing done in public could or should support or hinder the life they take to be alone worth living. As a consequence, they also have to adopt a stoic indifference to the world, whether they are rulers or ruled. Nevertheless, to obtain a desired position, each would have to struggle with and against what others demand. To that extent, at least, each would have to engage in distinctive, public tasks in order to attain a desired separation from particular, public involvements.

In direct opposition, both to those who see that life only to be of much good that is lived in absolute privacy, and to those who are absorbed in what is eternal, are those who find little merit in a life not devoted to the affairs of the state. What bureaucrats practice and politicians preach, these people attempt to justify. No room is made for or value given to private life; understanding is reduced to intelligence and private elections identified with selections.[4] Utilitarianism, instrumentalism, ritualism, and the use of common language are put in place of deontological considerations, speculation, imagination, creativity, and responsible decisions.

Once the Aristotelian and cognate positions take adequate account of those who are ruled, but who themselves do not rule, the differences between their views and the present will, in many respects, be mainly one of degree. There will still, though, be some signal differences, grounded in the fact that, unlike the others, the present takes explicit account of the reality of privacies, persons, the unions people form, the conditions which limit these, and the kinds of complexes which are produced through the interplay of the unions and the conditions.

So far as a state not only supplements but replaces a societal control, and thereby deals only with citizens, people will be subject to conditionings dealing with just aspects of themselves. These aspects will, in fact, be connected with others, not then considered. All are continuations of privacies. The clarity, persistence, and force with which a state deals with any of them makes, what otherwise might be just minor qualifications, sometimes be of considerable importance. The adventures of citizens affect people as they exist apart from a state, even though their citizenship is exercised only within the compass of one.

Interactions of states are carried out by those who act as their agents. Such agents are to be distinguished from those who act on behalf of the government, as well as from those who represent the citizens. All three, of course, may be carried out by the same individuals, thereby making evident in another way that roles are not to be identified with their bearers. The fact, unfortunately, is not always obvious to leaders, political commentators, or biographers.

3. REASONABLE PEOPLE TOGETHER

"Reasonableness" has related, but still different meanings, when used to refer to people in their daily activities; as together in unions, societies, or states; or to the activities of governments, states, or sov-

ereigns. A single core meaning is pertinent to all decisions and preparations and, most important, to actions carried out in accord with a
present that has been enriched by tradition and ideals. Quite close to
a daily life "commonsense", it differs from this primarily in its alert-
ness to long-established ways and to its openness to reasons. In a
union, it overlaps "morality", adding sound practical judgments
about the way to deal with instruments and things. It also differs from
an accord with social, political, and coercive demands in its changing
determinations of where, how, and why one is to act. Applied to the
decisions of a government or state, reasonableness takes account of
their likely effects, while showing little interest in what those decisions presuppose.

A state depends for its successful functioning on its citizens being
reasonable people, directly related to one another, independently of,
but still ready to act in accord with those requirements of the state
which must be satisfied if it is to continue and prosper. Were they not
reasonable, a state would have to compel its citizens to act for their
own as well as for its benefit. Conceivably, they might then be governed in ways which go counter to what they would have preferred,
and therefore may have to be coerced to do what was being demanded, even though this was to their advantage.

Reasonableness reduces the need to force people to act both for their
own good and for the good of the state. It anticipates, in consonance
with established practices, the actions which are desirable at a particular time so that maximum satisfaction is obtained by all. In some
states, the role that reasonableness plays is more prominent and important than the role it has in others, but each requires every person
to take such account of others that important common tasks are successfully carried out, and all are enabled to exist and act in harmony.

When a state builds on a society, or replaces societal conditions with
its own, it demands that attitudes and acts which may have been
appropriate in the society be so modified that they exhibit the reasonableness that the state requires. Those who do this are identified as
mature, public beings. They are not only taken to have passed
through a biological and psychological barrier separating them from
the dependent and undeveloped, but to be self-determined, expressing distinctive rights and duties in consonance with the continuance
of a well-functioning state. Unlike those who are successful in meeting only the challenges of Nature or in getting along well with their
fellows, reasonable people also carry out acts which the state requires,
experience supports, and reflection endorses.

Reasonable people work together with others who are reasonable. Sometimes, they confront some who are not reasonable, either because these operate in accord with the requirements of a different kind of state or because, while belonging to the same state, they do not know how to or do not care to adjust themselves to what others need, desire, and insist on. The reasonable look to the state to help bring the deviants in line or, at the very least, to limit their activities and reduce the losses that mig ht be produced. Although the reasons or causes of their behavior may not be clear, a reasonable person will still know that what these would do they cannot be allowed to do because it endangers the continuance and prosperity of the rest.

Reasonableness cannot be expressed in rules or formulae. Like a living language, it is carried out over the course of adjustments to the presence, actions, and requirements of others in changing circumstances, and then used without reflection to back assessments of what is done. It is also used to correct what seems likely to bring about the unwanted or dangerous, as well as to promote the welfare of both the people and the state. Those who engage in inquiries into the activities and the world where the reasonable spend their lives, should make use of the same ability, but mainly to guide and qualify their analyses, judgments, and use of factors having an application not limited to societies or states.[5]

Reasonableness keeps one close to the morality that an established union requires. Since each member of the union expresses a bodily mediated privacy there, reasonableness inevitably also has bearing on what these can privately initiate and therefore ethically decide to do. References to privacy, and the ethics which concerns it, though, are usually made only when what is publicly done touches on root human concerns. People then often become perplexed, for it seems as if they were being required to give up their reasonableness and allow more radical, absolutistic considerations to take over. But a truly reasonable person knows there are limits to reasonableness, no less than there are to rationality. This results in a reasonableness assessed by a privacy and, therefore, subject to the demands of what ought to be as well as to the exigencies of a present states of affairs.

Rarely do reasonable persons have or need to have reasons for what they do. This does not mean that their actions will be arbitrary or capricious; reasonableness stands in the way of such actions even more effectively than any reasons could. Neither arbitrary nor perverse, a reasonable person's judgments are grounded in established practice and funded knowledge, while account is taken of his rights, duties, and expectations. Like one who is rational, such a person may be guided by general rules, but these will rarely be consciously entertained, or used to obtain abstractly formulated or justified conclusions. Reasonableness is not a constant; the understanding of what is meant by "relevance", "cruelty", "slander", and "pornography" depends on knowing what people may be expected to do and accept at a particular time and in a particular place, as well as on knowing what the courts, with judges acting as reasonable people, will find acceptable or repugnant. Greater variations in conclusions become apparent when one compares what is endorsed or repudiated at times far apart. What would be reasonable for a Greek aristocrat in relation to foreigners or to those captured in war, would not be reasonable for a person in most states today.[6] Still, the reasonableness prevalent in one epoch is rarely much different from that characteristic of the epoch it replaced. Like language, reasonableness changes slowly, almost unnoticeably, with only an occasional sudden shift in perspective—and then usually in and after crises.

Laws codify reasonableness by making some of its demands explicit. They thereby impose sharp boundaries on what is permitted, required, and forbidden. Did the laws do no more than this, they would just affirm what some people together tend to do. If they did not even do this much, they would articulate arbitrary, authoritative decisions. Instead, laws attend to limited forms of the conditions which sustain and promote a people's joint reasonableness. On their side, the reasonableness of people enables them to be together in unions, societies, and states, and there act in pertinent and harmonious ways. While still subject to laws, the people carry out tasks and interact in accord with what tradition and ideals warrant in the present, and what the state presumably needs if it is to continue and to prosper.

Laws usually help people be reasonable in a state. Building on what humans are, need, seek, and deserve, they formulate prescriptions so that supportive responses are elicited or, at the very least, so that rejections and adverse responses are not provoked. Endorsing a reasonable concern with what humans are and might do, the laws apply to them as just publicly together, without making any explicit allowance for their privacies. Were the laws to oppose the ways in which they are vitally joined in a state and in other complexes, they would be required to be unreasonably reasonable, functioning reasonably only within unduly limited confines.

What is needed is a reasonableness that is not indifferent to any of the rights people possess. That reasonableness has no antecedently determinable extent, content, penetrative reach, or involvement with other ways in which people are together. Restricting it to proper ways of speaking a common language, acting in public, conforming to societal ways, or supporting this or that set of political demands, over-determines it. Reasonableness, though, is germane to more than political activities. It is also pertinent to what is to be done when initiating and pursuing intellectual inquiries, since inquiry begins and continues in a world where people act in established ways, not only with reference to one another, but with reference to what else they confront. It will always allow for contingencies and novelties. Blurred, without clear boundaries, not endorsed by analysts or logicians, it cannot be rejected without descending into foolishness, or ending with verbalities and abstractions.

The methods, earlier examined, which should be used in a study of sociological activities, are pertinent to reasonable people functioning in a state, when allowance is made for the fact that they there act together in some accord with what the state demands. Approaches to history, which are alert to the differences between historic and physical time, or such studies as Goffman's, which are sensitive to the ways people daily associate with one another, need to be qualified if they are to be pertinent to a people's normal functioning in a state. The distances maintained in queues in different countries—to take one of Goffman's examples—though mainly a matter of the ways various limited associations are formed, are determined in part by the degree of separateness that both a society and state require and permit, the society determining what is tolerable, forbidden, and the like, and the state providing definitions of tort and marking off areas of "privacy", etc.

A study of how people are to function in a particular society and state is a task for an as yet nonexistent discipline of political sociology, fragments of which are now scattered here and there in the memoirs of statesmen and the reports of observers. What mainly concerns reasonable people is usually something else—the occasions when they and others will be held accountable by the state.

4. ACCOUNTABILITY

People are accountable just so far as they are the objects of reward and punishment—and in the extreme case, of preservation and destruction. A state is needed to supplement a society's attribution of sources of desirable and undesirable actions, by means of clear, justified, neutrally formulated, enforced laws determining the nature and bestowal of rewards and punishments. On their side, the people assume accountability for some of the things they initiate. Since rewards and punishments by a state do no more than define who in fact is being held accountable by it—whether or not they did initiate or prevent the acts—and since people usually assume accountability only for what they recognize to have originated with themselves, it is possible for them to assume accountability for what they are not being held accountable, and to refuse to take themselves to be accountable for what they are held accountable.

Accountability is ascribed to public people by the state; people assume accountability privately. Ideally, not only will they assume accountability and so express themselves that a state's impartial determination of accountability is sustained, but their state's impartial determination of accountability will match the accountability the people assume. Ideally, too, people will assume accountability for other acts as well; a state, too, will hold them accountable not only for what they assume accountability but for what they must do to enable the state to function well. When people assume accountability for acts to which no accountability is publicly assigned, and when accountability is assigned for acts not accepted by people as really theirs, each makes evident that it is not only independent of the other, but may set itself in opposition to it. For the two efforts to be maximized in harmony, citizens have to be both well-habituated and thoughtful, and the state both fair and considerate.

One can do more than assume accountability. A state can do more than reward and punish. People think, believe, and hope in ways which make no reference to what is publicly done; states are not oblivious to the threat or presence of natural disasters. People decide and prepare, and states order and plan. If either fails to do these well, or fails to promote the other's being and effectiveness, it will not do all it could and should for itself. Each should so act that the other will be enhanced and so far be better able to help it.

The accountability people sometimes privately assume for what they publicly do may not coincide with what they are accountable for as citizens. They may privately reject what they are charged with, or may adopt as their own doing, what is due to others, circumstance, or inadver ence. We will not know for what any assume accountability unless they tell or show us that they do, usually by explicitly rejecting the rewards or punishments that the state prescribes. Their acts and remarks may then lead to an assignment of accountability where none had been made before, or to a cancellation of others previously assigned.

The assumption of accountability involves the exercise of a private power grounded in the self, and makes possible the achievement of a stage where one is responsible. Ideally, it accords with the accountability one has in an excellent state. On its side, a state is ethically justified in its determinations of a person's accountability, if it rewards and punishes in consonance with a arranted, assumed accountability, and makes it desirable for the person to assume accountability for whatever public acts he initiates. We have here another illustration of the principle that the proper way for independent realities to act on one another is for each to be so fully expressed that the others are maximally enhanced.

A person should both live a mature, private life and carry out public duties. This does not mean that only what is politically desirable is to be done, that a state's needs have a priority over all others, or that what alone is important is that for which the state rewards or punishes. Ideally, the assumption of accountability for acts for which the state holds one accountable occurs when other, non-political activities are initiated, some privately and some in areas demanding independent creative and original activity. Accountability is properly assumed for what one is held accountable by a state, so far as that state is promoting an end to which one is contributive.

A person is not to be used as a means only, but also not to be treated as just an end. Each is, and is to be used as a means by other people, a body, a society, and a state, and should promote their good as well. These are in turn to use the persons in such a way that they become better beings, able to be privately perfected and readied to live harmoniously together. Nor is the state to be used just as a means. People are to use it for their own good, but in such a way that it is strengthened. Consequently, it is no more proper to demand that a state act only in consonance with the accountability that people assume than it is to demand that people assume accountability only for what they are held to be accountable by a state. Neither is self-sufficient; neither is the inverse of the other; neither is a mere agent. Both are to contribute to the realization of a good greater than they severally or together could embody. Both, too, (as we shall see) occur in a larger whole, having a more comprehensive objective than that which they separately or jointly have.

The assumption of accountability is desirable. It shows a person not only to be a locatable origin of a public act or just a politically convenient object of reward or punishment, but to be a private, self-determining, independent source of actions as well. A state's ascription of accountability, also, is desirable, if the act not only advances its own interests but takes account of what people are, initiate, deserve, and ought to have.

When people assume accountability for what they do, they take their acts to be their own doing. Were they then to ignore the ways in which a state determines accountability, they would inevitably do what it does not permit, and fail to do what it demands. The accountability they are to assume is to be both produced freely and incorporated in the tasks that the state requires. On its side, a state may demand of people that they engage in particular work, or suffer penalty, but it should do this in such a way that their standing and functioning apart from it are also promoted.

The accountability that a society endorses entrenches on the accountability people assume. Although it will usually be more closely attuned to people's privacies than a state is, since the society does not make well-formulated demands, one cannot be sure just what it requires them to do. They must rely on experience, tradition, ideology, and habit if they are to act there as they should. If societal demands are supplemented by a state's general, neutral, distinct, articulated insistencies, the people will usually be more ready to assume accountability for the very acts for which they are taken to be accountable.

Although the satisfaction of a demand requires that account be taken of what is being used, and although something is used best when its nature is respected and perhaps enriched, and it is thereby enabled to be in a better condition, nothing may be done for the sake of the used. Things and living beings, and to some extent, people, societies, and states, are sometimes made to function as means without adequate account being taken of them. There are also onerous tasks to be carried out, debilitating work to be done, sacrifices called for. Some demands are imperious, brooking no denial. Whatever is used even at those times also deserves consideration. One should not over-consume, not only because this is bad for oneself but also because it uses more than need be used. One should not inflict pain,

be cruel, mutilate, corrupt, or waste, because these too unwarrantedly destroy or minimize what deserves consideration, and perhaps
preservation and enhancement.

Since what is consumed is not allowed to have the nature that it
had, one can never be properly said to benefit it. It may, of course, be
improved, on the way to being used to serve interests other than its
own. One might try to justify its consumption, whether it be animal
or vegetable, on the grounds that people have a right to use anything
as they see fit—which encourages ruthlessness—or on the grounds
that nothing is as important as human beings—which has a little
more plausibility. What is consumed could then be taken to be properly sacrificed as a necessary means for strengthening people or, at the
very least, enabling them to continue, and thereupon presumably
able and willing to help sustain and improve the rest of Nature. Such
a view, particularly when consumption is restricted to what is necessary to use or use up in order for people to exist, enables one not only
to treat carelessness, ineptitude, and gluttony as faults and sources of
wrongs, but to treat all entities as comparable and some perhaps as
interchangeable units. Groups encompassing greater numbers of
similar items could then be given proportionately higher values than
those with less. The view is difficult to maintain when one moves up
the scale of living beings, and deals with clearly irreplaceable, sensitive, individual animals. These surely cannot be injured or killed
without producing irreparable losses. Once this is admitted, it will be
found that there is no place where one can in principle stop. The use
or consumption of anything, no matter how low on a scale of complexity, intelligence, or sensitivity, involves a loss, incapable of being
made good as long as account is taken of it as concrete, individual,
intrinsically different from everything else.

One might defend some uses or consumption by people, like the
acts of a state in a crisis, as being justified because forced on them by
circumstance, and to involve only a sacrifice of some lower level beings in order to save and perhaps benefit the rest. That position, too,
is untenable. It cannot be carried out unless the uniqueness and integrity of what is being used is ignored, since the sacrifice depends for its
justification on a unique entity being viewed as though it were not
one, and then being quantitatively compared with what was to be
benefited. An item has the status of a sacrificeable unit only so far as
abstraction has been made from its irreducible, incomparable singularity and value. Because it is unique, a sacrifice of it produces an

irreplaceable loss. Consumption of any food and use of any thing involves one in the same theoretical problem that is confronted when dealing with the killing, enslavement, or instrumental use of some people to benefit others.

Things must be used. Food is needed. The unduplicable has to be sacrificed. In each case, the decision entails irreparable losses. The loss is increased the more surely one sacrifices more items when fewer would have sufficed; it can never be compensated for, as long as what is used is more than an interchangeable quantifiable unit.

Vegetarians sometimes speak as though they had avoided the problem, though the vegetables, fruits, and nuts that they consume have their lives cut short. Each one is distinct from every other, not duplicable, not really replaceable. Treating it as though it were a unit interchangeable with others, requires an overlooking of the rest of its reality, and a denial of some of its rights as surely, though not as poignantly as is done when animals or people are sacrificed. The theoretical difficulties are not reduced even when the practical acts do little harm, and may on the whole make great goods possible. The answer that alone is warranted is that no publicly maintained right is absolute, even though its denial involves loss. All such rights are inviolable only within limits. Bodies, communes, communities, unions, societies, and states, to function well, and therefore to serve many, again and again rightly deny a warrant for the satisfaction of some of the publicly maintained rights of others at certain times.

If one accepts a society's or a state's selection of what is to be sacrificed, one should also use the occasion to better other things, as well as the society or the state. The need to make such sacrifices should be anticipated, and their degree reduced. With equal warrant, a society or state should hold men accountable—and therefore, if need be, coopt their time, their property, and, *in extremis*, risk their lives. All will inescapably reduce values and can justify their acts only in the limited form of having made possible the preservation or promotion of greater values. This conclusion seems perilously close to the intolerable utilitarian view that one is justified in sacrificing some people if the greatest possible good (of all the rest) were thereby promoted. It is possible, though, to restrict the scope of utilitarianism to what is subhuman and needed in order for people, themselves outside the reach of a utilitarian view, to exist and prosper.[7] Since subhumans have rights, and since their use involves irreplaceable losses, their sacrifice cannot be ethically justified; but in a world where people are forced to make regrettable decisions, it is reasonable to sacrifice subhumans on behalf of what has higher value and cannot exist or prosper if the sacrifice is not made.

5. OBEDIENCE

In order for a state to achieve its objectives, people must so act that they help it do so. Were they completely opposed to their state's rule, this would at best be just a state for them, and it would have to spend its energies in making them accept it. Only when it had succeeded in doing this would its government be more than a channel for the expression of oppressive power.

Neither people nor governments are wholly passive or completely resistant. They are in a common present, share a past, and point toward a future pertinent to both. Each side resists and accommodates what the other insists on. Each would achieve more than it does were it to meet less resistance. Were it to meet none at all, there would either be no one governed or nothing that governed. An actual functioning state is the outcome of an interaction of a union of people and a government, an interaction in which each makes a difference to and conditions the other, and thereby produces a unitary, ongoing complex with its own nature and career.

From the standpoint of a state, people should so act that its decrees are carried out without undue delay or signal modification. Since the people are already involved in unions and societies, and since each is an individual, expressing a distinctive privacy, none can be counted on to function just as required. Consequently, if a state is to be a source of good for them, a good that they otherwise would not be able to obtain, they have to be controlled for their own sake, while they will be required to function at times in ways which sustain and enhance the state.

Although sovereigns may proclaim that what they demand is for the good of their subjects, rarely does any show that it has either the knowledge or the practical wisdom to provide what is needed. Indeed, the sovereigns are constantly on the verge of misconstruing and injuring their subjects to such a degree that these are unable to contribute as much as they possibly could. Rebellions and revolutions are among the agencies through which sovereigns belatedly discover that they do not have and, presumably do not deserve, support. More imagination, study, and energy should have been spent in getting people to so act that both political objectives and the people's interests were well-served. This would be more likely to occur were subjects accorded the status of citizens, and therefore were encompassed in a state which had long-standing and guiding ways for determining how rulers and ruled are to interplay. So far as they function as such citizens (or as units in a union or members of a society) they carry out public roles in relation to one another within a common setting. All the factors constituting a complex have values in themselves, as well as other values reflecting the extent to which they contribute to an excellent outcome for all.

The steady course of unions and societies depends largely on unreflecting, constant responses made to common cues in manageable circumstances. The training received from infancy on, the pressures exerted by those with authority, the effective insistence of elders, all conspire to keep people acting steadily along established lines, until they acquire a firm habit of obedience. That habit has two major roles: it readies a submission to the state's demands, and it assures a good, quick conformity.

The less certain it is that people will do what is demanded of them, the more time and energy will have to be spent to make them obey. States, consequently, try to build on a habit of submissiveness, initially instilled by parents and encouraged by others. This is not automatically carried over into the state. If people habitually obey one type of demand, they may not obey another. It is fortunate that this is so, for a state usually needs a different form of obedience from what is desirable elsewhere. It is not often that punishment elicits the nuanced responses on which the good functioning of a state depends.

People will be prompted to submit to a state if their submission yields an easier and readier benefit than neglect or rejection would; if the price of disobedience seems too high; or if their obedience permits an engagement in other activities thought to be important. If a state strengthens an existing society; allows a place for other complexes; presents itself as serving its people's objectives; makes their obedience seem to involve little or no sacrifice of dignity or aspiration; emphasizes punishments for deliberate deviations; and allows the obedient to engage in what is important to them, it will reduce the resistance of most and, more likely than not, will have its course sustained. It will, though, not yet be assured of all the support that could be given it, for this requires, not just obedience, but contributions freely made. Those contributions are more apt to be forthcoming if the goods people need and seek for themselves have been promoted and cherished.

Threat and fear of punishment loom large at times. Advocates of severe punishment for crimes occasionally claim that the threat and fear are enough to make criminals mend their ways, or at least avoid the most severely condemned crimes. The idea would have merit were crimes committed by reasonable people who weigh all the relevant factors before acting. This does not often occur. The advocates of the supposedly strong deterrents to crime do an injustice to themselves when they suppose that the spirit in which crimes are committed is like that in which those advocates believe they conduct their lives—judicious and planned, with a possible punishment for violations given due weight.

Obedience relates people to a demand. It shortens the gap between what is required of them and what they would otherwise be inclined to do. When it is exhibited, there is less need to compel, since some part of what compulsions would have had to bring about are already provided. Obedience is a person's gift to the state, expressed mainly in the form of a support the government needs in order to have its demands carried out; but it cannot be counted on, unless time has been spent in making people habitually ready to do whatever the government demands. If oriented toward governmental decrees, obedience will keep people in some accord with governmental changes. Since, to be most obedient, each person must also be able to remain in good accord with what others want done, and do this unreflectingly and well, a good government will avoid making many unpredictable moves.

People stop at a red light because they have become habituated to do so. There may have been a time when they stopped because they wanted to, or felt compelled to conform to what was required. There may be times when they consciously stopped at a red light because they recognized that this was demanded, and that it was better to do this than act otherwise. For the most part, though, such voluntary acts need not be considered. Governments usually count on habitual behavior, for what is to be done is then carried out in swifter and surer ways than could be expected were one to rely on voluntary acts.[8]

A habit of obedience, when expressed in a submission, is turned toward what demands; when keyed to a conformity, it keeps in accord with what is demanded. Conceivably, people could have the first form of the habit of obedience without the second. The timid and the fearful come close to doing so. Constantly modifying their ways to keep in accord with what they think is being demanded, they almost always do less than they could on behalf of government, state, sovereign, or themselves than is good for any of them.

A habit of acting in consonance with what is demanded may be bodily acquired, and may or may not be accompanied by a habit of obedience. Most people are brought up to behave in consonance with others, without having had to form a habit of obeying them. They are in fact usually oblivious of what they are required to do, and keep in accord with the ways others act, without having made themselves first yield to their or other demands.

Knowledge that a state is or is not primarily in a period of change is needed if a judicious choice is to be made between a stress on submission or on conformity. Changing states need people who readily vary in their functioning. Most states, though, are rather stable, with change subordinated and limited. They need people who readily obey, people with appropriate habits. The habits may make them act somewhat mechanically, but only by and large. One with a habit of smoking does not smoke incessantly, but still can be counted on to smoke over the course of the day, and to have smoked a number of times before the day is over. One who is habitually dishonest may sometimes tell the truth, keep promises, and the like, but over a period will lie and break promises more often than most of the others do.

While functioning habitually together, without thought of the state that needs them to so act, people are sometimes aware that their readiness to obey new demands is being counted on. From the standpoint of the state this is desirable, for it needs people who are able to break through their steady habits of action when it sets on a new course.

Socrates advocated an obedience even to unjust decrees; Aristotle defended an obedience even to bad laws. The first surely and the second perhaps took people to have privacies, yet both looked at them primarily from the standpoint of the state. It would be equally one-sided to stress the standpoint of the people and, with Locke, defend a supposed right to break laws deemed bad or unjust. The interests of people are to be considered together with the interests of the state.

Disliked laws may be good laws, deserving to be obeyed. Genocidal laws should be evaded and disobeyed, but not just because they are disliked. Both government and people are to be kept within the limits which, at the very least, make it possible for there to be publicly interacting people, where rulers and ruled all flourish, and the society and state are enhanced.

There is a constant danger that one will treat what is disagreeable or unfavorable to oneself or to one's group as being unjust and, therefore, justifiably disobeyed. What must be determined is whether or not people are being governed in such a way that both their good and the good of the state are being promoted or precluded, ignored, or misconstrued. If people do less than what is needed in order to have a flourishing state, they are to be brought to the stage where they will do more. If a state is not doing all that should be done for people, it should be made to change its ways. In any particular case, a sharp affirmative or negative answer about what is to be done cannot be given until one knows what is demanded and whether this is good or bad. If a law is foolish and its effects minor, it should be obeyed. If the dignity of the people is flagrantly denied, disobedience is justified. That disobedience, though, is to be qualified by the recognition that laws are needed if people are to function well together, and that what is foolish and minor is to be ignored or slighted. Some laws can be breached without being broken; others can be stretched or squeezed without being denied. One might reasonably refuse to take account of the exact wording of a law, since it might serve mainly to injure those who are to be helped. One can reasonably delay extending permits to suspect causes of unrest. These maneuvers could, of course, prove disastrous, since they could be used by both the well-intended and those who are not, and could promote indifference to people's rights and to the demands of law. There is no escaping the need for both the rulers and the ruled to be steadily reasonable and constantly concerned with the common good.

No breach or violation of laws can be endorsed, yet the reasonableness, which may have these as consequences, is rightly followed. This is but to say that there is no right to break the law, but that the breaking may at times be a consequence of the exercise of desirable acts. Every particular case mixes good with bad. If a law is good on the whole, it is better to accept it, particularly if one is prepared to work toward the stage where what is undesirable in it is eliminated. In a democracy, this is best done by so obeying that one promotes what deserves full obedience. If there are no acceptable ways in which a state's course can be peaceably changed, there will finally be no recourse possible but revolt. Since this is to risk the destruction of the state, and is usually bought with lives, it can never be justified as more than a last, desperate resort.

Both submission and conformity are eminently desirable in a state occupied with furthering the good of a people. Neither should be expressed if a state is destroying itself or the people. Actual states are in between these extremes, making desirable an obedience that is in consonance with what reasonableness demands. The obedience is to be habitually exhibited, subject to a sense of what is sanctioned by the past and the end that is sought, and modified in the light of what may ensue. The good to be achieved is to provide for the good of the state as well as for the good of the people, the former being promoted by the people carrying out a new attitude and eventually a new habit—loyalty, to be directed at a state attentive to the people's rights.

Loyalty differs from obedience in being both voluntary initially, and requiring an intent. It expresses a readiness to obey and to conform, and therefore to acquire a habit of obedience. Royce took loyalty (or loyalty to loyalty) to be primary virtue, but he did not show that the best and most inclusive encompassment of people, (to which loyalty for him was presumably due) might not urge what was unwise or wrong. What he had in mind, apparently, was the kind of spirit people would have in a world-wide commune, where they are harmoniously and intimately involved with one another. Loyalty there, though, is little more than a readiness to accept a guiding common value.

"Loyalty" is most appropriately used to refer to a faithfulness primarily toward one's state, backed by a readiness to act so as to provide a needed defense, aid, and support. It is surely desirable, particularly when emphatic and self-sacrificing acts are needed, or when habits of obedience or conformity are not yet in place, for such a loyalty makes it likely that the slack will be overcome by vigorous and emotionally sustained efforts. Those who change their allegiance, though they will not habitually act with the same alacrity and success that others exhibit, may make up their deficiency in the ways they express that kind of loyalty.

While one may have some habits whose exercise precludes the exercise of other habits, all may be equally firm, to be carried out at different times and on different occasions. Though more encompassing, more passionate, and self-sacrificing than these habits lead one to be, loyalty is not as strongly entrenched as they are, and cannot be counted on to withstand strong temptations or the unavoidable set-backs which a contingent world is likely to produce. Since it is a product of will, association, and tradition, loyalty will nevertheless tend to keep people functioning together in a way that their habits may not.

The final community with which Royce was concerned, and to which he thought loyalty should finally be directed—even when it is endowed with the consciousness he supposed it was—does not need people's loyalty in order to function well. If it did, it could get it only in limited forms. It would have to harmonize the people on its own terms, or they would have to give up individual differences so as to fit together. It would be a One which subordinated the Many who attended to it or, if it allowed them to exist and function apart, would allow them to specialize it, not necessarily in consonant ways.

The same objective, accepted wholeheartedly by a number, will not be promoted by all in harmony and to the same degree, unless all are steadily occupied with it. Loyalty and habit need one another. Together, they depend on individuals who have a common guiding goal. That, at least, is what Royce would have had to affirm had he adhered as closely as he wished to Peirce's ideal community (strictly speaking, a commune of scientific inquirers) in which all people are eventually to fit. Neither his nor Peirce's objective, though, is inclusive enough, for neither is able to encompass all those who are not only conscious and inquiring, but who have lived bodies which they use to enable them to function well together in multiple ways. The needed complex is one where people are joined in unions, societies, and states within a more comprehensive civilizing whole.

At its best, a state is a present object of a freely expressed, limited loyalty, promoting the likelihood and acquisition of a habit of obedience toward it as making possible a good common public life. That habit is possessed and exercised by individuals over the course of their joint lives, while their loyalty keeps them attentive to the merit of what does and is to encompass them. Together, the habit and loyalty enable them to be fulfilled in ways they otherwise could not be.

When people are trained, they also acquire habits, but the training, in addition, involves their subordination to externally defined re-quirements for the realization of limited ends. The training helps them produce a sequence of needed acts, at the same time that it turns them into carriers of what is demanded. If properly trained, the people become skilled, able to control their bodies, and sometimes the instruments and other means by which an objective is realized. Were they trained to obey, they would react somewhat as well-disciplined soldiers do to their commanding officers. Were they trained to function along some particular lines, they would do so more steadily and more single-mindedly than they would were they merely habituated to act in those ways, but they would then also make less use of individual judgments, and be more dependent on the wisdom of those who trained them.

Habits are too personalized to make possible more than a meshing together of a limited number of people. Training allows for greater cooperation and a better mastery of novelties. A training that enabled people to function on behalf of the state, somewhat as athletes function on behalf of a team, would therefore be most desirable, were it not for the fact that games take place only occasionally, while a state never stops functioning. Trained athletes have many opportunities outside their sport when they can act without reference to it. Trained citizens would have comparatively few opportunities to act apart from their state, except in those public areas where the state decided not to interfere, the so-called "spheres of privacy". A performance in a game, also, is directed toward an end that the players themselves want to realize together though mainly for themselves, while people trained to obey act as individuals but mainly on behalf of the state. From the standpoint of the state, such training would be most desirable, but not so far as it precludes people from acting independently of it, if only so that they could bring more of themselves to bear on what the state requires and would have them do.

While athletes voluntarily submit to training, a state has to demand it, and while athletes are permitted to outdistance those they can, if this promises success for the team, a state prefers uniformity, allowing for only incidental displays of great efforts. Heroic acts in times of crises may be encouraged by a state; sometimes successful new adventures are rewarded. On the whole, though, regularity, the routine, the quick, unthinking reaction, are preferred to a display of fallible initiative. If it would have people trained along the lines followed by those in charge of professional teams, a state would have to allow for more initiative and spontaneity than it now does and perhaps could ever safely permit.

Were all people trained primarily to become more mature and fulfilled, and thereupon able to promote the interests of their state, it would still be necessary to face the fact that few have the determination or dedication that is needed in order to assure the kind of success achieved by some who devote themselves to athletic careers. The most that a state bent on training can do, is what is done in the armed forces: train those in it to perform specialized activities rapidly and well, and allow a few who are in command to exercise some independence in judgment.

Training is sometimes provided in local political organizations. What most achieve there, though, is primarily an acquaintance with influential figures, and a learning of the rhythms of the organization, with some grasp of the ways use can be made of it. If people are to be trained to become good citizens, participation in local organizations will sooner or later have to be replaced with an actual participation in a larger, with its more powerfully backed demands.

Training makes individuals exemplify a conditioning; habituation awaits their reorganization so that a desired outcome is likely to be produced. Because training also results in some habituation, those who are well-trained will not only exhibit a common conditioning, but will be so organized that they will more likely do what is expected of them. Some of the rights people have may then be prevented from being well-expressed or satisfied. The better they are trained to carry out the work of a state, the more likely it also will be that the state will not obtain from them the kind of contribution that might have been made had they acted with greater initiative. It is best for a state to take people to be independent of it, while requiring them to so act that they bring their activities in closer accord with what it demands, and presumably needs. Training for full participation in the work of a state would be most beneficial were such training to overlay a freely expressed loyalty.

Were training mandated by a state, it would most likely be carried out with some reluctance, thereby requiring the imposition of force to compel greater acquiescence. If the training cost more in money, time, and energy than the results of skilled activity on behalf of the state would justify, it would, of course, be wise to slow the training and allow habituation to take over. The decision may at times be hard to make, requiring as it does a comparison between quantifiable costs and qualitative outcomes.

Through entertainments and minor benefits, some sovereigns seek to lull their subjects, and thereby keep them from interfering with or disturbing the ways they are being controlled. So far as the strategy is successful, there is little need to train or habituate people. Those sovereigns, of course, deny to themselves the gains that would result from the actions of self-mastered, willing people who both understand and are ready to do what they should. Modern states make the mistake in a subtler way. Their instrument is propaganda, constant assurances that all is going well, and that things are surely getting better—or, at worst, that the state is facing dangerous threats to its continuance, and needs the patience and help of its citizens, and perhaps even sacrifices from them to make it possible for it to hold on to some of the goods it and they have. Crises, of course, call for immediate action, and for the contributions people could quickly make to the preservation or strengthening of the state. When the crises are a result of poor government—often enough a reason why other states produce or contribute to the crises—people are suddenly called upon to do what better governing would not have made necessary. A good rule reduces the likely number and severity of crises and, therefore, the need to have people engage in heroic measures with a corresponding neglect of what enriches rather than preserves them and their state.

Bread and circuses are intended to keep people at a distance from political activities. Propaganda, instead, tacitly assumes that people have not been adequately habituated or trained to deal properly with what is politically crucial or of great importance, and therefore tries to manipulate them so that they contribute to the state to the degree, in the manner, and at the times demanded. Appealing to people's loyalty, sometimes directly and sometimes by awakening their national pride, and occasionally also by overcoming causes of signal distress, propaganda seeks to elicit people's attention and energy so that they will function as the state desires. Trying to make an immediate effective appeal to people to change the course of their activities, to cooperate, and to endorse decisions about to be or already made, the propaganda works best when it is able to elicit fear and prejudice.

In contrast with propaganda, education offers both ends and means. Tensed toward the production of what enriches people by what had been achieved in thought and act, it prompts them to ready themselves to make contributions of their own. Sharing something of the temper involved in training and habituation, it promises a steadier and better support for the state than propaganda could. It differs from habituation mainly in its addressing the mind and encouraging intellectual adventure, and from training mainly in its recognition of the right of each person to make what is taught be as much a part of a distinctive life as each desires. To say this is, of course, to view education from the standpoint of dedicated teachers; to depend on institutions where education can be carried out effectively; and to take account of the promise of students.

From the standpoint of a state, education is a means for preparing the young to become good citizens, living peaceably together under the limitations that the state provides. When a state takes over an educational system, it will, therefore, not be inclined to tolerate what fails to fit in with its plans. Inquiries into the natures of ancient civilizations, dead languages, theology, and philosophy will be tolerated by it only if they are supposed somehow to shore up other, more evidently pertinent studies. Usually, the state will not tolerate even accurate descriptions or practices of other kinds of economy, other forms of religion, or other standards of morality; it does not trust the independent mind, the fresh search, probings, questionings, doubts, hesitations, or radical honesty. The more firmly a state has education under control, the more ready it will usually be to see to it that everything taught is channelled toward the upholding of the course that the state is pursuing. Since the aim of education is to do more than prepare people to fit into a state, if a state intrudes on the educational process, it will inevitably hobble and pervert it.[9] At the very least, what should be provided is a means by which students are enabled to fit in the state as it is about to be. It would be better were they helped to function so that the ideal state is maximally promoted. But this cannot be guaranteed. Conceivably, education could prove to be an effective agency by which people were prepared to help in the achieving of noble political objectives and, at least, make it possible for a state to function better. Once this is admitted, it is but a step to acknowledge that there may be more political wisdom in allowing education to be carried out independently, and to want it to take fact and truth alone as its guide, than in forcing it to keep within narrow, externally imposed limits. Then, more likely than not, what the state really needs will eventually be provided.

Those who hold that a state should control educational programs, materials, and processes, apparently suppose that students are receptive to any type of instruction, or that they natively tend to oppose the state. When the first is assumed, the state is taken to be the locus of the best of a number of alternative goods to whose attainment the young might devote themselves; when the second, students are thought to be amorphous beings able to be molded as authorities see fit or to have an inevitable tendency to engage in selfish, foolish, or subversive pursuits, and, therefore to need to be corrected by a forceful orientation toward a well-defined political objective.[10] Neither approach exhibits a confidence that education, on its own, could produce good people who will promote a good state. No reliance is placed on the judgment of teachers or the maturation of students.[11] At the same time, the influence of teachers and the importance of specific affirmations and bits of knowledge are exaggerated. Worse, indoctrination is mistaken for education.

Indoctrination yields a submission to approved views, claims, and ideals. Not particularly interested in having its claims understood, it tries to have them responded to emotionally, unsullied by reflection. A form of training in the expression of key terms and practices, it is imposed in the belief that submission and conformity, with a consequent gain to the state, will ensue. plato was often on the verge of treating education in his ideal state as though it involved nothing more than such indoctrination. Aristotle avoided that extreme. Although he did not leave room for the learning of such subjects as logic and history, which he himself pursued, nor think that all men deserved to be educated, he did take some to require an education th at would lead them to live a virtuous life together under law, and thereby themselves be able to become rulers. A state should do more, but surely no less than that.

Because rulers rarely have much confidence that an occupation with what does not have a direct bearing on the state and its welfare will prove of value, they try to limit education's range and processes. As a consequence, they confine and cripple people on the mistaken supposition that this is the way to turn them into strong supporters, splendid humans, genuine contributors or, at least, into quiet or passive subjects. A state needs a well educated people, with a broad knowledge, who have learned how to judge and reason, know something about ideal goods, and have practiced the major virtues. Since they could conceivably help the state or its agents make and carry out sound decisions for its own sake, a state should promote education. This, though, directly benefits the people, not the state, and may in fact not help the state as it is then or is about to be.

Education needs to be independently carried out if it is to yield all the good it can. It is feared by those who want nothing other than to remain in control or to extend their dominance. That fear is justified, but the danger education presents may be less than that which its absence would. The fact that those in power are threatened both by an educational process freely carried out, and also by it as completely controlled and thus as not genuine education at all, points up the truth that they are caught in a dilemma from which they can escape only by making themselves be, or by being forced to become less insistent than they are or would like to be.

The educational process is neither inherently subversive nor innocuous, and this whether subject to powerful or weak control. Political leaders and educators tend to exaggerate both what it does and can do, the one unduly restricting or neglecting it, and the other offering it as the answer to all difficulties. Each needs the other in the role of a means enabling it to function better; each rightly objects to the other so far as this fails to do what it alone can and should do.

People who are not well educated are at best naively reasonable, reasonable in an unreflecting way, not thoughtfully reasonable, having some grasp of ultimate truths, at least as having pertinence to what goes on in the state. A good education acquaints them with fundamentals. Enriched by experience it becomes transformed into the grounded steady reasonableness of those well qualified to function as rulers or ruled. This result will be obtained only if carried out in the same spirit as that which animates mature public people; it must make use of imagination, risk error, raise doubts about what had been accepted, and reflect on what has had only a ritual support.

Well educated people usually lack the practical wisdom a good ruler has; they are rarely able to show these how to make good use of what is known. Political control of education's objectives, range, and processes usually results in the confining, distorting, and often the abuse of the educational process. Both fail to do all they could to enable the other to contribute to it to a degree and in a manner not otherwise possible.

People should be enabled to perfect themselves more than would be possible were they forced to attend only to what would benefit the state; a state should be helped to function well. One can envisage the double need as the primary concern of a large-scale education having two parts, one formal and institutionalized, the other an informal process. The first is to be left to experienced teachers whose task is to enable students to mature and to share in civilization; the second is to take place in a "classroom" as large as the state, with education carried out through example, mass media, and open discussion. If the students in that "classroom" were adult, self-maintained, independent persons, able to continue their own development and thereby be in a position to promote the state's, the curriculum there would have a place for whatever is pertinent to a full public life, and what is there taught would help them master the art of making sound practical decisions.

A state that would have people act in accord with its best interests would also allow for a free press, assemblies, forums, oppositional parties, and debates, trusting that these blessings of liberty will promote what it would have be. The program implicitly takes those representing the state to be able to learn what it needs. For its own sake, it therefore should encourage free inquiry with all its deviations and errors, thereby increasing the likelihood that unsuspected great discoveries will be promoted. This claim has a paradoxical air, since it asks a state not only to leave formal education to educators who go their own way, but also to leave a broader, publicly relevant education to custom, press, and assemblies, functioning independently of the state. Nevertheless, it is well warranted.

A state benefits most from people when they are enabled to promote its continuance and prosperity. Self-denial by it should, therefore, be recognized to be a necessary preliminary to its perfecting. That fact is occasionally admitted in those short, lucid intervals when a state does not take itself to be in or on the verge of a crisis. As has been noted, there is considerable risk in such self-denial. Education's appreciation of great achievements, its inescapable sceptical strain, its encouragement of a life focused on the pursuit of pure knowledge, art, relentless inquiry, and persistent experimentation, will lead some to spend their lives in pursuit of what is often indifferent to a state's expressed interests. Not unless a state were the locus of all that is good, or at least good for people, could it rightly ask all to occupy themselves with public affairs. Still left untouched would be the question of what a person is to do privately, and how the public expressions and outcomes then made possible are to be used.

The role of a state could be radically reduced if it gave education all the room it needs; more likely than not, it would then provide opportunities for the exploration of ideas and policies that might work to the state's disadvantage. Letting go, though, is part of a desirable act of receiving; whatever liberties a state grants may still be subject to limitation by it; those who are involved in the educational process are inevitably subject to the state. For its own sake, a state must risk being altered; there is no other way it could become perfected, barring chance and miracle.

Let it be granted that no one is ever all one privately should be unless he or she so acts publicly that the state is enriched, and this is thereby able to promote the attainment of good private lives; it would still be true that there are other goods which people privately cherish, and which they rightly pursue at the expense of an attention to what the state requires. The lives of artists, the speculative, monks, parents, and lovers are carried out in considerable indifference to what a state prizes and needs—and they should be.[12] Since if a state allows for these, it will allow for an ignoring and sometimes an opposition to some of its demands, a state is always in the paradoxical position of needing independent people for whom the state's good is only one of a number.

Every state must control the maturation of its people and thereby deny itself maximum help, or allow them to achieve whatever great goods they can, even though this means that they will not be fully involved in the affairs of the state, may treat it as but one of a number of goods, or may oppose it. Actual states in fact take some account of both objectives and, consequently, veer now toward one and then toward the other, and back again. The first, though, will be explicitly stressed by it since it usually takes itself to be more or less in some danger, from within or from without.

A good public life is eminently desirable, but it can be obtained only if people are also able to have rich private lives and engage in other than political activities. Were every other good, and all of them together, inferior to the good of a state, this would still be less than what it should be, if it does not include those others. Faced with this problem, states sometimes promise that the other goods will be readily and fully achieved under their aegis, or after political objectives had been attained. But the first is not possible unless the state relaxes its hold, while the second supposes that a state will be perfected if one now does what it prescribes, and therefore does less justice to other goods than these now deserve and require.

That a state should be taken to be only one good among a number is a consequence of the fact that it is in fact only one among a number. Like every other limited good, it must in the end make way for other goods, if only to be able to be at its best. The education it is to encourage, like the arts it tolerates and should promote, enable it to achieve only a limited kind of excellence—but that is the only excellence appropriate to it.

14. The Encompassed State

1. Morality

The core meaning of "good" is "excellence","the perfect". Unfortunately, it allows one to call an adroit thief a "good" or "better" thief, since he is superior to an inept thief, performing as he does with a degree of mastery beyond the capacity of the other. To preserve the desirable component in the idea of good, it is necessary to distinguish a mere perfecting of something, whether or not this be only in its role as means or as a mode of activity, from the making something be excellent in such a way that it allows for or promotes the perfecting of others. The former brings about a limited, relative, the latter an absolute, final, ideal good. The limited is a form of that ideal, absolute good, for it is a prospective excellence though realizable in some facets or items at the price of a necessary loss of others.

It is possible to satisfy a specialization of the ideal good and yet go counter to what should be done in a particular situation. A thief is "good" when free of the defects characteristic of inept thieves; but both prepare to act in ways which prevent the realization of the absolute good. Since both are obligated to realize at least that form of the absolute good which would perfect them as persons, the thieves will more or less conform to a specialized possible good, at the same time that they ready themselves to preclude the realization of the more basic, absolute, ideal, final good.

Evidently, there are a number of hierarchies of possible goods, in some of which the realization of lower forms stands in the way of the realization of others which are higher. This is a consequence of the fact that specializations are dependent on the realities which are to realize them. Only by allowing oneself to be guided by the absolute good will one be in a position to promote it maximally. Those who so specialize it that it expresses only the best form of what they then are or intend to do, may well be required by the outcome to act in ways which go counter to what the absolute good requires. Since the absolute good is pertinent to every privacy, those who act to realize what does not lead toward the realization of that good will not act in accord with what they already are natively directed toward.

"Good" thieves effectively oppose the realization of the ideal good. They are doubly directed, with a limited aim obscuring the apprehension of a good to which they are attached as private persons. A state also has its own proper good. So far as it is defective, it, too, will more or less obscure the fact that its being as a state necessarily relates it to a specialization of the good whose realization would enhance it. Its limited good guides its activities, and does so more effectively when directly aimed at. Aimed at or not, it does not control what is being done, and cannot therefore assure its own realization. Societies also have limited goods they are to realize. Were any one of them to succeed in realizing its good, it would not thereby promote the ideal good, unless it also made provision or at least allowed for the possible realization of the goods pertinent to other realities as well. If it did not do this, the others might conceivably both be hindered by and hinder it from being as excellent as it could be.

If the realization of the limited good of any one reality is to promote the realization of the final good, it must be so brought about that the limited goods of others are also promoted, or, at the very least, not precluded. Each good is realized through the performance of independent acts. To the degree that the acts impinge on others, an adjudication of the competing claims will be necessary. No success is to be expected unless a reference is made to a more comprehensive, and ultimately to a final measure of the merits of every enterprise, and their specialized goods.

Limited goods are designatable in terms appropriate to what is to realize them. The good of a union is an ideal union; that of a society, an ideal society; that of a state, an ideal state. Viewed from the position of people, the limited good of their union is a morality; from that of society, what is proper; from that of a state, the right. Viewed from their perspectives, the limited good of people is the people as moral, decent, and mature. Nothing less is required of them than that they help realize morality, the proper, and the right as instantiating and promoting the realization of the final good, in such a way that other, compatible goods can be realized within the compass of this.

An ideal union demands that a people conform to an ideal morality. An actual union, instead, requires that they act in accord with an established morality. This may require that the people be differentiated in a hierarchy on the basis of gender, color, or property. An ideal union has no place for these distinctions.

Morality has to do with the degree to which people are associatively and collaboratively together in an actual union. What is there required of them may deviate considerably from what an ideal union requires. Great spiritual leaders, on behalf of an ideal morality, sometimes point people in a direction counter to the prevalent, accepted ways; as a consequence, they and their followers may be condemned in word and act for deviating from what is currently approved, even when they claim religious or other strong backing.

Since no actual union is in fact ideal, every person is again and again faced with the need to decide whether to act in consonance with the demands of an actual or an ideal union. There is here no question of laws or explicit formulations, or even of ethics and its concern for what ought to be.

Usually people act as their present union requires, but they should do so in such a way that an ideal union and an ideal morality are promoted. Neither that ideal nor the prevailing morality specifies just what activities are to be performed at a particular time. Allowing for a plurality of individual outlooks and acts, they require only that these keep within the confines of and realize what is prescribed.

Societies and states set conditions with which unions interplay. As affected and limited by those conditions, the unions make different demands from what they otherwise would. Since an ideal union should be a component of an ideal society and state, people are consequently required to act in ways which depart even more from established ways than they would be by an ideal union, were it alone to condition them. No virtue, knowledge, or training clears a clean path through this morass. At the very least, each person must act in accord with what an actual union requires, and work to have that union perfected.

It is one thing to live in terms of what morality requires, and quite another to live in accord with the requirements of an ethics. Different unions define different moralities; the demands of each of these are directed toward limited numbers of people, and require consonant public acts from them. No one of these moralities can rightly claim to be superior to any other, except so far as it more closely approximates what an excellent union demands, or because it measures up to the demands of a state, and finally an ethics, better than other unions do.

"Ethics" is the Greek term for "morality", but over the years there has been a gradual differentiation of the two. Today it is not infrequently used to refer to assessments of actions in terms of an absolute good pertinent to people. Since these are both private and public beings, and since each has an appropriate good, it is sensible to extend the meaning of the "ethics" so that it embraces that final ideal good of which the goods of private and public persons are specializations. Since unions, societies, and states have their own limited goods, and since it is not improper to speak of them as "bad" if they fall short of what such complexes should be, and to do this without then attending to the good people ought to embody, it is desirable to go still futher and use "ethics" to refer to the good that assesses whatever there be in terms of the ideal, final good. One would then return to something like the view Plato entertained.[1] The primary warrant for making such a move is that it also allows for the determination of the claims of what is not human—subhumans, unions, societies, and other complexes.

At the same time that ethics determines the rightful tasks and limits of people, unions, societies, and states, it both depends on these for its realization,[2] and assesses moralities, social practices, the status of actual states, and the merits of people separately and as publicly together. A desirable morality is one whose presence and strengthening is ethically endorsed, and which promotes the realization of the good in individuals, unions, societies, and states.

Ethical demands are not met unless whatever there be is perfected. They surely cannot be met if people are in conflict with one another, or if their unions, societies, or states are defective. We are, today, far from fully satisfying such conditions. It is unlikely that they will ever be completely satisfied, but that is only to say that what occurs is not, and evidently will not become perfect in a perfected world. Ethical considerations, though, are not unnecessary or unwarranted, for in their absence there would be no determining the relative merits of people, unions, societies, and states, and of the values resulting from their interplay.

A morality is to be ethically assessed as good or bad, depending on how it accommodates, preserves, and enhances people, and promotes a perfected society and state. Each of these, in turn, is to be assessed not only as more or less being and functioning at its best, but as making possible the existence and functioning of the best of unions and their moralities.

2. The Right

Everyone is ethically required to attend to the needs of a common union, to what a perfected union requires, to what actual and ideal societies and states prescribe, and to the larger world in which these fit. Conceived narrowly, that larger world reaches no further than to what is pertinent to what has bearing on human concerns. This, to be sure, is very far, encompassing as it does all actual societies and states, what they ideally could be together, and the civilization that now exists and is being added to. It still leaves out much of the entire universe, with its distant unknown stars, ultimate particles and waves and their combinations, and ignores most subhumans. To deal with these one would have to leave such a study as this behind, for, instead of moving progressively from collaborations and associations, to unions, societies, and states, and eventually to these as perfected together, one would attend to the natures of ultimate realities and the ways these interplay.[3]

What a state demands is right—not absolutely right, but right for those who live within it. The requirements of that right pass beyond the demands of morality to the people as able to make a difference to the ways they are to be together under a common governance. If the people do not act as the right demands, this still continues to be operative. It not only makes demands on their union but acts on this under the guidance of the ideal state.

Not a utopia, the ideal state is realizable, and then not instantaneously but over the course of history. Marx thought that it would eventually be realized as a result of violent revolutions, historically necessitated. History, though, is forged every day, guided by, but not under the complete control of desirable prospects pertinent to what is operative there. Like these, the ideal state awaits the performance of specific acts. Whether peaceably or violently brought about, and no matter how excellent the result, it will embody less good than what an ethics demands, for ethics is also pertinent to what people are privately, and apart from any state.

Turned toward a union of people, a state prescribes what it is right to do. When it refers to what is right to do in some limited situation, it gives the right the status of the appropriate. This may at times be at odds with the proper, that which is determined as appropriate in a society, apart from what a state might prescribe. It is proper to feed a horse, give milk to a cat, or take a dog for a walk. But when people are starving, milk scarce, or a curfew in force one should yield to the right that a state defines, the subordinate rights is authorizes, and, always of course, to what ethics demands.

In order that right prevail, imagination, experience, and thought, admonition, criticism, and the prospect of reward and punishment may have to be used to direct efforts in the desired ways. Nothing, though, enables one to take account of all details. Both the right that a state endorses and the right an ideal state defines are involved in adventures no one can completely anticipate. They are indeterminate prospects to be actualized in determinate, not wholly predictable forms.

Those who are familiar with the usual course of things, and who are aware that what is amiss at a particular time and place is to be corrected, should also be alert to what will most likely affect the lives of others in basic ways. If they have good characters they will be ready to do what is right, so far as this is consistent with what ethics requires. Did they have good characters, but were without the requisite knowledge, wit, or strength, they would fail in another way. Circumstances, though, may not allow them to make both what is politically right and what ethically ought to be, fully present in a particular situation, while Nature's power and human weakness will sooner or later put a stop to what even the wisest and best of people can do. The right will still make its demands; there will still be appropriate as well as proper ways to act, for what a state and society require does not vary in accord with a people's willingness or competence.

What mature, reasonable people of good character are readied to do in a union conforms to what a state defines as right, just so far as that state acts in accord with what the ideal state requires. What one person there does, other mature reasonable people of good character will, more often than not, endorse. The judgments made by these are no more infallible than the judgments made by other people; they are surely no more infallible than the judgments made by scientists and mathematicians. Still, since they share in a common tradition and pursue similar objects, adjust their acts and thoughts to fit together in a common union, and keep in consonance with daily experience, despite the fact that they do not follow well-tested methods nor are as well disciplined and critical as the scientists and mathematicians, they may nevertheless agree no less insistently and effectively than these others do.

Since what reasonable people of good character endorse, other reasonable people of good character will also endorse, to be of good character evidently is to be enclosed in a circle, endorsing and doing what is right, and being endorsed by others for doing what is right. The circle is entered by gaining a sense of what particular situations in the state require, and what is beneficial and hurtful to it and, therefore, of what is to be done in, to, and for the state. It can also be entered by forming needed habits. Both processes are gradual and accumulative. Neither ever comes to an end. There is always more to learn about what others will do and endorse; there always are endorsements and condemnations, situations, and demands for which one is not adequately prepared. Teaching and example help a person anticipate what will occur; they should be accompanied by a readiness to modify actions so as to satisfy a greater rather than a lesser right. Each is occupied primarily, not with what are objective truths, but with conformal and embedded ones, truths which are involved with and affected by that with which they deal. As we have seen, such truths are inseparable from themselves as having an objective role.[4]

Stated abstractly, just thought about, the right lacks definiteness and content. Were every situation radically new, with little in common with any other, experience and habit would consequently prepare one to deal with only superficially common aspects of a number, leaving the particularities unanticipated and untouched. Fortunately, it is not usually hard for most people to discover to what group a familiar object is commonly taken to belong. Even a child does not take long to learn how to distinguish actions having to do with parents and other members of the family from those appropriate to neighbors, strangers, or those encountered in daily life. Not long after, the child is also able to discern what actions are appropriate when dealing with the military and officials. Without hardly knowing it, as a person matures, much more is learned, and particularly how to fit well in the society and the state. An interest in what is best for the members of that state may lead to a search for a better, more intelligible, and justified way of promoting the right, while tradition, experience, the course of daily living, and the kinds of relationships endorsed as proper to maintain in the family, daily work, and the larger community, will dictate the terms on which different kinds of acts are to be assessed.

Anglo-Saxon thought emphasizes fairness, equality of opportunity, freedom of expression. It makes hardly any reference to ancestors, extends only a grudging respect to officials, expresses little more than a minimal concern for elders, and leaves the relations to parents and teachers ambiguous. Nor is it sure just how to deal with those who are immature or perverse. To replace its morality and right by others is to require changes in a thousand directions, the breaking of established habits, and an ignoring of distinctive traditions and prospects. This obviously would not be desirable unless the outcome were really better than what it replaced. Infusions from other approaches might help, provided they could then preserve what had been deservedly cherished.

Sanctioned exhortations are tradition-bound, leading to a stress on some type of activity in one place, and quite others elsewhere. As long as there are no great upheavals or crises, and situations are clearly marked off from one another, the exhortations could lead to the doing of what must be done if one is both to belong with others and do what is right. Usually a counter-tendency will be exhibited by those in power, serving to shore up their privileges and to protect their advantages, at the same time that the unpropertied and the insecure, inferiors, minor groups, those whose religious practices are viewed as being blasphemous or superstitious, and those with a disliked ancestry, are denigrated. What is right to do in a state is not always sanctioned by those in charge.

Since people form only a tiny fraction of all the beings there are, principles which apply only to them and what concerns them, are necessarily quite special, having no necessary application to the vast indifferent world outside their interests. To concentrate on people, and what they must do, so that a politically relevant right prevails, it is necessary to operate within a limited part of the universe, to ignore many of the needs of animals and plants, and to sacrifice of what should and could have been saved. Naturalists and environmentalists have tried to remedy the imbalance, but with comparatively little effect. Until they succeed, people will do much that should not and need not be done, even while doing what is right inside their state.

If a people is to be helped, without others paying an undue price, what has bearing on these must be recognized and respected. One must learn what should be done in situations which affect the interests of others as well as one's own. That is a minimal requirement. One should also know and be prepared to do what will benefit the others, since otherwise the outcome will be less good that it could have been.

Doing what is moral and right, people are to be alert to what is required from more basic and comprehensive positions. From such positions, it may be discovered that what is both moral and right may have to be qualified. So far as one is occupied primarily with doing what is right, what is needed in and by a state will of course have precedence. Although account will still have to be taken of the interests and claims of others, one will tend to do this in limited ways, unless those interests and claims are faced in areas in which the state had no or little interest.

It is often assumed that the interests of people are always paramount. I have found reason to question that assumption, and to maintain that unions, societies, states, and subhumans also have rights. It is necessary to go still further, and take account of the values and claims of whatever exists. One should then be alert to the possibility that their importance may be exaggerated, with a consequent minimization of the rights and deserts of others. Extremes will be avoided if one takes account of the good that all beings instance in different ways and degrees. It is, though, one thing to recognize that fact, and another to do something about it.

We live and function in a state. The recognition of a good pertinent to what is also outside that state can rarely be implemented by us in complete independence of our position there. The ideal good deserves to be viewed from a neutral position, but we can realize it only as people who already do, and who will continue to act together under special established conditions, demanding that we take account of specific issues. The recognition, that there is a good greater than that which a state could embody or allow, should therefore be a signal, not to abandon the state and its pursuits, but to modify these so that greater provision is made for the satisfaction of other rights than those which a state can provide.

Appeals to natural law or the commands of a God prompt some to set themselves in opposition to the state. They do not then express a warranted right to disobedience. As we have seen, there is no such right. All that can be claimed is that one has a right to other goods than those a state acknowledges, endorses, or even tolerates. Abolitionists helped runaway slaves; pacifists defy a call to arms; reformers distribute land and property. All appeal to a higher good than that which their state acknowledges. So do revolutionaries. On behalf of their objective they rob banks, terrorize the countryside, assassinate rulers. A similar appeal to a supposed primal justice can be made by thieves. They can and occasionally do claim that their acts are ways of redressing an inequitable distribution of goods and income.

Had the abolitionists paid the slave holders the going price for the slaves that they helped to escape; if a distribution of land and property were carried out with some regard for the rights and expectations of those who owned them; if an assassination could be shown to be the only means for producing a good that more than compensates for the loss of life of those in charge; if thieves were to distribute what they had taken from others, and do this wisely and well, some kind of defense could be provided. It would still remain true that what was done not only was not ethical, but perhaps neither moral nor right. Whatever the form one's opposition or resistance takes, one will have set oneself against the state and many of the stabilized expectations and acceptances of most of those who are governed. The result will be a conflict, to be settled by force, or by both sides submitting to the demands of what is able to determine their merits.

Oppression and denigration, the revolutionaries say, can be adequately countered only by a greater force or, at the very least, by a persistent opposition maintained with a passion and degree of self-sacrifice beyond the capacity of any who defend the state. Fire, it is said, must be fought with fire. But water will sometimes serve. Is this not to overlook the Holocaust, the inhuman destruction of lives and what is deeply cherished? Is it not to forget that bad people can control a multitude and turn them into slaves, hardly more than animals, puppets, or things? Were these truths slighted or ignored, one would deserve to be charged with insensitivity, and perhaps also with stupidity. Once such horrors are upon us, there is no answer but revolt, rebellion, war without remission. Well before that time, though, people should have been alert to the good a state can promote, as well as to what lies outside its provenance, and to what should have been done to prevent the deplorable situations from arising.

Those who are in rebellion are not altogether innocent; their acts are belated responses to what should have been curtailed or stopped earlier. The rise of Hitler was not possible without a wide-spread toleration of his early acts and an ignoring of his stated plans. Those under his rule had a right to revolt just so far as his decisions, though evidently authoritative, were without legitimacy, going beyond the limits of warranted governing action.

One who, on acquiring power, proceeds to reduce the good of the people, severally and together, on behalf perhaps of the glory of the state or for personal benefit, has to be opposed. The opposition can be justified if it is the best means for preserving or achieving a precious good. Strictly speaking, the new and the old are incomparable, and can be equated only by being quantified or dealt with as parts of better and worse totalities.

All rebellions come too soon, since they destroy the irreplaceable; all rebellions also come too late, evidencing a prior neglect of what should have been acknowledged and used. Well before there was a need to rebel, one should have moved to the position where this was not necessary. And once the need has to be met, what is done must not only be tailored to the task, but must lay the ground for a better outcome to be produced.

The prospective good a state faces is a subdivision of a more basic good. This is the inescapable prospect facing every state. It is like the tautological consequence that is entailed by every premiss, that to which all are unavoidably and necessarily related. Like inferences, which get to entailed conclusions in different ways, states have to move along different routes to realize it. But not unless the prospects they are to realize are realized harmoniously, will the good of all be properly promoted.

The transformation of present states into a single ideal state, embodying the common good of all of them, requires the overcoming of obstacles and the transformation of present occurrences in such a way that the good is filled out, made concrete, detailed, and present. Not until people take it to be that which is to be realized, though, will they deliberately so act that they will help their state do all it should. The achievement of an ideal outcome, of course, will come, if at all, only at the end of a long and laborious process, dependent in part on the mastery of the art of politics, followed by an adventure in so adjusting the various components of a state to one another that each is maximized, is supportive of the others, and is enabled to function as an excellent part of a single, perfected complex. At every moment, there will be a need to emphasize some factors at the expense of others. At every moment, the outcome achieved will make necessary another effort to realize the ideal. At any particular time, though, nothing more can be done than to produce a better outcome than that which had been achieved.

Artists, philosophers, scientists, and political thinkers who are forbidden to engage in their enterprises with the freedom they need, by a narrow-minded, totalitarian or misguided state, have a choice of joining an oppositional political endeavor, of conforming to the state's decrees, or of finding ways to continue their work within the narrow confines permitted them. The last is the obvious solution, allowing them to continue, though under regrettable limitations. Suppose, though, that they were forced to spend their time at exhaustive hard labor, deprived of the materials and instruments needed to carry out their chosen endeavors, or threatened with death if they did not submit to imperious, oppressive demands? They will then be faced with a choice between engaging in a persistent, effective opposition that will, more likely than not, result in serious losses on both sides, or in modifying and eventually eliminating the oppression. Only the latter can be justified.

There is no escaping the fact that every state depends on contributions made from multiple directions. If it is not appreciative of the contributions which artists, philosophers, scientists, the religious, and others make to the improvement of people and thereby the production of better contributors to the state, it will have to rest with what its rulers are able to discern, unaided by those who know more basic values, more lasting truths, and better means for producing a wellrun state. The appeal, though, must not be just to cherished objects, but to a good that makes provision as well for the existence of an excellent state. If this be so, those who oppose a particular regime must work to realize a greater good. That requires the oppressed, while attending to their own desirable objectives, to make possible the realization of one to be realized by the state as well. Political opposition no less than suppression should never be more than a means; it should never preclude anyone from engaging in more important, nonpolitical tasks.

A better state can be reached through a transformation of a bad, if one works in accord with the requirements of a greater good, of which warranted political, social, and individual objectives are specialized subdivisions. The outcome, sadly distant and painfully difficult to realize, is the best of a number of undesirable alternatives.

The good is what ought to be, a possibility whose realization so unifies what it encompasses as to make each part both enriched and sustained by the others. Conceivably, what might be right at a particular time may not be very good, but only better than the best realizable alternative. If the only right that is possible at a given moment requires injury for some but is needed in order that great benefits be obtained or great losses avoided for a greater number, the doing what is right will, while good so far as it is better than any other alternative, be bad because it involves those losses. A greater good might have been produced had the requirements of the right been ignored, but what is done will still not be entirely good. Utilitarians emphasize the greater good that is to be produced. But, because they ignore the fact that its achievement may also involve loss of irreplaceable goods, their program is rather callous, despite the cheery talk about the greatest good for the greatest number. To stop a raging fire, it may be necessary to destroy some of the houses in its path. It is good to do this. But it is also not good to do it, unless it would be good to do what is not good.

From the standpoint of a final good, whatever it requires is good. It assesses the right in terms of its compatibility with other kinds of demands, and requires that it give way if greater good could thereby be obtained. It is never right to overthrow a state, but greater good might be produced were this done, since the state might block the achievement of greater goods people should have and could obtain.

It is good that right sometimes prevail. The fact subordinates that right to the good. It is also true that it may sometimes be right to have good realized. But if it is sometimes good to do what is right, and right to do what is good, it may sometimes be good to do what is good. And if it is sometimes right to do what is good, and good to do what is right, it may sometimes be right to do what is right.

There are admonitions to heed but no rules to follow in order that the right prevail. But there can be rules to follow in order to realize the good, since this is a prospect implied by what in fact occurs. That implication can be formulated, and the result used as a rule to follow. Wittgenstein seemed to deny this. He maintained that it makes no sense to speak of following a rule because there was no way of comparing the activities in which one engages and the rule that one is presumably following. He overlooked the fact that the activities involved in following a rule are guided by the very ideal that terminates the rule's relating of what had been accepted to what can be. Understanding a rule and following it are two sides of one act, the one envisaging the implied prospect, the other progressively realizing it. That the two are in consonance cannot be known by comparing them; here Wittgenstein is surely correct. One can, though, know of their consonance by dealing with both from the same perspective, since they both deal with this, though in different ways.[5]

It is not always clear whether or not some of the great political thinkers thought that the state they urged prescribed the good or the right. Plato, Aristotle, Hobbes, Rousseau, Kant, and Bentham usually spoke as if they were concerned with a state that prescribed a special kind of good. They also took account of the nature of humanity, sometimes in an idealized, and sometimes in a familiar form, and seemed to be concerned with treating it as the source of the right that would, in fact, exist were people both mature and of good character. Their ambiguity was due in part to the fact that they were concerned with what was an amalgam of both the right and the good.

Like the right, the reasonable is exhibited in particular situations. Like the good, it offers a prospect to be realized. At one moment, it stresses the right, and at another the good in the attempt to achieve a maximum outcome of the two together.[6] Were people more than politically reasonable, they would take account of the need to achieve and preserve economic health, organizational efficiency, and social solidarity, at the same time that they promoted the prosperity of their state.

An excellent state is a perfected state. It can never realize more than a limited good, within which a number of people are ruled justly. What the people and the government of one such excellent state do not embrace, may be dealt with by other limited states. There is no assurance that all of the states will function in harmony, or that they will always be able to counter external challenges. Neither separately nor together do they make adequate provision for all the achievements of people, or take account of what they privately are and need.

One way of discovering how such limitations are to be overcome is by attending to the neglected factors and seeing how they must be specialized and qualified in order to be appropriate to actual states and their perfected forms. That approach will sooner or later lead one to consider the nature and role of mankind, a constant in every person; an historic mankind in which the constant is supplemented with what is done over time; a humanized world in which the achievements of people are preserved, function as conditions, and are joined to historic mankind; and an evaluated world where people assume accountability for what occurs in the humanized world. The Commonhealth is that evaluated world in a political form.

3. MANKIND

Each human is radically different from all others. Self-identical over an entire career, with a distinctive mind and will, each is responsible only for what each privately initiates. No study of bodily parts, no examination of the brain, no accounts which refer to duplicable occurrences will do justice to what such a person is. At the same time, despite a radical singularity, grounded in an irreplaceable and unduplicable privacy, each must be recognized to be like the rest. Were this not so, it would be incorrect to say that any one was the equal of others; each would just be incomparable and that would be the end of the matter. Nor will it do to take each to be unduplicable in privacy and duplicable in body. Not only does this lead to a division of each into two realities; it overlooks the fact a body has its own unduplicable components joined in an unduplicable way. What is common is something general. This is present in each, privately accommodated, and expressed in and through a privately possessed body.

Every human is both a private and a public person. Viewed from within, each is singular, incomparable. Viewed from without, each is like every other, a locus of the same kinds of private and public powers, due to the presence of a common mankind. This is distinct from but operates in every human, and is wholly absent from other kinds of being. It is a common essence, possessed by each in an individual way.

What is abstractable from a person is "personhood", a person shorn of all individuality. Mankind, instead, refers to a constant nature ingredient in every actual person. Where "personhood" just isolates what is common to all persons, "mankind" refers to what makes each person equal to every other. The two ideas meet in "human". That is why the same "humanity" is abstractable from every individual, and is also locatable in a specialized form in each.

Dogs have common traits not present in other beings. So do cats, horses, mountains, beaches, and clouds. Each incorporates a counterpart of mankind; each also yields an abstraction from its singularity, the counterpart of personhood. Humans differ from these others in radical ways, their mankind and personhood having features which these others do not have. Those features are not equatable with what happens to be common to a number, for what is so common are only duplicated aspects of the members of a population. Such common aspects may be adventitious, unrevelatory, merely what happen to be present in a number of cases; they need have no relation to or what is private.

Dogs and other organic beings have privacies, but are unable to exercise any epitomization of them, apart from their bodies. Unlike people they have no responsibilities, obligations, concepts, theories, superstitions, appreciations of art, or traditions. They have no ideal objectives, and are not joined together under rules and laws formulated by some of them. Their sensitivities are expressions of their privacies, unaffected by any of the developed, privately exercised specializations of privacy that people are able to achieve.

Subhuman sensitivities are so firmly and insistently expressed in bodily ways, that they prevent other aspects of the privacies from being expressed in any but bodily ways. Because the sensitivities of people do not prevent them from also exercising their privacies apart from their bodies, people are not only able to think and will, but make it possible for a common mankind to play a role both in their privacies and their bodies.

No matter how abstracted a person be, each is always sensitive, one who expresses a privacy in and through a possessed body. That sensitivity is the agency by means of which pains and pleasures are felt. In the absence of these, the sensitivity still keeps one from being wholly involved with the adventures of that body by itself or as connected with others. That is why each human is not only a person privately, but also a person in a world where each acts in bodily ways, and there provides an instance of the very mankind that is instanced by every other person.

Mankind is a combination of the constant and changing—constant because it is a single nature present in every human, and changing because it is affected by the way people use it in making themselves public and when acting on one another. Because mankind is also affected by shifts in people's relationship, mankind has a different public tonality at different times. And, since people form limited groups, some of which have no relation to others, the single mankind of them all has intensifications and qualitative features in one place that it does not have in others.

Human races do not make a difference to mankind. Still the people in them may utilize it differently, using race and other variations in bodily features to dictate the ways they behave toward one another. Were the idea of mankind in better focus, differences in ancestry and appearance would not loom as large as they now do.

The idea of mankind has been so rarely explored that it is hard to be sure of the adequacy of one's understanding of it. Yet everyone makes reference to it when speaking of other humans as persons, despite their differences in color, gender, age, and ways, and despite variations in the rights they are acknowledged to have.

The changes that varieties of dogs introduce into the nature of a collection of them is parallelled by the changes people conceptually and practically introduce into mankind by their reactions to those of different races, gender, ages, and customs. This need not occur, but there is no avoiding the difference that the varieties of dogs make to the nature of a collection of them. The bodies of dogs determine how they are to be grouped. People instead, belong to a single mankind. No matter how they differ all are persons. An attempt to reverse this observation, and claim that dogs, no matter what the breed, are all equally and intrinsically dogs, and that people, despite their equality as persons, differ essentially because of their differences in virtues, abilities, and effectiveness, is up against the fact that the privacies of dogs are overwhelmingly subject to the bodies in and through which they are expressed, while the privacies of people not only act in and through their bodies, but assess, control, and use them. Mankind is a constant and operative condition, enabling each human to have the status of a private person with inalienateable rights, and a bodily existence as a public person with inalienable rights. Canine is at best a condition always diversified, having no bearing on privacies or rights.

4. HISTORIC MANKIND

Were there no mankind, limited groups of people and their achievements would be sealed off in societies and states, and there would not be a single historic mankind, encompassing all people and their achievements. There is such a historic mankind because people live in an accumulative time. No dialectic could do justice to its course.

Whether purely formal or historical in its development, or the two somehow combined to constitute the next stage of a necessary course, a dialectic will always fail to take adequate account of the actual struggle, contingencies, and creativity that people express over the course of history. Nor will it allow for the fact that lived time is worked out through the performance of particular acts in which mankind is involved with multiple adventitious occurrences. What takes place at subsequent stages is not predestined, coming about no matter what is done; at best, it is only predictable, implied by what is present.

At the opposite extreme from the supposition that the future of mankind is predestined, is one which allows no place for the idea of mankind, or denies that it is distinct from and able to affect individuals. The acceptance of such an idea, more likely than not, is a con-

sequence of a common tendency to suppose that whatever is distinguished must be due to another particular, perhaps at a distance
where no one could encounter it. Even those who say that God is
omnipresent often speak as though he were off somewhere in or
above the heavens, while those who affirm that time is unlike space
sometimes envisage it as having a past and future spatially or temporally distant from the present. The required move takes one instead
into what is a more intensive version of it.

Space and time cannot be arrived at by going through time or space.
They are present conditions enabling different actualities to be located and thereupon separated from, and extensionally related with one
another. The integrity of neither space nor time is compromised by
being occupied. Like mankind, they are distinct from individuals, but
not set at a distance from any.

Human history extends over a region of space as well as time.
Since some of the things people do, occur independently of what is
occurring outside their societies and states, human history necessarily
encompasses less than the entire scheme of things. Since in the areas
where that history does not extend, time continues to pass, it is also
true that human history is necessarily confined to only part of a larger
temporal ongoing and can, therefore, never provide the final comprehensive word about reality. So far as it is restricted to human affairs,
history necessarily presupposes mankind as that into which it introduces its transitoriness, though only so far as mankind is expressed in
action. At the same time, mankind presupposes history as a field in
which the actions of persons are expressed.

Recognizing that words, and perhaps even theories, concepts,
and affirmations all have a history, there are some who take history to be the locus of whatever occurs. Everything that is affirmed,
it is thought, is fully embedded there. Such a claim, as we have
seen, requires its own denial. To say that all truths are fully embedded, that everything said, known, and perhaps real, is a function
of its historic time and place, is to offer an objective truth all are
being asked to accept, no matter what their time, place, and historic
setting.

Historic mankind encompasses states and societies functioning in
limited regions of space and time. It has a place for the products of
individual action, both as affected and unaffected by the complexes in which they are produced. It stretches backwards in time
toward a period when there were no states, and forwards toward a

future when there may be none, a plurality of them, a single one embracing a number in subordinate roles, or perhaps just one in which all people are encompassed and there function in a way not possible otherwise. Within that history, different states interact, compete, fight, and coexist. There, the sciences and arts are produced, preserved, enjoyed, corrupted, sometimes censored, and brought into relationship with other human achievements and activities. There, some of the past is given a role in what comes later, thereby making it possible to understand what happened by making use of what it is in its present form.

Were mankind without a historical role, what people individually and together achieved would do no more than add transient irrelevancies to a fixity. Were there a history and people, but no mankind, people would produce what was more or less preserved and used, but there would be no referring of this to a constant. Humans would be equals only as biological entities, not as persons.

It has been occasionally thought to be illuminating to imagine all people to be in history as though they were afloat on an open sea, having to do everything, including their "repairs," then and there. No recourse, it is supposed, should and presumably could be had to anything but what was then and there available; all references to anything outside the historic "ship" are therefore to be dismissed as futile. The image is supposed to justify the claim that people are inescapably forced to think and act as creatures of their time, and to justify the dismissal of all formalisms and references to ultimate conditions as idle or distracting. What is overlooked is that what is done is done by beings who exist apart from, and make use of a knowledge and skills that are not part of the "ship"; that the "sea" continues to exist and makes its own demands; and that instruments and energy will be used on what is distinct from them, coming to them from positions outside them. A ship in an open sea is repaired by making use of what it does not contain—knowledge, energy, the sustaining sea, and objects able to function as instruments.

The image of a ship on an open sea underscores the fact that what people do as well as know is embedded in history. Yet it is only because their actions and knowledge are also conformal that people are able to act pertinently toward what occurs or "needs repair". If they are not to work without plan, they must also be able to stand apart, and deal appropriately with what is objectively the case both before and while they act. Everyone, to be sure, is in history and refers to other parts of it, but if one wishes to speak of the nature of history, of a person's place in it—or of any other occurrence—in terms which do more than reflect a momentary position there, each must stand away from that particular public place and time. References to particular places and times, and to these as within a single space and time, are all made from a position outside every such place and time. One immersed in history is, so far, not in a position to say objectively what it is or what occurs there. While historically conditioned, we are able to know both the nature of history and items in it only because we are also able to stand away from ourselves as historically conditioned, and see what all are like when in it. If at least as much weight is given to mankind as is given to the particularities of history, we will, in addition, be able to envisage both from the position of their product, historic mankind.

Mankind has no analogues elsewhere. Nor has human history. The one has an affect on human privacies; the other is constituted in part by people privately bringing, what had been cherished and ought to be, to bear on what occurs. Historic mankind, as a consequence, also lacks analogues.

5. THE HUMANIZED WORLD

What is constant in historic mankind is a single space and time joined to a single mankind. What comes to be and passes away are particularities in it, the result of the interplay of its factors. Stopping at a red light, casting a ballot, obeying a curfew all occur at particular times and places framed within a constant mankind joined to history.

What is occurring passes away, but it will usually be produced by what outlasts that moment, and will itself continue to be in the present as a determinate fact. In that present, some items stand out from the others as important, while continuing to have the status of facts alongside others, thereupon giving these a distinctive tonality and enabling them to be connected in a distinctive way. When joined to historic mankind, the outstanding occurrences acquire the additional status of conditions governing what is to be done. The humanized world is historic mankind as conditioned by such occurrences.

The situation is somewhat like that which occurs when one speaks and writes. Each word is a particular, locatable at some time and place; each also has a meaning that may provide a connection for other words. When the meaning is sustained by a group, a society, or an individual, it prescribes to the words that follow, defining some of them to be appropriate and others not. In the humanized world, the prescriptions do more, determining the importance of the items embraced by historic mankind.

Outstanding occurrences joined to historic mankind constitute the dominant conditions of the humanized world. Those conditions have specialized forms governing the arts, sciences, technology, invention, religion, politics, and other specialized ventures. Today, it is common to speak of such conditions as "paradigms", and to concentrate on those which are applicable primarily to science. They are also spoken of as though they had no grounding and therefore as though no explanation could be provided for their singular status. This is a singular position.

Each enterprise makes use of distinctive "paradigms". A succession of these is conditioned by a still more basic condition, just as surely as more limited occurrences are conditioned by them. To hold that scientists always work within the confines of some such paradigm, having only a limited duration, is to overlook the condition under which different scientific paradigms occur. That condition is definitory of the nature of science, and is itself alongside other conditions pertinent to other disciplines.

Paradigms are a limited selection of crucial achievements germane to special groups. A humanized world not affected by these would be indistinguishable from historic mankind—mankind in history. Were they alone focused on, the humanized world would be just a series of outstanding achievements, bearing no sign of their human origin, and no dates marking out their time of occurrence or dominance.

The humanized world is historic mankind joined to outstanding, pivotal occurrences. The works of Homer and Aeschylus; Newton and Einstein; Plato, Aristotle, Kant, and Hegel; Bach and Beethoven—to choose but a few—are produced at particular, limited places and at specific times, but all qualify a host of occurrences over a much larger space and time. The French Revolution, the world wars, and the nuclear bomb play somewhat similar roles. Concentration on one of these leads to the separating out of a special historic set of events. Concentration on a plurality of them as belonging together, instead, leads to the demarcation of an epoch.

Narrative historians differ on the weights to be given to different contributors to an epoch. Some emphasize science, some politics, and some the arts, without necessarily denying room for others. Broad-gauged historians emphasize the unitary meaning of an epoch, and thereupon take different contributions both to be affected by and to have different degrees of importanace in it. Monographists, instead, concentrate on particulars and, often enough, ignore the divisions and connections the others introduce. All, of course, can promote knowledge and understanding. If, though, any is taken to set the limits of knowledge or action, what is claimed will lead to a misconstrual of what occurs in particular fields or over the course of a single histor y, and perhaps both.

Signal achievements must not be taken to be absolute conditions. Nor are they subordinate to nor unaffected by others occurring independently of them; to suppose that is to overlook the influence of other outstanding occurrences, and the constant in all. Nor are particular occurrences to be treated as though they were completely isolated unit items; that would be to overlook the connections they have to one another—connections which enable them to form significant wholes rather than just aggregations of distinct items ordered in time and related in space.

Were one to affirm nothing more than that workers in a given field operate within the confines of a limited outstanding occurrence having the status of a common condition, one would neglect the outstanding occurrences which are conditional for other enterprises, as well as the fact that the various conditions in a particular field and all the conditions together are subject to a more inclusive condition. At the same time, one would ignore the independent activities, resistance, and modifications to which those occurrences subject the common condition. The humanized world, as a unity of historic mankind and its outstanding occurrences, must be acknowledged if these results are to be avoided. That world is neither a society nor a sequence of societies, neither a state nor a sequence of states. Regardless of how these function, the humanized world subjects a multiplicity of occurrences to conditions grounded in what is outside them, and enables them to be interconnected with one another in a distinctive way. None of the achievements may be fully appreciated. Attended to, though, they will enable people to focus on what deeply affects historic mankind, sometimes over the centuries, though never able to fully determine what is there done.

Although communicated knowledge and truth cannot avoid being colored by terms used by historic mankind, or avoid being qualified by the humanized world, they still allow room for what is outside both, to be grasped by people making private use of their minds. The distinctive languages used to express what is then known need not alter the nature of what is being conveyed. That fact, of course, is known only because one employs powers outside the reach of a language. That is why one is able not only to use it, but to understand what it is and does.

People live together in a common humanized world and within limited portions of this. So far, they are closed off from the rest of the universe, but still impinged on by external forces. The very earth on which we live has its movements determined and its weather and seasons affected by what our humanized world does not contain. What happens inside it cannot, therefore, be understood solely by attending to what is done there. Nature goes its own way, no matter what people would prefer to have it do, or the use to which they would put it. When they act on it, they act within their humanized world, but not without impinging on what continues to be and function regardless of them. When the objects in the universe become part of that world through their bearing on people, they continue to exist independently, with distinctive natures and careers. Evidently, whatever occurs in the humanized world has a double role: each item there has its own nature and career, as well as a bearing on human affairs. A plant has a place in a home, where it is cared for and appreciated in ways it would not be, were it to grow up unattended; but it still grows as that kind of plant, and not some other.

States exist within the confines of the humanized world, where they are together with a multiplicity of items in which the states usually have no interest—art works, sometimes religion and sport, surely philosophy, and usually most personal relations. When a state brings these under its control, it so far limits expressions of creativity, and restricts the range of appreciation, but it still is unable to prevent them from having a conditioning role with respect to other occurrences, the state itself, and other states as well.

Unlike states, the humanized world makes no expressly formulated demands. Nor does it have any power by which such demands could be enforced. More inclusive than any other way of encompassing people and what concerns them, it is unable to stand apart from either except by being externally maintained. At the same time, tradition, myths, customs, unions, societies, and states, as well as the sciences, arts, religions, inquiry, and morality, have roles inside it (and smaller areas within this), making a difference to the people in them, and to that on which these act.

One bent on improving a state must sooner or later take account of that portion of the humanized world that is outside the state's interests and control, and bring it to bear on the way in which the state is to be enhanced. To do this, one must, for a time, neglect the state and its concerns, if only as a preliminary to a better occupation with what may benefit it. One then offers a plausible justification for those who occupy themselves with the pursuit of truth, goodness, virtue, beauty, the preservation and enhancement of the environment, subhumans, and the like, as having to ignore the state's immediate problems so as to attend to what may eventually benefit it. It is possible to improve the state by working on behalf of non-political goals, and ignoring and perhaps occasionally opposing what even the best of states might demand.

An occupation with a distant objective, requiring a comparative neglect of more readily realizable ones, and an occupation with objectives not directly relevant to the interests of a state are, of course, quite different. The difference is both one of degree and of kind. Were it only a difference in degree, political and nonpolitical objectives could be scaled in relation to one another, thereby allowing for a comparative justification of the pursuit of the latter as having pertinence to what a state is and does. If they differed only in kind, an adjudication of what was pertinent to the interests of the state with what was not, would require a reference to a good distinct from both, in terms of which the different concerns could be assessed. They do differ in kind but, from the position of the good, they differ only in degree. Because it occurs within a part of the humanized world, a state always makes some use of that good, and it is necessarily dependent on those who attend to it.

A state's interests are best served if some people devote themselves to promoting the good it should embody. Even the pursuit of a nonpolitical objective depends on some making sure that the pursuit is carried out in relative peace. At the very least, all concerned with what does not directly bear on the problems of the day need to make room for one another, and together should, at the very least, not prevent the state from carrying out its needed tasks.

What is to be attained subtends both the good of the state and the goods pertinent to other enterprises. It is not necessary, and often not feasible, though, for those who are occupied with the one to attend to what occupies the others. Each requires a concentration on its own problems, but in such a way that there is also room for the others to function, for these, too, have their rights, and deserve satisfaction. It is not possible to do full justice to all. The determination of what should give way and what is to be insisted on should not be left in the hands of one or the other of the contenders; each not only should leave openings for the others, but is itself to be pursued under conditions set by what is outside all. Inevitably some people would have to devote themselves to the consideration and use of goods more comprehensive than those which concern either, thereby risking the introduction of still another factor, requiring another adjudicator, and so on without end. This regress is avoided with the recognition that the various limited goods are specializations of and inseparable from one encompassing them all.

The humanized world contains what is available from humanity's past, the future as then effective, and what is now being done. Since it has no control over what occurs within it, it is unable to provide the kind of benefits a state can. Others, though, would be possible in it, were the requirements for the realization of an excellent future of the humanized world accepted by people as binding on them, since they would then act in terms of a self-imposed demand that they realize a world where great achievements in multiple areas are preserved and promoted.

When it is said that people are affected by their society or state, or by the language, power, or practices dominant in them, a society or state is treated as a conditioning achievement, perhaps placed alongside others, but sometimes subordinated to more comprehensive ones. Independent conditioning contributions may still be made to those who live in a particular society and state. Discoveries in mathematics take place at particular times and in particular societies and states; sometimes they show the effects of transitory notations and outlooks. Nevertheless, mathematics has the role of a condition applicable to all societies and states, and to what is within them. It does not, of course, impinge on more than an aspect of what occurs and is never able to do justice to acts of creativity, the qualitative, to beauty, virtue, or affection; but even if it could exhaustively explicate these, it would continue to have the status of a condition having a wide range, far greater than that possible to any society or state. It would also be both carried out in these and to be expressed in the particular ways these help determine.

In the humanized world, great occurrences all have a place. If, then, we attend to nothing outside the particular occurrences in a society and state, we will necessarily miss some humanized occurrences which affect those societies and states. Did we wish to know what those occurrences presuppose, we would have to find evidences in them of more ultimate realities. If, instead (as here) knowledge of the humanized world is to be used so as to obtain a better understanding of the state, attention would have to be directed at only that part of the world that is qualified by people's evaluations. Keeping focused on the humanized world, constituted by mankind, history, and conditioning achievements, but as confined within the limits of a state, allows one to know only a specialized fragment of that humanized world.

Were people to assume accountability for whatever happens in the humanized world, they would turn this into an evaluated world. To confine themselves to what occurs within a state, having the status of a subdivision of such an evaluated world, they would have to assume accountability for occurrences there. Were they to so confine themselves, they would live in a Commonhealth, where mankind and history (historic mankind), conditioning achievements (which, with historic mankind, form a humanized world), and the assumption of accountability, (adding evaluation to the humanized world) join to constitute a state.

The Commonhealth is that portion of the evaluated world where people are well-governed. A constant, behind and operative through the limited ideals which are pertinent to different actual states, its realization requires the subordination of all states to it. All the while, people will continue to possess privacies and rights of their own, able to be effectively exercised against both the Commonhealth and those actual states.

6. THE COMMONHEALTH AND BEYOND

Morality, religion, art, science, and economics loom large at different times, allowing for a characterization of historic periods primarily from the perspective of some one of them. As a result, we have moral, religious, and other ways of characterizing times different from our own. Occasionally, one of these special enterprises is taken to provide principles in terms of which the others are to be understood. When this is done, history, politics, and the humanized world are dealt with primarily in moral, religious, economic, or similar special terms. As a consequence, we get theories of art grounded in politics or economics; treatments of religion based on what has been learned from anthropology, psychology, or astronomy; and political theories revolving about what has been held to be true in business or the army. All are appropriate only to special areas or phases of that on which they are being applied. Sometimes they provide insights and permit one to assume a standpoint that is not altogether alien to what is being studied; but distortions and omissions inevitably occur. Art is never just a matter of economics; institutionalized religion is not just an odd way in which people act together; politics is more than technology carried out in limited and inadequate ways. Each has a nature and career of its own; none is just a function or a variant of some other.

The roads to the attainment of final goods, not the goods themselves, are correctly characterized at different times in terms of whatever factor is dominant, even though it may have been only thrust upon what is occurring apart from it. It should, though, not be forgotten that, at each step along the way, less conspicuous factors are also operative and contributive, and that there are many types of occurrence, each with its own nature and career. This would require a plurality of completely detached studies, were it not for the fact that the occurrences are all subject to the same conditions.

What is amiss in dealing with one enterprise in terms provided by another is not only that the terms are different, but that they have restricted scopes leading one to blur the fact that all are dependent on the same principles. We gain little by dealing with some topic in terms which are restatements of what occurs there. We gain a little more by dealing with it in terms which have been successfully applied elsewhere, particularly if backed by a testable method. We deal best with it, when we understand it in terms which are appropriate, provided that the differences, which further specializations introduce, are not overlooked.

Mathematics' austere objectivity, clarity, and necessity gave it a preferential status over the last centuries, and will undoubtedly always recommend it as a proper guide to the understanding of many types of occurrence. Unlike more empirical disciplines, it is not well geared to deal with the contingencies, qualities, and the ideals characteristic of the unions, societies, and states where people spend most of their lives. History is.

An acceptance of dominant outlooks at different times, as providing proper characterizations of some state, makes it possible to take the historic course of this to have a plurality of different, independently constituted periods. If this is done, one will be able to remain in rather close consonance with the obtrusive facts. But provision should also be made for what does not pass away.

To have a single history, reference must be made, not only to changes, but to a constant. If the history is to embrace all people, a reference must be made to mankind. Without it, the history would lack unity. Some of the occurrences in it might persist for a long period and affect what comes later, but what continues for a while may not be permanent, and might change at any time. Mankind, when expressed in what people do, does provide the needed constant, thereby making possible the encompassment of the adventures of humans over the ages.

Mankind provides history with a fixity in which all its changes are embedded. Conceivably, there could be a constant, other than mankind, that was unaffected by the changes occurring in the history with which it is joined. Some have supposed that such a constant has the form of a scientific or economic law, a nisus toward blissfulness, or a divinely sustained purposiveness always operative and effective. It is hard to know whether or not these just express hopes, are idle fictions, or do play some rol e. Whatever the answer, reference still has to be made to mankind. Only this is a constant that, while necessarily involved with individuals, each with an irreducible privacy, is so joined to history that all people and their activities, past, present, and future, are encompassed. The result is historic. When great occurrences are added to this, the result is a still richer whole—a single, ongoing, humanized world.[7] Within this, every empirical occurrence, qualified by people and their activities, occurs. It is, though, too broad in scope and too general in meaning to be of interest to one concerned mainly with understanding or producing an excellent state. Since the humanized world is presupposed and partly utilized by every state, it nevertheless should not be neglected; to do so, would force one to leave out references to what has an important bearing on the state's functioning.

By being affected by the humanized world in which it is located, a state is able to have a single history where great achievements play a conditioning role. Outside that state, there is also a cosmos and its raw materials—as well as people in their privacies, with their native rights, able to assess what occurs, and thereby readied to support, oppose, or be indifferent to what the state requires.

A state deals with people as public beings; they are there because they have independently expressed their privacies. As a consequence, a state not only presupposes and makes some use of the humanized world, in which a constant mankind is joined to a history of great human achievements, but is also affected by what people privately initiate and privately judge.

The humanized world exists whether people would have it occur or not, since it is the product of mankind, history, and significant products, each functioning in considerable independence of what people desire or endorse at a particular time. A state, though, depends on people acting together. Affecting them through rewards and punishments, and its distribution of privileges, goods, and opportunities, it defines individuals to be publicly accountable beings, whether or not they did anything to produce what it ascribes to them.

A distribution of advantages and disadvantages are a state's way of expressing for what and to what degree it holds people to be accountable, whether or not they brought it about or had anything to do with it. To the degree that people take the distributions to be justified, to that degree they privately assume accountability for it; to the degree that they assume such accountability, to that degree they privately accept what the state does, and thereupon turn it into part of an evaluated world.

The best of states has no more than a limited range and duration. Were there a single perfect state, encompassing all people, and having a place for all their achievements, it would still fail to embrace privacies and what takes place in them. By assuming accountability for what is done in a state, people are not only able to live under a governance within a part of the humanized world, but will endorse what occurs there as conforming to their own evaluations.

When people assume accountability for what a state does, they privately make themselves be in accord with it. Were they to assume accountability for what occurs in an excellent state framed within the humanized world, they would be well-governed, and both freely and effectively exercise their privacies in consonance with what that state does. They would then live in a Commonhealth. Viewed from without, this is that part of the history of mankind, with its conditioning achievements, whose activities are privately approved. Viewed from within a state, the Commonhealth is an ideal for it and all other states whose members privately endorse what there occurs.

The humanized world gives the Commonhealth a place in a larger history and in an area determined by the range of human nature, interests, and influence. That humanized world lacks the definiteness and power that an actual state has, but is more comprehensive and longer lasting. Not even a Commonhealth could do justice to it, for even if this were to include all people at some later date, it would not embrace all who had existed over the course of history.

To make a particular state as good as it could possibly be, is difficult enough. It is more difficult to get different states to function compatibly, even when account is taken of the fact that their particular ideals are specializations of a more basic. There is therefore little likelihood that the Commonhealth will be realized in the foreseeable future. That does not diminish its status as an ideal, subtending the ideals of all particular states. Nor is there an assured way of preventing the Commonhealth, once realized, from becoming tyrannical and, thereupon, provoking rebellions by subordinated sovereigns or the people. There is also no way to preclude the possibility that people may heed different and perhaps opposing recommendations by local authorities, sages, religious or other leaders.

The Commonhealth is a prospective, excellent state whose members accept the way it functions and its distributions of goods, honors, materials, and opportunities. It never can have more than a limited scope, fitting as it must within a larger humanized world.

The Commonhealth will exist only if people assume accountability for what is authoritatively done in the best of states. Were they to assume accountability only for this, and therefore only for the distributions that the Commonhealth makes in accord with well-enacted and justly administered laws, they would, though, inevitably ignore and perhaps oppose some acts and demands by the actual complexes in which they live, unless the Commonhealth dictated and controlled what is done within those limited area.

There is no Commonhealth unless actual states are perfected together, as a result of each being backed by people of vision who are guided by and live in accord with its requirements. That Commonhealth, dependent as it is for its realization on actual states and actual people, will remain a remote prospect as long as people do not know who they are or what they should do, for they then are not able to function properly as self-determining members of a part of a single, evaluated world. Whether it is known or not, striven for or neglected, the Commonhealth nevertheless is a realizable ideal inseparable from the good of every state and, through this, making a difference to what these do.

Were the Commonhealth accepted as a guide by states today, it would require these to attend to one another. Only then would it be possible to achieve a single, public ordered whole in a humanized world where people are held accountable and assume accountability under the aegis of a legally mediated justice. All that can now be done, however, is to so act that the realization of the Commonhealth is promoted, while it continues to act as a guide. People have to maximize themselves as private beings while acting in accord with what is required, if that comprehensive common excellence is to be realized. The result would still be less than what ought to be, since it does not encompass all that people privately can and should do.

Humans together, the complexes they help form, and what they produce, work themselves out in a present by making use of the past and the future. Inventions, explorations, philosophies, scientific theories, and art set much of the tone and pace of the day. Hero, genius, saint, and sage serve as models for the rest, providing standards for their lives and work. All play a role in the realization of the Commonhealth. They do this best, though, only if they act in the light of what the Commonhealth demands.

Today the Commonhealth is an ideal awaiting the maturation of people to the point where they know and accept accountability for what is done in a limited part of the humanized world. Those who concern themselves mainly with making use of their privacies so as to become greater masters of truth, beauty, and themselves, can be as fully a part of the Commonhealth as others can, and those others can enrich their private lives as surely as the former can enrich their public lives, for the Commonhealth can become a prospect whose realization allows everyone to do what he does best in such a way that he supplements the rest. Unfortunately, since the more remote and comprehensive a prospect, the more indeterminate it is, an understanding of the Commonhealth will not enable one to know exactly what it is now best to do.

No one concerned with solving the practical problems of the day will find that thinking about the Commonhealth is of much help. We would gain more if those concerned with perfecting particular states were to concentrate on achieving the limited objectives these could realize. Sooner or later, however, even the most short-sighted and parochial of people in these should be made to realize that their state must mesh well with others, if only to be able to function as well as it can. At that time, it might be desirable to attend to the Commonhealth in the form of a prospect. Indeed, no one with political concerns can fully ignore the Commonhealth's insistent, guiding presence, since the prospect of no state is altogether separable from that which encompasses them all; but there will always be a problem of getting the Commonhealth into better focus and the difficulty of assuming sufficient accountability for what is publicly done. The Commonhealth is an ideal guiding all states through the mediation of their more limited ideals, and requiring acceptance by privately governed people. Able to include only part of the entire evaluated world, it will, though never have room for all that is of importance to humanity.

Men assume accountability only for what comports with what they take to be right. If then they are to assume accountability for what occurs when they function harmoniously together under a common rule, this must limit its activities to what they will accept as their own, or they must accept what it requires as expressing what they really intend.

Although the claims of religion, art, and free, open inquiry are no less imperious, and may at times set justifiable limits to what the Commonhealth demands, it is ethics alone that is directly pertinent to what people do privately and publicly. Other claims, of course, are also to be taken into account, and the Commonhealth is itself open to a final, ethical assessment.

Ethics assesses every occurrence in terms of a final good. It evaluates private and public individuals, as well as the Commonhealth. The Commonhealth is a perfected state, but even if it encompassed all people, it would not do full justice to the demands of ethics. Imperious with reference to more limited states and what is in them, the Commonhealth needs supplementation by beings and acts which independently meet other demands. A perfection relevant to but always beyond every limited state, it still has beyond it a more encompassing, greater good, pertinent to whatever there be.

Action in an actual state must be carried out in such a way as to promote the realization of it as perfected, in a world where there are other states needing to be perfected as well, at the same time that the requirements of a Commonhealth and an ethics are respected. Conversely, were one bent on doing what ethics prescribes, one would have to accommodate or, at the very least, not stand in the way of what must be done in and for actual states and the Commonhealth.

Provision for the satisfaction of justified demands other than those with which one is directly concerned, may be minimal, no more than a reluctance to intrude into another area, or maximal, attended to as making claims not to be questioned or limited. Most desirable is a concern for what subtends both that in which one is interested, and that which concerns other claimants. The latter is what is done when, in the attempt to keep close to what people could accomplish together in a Commonhealth and to what an ethics requires of them, one takes account of the nature and needs of civilization. This provides both the historic course that could lead to the establishment of a Commonhealth, and makes room for ethical demands. A medium through which ethics is brought to bear on an evaluated world, civilization also provides humanity with a guide to the ways it is to act.

People can be said to be part of civilization today only so far as they act in accord with what both the Commonhealth and ethics demand. That they so act only occasionally, and then poorly, testifies to the fact that we are not yet fully civilized. A fully civilized people would function as historically significant public beings harmoniously together in consonance with an assumed accountability for demanded activities, producing both what then has to be done and what ought to be realized.

The largest arena having a history in which humans can live together, and produce works conditioning what they subsequently do, is an evaluated world. A Commonhealth is that evaluated world, kept within the borders of a state. Whenever people do what is both right and good, they act as prospective members of that Commonhealth, as embedded in an ongoing civilization. Its recognition makes it not only possible to see how present states are to be improved, but how a rich life might be possible for all.

NOTES

CHAPTER ONE

1. The lower living beings tend to answer challenges with immediate responses. Reflection occurs when the demands and the replies are separated. The higher animals use the time as an occasion for reorganizing their responses; humans occasionally use it as an opportunity to think, sometimes about what they are to do, but sometimes about other matters instead. The further back they begin, the more likely it is that they will think before they act, and sometimes about what has nothing to do with any act. Studies about action, as well as those having nothing to do with action, should take account of what occurs in the interval between demands and replies.

Associations are usually formed independentiy and without delay. Thought about them lags behind and depends on the ability of humans to maintain themselves apart, even while they are involved with one another and other beings. Combinations of collaborative and associative moves are carried out at positions behind both in privacies, which these activities presuppose, evidence, and jointly depend on. The most acute observation will fall short of noting what in fact occurs when people collaborate or when they join a collaboration to an association, and thereby are able to form communes, communities, unions, societies and states, or to understand how people are able to function together, it is necessary to take account of the fact that they exist apart as well, and, to understand what they there do.

2. A collaboration is subject, in a limited, specialized form, to a number of final conditions governing and interplaying with all actualities. (See, e.g., *First Considerations*, pp. 107 ff). Together, the conditions and actualities produce phenomena and appearances, and constitute a cosmos. In accounts of nature, one of the final conditions is emphasized in the guise of laws. These join space, time, and causal activity to produce effective structures limiting the course of actual occurrences.

I have elsewhere offered evidences and reasons for acknowledging a number of final conditions, all effective at the same time. Each determines a distinctive way in which actualities are together. Physics, art, and history make respective theoretical, creative, and guiding use of specializations of final extensions. Other enterprises take account of other conditions, or of specializations of them. Religion is occupied with a final governing value; mathematics concerns itself with a distinguished rationale; social thought is primarily interested in instances of a final determinant of mutual references; cosmology takes account of what enables individuals to interact; laws have as a primary task the effective use of a principle of justice which respects the equality of persons.

To attend to any one condition without taking some account of the operation of others is to risk distortion. An emphasis on value, e.g., if not suppiemented by references to possibility, promotes a neglect of the role that ideals play in the evaluations to which people are together subject.

Each actuality has a privacy that is more and more in control, the more advanced the actuality is. Indeed, its superiority over others is one with its ability to realize more and more self-determined specializations of its privacy, while its capacity to be an effective part of a common public world is one with its ability to impress itself on and express itself through its body. When and as a privacy is impressed on and expressed through a body it acts as an individual, dictating to but also limited by that body.

Privacies are insistent powers; bodies provide loci in and through which those privacies are expressed. Classical thought reflects, but also exaggerates the fact in its characterizations of bodies as essentially passive and of 'souls' as essentiaily active. It does, though, avoid the modern error of supposing that privacies and bodies are entirely separate realities; that only one of them is real; or that some third reality joins them. When we free ourselves from these errors, we should of course also avoid losing the insights which have been achieved in modern times—e.g., the wrong of slavery, the status of women, the diversity and possibilities of art, and the reality of submicroscopic realities.

Privacies are units expressed in and through bodies. The energy that is contained in those bodies and which, to our regret, we have learned how to release with explosive force, makes evident that the bodies may function at times in such a way as to require them to give way to multiplicities of smaller units each with its own privacy and body. These had their activities partly limited by the larger privacy and its body. To know where the smaller bodies are to be found, we must attend to the larger, and to the place it occupies; if that larger is an organism its movements will result in the smaller units within it being at places they would not be were they to act on their own—a fact that reductionistic theories, which take all changes in place to be due to mere unit bodies acting in conformity with physical laws, overlook. It is also true that the most advanced of individuals, with mind, will, virtue, and insistence, falls from a height at a rate determined by the unit entities it encompasses. Evidently, privacies make a difference to the functioning of unitary bodies and what they encompass—but are not in full control.

Although the present account requires no mastery of final conditions, or a detailed knowledge of the nature of privacies, the presence and operation of these are inescapably presupposed by it—as it is by every other enterprise. References to them, though, usually need be made only when we seek to know what is always being presupposed.

3. I was alerted quite a while ago by Nathan Rotenstreich to the importance of tradition in the understanding of people. Anthony Cua, Jude Dougherty, and Dan Dahlstrom have kept me attentive to it. The preservation of that tradition in the present must be accounted for. A recent effort (in some accord with what is here being maintained) has been well stated by Edward Casey (see note p. 394).

An emphasis on tradition should not be allowed to obscure the roie that the future plays in the present nor the ability of an objective present moment to sustain both what is inherited and what is prospective. What had been and what will be, both effectively dictate to people in the present. These respond to the resulting enriched condition, while adjusting to one another and directing their efforts at meeting a common challenge. But the past is usually more conspicuous and effective in the present than the future is, even though the past's effective presence there depends on this. The past, therefore, deseves to be stressed, at least in the beginning of a study of the nature of collaborations.

4. Hobbes played a variation on an old Biblical theme. Just as Adam was supposed to obligate all posterity to seek forgiveness by God, so Hobbes' savages were supposed to obligate all posterity to obey a sovereign. True freedom was granted only to some supposed ancestors, and was said to be given up forever because of a supposed sin or a supposed contract. Posterity does benefit—and also suffer—from what its predecessors did. That of course is not a sufficient reason to hold that it is obligated to accept what had been previously accepted in order for it to obtain what it needs. Posterity is obligated to give full weight to what enables it to get what it otherwise could not. It not only begins at a different position from that occupied by supposed predecessors; it may have a different sovereign and face different demands. The challenges it meets and what it seeks may be quite different from those that concerned those predecessors.

To justify a submission to a present power, one must show that it is legitimate and that its demands are authoritative (see part 2, chapters 9 and 10). But even a presumed ancestor's disobedience to a God should not be taken to mean that all thereafter have no right to decide how they are to respond. Granted that an absolute sovereign has legitimacy and authority, and that those who follow are to yield to it because the sovereign and his agents or heirs continue to have the same legitimacy and authority, those who come later still have the right to determine how they are to respond. They have no duty to respond to their sovereign the way their predecessors did. The response required by a legitimate and authoritative power to whom absolute obedience had been pledged by predecessors, is not identical with the response required by an equally legitimate and authoritative power faced by those who did not make that pledge.

If it be granted that disobedience by one's predecessors would break a pledge to one who may have taken them out of a savage state, it still would not follow that the successors were similarly obligated. The disobedience of those who come later presumably returns them to the state of savagery in which their predecessors were once mired, but where the disobedience of predecessors would involve a breaking of a pledge, the disobedience of their successors would instead involve only the loss of a benefit.

No people today are free to do as they like; they are obligated to act on behalf of those who benefit them, and therefore on behalf of those rulers who have made it possible for them to live in peace and to take advantage of the great gains their civilized ancestors achieved. But a present ruler, in turn, has the obligation to take account of people as they are today, with their own rights, needs, tasks, and objectives.

5. See *Privacy*, particularly p. 21. A comparatively easy means for making a penetrating contact with the *dunamis*, and to realize that this has been done, is to attain the state of being peaceably alone at the end of a fine musical performance, or by becoming involved in that or some other ab-

sorbing work of art. Sitting quietly in a great cathedral or in some other evident place of worship, on a lonely beach, in an open field, in a desert, a person has other opportunities for becoming aware of a vast reality whose boundaries are not discernible, and which seems to vanish when one tries to conceptualize it. In fact, one always merges with it.

The *dunamis* enables one, while radically alone, to continue to be together with all other beings. That power makes it possible for a human to belong together with everything while remaining apart from all. Participation in a collaboration, directed at meeting a common challenge, does not match the range of such an association.

People both belong and act together from separate, unitary privacies expressed in compatible ways. As will become evident, they join one another primarily in unions, where they are both collaborative and associated, without losing their status as independent and unique beings. In those unions they both collaborate more or less, and more or less share in a common spirit. In daily life, the two modes are intermixed in various degrees. To understand what is there occurring and what in fact should occur, it is necessary to separate out the two, understand what each is and can do, recognize a distinctive insistence in each, and use the result as evidence leading to the acknowledgment of the other. Once the opposing factors are isolated, it is possible to see, not only how they composed the initial mixture, but how they could be joined in better ways.

Collaborations, though inseparable from associations, need to be carried out independently and to be effectively joined with them, if there is to be a satisfactory union. That union must itself be distinguished from itself as involved with externally maintained conditions. The more surely the union and the conditions function independently but in harmony, the more surely do they make possible healthy societies and states.

6. See *Privacy*, pp. 20 ff.

CHAPTER TWO

1. Hegel, in some accord with classical views, held that individuals were localized forms of a primary whole. Yet he entertained this idea on his own and carried it out on his own responsibility. Some existentialists assume the opposite, taking people's common public existence to lack reality, while communicating their view by using a common language inside an arena shared with others. Living individuals make evident that these opposing accounts are supplementary.

2. Law, concerned as it is with the use of publicly available evidence and the established machinery for determining guilt and innocence, never goes beyond accountability. It cannot understand how people can with justice complain that, despite the fact that a verdict has been reached in complete accord with the prevailing rules and methods, a condemned person is in fact innocent. Those who do not permit a move beyond the consideration of

private intentions and private initiatives have the reciprocal difficulty of being unable to understand why law is ever necessary, or why legal decisions should be confined to what publicly available evidence sustains.

3. The fact that people can contribute unequally to a common union points up the fact that a union has a minimal reality, determined by an equality of contributions by different people, as well as a richer nature, determined by what people do above that minimum. The one defines the steady nature of a particular union, the other a fluctuating union with a consequent variation in the nature of a morality. The first marks the point below which people are immoral; the other, a shifting morality with which many may fail to accord at a particular time. Both will be tolerated in quiet periods, but will be condemned when crises loom.

One can view a failure to contribute maximally to the constitution of a union to be a mark of immorality and therefore to define a person's unworthiness to be considered as coordinate with others. To ask whether those who contribute less should benefit from a union as much as those who contribute more, if ethical considerations be ignored, is to ask if those who make lesser contributions are as full members of a union as the others are. They could be taken to be persons on a footing with all others, but not to express that fact in what they do, either deliberately or due to incapacity. The deliberate ones take themselves out of the union to some degree and can be dealt with in consonance with that fact. But the others may continue to be in the union. It is because they do not help constitute it to the degree that the rest can and do that the problem arises. To say that they are to be helped is to tacitly hold that there is a normative union to which all who do not withdraw belong by virtue of their being persons, and that whatever additional goods such a union possesses, due to the activities of a few, belong to all in the union. This allows for any one of a number of ways in which the additional goods may be distributed.

Those who contribute more than others often protest that if they are treated as equal to the rest they are being denied what rightfully belongs to them. They overlook the fact that whatever they achieve is but a tiny part of a huge common inheritance on which they build. They take advantage of roads, bridges, clearings, the absence of wild animals, and an established language they did nothing to produce. If they were to receive in some correspondence to what they give, they would rightly get but a small fraction of what was available.

Present collaborations and associations occur within settings jointly inherited and jointly focused on, belonging to all, but of which some have been able to make better use than others. What they achieve could be said to be just a means for making a great hoard more available to all. They could be rewarded for this, but the reward should be far less than that which is usually given or taken. From this perspective, those who contribute most to and those who gain most from their participation in a union are mainly channels through which, what all have received without asking or work, is vitalized in the present and provided with minor additions.

The text deals with the more practical issue of present inequalities and the remedies which are to be provided for those who in fact are unable to be as effective or successful as others are. The outcome, though, is the same. Benefits are opportunities to shorten the gap between the advantaged and disadvantaged. When emphasis is on individuals in the present, consideration is to be given to the maintenance of a common strong union. When, instead, attention is paid to people as living in a common present and an enriched place in ways some are able to utilize but others cannot, consideration is to be given to the fact that the union people constitute is a means by which greater goods belonging to no one are transmitted and made available to all. Those who so use it deserve honor and reward, though what they provide is no more than a minute fraction of what is there for everyone.

4. Sometimes the intimacy people enjoy with one another prompts them to attend to the same focal object; sometimes the fact that they are occupied with the same focal object leads them to become more and more intimate. Still, it is not uncommon to find members of a synagogue, church, or mosque, while professing to worship the same God, distinguishing themselves sharply from those who attend some other synagogue, church, or mosque. Nor is it uncommon to find well-integrated families, where the members are strongly attached to one another, attending to different Gods or having different ideal objectives. Evidently, though a commune has people intimately together and focused on a common object, the two aspects are able to be effective in some independence of one another.

Were a focusing on some common object carried out in the absence of any intimacy, people would be associated adventitiously and prospectively; were they intimately involved with one another without having a common focus, they would be associated only as comrades in a limited area. The intimacy and focus are both present in and affect one another in a well-functioning commune.

5. Charles Sanders Peirce was here, as he was in other areas, a pioneering spirit whose views are becoming more and more reflected in current discussions. He held that experienceable, accumulative knowledge is possible only to an ever-expanding and continuing 'community'—strictly speaking a 'commune'—of scientists. Unfortunately, it is not entirely clear whether he thought that they constituted that truth, possessed it, or provided the only adequate formulation of it. Nor was it clear whether or not he thought there ever would be a time when the final truth would be attained, even in principle and in general, if not in details. See, e.g., *Collected Papers* 5.353, 5.407. But Peirce never confused it, as some of today's philosophers of science do, with a collaboratively constituted whole that lasts only as long as people happen to accept some common theory. The commune of scientists is centuries old, and has an apparently indefinitely long future, joined to a sequence of collaborations, each having a much shorter span.

6. A sustainer of a supreme value might be known through a contact made possible by prayer. People might be led to acknowledge it by having prophesies confirmed. Although their acceptances may not be able to withstand the scrutiny of a sceptical reason, they may still be no less reasonable than hundreds made in the course of daily living or than those which back the scientific assurance that nature is intelligible, and can be known through a use of scientific method quickened by insight and the imagination of gen-

iuses. Of course, all communal acceptances may be mistaken, thereby revealing them to be mainly maintained through shared attitudes and a common focus. That need not jeopardize their existence or reduce their efficacy.

7. There are many today who hold that all knowledge is theory laden, precluding a knowledge of anything, except from the perspective of some theoretical account. For them, facts are qualified by theories but not conversely. But it surely is true that many theories are the outcomes of attempts to provide an explanation for what is encountered. At both times, theories and facts are acknowledged in different ways, and in some independence of one another. When brought to bear on one another what results expresses something of both. Theories and facts yield a factualized-theory or theorized-fact, depending on which is in ascendancy. Ideally, each will be given full weight, and will be accepted only so far as it allows for the full presence of the other.

One betrays a formalistic mentality by insisting on the dominating presence of theories. Nothing is changed in principle when the theories are allowed to be smudged by being expressed in daily language, or the facts are selected under the guidance of some accepted categories. A radical empiricism, instead, over-insists on the dominant presence of facts. Nothing is changed in principle when the facts are translated into logical expressions, or the theories are reached through an abductive inference.

Theories and facts have different origins, and different degrees of effectiveness. The outcome of their juncture is something new. It is this which pragmatism attempts to express by remarking on the transformation that formalisms undergo when applied. Pragmatism, though, will never be more than a half of a philosophy if it fails to allow that both what is expressed and what is encountered are changed on being joined. It is necessary to acknowledge the independence of both sides, and also to affirm that their combination yields a new result, itself able to be formally restated and experienced. All the while the contributing factors will continue to have a status apart from the combination they make possible.

Formalism, empiricism, and pragmatism all attend to genuine occurrences, but arbitrarily take what is focused on alone to be, or to be basic. They have their counterparts in social and political accounts which place primary emphasis on or give a dominant role only to laws, custom, ruled-governed customs, or a 'living law'. All tacitly assume a position in a privacy, and there attend to what everything specifies—ultimate conditions, irreducible actualities, and the *dunamis*—in different ways and degrees. The refusal of current thinkers to deal with metaphysical issues, or to accept the results of those who do, is evidenced by their radically one-sided, truncated accounts.

8. Some neo-Marxists have discovered that art and other parts of civilization are not functions of economic forces. The point, won over a long course of struggle among different branches of Marxism, would have been obvious, had attention been paid to the nature of human beings and all the different things which concern them deeply. An interesting summary of some of the basic issues is provided by Wm. J. Morgan, "Social Philosophy of Sport: A Critical Interpretation," *Journal of the Philosophy of Sport*, X, 1984.

9. People who face a common challenge may, of course, act at cross

purposes, and people who mesh well together may not attend to a common challenge. They may act selfishly when cooperation would be most to their advantage; they may work well together but for no discernible reason. Alliances collapse because of the first; over-trained teams fail because of the second.

10. There are too many variations, similarities, cross-currents, and interchanges between East and West to allow for a rigid division between them. A concentration on these two regions also invites a neglect of the rest of the world. Communes and communities are to be found in all; in all, too, there are nations and organizations. Distinctions made between East and West reflect more their long traditions and hallowed teachings than radically different ways in which those in them exist and function together. The sharpening of their differences and the ready location of them in separate areas, though, helps make the differences between a commune and a community more evident, and thereby makes possible a better understanding of both. F. S. C. Northrop's *Meeting of East and West* presents an arresting, original account of basic differences between East and West, with an illuminating treatment of variations within each, but at times tends to oppose them too sharply.

CHAPTER THREE

1. Humans are not just bodies. Nor are they just public beings. Each lives a body and acts in public by insistently expressing an irreducible privacy in and through it. The origins of each individual and the explanation of the ability to make intimate contact with others, as well as of the ability to create and appreciate works of art, find explanation in the acknowledgment of the *dunamis*. (See above, p. 22ff, and *Privacy,* pp. 21.) Most of those who have signalized the *dunamis* have been content to deal with it as an essential contributor to ontology (Plato), tragedy (Aristotle), metaphysics (Taoists), politics (Rousseau), music (Schopenhauer), psychology (Jung), time (Bergson), or cosmology (Whitehead), though not always without some regard for its presence elsewhere. Its acknowledgment, as we have already seen, is required if one is to understand any union, and, therefore, eventually the societies, states, and other complexes in which unions are constituents.

2. Edward S. Casey, taking a quite different, phenomenological route, has come to a somewhat simiiar conclusion. (See *Review of Metaphysics,* vol. 37, 1983; pp. 77 ff.) To explain how we could know the past, he found it necessary to refer to a "place-oriented" memory, able to operate apart from a mental act of recollection. Provision should also have been made for the "memory" that a union uses. And an occupied grounded space—the locus of the contrast that objectively sets human beings apart from all else—should also have been acknowledged. When this is done, one is in a position to see how it is possible for a society to provide a way in which people can be together in the present as beings who are affected by what had been and might be, as well as by the territory in which they live.

A present, having a past and future ingredient in it, when joined with a region of space, is spread out as single and undivided, and the region is given a role in the present. The sun, moon, clouds, and oceans are there dealt with as pertinent to people. When faced as sources of the benign and malign and joined to an enriched present, despite the fact that they are not within human control, they become part of an effective relevant condition affecting the way people act together. That condition, with those joined individuals, helps determine the nature and course of a society.

    3. A tradition is inseparable from what should be. When this dominates over the inherited past, it takes the form of an ideology, to be maintained against oppositional natural forces.

    4. In various books, but most particularly in *First Considerations*, actualities were found to yield evidences that there are final conditions effectively governing all. In *Beyond All Appearances*, what was empirically known was discovered to yield evidences of people and other actualities, as existing apart from one another. In *You, I, and the Others*, and especially in *Privacy*, the use of such evidences made it possible to note the various distinct private powers that humans possess.

Since the present study is concerned with people as together in various basic ways, it properly began with them as they daily exist, at once interacting and belonging together. Instead of envisaging them solely in their ideally pure forms and examining the ways these could be ideally joined, account is then taken of the main combinations their collaborations and associations actually yield, while remaining alert to the existence of their privacies and the fact that they are together in many different kinds of complexes, among which societies and states are the more conspicuous and important.

    5. Rousseau's "Men are born free and are everywhere in chains" is obviously untrue. A child is born into a family, a commune, a community, and other complexes; it is legitimate or illegitimate, free or enslaved, to be fed and taught along special lines, addressed in a particular language, etc., etc. It could not be born free unless it could be born as just a private being; but it immediately enters a public world with well-established ways into which it must be better fitted. What is needed is a change from the onerous, discriminatory, hurtful limitations to which some infants are subject from the moment of birth, into others which allow them to mature both as individuals and as members of a union, society, state, and other complexes.

    6. A person can be *of*, *for*, *in*, *with*, and *within* a union. As a father *of* a family, he is a demarcatable portion of it, without a status of his own. *For* the family, he is a representative of the whole. *In* the family, he interacts, usually with his children and their mother, producing a family with them. *With* the other autonomous unit beings there, he divides his family into a number of interacting parts. If he is the financial support or a disciplinarian, he is *within* the family, exercising some autonomy, while epitomizing the family from a distinctive angle and with a distinctive emphasis.

These different ways of belonging to a family have counterparts in the ways people belong to a society. Not only are they distinguishable there; they can also represent, and therefore be *for* the society. They are *in* it, as well, able to act on one another. *With* the others, they make possible a way of subdividing the society. And, since they are autonomous, they are also able to be *within* it.

Individuals, though, cannot be *with* a society, since they do not subdivide it. Nor can they be *of* a society, for they are not demarcatable portions of it. So far as they are accountable for their unions, they are *for* a society; as constituents of a union, they are *in* a society; and as exercising some autonomy, they are *within* it. Since institutions are constituted in ways somewhat similar to that in which society is, one can properly identify a similar set of ways in which individuals are related to institutions. No account will have yet been taken of them as private beings, or of their status as distinct unit members.

7. A power is an ability to compel something else to exist or act in a particular way. Since everything makes a difference to whatever it encounters—even to what dominates it and effectively dictates how it will function—the most feeble and malleable of entities must be credited with power enough to be able to qualify whatever acts on it. The fact is embarrassing to those who credit all power to a complex, whether this be a commune, community, social union, society, or state. If, as is sometimes done, individuals are taken to be localized inversions of the power of some such complex, it will still be necessary to credit them with power of their own, enabling them to act on one another and to make a difference to the outcome of the complexes' action on them. If, instead, all finite beings are taken to be created, it will have to be said that they inescapably resist any intrusion by that creator, and will themselves affect and be qualified by it when they deal with it. If they did not resist it, they would be indistinguishable from nothing. And if their presence made no difference to their supposed creator, they and it would have had to be completely cut off from one another.

A theory of creation necessarily ends with a creator and created relevant to one another, with powers independently exercised. To maintain, then, that a God, as before or apart from an act of creation, is exactly what he had been before or in the absence of creation, is in effect to hold that nothing was created.

8. The copresence of sequential items within an indivisible present is a central idea in Whitehead. The fact that he was here deeply influenced by Bergson and perhaps Alexander does not detract from his recognition and clear original use of the ideas. He did not, though, make evident how different moments, distinct from one another in a sequential order, could also be indissolubly together within a larger stretch of present time. For an attempt to deal with that issue, see *History: Written and Lived*, pp. 145 ff. Related observations are applicable to space. An occupied region is only mathematically divisible, but there could be smaller actualities within the confines of a larger, each of which occupies its own indivisible portion of space. As possessed by the larger being, the smaller are distinguishable, but not distinct parts of the larger. See *Reality*, ch. IV.

9. On the distinction between accountability and responsibility, see particularly *You, I, and the Others*, pp. 29-38; *Privacy*, p. 173.

10. The topic is explored in *History: Written and Lived*, ch. 6.

11. We here come close to the position taken by astrologers. They

too take the course of astronomical bodies to play a role in human affairs. They also claim that what they say is precise and therefore scientific. For them, it is primarily or only related planets that exert an "influence", and which directly affect individuals because of their date of birth, and crucially affect their later activities. The recognition of the relevance of astronomical bodies (and geographical locations) on human affairs, does not, though, require one to subscribe to such or other types of determinism or fatalism, or even to suppose that the bodies and locations are any more than conditions with which unions interplay, and then only so far as they are societally qualified, and prompt responses from those who are together in the union.

12. Jainists are dedicated to the truth that every living being has value. Their refusal to extend the acknowledgment of value to what is not alive, forces them to suppose that there is a deep chasm separating one part of the universe from another. Panpsychists avoid that difficulty by taking everything to have a "psyche"—and therefore in some sense to be alive and sensitive—but at the price of being unable to allow for genuine nonliving beings, as irreducible and as real as the living.

An acknowledgment of a difference between the living and nonliving does not require a denial of the ubiquity of value, or the fact that living beings both express themselves in and through, and are limited by, their bodies. People interact with inanimate beings, and these interact with one another. To scale the values of the inanimate in relation to humans and to the other animates, it is not necessary to suppose that all of these are parts of a single continuum; differences in grades of value can be possessed by entities disconnected from one another and quite different in kind.

The issue is bypassed when what is inanimate is taken to have a value only so far as it serves the ends of humanity, and perhaps other living beings, or when inanimate beings are taken to be arbitrary, demarcated portions of a single, indivisible field. It is hard to determine the value possessed by a mountain in contrast with a lake, but their encompassment of different things in different ways testifies to a difference in them, just as their independent functioning makes evident that they are not arbitrarily carved out by us from an undifferentiated whole. The differences they make to what they encompass differ in kind and effectiveness from those which living beings introduce. The living locate what they encompass in a gross macroscopic world, and also impose new determinations on the items within their confines. Where the one inevitably sets its parts in a frame having its own nature and relations, the other at times also qualifies and limits the activities of what it encompasses. Natural beauties are like the former, created beauties like the latter. In the first, a unity provides limits for an embedded multiplicity; in the second, a unity is so imposed that the parts are related in new ways, without abrogating the relations already connecting them.

Unless realities are all unrelated and therefore have no bearing on one another, they must belong together in a single unity constituted by themselves and a relation. Unless they could not ake any contribution to any whole in which they were located, they must have some status apart from one another and every whole.

Ultimate particles are distinct entities; they are also related in space and time. Their activities as distinct units need not be affected by the ways they are related, but if they are within organic beings or in beautiful wholes, they will inevitably be affected by the adventures of these. Where people move, there their particles will also be; when flowers attract birds and insects, the particles in both are subjected to new adventures. All the while the particles have their own status and adventures in a free fall e.g., they will make the whole in which they are interrelated undergo changes in position.

Reductionisms overlook the constraints and transformations to which parts are subject by the wholes in which they are, as well as the complusions to which the wholes sometimes subject them. Monists overlook the difference that ultimate particles make to the movement and changes of the whole. Both so exaggerate the role of one factor that the truth underscored by the other cannot be accommodated. Neither, therefore, is prepared to deal with the difficult issue of determining when and how and to what degree their acknowledged entities make a difference to one another.

13. A privacy acts in accord with its acceptance of the body, and thereby achieves a public role; a body acts in accord with its acceptance of the privacy and thereby makes a difference to the way a person lives. Guided by the prospect of being private and public maximally, each individual can become a well-unified private and public person. Because the body is relatively passive with reference to the privacy, some control is always exhibited; so-called "incontinence", or lack of control, is control below a desired maximum. So far as a body is affected by a well-directed privacy, virtue is expressed; so far as the privacy is affected by a controlling body, an attitude of practicality is encouraged. Character is formed through a union of the two.

These characterizations partly coincide with some of Aristotle's primary distinctions. For an excellent, more classically grounded account of the nature and import of virtue and vice, and related issues, see Robert Sokolowski's *The God of Faith and Reason*, chapter 6.

14. This is not Rawl's version. His people, in a supposed initial stage, are rational, aware of one another and of the diference between social advantage and disadvantage. Evidently they are already socialized. The contract they are imagined to have made certifies what they decided to do, and then is supposed somehow to achieve the status of a pledge that is never to be broken. More traditional theories of the contract, instead, assume that people are asocial before they contract with one another, but somehow are able to agree to agree. Although he avoids that flawed idea, Rawls does not advance our understanding by his imagining isolated rational and decent human beings promising one another that what they decided was right to do will be carried out in fact. The imagined situation allows one to see what the noble might endorse; it does not tell us how actual societies or states originate, what they can do, or how actual people can and should act in them.

15. Any view that takes seriously the existence of a plurality of distinct beings is inevitably driven to acknowledge final conditions able to relate them. Recourse need not be made directly to those conditions, however; attention can be restricted to limited portions of the world where some finite entities are identifiable as instances, loci, or mediators of those conditions.

If accounts of society and state are to be completed, it is necessary to acknowledge that what is distinct both from unions and the people in these, are such instances, loci, or mediators of what is irreducible, insistent, and final. Descartes saw the issue with a clarity his successors did not. Taking mind and body to be finite "substances", exhaustive of what exists through time, he looked to a transcendent God as alone able to relate them. Existentialist also try to acknowledge human minds and bodies without taking account of the control the first exerts on the second, and the limitations to which the second subjects the first. One consequence is that they find themselves unable to cross the gap between humans and what else there is.

It is of course not necessary, with Descartes, to suppose that the universe is divided into minds and bodies, nor to suppose that the only transcendent condition able to join them is a God. Nor is it necessary to suppose that privacies are only incidentally and avoidably connected with bodies. People are unities in which privacies, while able to exercise some functions without any public role, always partly express themselves in and through their bodies.

16. In his exhaustive, and sometimes exhausting examination in *A Study of War* (the enlarged second edition of 1965), Quincy Wright takes wars to be due to a failure to preserve an equilibrium in a number of areas, one of which has to do with values. It is not evident from his account whether the other reasons are supposed to be altogether distinguished from this; nor is it clear just how seriously opposed outlooks must be in order for them to provoke violent acts by one or more. Greater weight should have been given to the roles that stupidity, ineptitude, and ambition play, and the fact that some think war is an eminently desirable way to obtain what they want or for making a people associate more firmly and on a deeper level than they had before. These observations should not be permitted to obscure the importance of Wright's basic, wide ranging study.

CHAPTER FOUR

1. There is an old puzzle, focused on by Plato, as to how there could be more than a single mathematical one, and how anybody could arrive at it by adding or subtracting from some other eternal number. The problem arises because numbers were conceived by him to be in an eternal realm, allowing for neither change nor action. The difficulty is avoided with the recognition that mathematical truths and operations occur in a domain in which fixity is joined to a root transience. That domain does not reinstate the society in a formal guise; it has its own distinctive nature and content, produced through the interplay of the *dunamis* with what abides forever.

2. What truth is in the realm of knowledge, conditioning is in the realm of social life, at once referential, operative, and involved with what has a reality apart from it. We have here another illustration of the fact that whatever there is has a nature of its own, makes itself manifest, and is involved with others.

3. Adumbration is an inseparable part of an objective truth, being

the means by which the copula and its cognates enable the components of the truth to converge on the object that the truth articulates. See *Reality*, pp. 57 ff., *Modes of Being*, pp. 62, 63; *Beyond All Appearances*. pp. 106-7. The idea is critically examined by Robert E. Wood in "Weiss on Adumbration" *Philosophy Today*, winter, 1984, pp. 339-348.

    4. Hegel's recognition of the inescapable universality of such supposedly indicative terms as "this" and "here" began a dialectic in which universal was added to universal until they somehow summed to or terminated in one that was all-inclusive. The acknowledgment of the adumbrative dimension of objective truths stops his juggernaut at the beginning. If this could not be done, it is hard to see how it could ever be brought to a halt.

Contemporary thinkers, who hold that all knowledge is confined within a single theoretically or linguistically expressed whole, stop where Hegel found it possible and necessary to move on to better and better embedded forms of what was for him also radically conformal and objective. He saw, as they do not, that if one wishes to encompass universals of a particular kind, such as those expressed in a language, one must make justifiable moves beyond them. I think, though, with Kierkegaard, that Hegel cannot, any more than those contemporaries can, find a place for the existence and activity of individuals.

    5. The laws that the sciences state, if actually operative, necessarily dictate how one will conduct experiments and use instruments. Directly, or through the help of technology, the knowledge of such laws helps people to fit better into the scientifically known world.

It is unfortunate that the current recognition that scientists form a "community" of investigators is thought to compromise the objective truth of what they embed in consonance with their community's outlooks and practices. It is no less unfortunate that Galileo, Descartes, Leibniz, and Newton did not see that their objective truths were also both embedded in and conformal to the world in which they lived. The fact, though, that scientific theories are subject to practical and social conditions, values, meanings, and roles, does not mean that their objectivity has been compromised.

    6. An examination of some of the main similarities and differences between art and other disciplines is discussed in *The World of Art*, chapter 2. Chapter 3 pays particular attention to the similarities and differences between science and art.

    7. In *Reality*, pp. 144 ff., it was shown how one could understand the law of contradiction to be specialized by every assertion and the reality to which this answered. In *Modes of Being*, and in subsequent works, it was shown that ultimate conditions play a role in the constitution of familiar objects, and contribute to the nature each has as a unity interrelated with others.

What we think and know are affected by ultimate conditions. These enable thoughts and knowledge to have an inescapable universally operative sanction. It could be plausibly claimed that knowledge will so far be a function of an alien influence, precluding it from being appropriate to what exists apart from it, were it not for the fact that the ultimate conditions govern both knowledge and the known.

Metaphysically-tempered thinkers, concerned with obtaining final answers, would here remark that what the ultimate conditions affected must have a knowable nature apart from these, or could not intelligibly be said to be present and able to be affected by those conditions. It perhaps suffices now to reply that knowledge relates items which are distinguished but not separated from denser versions of themselves. Making use of ultimate conditions to connect the knower with an aspect of what is external, knowing always thrusts beyond that with which it is explicitly concerned. What it reaches is known as apart from but accommodative of it.

Similar attempts to look at particulars in fresh ways, and to provide reports which embody, while leading one into what is basic and permanent, are prominent in theology and religion. They are carried out in other enterprises as well. Psychiatrists make one of the attempts evident in their efforts to note the inadvertent gestures, slips, and errors of their patients. The closest most of us come to what these do, is to make ourselves attend to what occurs in new and unexpected circumstances. Were we to make better use of other inquirers as teachers and guides, we would undoubtedly make fresher, subtler, and more arresting observations in society and elsewhere. Because all people are at least dimly aware of what is partly captured and focused on in whatever is done or understood, all are able both to appreciate what others have achieved and to benefit from the openings into reality that they provide.

Since what is at the fore and what remains behind are connected, it is not correct to set the topics of any discipline in radical opposition to others. The humanities, though, since they are mainly interested in what occurs in the human milieu rather than in the cosmos, and in teaching rather than in training those who are to benefit from them, remain alert to the connection between what is and is not to the fore to a degree that those involved in other enterprises usually are not.

Social study's occupation with particulars does not require that one be ignorant of or ignore the realities already involved with these, or to be unaware that there are other realities besides the investigator, able to be better known than they initially were. Like all empirically oriented inquiries, social study rightly looks to other sources for knowledge of what else is relevant to the presence and functioning of the items with which it is concerned.

8. The adjustments required here exhibit one form of a more widespread type of activity in which entities take account of one another. In some of these, one side is overwhelmingly dominant, but the outcome of its activity necessarily depends on its acting in some accord with what is being dominated.

When people creatively produce works of art, overcome scientific difficulties, or solve mathematical problems, as well as when they work and pursue crafts or act responsibly, it is they who are dominant, and their contribution to the result conspicuous. When, instead, they interpret a text, make discoveries in nature, or adapt themselves to circumstance, the emphasis is on the confronted. At both times, they begin by guiding themselves by what is able to satisfy a lack in them, while what is external is faced as having no need of them.

Artists begin with a felt lack in themselves that nothing available could ever fully overcome. Their experience of that lack is undergone as a distinctive emotion, requiring and quickening the artists' actions. That emotion is expressed in acts of creativity in which the artists' insights, objectives and rhythms are united in the course of the production of a unified work.

The texts that people interpret are like the world that is to be understood, in having problems and solutions dictated primarily by what is confronted. An interpretation of a text involves a yielding to it at the same time that meanings are produced which the text is to sustain. Success in producing a satisfactory interpretation is attained when it enables a text to remove blocks to understanding how humans belong together and interact with one another in special circumstances.

9. This idea of commonsense is close to that which Aristotle identified as enabling us to understand how we knew that what we touched was the very object that we saw. Neither seeing nor touching by itself could tell us this. Recourse has to be had to what is distinct from both, able both to contrast their objects and to identify what could have them as aspects. Were the contrast and identification intellectually produced, one would not only often do so comparatively late and might introduce alien notions, but would not yet reach that which was sensibly known. The common locus of the touched and sought has to be identified by a sense, less specific than, but pertinent to these. "Commonsense" as I am using it, though, is not limited to what is sensed. In closer accord with modern usage, it refers primarily to the unreflecting, habituated, more or less successful ways in which we identify and adjust ourselves to what is daily confronted; sensing is one limited way in which this is done.

10. For a collection of Peirce's observations about the way to obtain explanations, i.e., to carry out abductions, see my "The Logic of the Creative Process" in *Studies in the Philosophy of Charles Sanders Peirce*, edited by P. P. Wiener and G. H. Young.

11. See *Collected Papers*, 1.121, 1.316, 2.212, 5.47, 5.603-4, 6.418.

12. The trickery to which gamblers are alert is matched by the social inquirers' "unrepresentative sample", and their "lady luck" is matched by a "fortunate discovery of a meaningful correlation". Students of society abandon theories that are no longer successful; gamblers do something similar when they stop frequenting a particular casino or racing track as one where their successes are no longer likely. Both so far allow that a theory that had worked for a while may work no longer. At those times it may be thought that the theory is not applicable, because this was not the time or place for its application.

13. Observation, too, can be viewed as a type of inference, even of an abductive inference, if one follows Peirce's lead. (cf. *Collected Papers*, 5.181) But that will preclude our ever observing what it is from which an abductive inference takes its start.

14. A careful characterization of what is used in rules and inferences leads to a distinguishing of three ideas: the truth of a P or a Q as directly referring to something making it true; the truth-value of P and Q in "If P then Q"; and the truth-claim that is made by the premiss of an inference and

transferred to the conclusion, preliminary to making the Q a bearer of a truth referring to something apart from it.

To move validly from the truth of P to the truth-value of P in "If P then Q", we follow a rule for converting the truth of P into a truth-value and this into the truth-value of Q; we then proceed to convert the truth-values of P and of Q in "If P then Q" into truth-claims by P and Q in the inference. Each step involves an inference. We will not yet have inferred to Q. To do that we not only have to pass from P to Q, but will have to reverse the process (for Q) which we followed when we moved from P as true to P in "If P then Q". Only if we convert Q's truth-claim into the truth of Q, do we make it parallel to the P we had initially taken to be true. If the P with which we began was not true, the Q at the end of the inference could not be certified as true. Validation of inferences do no more than justify truth claims. When we reason from a premiss P which is true, we wish to end, not with a Q making a truth claim, but with a true Q, on a footing with the initial true P.

No actual infinite regress is involved in holding that each step's validity itself depends on the acceptance of a truth, the use of a rule, and the carrying out of an inference, for the validations need occur only after one has in fact made a single, unexamined inferential move from the truth of P to the truth of Q. Valid inferences need not be preceded by validations of distinctive stages in them.

Chapter Five

1. A more extended examination of the topic is to be found in *Nature and Man*, pp. 3 ff.

2. Features present in an actual occurrence are not present in the possibility being realized. A critic will be quick to ask whether or not those features were possible. The question is equivalent with one that asks whether or not a possibility is realizable, for realizability is one with being able to acquire determinations.

The determinations of a possibility are that possibility in a limited form, the possibility realized. From the position of the possibility its realization is just a subordinate possibility, and therefore not able to make the possibility be actual and determinate. As outside the compass of the possibility altogether, the realization is unanticipatible and, of course, not explicable from the position of the possibility.

From neither the side of the possibility nor the actuality, can full account be taken of the other. The acknowledgment of both requires the acceptance of both of them as terms in a relation not adequately characterized from the position of either. The determinate features present in an actuality were possible; so far, they are the possibility in delimited forms. They are, though, not part of the possibility before it is realized, being produced only in the course of its realization.

An actuality continues into a possibility as an indeterminate version of itself; a possibility is the inseparable terminus of a present actuality's thrust. If we take our stand at the relation, we adopt a position where the actuality and possibility have the status of terms, connected implicatively. In a process of causality they are connected dynamically and progressively. A consideration of prospects—i.e., possibilities as relevant to human concerns—adds to this account the fact that people in the present both focus on possibilities and use them as guides.

3. An examination of the nature of the Golden Rule and the subordinate cases for which it allows is to be found in *Man's Freedom*, pp. 151 ff.

Chapter Six

1. The right of a person to have a publicly appropriate life is grounded in a privacy involved with a body and expressed in a public world. That right does not follow from the nature of privacy. If it did, a privacy would define the merits of what occurs publicly, or of what enables one to live with others. Nor does the right follow from the nature of a society (or state)—that would preclude a warranted objection to what prevents one from developing as a private being while living under a common governance.

Private beings have inalienable rights so far as they express their inalienateable rights in and through their bodies. Both kinds contrast with a bestowed right, a right that is no more than a privilege a particular society (or state) finds it desirable to grant at a particular time.

There is neither an inalienable nor an inalienateable right to marry one's cousin or to vote. These are rights bestowed. Tradition helps determine whether or not the first is acceptable; a publicly maintained justice determines to whom the other is to be extended. For a further examination of rights, see *Our Public Life*, chapters 2 and 3.

2. If posterity had no present rights, we would not be obligated to make provision for posterity's healthy existence. We are obligated; we do have a duty toward posterity. Since it does not exist, a society (and a state) must serve as a reservoir for the rights posterity may exercise. Although we cannot satisfy the rights posterity will in fact possess, we now have a duty to see that those rights are also respected and satisfied in the form that they now have. Since we hold those rights in trust for those who may later be able to exercise them on their own, our relation to posterity is, therefore, somewhat like our relation to those who are our wards. We should act as surrogates on behalf of others not now able to exercise their rights.

3. Privacy and body, thought and action, laws and occurrences, societies and states are mutually relevant, and therefore able to make a difference to one another. Whether, as is the case with privacy and body, one dominates over the other, or whether (as may sometimes occur with societies and states) they are close to being equally effective, each must be pertinent to the other. Otherwise, they would not be able to be together in a single

unity. Both when one of them is dominant, and when they are more or less equal in effectiveness, something produced by the one is used by the other.

4. The acknowledgment of rights need not and should not be taken to apply only to people or to the living. Every item has a nature making an essential claim to be and to continue. Waste is wrong, not only when it does away with what might be of value to people, or because it reduces what is thought to be God's bounty or property, but because it destroys something of value and an entity's right to this, without an adequate redressing of the wrong. The fact is not to be exaggerated, a prospect always tempting to defenders of animal rights and of untamed wildernesses.

5. If entomologists kept their terms neat, they would not speak of "social insects." Insects are not in societies; they have no morality, traditions, or myths. Colonies of ants are just that, colonies. There, a number of inter-locked, distinct individuals are subtended by a single, ineffective privacy. On this, see *Privacy*, pp. 22-23.

CHAPTER SEVEN

1. I have found, in speaking to those who are experts in the thought of some great thinker, that there is no criticism, suggestion, or novelty that can be mentioned without one being confronted with a text, a turn of phrase, or a reasonable interpretation that can be understood to have anticipated what is being said. This shows, I think, that great thinkers do not fit neatly within the frame their disciples or tradition impose on them. It is also true that the defenses offered make it difficult to provide a coherent, warranted statement of the thinker's view. Although Plato is no Platonist, Aristotle no Aristotelian, Kant no Kantian, and so on, and therefore in fact different from what text books and histories describe, it is also true that each has some important and distinctive things to say. The criticisms in this work are direct-ed at some of these. If the criticisms are justified, qualifications and counter-examples will help one develop another, better view.

Were every fundamental truth already discerned by some great thinker, it would still be necessary to engage in the philosophic quest afresh, in order to provide a coherent account that brings to the fore what had been slighted, and qualifies what was central but has little merit. The new account, though flawed, may still constitute an advance in its concern for what is important, but that had been not dealt with adequately. If the whole makes an advance, it will require engagements in subsequent intellectual adventures on behalf of what should have been emphasized—a matter that will not usually be known until one has the new account well-worked out.

2. It has been held by some jurists that the Ninth Amendment re-spects a "right of privacy", "privacy" for them, apparently meaning a public region outside the provenance of normal regulation. Actually, in the so-called privacy of one's home, to which those jurists refer, one is very much exposed, as public as one ever is. When jurists refer to what people do privately, they

refer not to privacies but to public areas not taken to be properly brought within the scope of enforceable law. That people and their acts are recognized by those jurists to be in a public area is evident from their refusal to allow all occurrences in the home to be beyond the law's reach. They recognize that murder and other crimes committed there are no less within their jurisdiction than similar crimes committed in other areas. At the same time, many things occurring outside the home—unavoidable jostlings, contacts, noises—are identified by them as being "private," in the sense that no legal account is taken of them.

3. The term "sovereign" has unpleasant associations in the United States. As was remarked in Chisholm v Georgia (US) 2 Dall 419, 454, I L Ed 440, 455 "To the Constitution of the United States the term sovereign is totally unknown. There is but one place where it could have been used with propriety. But even in that place it would not, perhaps, have comported with the delicacy of those who ordained and established that Constitution. They might have announced themselves 'sovereign' people of the United States. But serenely conscious of the fact, they avoided the ostentatious declaration."

Nevertheless, the United States courts have credited the various states with a "sovereign immunity," denying people the right to sue them in their own courts or in any other without their consent. One comes close to both this usage and the classical, where it referred to the unquestionable position of a king over and against all others, by taking "sovereign" to refer to any power, human or institutional, that determines what anyone, citizen or not, may do without penalty. Such a sovereign may or may not express its intent, power, or demands through a government and its laws.

4. It is not possible to understand what Law is or how it could exist apart from and thereby be able to dictate to a state and its constituents, if there were no condition beyond them with its own nature and warrant. Reference has to be made to what in various works I have called "Being", a final condition whose insistent presence makes actualities be coordinate, equal in status. The Law is constituted by divisions introduced into Being by actualities. Historically, it has been identified with "natural law", having its ground in God, or with civilization's understanding of what is right and wrong. It does not, though, depend on a divine act, nor is it limited to issues of right and wrong. Instead, it embodies the idea of justice or the equality of actualities, and the right to have merits considered in the determination of what may or may not be done. Actual laws take account only of a limited number of people and institutions, but the Law, that those laws are intended to incorporate, is pertinent to all. Each distinguishable item is accepted by Law as equally deserving to have its claims considered from the same impartial position. There is no consciousness or intent involved here. Law, like gravitation, is operative everywhere but diversely specialized at different places and times.

5. In article 1, section 7, of the United States Constitution it is said, "Every Bill which shall have passed the House of Representatives and the Senate, shall, before it become a Law, be presented to the President of the United States; If he approve he shall sign it, but if not he shall return it, with his Objections to that House in which it shall have originated, who shall

enter the Objections at large on their journal, and Proceed to reconsider it. If after such Reconsideration two thirds of that House shall agree to pass the Bill, it shall be sent, together with the Objections, to the other House, by which it shall likewise be reconsidered, and if approved by two thirds of that House, it shall become a Law. . . . If any Bill shall not be returned by the President within ten Days (Sundays excepted), the Same shall be a Law, in like Manner as if he had signed it, unless the Congress by their Adjournment prevent its Return, in which Case it shall not be a Law."

Later, when John Marshall refused request for advice on a proposed piece of legislation with the comment that the Supreme Court does not entertain hypothetical questions, that Court became one of three equal branches determining whether or not an enactment is a law. Should an enactment have the support of the President today, despite what is said in Article 1, section 7, it will not be a law, if the Supreme Court rules that it is not. One convicted under it could have his conviction overturned. In the absence of an adverse Supreme Court decision, article 1, section 7 prevails. But it is then only a putative law, a law by default of not having its legitimacy confirmed as that which had been produced in consonance with the requirements set down in the Constitution. The first Amendment put a constraint on the government of the United States of America. It did not proscribe the establishment of a religion in any one of the states, nor deny them the right to prohibit the free exercise of religion—unless one accepts Justice Black's view that all the Amendments applied to the several states, well before the due process clause in the Fourteenth Amendment was taken to justify (through the agency of the same clause in the Fifth Amendment) the application of all the ten Amendments to the several states.

The "free exercise of religion", moreover, must be understood to be an exercise in consonance with the rest of the Constitution; religions enjoining polygamy, cannibalism, and similar practices contrary to the traditions of the United States or going counter to what Law and justice require, are evidently precluded. Other religious practices, and the religions endorsing them, might also be denied a warrant, depending on what the government decides is a true religion and what an appropriate free exercise permits. That decision will require the concurrence of all three branches of the United States government.

Each branch of the United States government has a limited provenance: the Congress' decisions may be stopped by a veto it cannot muster enough votes to override; the President may be stopped by an overriding of his veto; and the Supreme Court, while passing final judgment on the validity of what the other two do, may have its decisions subsequently nullified in new Amendments.

6. The method was examined and followed in *Modes of Being, First Considerations*, and *Privacy*. In the first two, attention was paid primarily to the way in which one comes to know final conditions, and the language that is to be used; in *Privacy* there was an emphasis on the discovery of the different basic powers people have and the ways these are exercised. Following the lead of the first two requires the use of a new vocabulary and an adventure in speculative thought; following the lead of the third requires a participation

in the adventure of knowing oneself and others. The practioner of civil dis-obedience goes at least part of the way in each direction, appealing both to Law as certifying what is privately grasped, and to a sense of what it is right to do.

CHAPTER EIGHT

1. One of the most startling phrases in all of Augustine occurs near the beginning of the eleventh chapter of his *Confessions*. He there speaks of time as a "distension of the soul". The observation has usually been allowed to pass without comment, in good part because time was taken to be entirely independent of privacies, but in part also because the idea of "distension", was not recognized to open up a new way of viewing volumes. A distension is an indivisible voluminosity; occupation of an extended region, whether it be that of time, space, or causality, results from the filling out of a divisible, measurable, objective extension by a singular, private voluminosity.

In the absence of a privately possessed distension, a being, even one that was inanimate, would not be able to occupy a divisible region. There would be no way of accounting for motion, or for the successive occupation of adjacent regions. One would, therefore, have to deny that anything ever occupied an extended region; would have to suppose that all individuals were divisible; would have to treat occupied regions as indivisible; and would have to hold that nothing ever moves.

Once the indivisible distensions of unit beings are acknowledged, it should not be difficult to see that governments have distensions of their own. Their distensions have a larger spread than persons have and which they always manifest in the form of controlled, extended bodies. Governments are there-fore able to provide places for those who already privately occupy extensions in a public space and time, and who are therefore able to provide the disten-sion of their government with limited, extended avenues through which it can express itself.

2. What is earlier is replaced by what is later; what is before may be copresent with what is after. Yesterday is earlier than today; the number twenty-three is after twenty-two in a series of numbers. Those numbers, when attached to actual objects, may be temporally presented in that order, a reverse order, or conjointly, thereby making evident that it is an ongoing time and not its formal nature that is relevant. The observation entrains a difficul-ty: How could one item with a present longer than another—a war, let us say, compared with a battle—take place when the shorter does?

While a war continues, not yet completed, extending over a single indivis-ible present, one battle occurs after another. Those very battles, as part of an ongoing war, are part of the indivisible present of that war. Evidently, the present of the war, and the presents of the battles as distinct occurrences taking place one after the other, are temporal in different ways. As in the present of a war, the battles are there in outline only, conceptually distinguished, not yet determinate and bounded off from one another. There, they are not identifiable as distinct occurrences, following one after the other, each in a present of its own, sequentially determining the course of the actual war. Each battle, though, is a distinct occurrence; it takes place in its own indivisible present, embracing undistinguished skirmishes. As single units, the skirmishes provide external determinations for the single battles, and the distinguished battles provide external determinations for the unitary war.

Ongoing battles and an ongoing war are indivisible unities. Sequences of skirmishes and battles occur outside these in a series of presents. The primary fact is the unitary war, the unitary battles, and the unitary skirmishes together. In each, and in all of them together, a One and a Many, a separate unitary nuanced nature and sequences of distinct presents, are progressively united. Similarly, a government and occupied positions, both with their distinctive natures and spans, are joined in a single ongoing where the one becomes progressively determinate, and the others achieve places within a larger, single whole.

A war in which there are battles is not divisible into a separate, indivisible present and battles coming one after the other. Each has a status of its own, but each, too, is part of a single war embracing unseparated battles.

As long as a battle continues, it has no final boundary, and is so far indistinguishable from itself as part of a present war. Coming to an end, its final boundary enables it not only to be distinguished from the battles that follow, but to provide the ongoing war with an externally maintained distinct subdivision. Without a boundary, a battle is in the present ongoing of a war; with boundaries it is a separate occurrence. As the one, it is in an integral part of the war; this contains it as not yet determinate. As the other, it is distinct from the war, as well as from itself and other battles which are integral parts of that war. An ongoing war, with its sequence of battles, is a single whole made determinate by actual battles. What happens here has counterparts elsewhere: indeterminate presents embrace aspects of single ongoings; a plurality of bounded, limited occurrences must be joined to those presents if there is to be a sequence of present ongoings.

A clock has mathematically subdivided units. As a consequence, it inevitably exhibits the undivided larger presents of some beings as taking place in smaller separated presents. But no present depends for its existence on an external measure. No such measure deprives what is measured of its unit span, though it may refer to mathematically smaller segements of it which are not in fact present there as distinct units.

The issue, as has been remarked, is dealt with at length in *History: Written and Lived*, pp. 141 ff. What is there said will have to be appropriately modified to be able to apply to the special rhythms and units of history, clocks, the arts or, as the text makes evident, to politics. All require that a distinction be made between "before and after" and "earlier and later", and the two reconciled. Reference has also already been made to Whitehead's view that subdivisions of a present moment are merely conceivable, not separately bounded components in it. Since he ignored the related questions of the spatiality and causal power of his unit occurrences, and since the occurrences were taken to be all of the same minimal temporal magnitude, his account was arbitrarily restricted to the temporal nature of occurrences with unit, indivisible temporal spans. If no provision is made for the extended presents and reality of real complex beings, one is faced with the counterpart of the difficulty that would arise were it maintained that battles alone had indivisible presents. That would require the denial that there could be real forays and feints and that a war was more than a string of battles, with a distinctive rhythm, and a beginning and ending of its own.

Whitehead made some provision for the second of these issues by referring to "societies", in which his various atomic units were strung together as singularly relevant to one another. This, though, is far less than what is needed if one is to take account of unitary occurrences whose presents (and places and actions) not only have greater extensions than some others, but are both distinct from those others and sequentially acquire determinations. His view allows no place for the ongoing of an actual government or state, and therefore for its time, its space, or its dynamism.

3. For a detailed examination of "we", see *You, I, and the Others*, chapter 4.

4. Aristotle *(Ethics*, 1130 b 31 ff), after distinguishing general from particular justice, divides the latter into distributive and rectificatory forms, the one having to do with the distribution of honors, money, etc., among citizens, the other with redressing wrongs. But distributions are to be made among all those who are ruled and also among rulers and ruled; and rectifications should counterbalance, not only wrongs but natural disadvantages, as well as unjustified discriminations.

The justice that is pertinent to those who are governmentally ruled is a special case of an impersonal demand that people receive what they deserve as persons publicly together. What the more general form requires is not restricted to citizens or to the redressing of wrongs. Were it identified with fairness, it would act without regard for private persons; were it only an ideal, it might simply assess acts and people. Made the concern of a government, sovereign, or state, justice is a limited, effective, equilibrating condition affecting different facets of a limited number of ruled people, subjects, and citizens.

The confidence people have, that they deserve more than they get, may exist together with lassitude, subservience, or an acceptance of their station. Often enough, acceptance of themselves as irreplaceable, allows them to be content with themselves, and yet to take themselves to be denied what they deserve, the first emphasizing their privacy, the second, their need and right to be perfected. Justice requires that claims be dealt with impersonally, in the face of claims made by others.

CHAPTER NINE

1. Richard J. Bernstein, in his review of *You, I, and the Others (The Review of Metaphysics*, December, 1981) backed the Hegelian-based claim that even the most fundamental categories are dialectical opposites of a time in

which everything undergoes change. Such opposing categories and time, though, could not be reconciled except in what is itself fixed and outside time—or is passing away—and leaves one faced with the same issue again. It is more correct to say that what is fixed has at least two different forms— what is final and forever, and what people apprehend. Language offers a good illustration of the point. The fact that words have a history does not compromise their reference to constancies. Just as people can speak with different emphases and use different expressions to greet one another in the same ways, so they can use different terms to refer to themselves and other realities as existing outside a public time. The presence of a term in time does not preclude its being used by and with reference to what is outside that time.

When this issue is dealt with ontologically, passing temporal beings are seen to be dependent on both final conditions and finite actualities, each maintaining its integrity apart from the other, at the same time that their combined expressions constitute transitory, public extensions, to which some of their other expressions are subject. See *First Considerations*, pp. 149 ff.

2. A reasonableness, that is the outcome of a meshing of reason with the lessons of tradition, is both guided by ideals and backed by the customary behavior of a people. It therefore can enable one to forge sound judgments about what occurs and should occur in society and state.

3. When an enriched present for a union of people, as habituated and expectative, is joined to a place possessed by them together, the outcome is a homeland. Each one of the people, though born naked and defenseless, is conditioned together with others living there at the time. As individuals, as together, as inheritors and predecessors, and as locatable, they are inevitably in a present different from any which had been before or will be again. That present has the three-fold status of a condition, a component, and the two together, each qualified by a past and a future.

It is necessary, therefore, to take a stand somewhere in between Whitehead and Heidegger, when the one supposes that the present swallows the past (and possibly the future as well) in an act of self-creativity, and the other supposes that the past (but perhaps not the future) may occasionally overwhelm what is present. Neither allows for an enriched present functioning just as a condition; neither provides for the fact that a union of people is in a distinctive present at a rather constant, meaningful, accepted place; neither sees the present of a society to be a product of the other two.

The present in which people are together, and the place of their union, have distinctive tonalities, stemming from the way in which past, future, and place affect the meaning of a condition, the people as joined together, and the interplay of the two. Whatever legitimacy either of these had, precisely because it is never wholly subjected to the present, could be maintained for an indefinite time. Since it is never unqualified by the future, and depends on what is present in order to be effective, the force and meaning of that legitimacy will rarely be constant.

A legitimacy that remains identical over time is a component in a legitimacy that changes in weight and meaning. It is therefore readily identified with rules, laws, or essences, as unaffected by time. A legitimacy that plays a role in a state is always more than this. It is a constant with a constantly changing tonality, and is able to be expressed in distinctive ways at different times.

The legitimacy of a rightful heir to a throne is less than that of its predecessor just so far as it is dependent on this. The heir need not have the merit that the predecessor had intrinsically, or the degree of legitimacy that this may have inherited. Its legitimacy may also be more than its predecessor's; dependent on this, it may not need to have the merit the other had to have in order to establish itself. Its legitimacy can also be said to be equal to that of its predecessor, so far as the legitimacy is a constant, legally continued. Its legitimacy is nevertheless different, possessed and expressed in a different way. The present Queen of England is legitimate, just as surely as other queens and kings of England were in modern times. But as a functional sovereign, her legitimacy has a more limited range than that which many of her predecessors enjoyed. Tradition, law, and rituals emphasize her inheritance; the growth in the power of the prime minister and the parliament partly account for the narrowed range of her legitimacy today.

4. Such distinguished thinkers as Kant and Hegel have denied that there were any real possibilities. But if there were none, there would be nothing future that would be relevant to, limitative of, and capable of being realized in the course of action. There would be no effects to be brought about, but only actions performed in the present, perhaps accompanied, in the case of people and some of the higher animals, with an expectation of what might ensue. Imagined goals and ends would be realized without having the status of objectives, and therefore without having any affect on what was done in the present.

Real possibilities do not exist at a later moment of time, somehow related to the present over a temporal stretch. That would paradoxically make the future be separated from the present by the future. The future is not to be envisaged as being at a temporal distance from the present, any more than the past is to be taken to be distanced from it. Both are at the limits of the present, the one in the form of an indeterminate possibility, the other in the form of facts.

5. The realization of a future prospect is one with the conversion of it, as a possibility at the limit of the present, into an extended present with its own distinctive nature and limits. What occurs through action has a counterpart in an historian's conversion of the available past into an extended concatenation of distinct, ordered items. Could one interchange these conversions, the past would be a reality produced by the historian, and future occurrences would be constructions produced by present people. Adam presumably did the one when he identified a tree as old enough to bear fruit; an omniscient God would do something like the second when he thought about the day of last judgment, since he would confront the future without having to reach it over the course of a passing time.

6. The acts of people, unlike those of machines, occur in contexts which extend backwards and forwards, and thereby give a meaning to what is done that could not be obtained be examining what is being done. Subhumans also act in contexts, but unlike a people's, these are limited to what is pertinent to their welfare. Humans live in an open world which they delimit not only by what they do but by the context from which the act is inseparable

and which fits within a more stable context produced by them together.

A computer, being a machine, can never duplicate what a person does. Where a person's sentence is freshly created out of the available vocabulary and grammar, and thereupon bears on what had been and what will be said, a computer's "sentences" are units set alongside others. What it does is even less than a copyist does for, while adhering to the original, a copyist produces a new entity for pleasure, the market, art classes, and so on. Computers have no aims.

The acts of people bring an enriched present, with its ingredient past and future, together. They also project backwards and forwards and thereby define a pertinent past and future which rarely coincide with the past and future operative in the act itself.

7. The posterity that the authors of the United States Constitution had in mind, evidently, was not just their offspring. There might not be any, or they might emigrate and give up their American citizenship. "Offspring," moreover, does not make provision for foreigners who become citizens. It is doubtful, too, that slaves, Indians or their progeny were being considered. What apparently was intended by "our Posterity" were those who lived later in the territory of the United States, and had special rights protected by the Constitution.

The Constitution provides a legal link between those who live at different times and who are to be identified as predecessors and successors under a common rule. "Posterity" adds the additional note that those who come later are being kept in mind, "the Blessings of Liberty" being secured through the Constitution both for those who will then live under it and for those who will do so later.

8. The necessitarianism that was so prominent in the last century and still is maintained to some extent in various sectors, including social and political study, has at least six serious defects. (1.) It cannot distinguish between possibilities and actualities. The two are held to be simply located at different dates, which are identified with numbers and thereupon not taken to be in an order of earlier to later. (2.) It has no room for contingencies. These are supposed to be necessities which had not been adequately analyzed, with the consequence that theory is allowed to deny the deliverances of experience. (3.) It cannot, as Peirce observed, account for the distribution of its units. The later theory of a "Big Bang" occurring "at the beginning" takes the distribution to have occurred suddenly at some point of time; it does not explain why it occurred or why it took the form it supposedly did. (4.) Necessitarianism permits one to move backwards and forwards in time indifferently, unable to say in what ways past, present, and future differ. (5.) It has no place for movement, passage, action, the bringing about of anything through effort, backed by decision, maintained through determination, and ending with what is sought. (6.) It cannot account for the dislocation of some of its units at various times. Yet the particles in an organic body are where this is; when it moves in pursuit of food, the physical units in it are found wherever it goes. This will be to a place reached through acts and at a pace not possible to what it contains.

It is not enough, with Peirce, to introduce the idea of chance. That might allow one to accommodate variations beyond the capacity of a necessitarianism; it does not meet the above-mentioned difficulties, with the possible exception of the second and third.

Every act and movement produces unpredictable details in, and thereby realizes indeterminate, relevant possibilities. There is a formal necessity connecting these with what terminates in them, but that necessity is just one component in a single action in the course of which details are introduced into the possible, unavoidable outcome, to end with this filled out in ways that had been then and there produced. All actions combine a formal necessity with a freshly constituted way of transforming the necessitated possibility into an actual, produced, present occurrence. This can then be exhaustively analyzed, but that is only to say that the past, unlike what is occurring in the present, is dissectable into an aggregation of distinct facts. An apparently simple occurrence, such as the transfer of legitimacy from a monarch to an heir, has its unpredictably produced details, making it have a new concrete status, both because it is in a new present and is there through acts then produced, giving the result a distinctive particularity.

9. Whatever the method be by means of which positions in a government are filled, neither the positions nor the filling occur in isolation from one another. The different positions are together in and conditioned by the government as a unity, and the people together constitute its work force. Their interplay results in a functioning government.

This situation has a counterpart in the interplay of employers and employees, but with important differences. Few are interested in the ways positions are filled in a government; almost everyone is concerned with the ways the outcome affects those who are ruled. Almost everyone involved is interested in having the available work force employed; only a few are interested in the ways the force is subdivided.

Questions about legitimacy arise for both employers and employees, but mainly in connection with the kinds of actions they carry out in relation to one another. If an employer reached the position through fraud or an employee was improperly replaced by a relative, the issue may have to be settled apart from both. A legitimate and even an illegitimate government is more than an employer; it may be effectively, properly, and directly questioned by those who are ruled, and if it has branches, each of these may be required to assess the legitimacy of what is done in the others.

A government affects both rulers and ruled. A corporation, in contrast, whether it has or does not have regulations which govern managers and managed, acts under the aegis of a government and state. Were a government like a corporation, its status as an interlocked set of positions would be distinct from, but still a related part of some larger whole, instead of being a whole under which people, and corporations as well, exist and are regulated. In either place, though, a characterization of particular positions as unoccupied may not be appropriate to what would be appropriate to them as occupied. Nor need a characterization of occupied positions be appropriate to what would be appropriate to the outcome of a confrontation with those who are ruled.

10. On the nature of such health, see *Privacy*, pp. 295-6.

CHAPTER TEN

1. Wittgenstein held that there is nothing to be known except by using evidences available to others. Still, anyone using publicly available evidence must do so as a private being, and offer knowledge to other private beings for acceptance or rejection as true or false.

What another knows is sustained by what is a "you" for oneself. What one knows of oneself is confronted in a "me" sustained from within, while it is being faced from without. The fact that it was so sustained is knowable by others just so far as they can know that it is in a me different from their own. That is possible so far as they know, not only that what they confront is not produced by them, but that it is privately maintained apart from them. See *You, I, and the Others,* chapter 2; *Privacy,* p. 34.

2. Their capacity to interact, most sharply distinguishes states from a primary universal determinant of the merits and limits of what people are and do. Were one to assume, with idealists, that a state is the Hegelian Absolute in lower case, it would have to be added that, unlike the Absolute, it is opposed by effective powers distinct from it, and outside its control. The Absolute's concern is with recovering itself via limited self-expressions. Both outside all limits and determinative of the limits of all else, it is like but not identical with that which can assess whatever there be, for instead of just being beyond all limited entities, it creates them, determining not only what they can properly be and do, but what they in fact are.

Once it is realized that some finite occurrences are irreducible, and both are and act independently of what comprehends and conditions them, it becomes evident that a supposed Absolute must lack some reality and power. The present acknowledgment of a determinant of the merits and proper limits of contenders, carries that idea of a lack to its limit, crediting the determinant with the status of a possibility having minimal effectiveness.

Might not one add individual efforts to such a possibility, and thereby give it an efficacy it otherwise would not have? If this were done, needed energy and interest would be taken away from a contender and this would, so far, keep it from finding a proper place in a challenging world. To realize what ideally measures all else, and thus to have each acting properly according to its nature and in harmony with others, a possible measure must have an effective role in what is occurring. It is not to be aimed at. Rather, it is to be used to guide the course of each activity, but not treated as a control or an objective with which anyone is to be primarily occupied. The good to be realized by a multiplicity of contenders is a constant already involved in their different, limited activities.

It is not possible, on behalf of the vision or ideals cherished by a religion, ethics, or a perfected world of publicly related people, to act solely to rectify what is amiss elsewhere. Such a rectifier is still a contender and, so far, itself needs rectification. The right of a church, speaking on behalf of the commands of its God, to complain and act against omissions and commissions of a government, is not entirely separable from its duty to complain against itself, as one of the actors in the world.

There is only one ideal pertinent to everything whatsoever; there are a number of others having more limited ranges. The Commonhealth is one of these, being pertinent to public men already living in states.

Those who take the position of a religion, ethics, art, etc., to be sure, do not usually suppose that they are offering an alternative to be set alongside a government of law, but instead take themselves to be appealing to what assesses all on the basis of what transcends everyone. Those who hold such a view, instead of opposing a government, should then take a stand beyond this and any other specific determinant of what people ought to be and do, and from there determine the limits within which different contenders must act. Government and its laws will then be assigned inviolable spheres of activity.

The Roman Catholic Church takes itself to judge in terms provided by a primary assessor which is not in competition with any other way of determining what people are and how they are to act. (The position is not to be confounded with Pope Gelasius' doctrine of two swords, where the Church takes each side to have its own proper sphere of influence.) Today, with the dominance of the state over religions, the position has been reversed, with the state deciding where to place the limits of religion as well as of itself.

The determination of what a contender may and may not do cannot be properly decided by it. Appeal must be made to what is able to assess it and others, and to which all must yield because of the authority it possesses, an authority superior to theirs.

3. Bodily health is not an entity, set alongside of or over particular bodily parts; it is a condition effectively determining the ways in which different parts of the body function. Instead of just operating indifferently on all, it uses some to condition others. Heart lungs, and liver, in addition to being parts of a body alongside one another, function as its primary a gents, through which its influence is transmitted to other parts. A state operates on a govenment and a union of people in somewhat the way a human being acts on his or her various parts. Lacking consciousness or intent, a state though, is not more real, nobler, or more concrete than its encompassed govenment or people.

4. Social and idealistic theories of knowledge and language deny authority to individual assertions, the individuals supposedly introducing only confusion or error, and having only as much authority as a society or some whole extends to them. This is surely to turn things upside down, and to back the move by a supposed authoritative individual claim.

It is odd that individuals self-confessedly without any authority for what they affirm, should hold that no one has the authority to say what is true. Despite the apparent modesty in holding that only a society, common language, an Absolute, a scientific community, or a shared theory is intelligible, legitimate, authoritative, and the like, the defenders of the view ask others to accept as true that for which there is supposed to be no authority. They and those who disagree with them presumably can do no more than exhibit the effect others have on them.

5. The reductionistic procedures characteristic of behaviorism allow one to treat persuasiveness as a degree of transformation undergone in the presence of something else. The acceptance of such a behavioristic explanation will not eliminate the need to take account of the presence and con-

tribution of "psychological" private activities; it does no more, in fact, than make provision for a persuasiveness that may not be affected by these.

A private accommodation to what is persuasive may occur before there is any public evidence for it. Its presence may sometimes be detected when responses continue in a particular direction despite obstacles and opposi- tions, or when people change their course despite prevailing constancies. If no account is taken of the occurrence of private accommodations, the steadi- ness of people's responses in the face of changes in what is impinging on them, and changes in their responses to the same conditions, will be left unexplained.

6. A lie is authorized by the liar; another can therefore use it as evidence of the liar's character or intent. What the lie says, therefore, has to be traced back to two sources—an intent to deceive and a presentation of what looks like a truth. To understand that it is a lie, it is, therefore, necessary to distinguish the fact, that is expresses the liar, from an articulation of what the liar in fact intends.

7. for a discussion of the difference between tools and instruments, see."An Introduction to a Study of Instruments", *Philosophy of Science*, vol. viii, no. 3, (July, 1941), pp. 287-296.

8. This is an old question. Cf. Aristotle *Politics* 1284 b. 14, " . . . with the words used by the lions in the fable of Antisthenes, when the hare were making orations and claiming all the animals had equal rights, ["Where are your claws and teeth?"]" Ernest Barker's translation and bracketed addition.

9. Might it not be true that though governments and states ought to have their expressions respected, they do not have as much right as people to express themselves as fully as they can? Alternatively, might it not be true that they should express themselves fully but that people should not? Affir- mative answers would be required if any of these were latently evil or, at the very least, if their expressions beyond a certain point were injurious to them- selves or others. Claims that a government should govern less accept the first of these; claims that people are natively savage accept the second. Neither should be allowed. If they are, it will still be true that both sides, so far as they are constituent factors of a state, are to express themselves as fully as it is possible for them to do, consistent with their need of one another.

Chapter Eleven

1. Religious thinkers speak of divine laws, economists of the laws of the market, philosophers of the laws of logic. These and various other types of "law" lack the rational structure of the laws of Nature or the humanly enforce- able nature of the laws of a state. They too, though, are prescriptive, and are also taken to be effective enough to assure that required consequences will usually ensue. In all, outcomes are assured because prescriptions are in full control—the divine laws; or because they so limit the activities engaged in, that designated outcomes are usually produced—those laws which govern sound inferences as well as those formulated by legislators.

Natural laws are specialization of more ultimate effective conditions. Contingent occurrences in Nature make those laws fall so short of unqualified effectiveness that the modern scepticism about their existence is not disturbing. What is disturbing is the accompanying supposition, that Nature and people, and perhaps the state, are imaginary entities, minor products of individual experiences, or just terms in a common language.

2. See particularly Jerome Frank, *Law and the Modern Mind* (1930).

3. "Living law" is a recurrent topic in F. S. C. Northrop's various studies. See e. g., *Philosophical Anthropology and Practical Politics* and *The Taming of the Nations*. He credited the use of the term to Eugen Ehrlich, but took it to have been recognized by a number of other political thinkers, particularly those who were interested in sociology. It coincides somewhat with the idea of Law, a final justice limited to what states and governments decree and do, differing from this primarily in suggesting an involvement with people who form intimate bonds with one another.

4. Most of the work of lawyers and the courts has to do with rulings determining how opposing claims are to be assessed. Laws are taken by them to be means for reducing conflict, determinants of remedies, and mediators. Positive law can be said to have these roles when it is understood to require that possible conflicts be settled peaceably, with the government seeing to it that this is done expeditiously and well.

5. "*I, thou, that, this* . . . indicate things in the directest possible way." *Collected Papers of Charles Sanders Peirce*, 2.287 n. See also, *You, I, and the Others*, pp. 261 ff., and *First Considerations*, pp. 68 ff., on the nature of proper names and pronouns.

6. To hold with some that the authority of laws is due simply to their incorporation of a principle of justice, or on their having rational, communicable forms, is to claim too much, since such an authority would not necessarily be restricted to dealing with occurrences inside a state. If, instead, it is maintained that laws have authority on their own, but limited to covering only what occurs inside a state, one will be faced with the fact that laws are contingent products, formulated, mandated, and insisted on in alterable, and sometimes questionable ways. Laws have an authority because of their justice, rationality, and nature; but this is an authority that awaits and adds to the authority they possess as agencies of the state. As just agencies, the laws have acquired some authority, even when they are not well-stated, fair, or respected. Were it maintained, instead, that all laws, even though formulated and enforced by a legitimate government, owe their authority to the people, laws which go counter to the people's interests would have to be said not to be laws at all. Authorizations traceable to those who are being governed can, at best, be only part of the authorization laws possess.

7. Because proper authority, desirable prospects, and a cherished past all have some effectiveness, the grounding of laws in these is one with the derivation of an "ought" (strictly speaking, a "should") from an "is." Hume, who denied that such a derivation was possible, took "is" to refer to an unrelated matter of fact. But even if this restriction were accepted, it is possible to derive an "ought" from an "is". All people are imperfect, lacking much that would enable them to be happy, to prosper, or even to continue to exist unruffled and at ease. What would help them overcome their lack is

what ought to be, the "ought" measuring the distance between what is present and what would remedy some defect in it. The fact could not be acknowledged by Hume, for he took the future to be entirely disconnected from the present, and thereby implicitly supposed that nothing in the present could be said to lack anything. Were a lack, instead, a present condition making no reference to what might overcome it, appetite, need, desire, and planning would cease to be.

What "is" is something present, related to what would make good its lack; what "ought" to be is what would make good the lack. "Ought", because it characterizes a present lack that should be overcome is, evidently, "is needed" read backwards.

"But", it will perhaps be objected, "there can be lacks without there being anything to satisfy them. People lack food and die of starvation; governments need support and are met by opposition." It is not being contended, though, that what ought to be does in fact overcome a lack. Were it realized, it would do so, but not otherwise. Food that is needed is not food awaiting use; it is a possibility that ought to be realized. A lack both characterizes a living being and relates this to what could overcome that lack; what ought to be is the correlate of something actually present as sustaining a deficiency related to what, on being realized, makes the deficiency vanish.

8. See below, note 8 of the next chapter, for a further consideration of the rights people have in a state, apart from both those which express inalienable rights and those which a state might bestow.

9. "Being", "existence", "intelligibility", and "unity" are transcendental terms whose referents are pertinent to every actuality. "Beauty", "truth", "goodness" are more limited transcendentals, with referents pertinent to art, assertions, and human acts. "Justice" belongs with this group. Its primary referent is a transcendent reality able both to condition and to make itself present in pluralities. Not restricted to the world of law, "justice" still has primary relevance to this and, so far, to what does not range as widely as it might, and surely not as widely as do the referents of "being," "existence", and similar transcendentals. Those enactments which do not permit a place for it, or do not possess it to the degree that an enactment should and can, are defective, lacking a necessary ingredient. Despite all talk about "justice" in every branch of government, adequate account is not taken account of it in any, precisely because no attention is paid to the nature of transcendental terms, their referents, and on what these bear.

That justice is always operative and not altogether neglected is due to the fact that, like the referents of other transcendental terms, it is always present in particulars, though only in attenuated forms, and usually not in clear and dominant ways. Always outside all laws, it is also present in every one as a specialized form of a constant, effective condition.

A person may be just to his or her sense of self, refusing to slight talents, or to exaggerate virtues or vices. None of these, or deviations from them or other forms of justice, need fall within the provenance of law, or elicit a force that might make a person behave differently.

Were justice simply an idle ideal, it would exert no control; did it not play a role in ideal assessments, these might not be equitable. The recognition, that the boundaries and status required by justice should be accepted by all competitors, is possible to all of them, because justice is always available, a more or less evident ingredient in every situation where a number of items are together no matter how opposed they in fact are.

10. In *Modes of Being* this equalizing condition—"Being" it was called—was dealt with in a confused way. Its nature comes into clearer focus in *First Considerations*, pp. 121-131.

CHAPTER TWELVE

1. I make no claim that this hierarchy was clearly seen and deliberately presented, but only that it can be discerned, and that it makes good sense to emphasize it. Nor is any claim being made that the document is perfect, or even superior to any other that might be produced. It is, though, being maintained that the "Preamble" offers a splendid entrance to the rest of the United States Constitution; promotes an understanding of the nature of any state and what should be its primary purposes; and provides warrants for the existence and functioning of a decent state. An examination of the salient features of the different phrases will also provide an excellent occasion to inquire about other objectives, not there stated, and about some of the supplements and aids every state needs. That is enough to make the "Preamble" worth examining, apart from the fact that it guided an expanding, changing, large State for two hundred years, has been widely copied, and has sometimes guided other successful political adventures.

A bolder, but I think still proper claim, is that "a more perfect[ed] Union" is the precondition for the other objectives, limiting the United States from within and bounding it off from other States coexisting with it. On this view, the other objectives are specialized ways of enabling that State to be more and more involved with its people. Just as people have privacies, unions limits, societies closures, and rulers and ruled a need for equilibrium, a State has a boundary internally defined.

2. In United States v. Darby, 312 U.S. 100 (1941) the Court held that the Tenth Amendment . . . "states but a truism that all is retained which has not been surrendered. There is nothing in the history of its adoption to suggest that it was more than declaratory of the relationship between the national and state governments as it had been established by the Constitution before the amendment or that its purpose was other than to allay fears that the new national government might seek to exercise powers not granted, and that the states might not be able to exercise fully their reserved powers."

A sovereign State need not, of course, be a One for Many subordinated but still sovereign states, since there may be no such states. There will, nevertheless, always be a Many with which it interplays. It is a One for many subordinate, independently functioning entities, all able to act on their own and oppose it. These may be, but need not be, states. Were every subordinate state eliminated, the State would still be left with ruled people and a ruling government, separately functioning in relation to it.

The United States, evidently, is a One in a number of different senses, depending on the nature of the Many with which it interplays. As joined to a federal government and the people, it has the status of a One for the several states. Were the government and the governed ignored, it could be no more than a sovereign One for those Many subordinated sovereign states. If a government and governed are acknowledged, the United States will be a One for both, as well as for the subordinated states.

An extended examination of the problem of the One and the Many is to be found in *Modes of Being,* chapter 10.Refinements and modifications of what is there maintained are scattered throughout the various volumes of *Philosophy in Process.* At all times, the mutual involvement of the One and the Many is maintained, as at once unavoidable and incapable of being denied without producing intolerable consequences.

3. "Union" here evidently refers, not to the One together with the Many, but to the One alone, and therefore not really to the "more perfect[ed] Union" that the Constitution that was "to form". If there are no limits to the federal courts' reach except those that they impose on themselves, and therefore which they might subsequently abrogate, justice is not established. An established justice must fit within the Union of One supreme and Many subordinated sovereigns.

4. If this is so, why should ethics not respect the limits within which people necessarily operate, and hold that anyone is perfect who does all that could possibly be done in the circumstances? Because this would require us to give up the idea that people are obligated to realize what ought to be.

"Ought" does not imply "can". If it did, incompetence would free one from obligation, and provide a perfect excuse for habitual carelessness. People ought to do much that they cannot.

When a state fails to do all it ought, we can attribute the fact to circumstance. The outcome would be regrettable; it might even be tragic, but there might be nothing other than the course of the world to blame for the result. People are condemnable for not doing what they could not, because they are obligated to realize excellence. A state, though, is not necessarily condemnable for being less than perfect, for while measured by and related to an ideal state, it is not obligated to realize this, having neither knowledge nor will. Every human being has a possible perfect human as an essential factor. A state dictates to government and people in whatever way it can. Although it would be better did it realize more of its ideal than it does, and though that ideal is inseparable from and inevitably guides it, if only weakly, the ideal is not a component of the state as that state now is. And while the deficiencies of an actual state make it less than some other having fewer deficiencies, the deficiences of an actual person do not compromise that person's status as equal to every other.

The ideal state is external to every state; ideal humanity is both external and internal to every human. As a consequence, a state falls short of being a true state just so far as it falls short of the ideal, while a person remains fully human no matter how evil. The ought to be that is to be realized by humans is already internal, though not entirely in the way it should and could be. All humans are unequal in excellence and equal as persons; states are unequal as states because and so far as they are unequal in excellence.

We can take a state to be no less a state than any other only by taking account of an ideal that continues to be unrealized, but each person is intrinsically just as much a person as any other.

Since an actual state, no matter how defectively its government and men interplay, is a state as much as any other, the ideal of their proper interplay can, therefore, be said to be ingredient in it, in the same way that what a person ought to be is an ingedient in him. Only if the ideal state were a present requirement that a government and people mesh perfectly, would it be proper to say, as one can of a person, that an ideal is an inseparable part of it as it is here and now.

A state has its center of gravity in an actual interplay of its components, while being related to an ideal state not yet realized. People have another, distinctive center of gravity; each is in a tension between what is and what ought to be, a tension that must be reduced if one is to become the person one ought to be. Whatever the degree of success, each person is related (as a state is) to what ought to be realized; but a person is also required (as a state is not) to so act that what ought to be is exemplified elsewhere. An ideal is always a constituent of persons, and only of them; because of it they, and only they, are obligated to realize what benefits others.

5. Were people required to do only what respects the rights of others, or to carry out their duties as far as they are accustomed to, acts of generosity, altruism, and self-sacrifice would be gratuitous or supererogatory, going beyond what is required. (In Roman Catholic theology, supererogation has reference to good works performed by saints over and above those commanded by God.) But the fact that there are acts not usually performed, not explicitly commanded, or requiring unusual effort, does not mean that there is no obligation to engage in them, unless it can be maintained that people who do not realize what ought to be are not less than what they ought to be.

In ethics, the idea of supererogation serves to keep ethical acts within the limits of usual practices, specific commands, and even niggardly attitudes, requiring less than maximal efforts. The idea takes ethics to have no room for what ought to be done, though this is beyond anybody's ability at that time. Since it is surely tragic that a person may be able to rescue only one of two children from a burning house, evidently what a person is ethically required to do, may sometimes not be possible.

To this, it would not be unreasonable to reply that ethics does not condemn people for failing to do what is impossible. One does not do what is ethically wrong because one cannot be present in two places at once, or because one cannot fly by flapping one's arms and thereby arrive rapidly at the place where help is needed. But people are not here being said to be ethically in the wrong just because they are not able to do what is outside the range of human ability. They are ethically in the wrong because they are obligated to realize what ought to be, and fail to fulfill that obligation.

Politics is the art of the possible, but ethics may ask the impossible of people just by demanding that they realize what ought to be. Since the tragic failures, which result from the inability in some circumstance to bring about what ought to be, may be lessened and even eliminated by the use of technical devices and adequate preparations, there is an ethical warrant for forging grounded expectations of what will ensue, and making the needed preparations.

It does appear wrong-headed, though, to condemn people who lived in a less developed age for not achieving what could be achieved only in ours. Yet were the idea behind that thought carried out in our ethics, we would have to excuse the Greeks for the practice of slavery, their subjugation of women, and their attitude toward barbarians. We would also have justification enough for excusing our forbears for their attitude toward the slave trade, and ourselves for the wars we blundered into. The fact that people do not do all they ought and in certain circumstances cannot do it, requires one to say either that people are not required to bring about what ought to be, or that that they are tragically unable to do so, except fragmentarily and in part. Tragedy does not eliminate ethical failure; instead, it makes this poignantly evident.

6. If the first two provisions listed in the "Preamble" were carried out, there would be less need "to insure domestic Tranquility", were it not that a more perfect[ed] Union might stand in the way of an establishment of justice, or that the establishment of justice might preclude a more perfect[ed] Union. The first of these alternatives would come about were energy and attention concentrated mainly on the achievement of a proper relation between the One State and the Many subordinated states; the second, were the establishment of justice to jeopardize the continuance of the One or the Many. An undisturbed public life is promoted if the demand for a more perfect[ed] Union allows for the people's need to have an established justice. But, since there are other sources of unrest, having to do with the frustration of the desire of a people to live with dignity together, there will always be a need to have tranquility treated as a distinct objective of the One State.

7. When a similar approach is taken toward society, this is seen to have as its primary objective the achievement of cohesiveness. A union of people and the homeland can then be recognized not only to interplay, but to be guided and affected by that objective. The bounding of a society from within, though, does not make it coordinate with other societies; it just sets it apart. A state's objectives can also play a more effective role than a society's does in determining what is done by subordinated sovereignties. More important and conspicuously, its objectives characterize a state as a unit, bounded off from other political units, one or a number of which together might be able, and are usually identified by it as ready to set grave obstacles in the way of its continuance or prosperity.

8. The promotion of the general Welfare and the securing of the Blessings of Liberty can be thought of as taking account (perhaps also with the establishment of justice and the insurance of domestic Tranquility) of rights people possess in opposition to the State and its government. The so-called "Bill of Rights", was written with an awareness that people have such rights.

The free exercise of religion, freedom of speech, the right of the people peaceably to assemble, and to petition Government for a redress of grievances, the right to bear and keep arms, the needed consent of the Owner before a soldier can be quartered in a house in time of peace; the right to be secure in "their persons, houses, papers, and effects, against unreasonable searches and seizures"; the way a person is to be held to answer for a capital or otherwise infamous crime; the right not to be subject to double jeopardy, to be denied due process of law, or to be deprived of property for public use without due compensation; the right to a speedy and public trial by an impartial jury; the right to be informed of the nature and cause of an accusation, to be confronted with witnesses against him, and to have the assistance of counsel for defense the right to trial by jury in suits at common law, the right not to have excessive bail or fines required, are all evidently possessed by everyone. They are not native rights, i.e., rights ingredient in people as private beings, existing apart from any state. Like the right to vote, they exist only so far as people exist in the State and are, so far, correlative to the powers this enjoys. They are not simply bestowed rights, rights which people have only because they are granted to them by the State, for such rights could be taken away by the same power and, presumably, with the same warrant that lay behind their bestowal. They are bestowed, adherent rights, rights people in fact inescapably possess as their own, but only as and so far as they exist in a State.

The native rights people possess are theirs no matter what the State decrees, but their exercise depends on what people are as constituents of the State, contrasting with and interplaying with its government. Those denied the right to vote, to assemble, etc., still have these rights but only so far as their denial conflicts with the existence of a well-functioning government. If publicly viable rights are grounded in private rights, or if their denial conflicts with the very existence of a government for all, it would be wrong for a State to deny any of them; so far as the rights are correlatives of the powers of a government, they will, instead, necessarily vary with the kind of State in which those correlatives exist.

Adherent rights are bestowed rights which belong to people so far as they are subject to a government, either as it essentially is, or as it happens to be. If the former, those denied the right to vote are denied what is essential to their being governed; if the latter, some or all may be defined to be people without certain rights. The blacks in South Africa insist on the first of these alternatives; South Africa on the second. Both take voting to be an adherent right, the first treating it as a consequence of their being governed, the second as dependent on a governmental decision. The blacks have a better warrant than South Africa because they not only ground the right to vote in their privacies, but identify it with the right that an ideal state, inseparable from every actual state, defines as being adherent for all those who are governed.

To know whether or not there are other adherent rights (and thus whether or not the rights, said to be retained by the people in Amendment Nine of the United States Constitution, are native rights having a possible public expression) one must know the essential nature of a state, with its government and correlative governed people. Do these include the right to work, to help in old age, to the exercise of sexual preferences regardless of gender or degree of consanguinity, to attempts at suicide, or to any use one would like to make of one's body if no one else were harmed? It is not evident that all of these are public expressions of private rights, though a right to gainful work seems to be implicated by the right to life. Nor is it evident that all of them would adhere to people in a splendidly governed state. We must wait, I think, until we have made greater progress in realizing the ideal state before we are in a position to be sure that these, and other claimed rights, do adhere to well-governed people. And, then, perhaps still others will become evident. All the while, it will be true that individuals have rights of their own, whose public forms deserve satisfaction, no matter what a state can or will do.

9. The "Preamble" begins with a reference to the people of the "United States"—the Many states together. It ends with a reference to the Constitution for "the United States of America". This, strictly speaking, is The United-States-of-America. Not until it is joined with the Bill of Rights, expressly stated or tacitly understood, is there a United States of America in which there are a One and Many states and a people, each with its own rights, working toward the realization of common objectives.

The sought perfected Union was intended to join the one State to a plurality of limited states so as to constitute an actual, single, ongoing United-States-of-America, kept steady by a prospect of an excellent harmony between the two sides. That prospect is an objective having the primary form of a perfected Union, and the various subordinate forms listed in the "Preamble".

The United States of America embraces the United-States-of-America and the people functioning as correlatives. It is a single ongoing State having its own objectives. Those objectives guide it as well as the United-States-of America and the people as they interplay. When the objectives listed in the "Preamble" are treated as referring to the powers of the United-States-of America, and the "Bill of Rights" is taken to list the correlative rights possessed by the people—the position here defended—the United States of America has the status of a single ongoing State, guided by a splendid matching of powers and rights in an ideal, realizable State.

10. Superpowers do not take kindly to the idea that they should submit to the decisions of some neutral power, able to limit and perhaps punish them. Despite that, there are projects they could beneficially carry out together which could lay the ground for the existence of a State over all; they could together explore outer space, the oceans, and the arctic regions; they could together prepare for a posterity which encompasses both their populations and others besides; and they could take themselves to be jointly prepared to keep peace everywhere. There is little hope that anything like this will be done until all humanity, or at least the superpowers, face a serious common crisis. It may then be too late. Efforts must now be made to promote the desired outcome, and whatever little success is achieved should become the occasion for the achievement of further, greater successes. European nations are today pointing the way, hesitatingly, and in only limited areas, but clearly enough to make evident the direction in which all States are to move for their own benefit, their people, and most surely, humanity.

CHAPTER THIRTEEN

1. People are responsible for what they privately intend and for what they privately initiate. If they carry out what they began, they tacitly assume accountability for what is done. If they are rewarded or punished, they are held accountable by the society or state. Were they to approve of what is then done by the society or state, they would assume accountability for the very acts and outcomes for which they were held accountable. Evidently, they may be held accountable for acts for which they are not responsible and for which they have not assumed accountability. Just as surely, they may not be held accountable for what they are responsible and for which they may have assumed accountability. One is responsible for intending to lie, and assumes accountability by telling the lie. Yet neither society nor state may be interested in the fact. An employer may be held accountable for losses caused by poor workers despite the fact that he or she had no responsibility for their acts nor had assumed accountability for them. See *Privacy*, pp. 171-3; 183-4.

2. The Confucian tradition is splendidly illuminated by Antonio S. Cua's "Dimensions of *Li* (Propriety): Reflections on an Aspect of Hsün Tsu's Ethics", *Philosophy East and West*, 29, (1979); *Dimensions of Moral Creativity*, chapters 4 and 5; "Reasonable Action and Confucian Argumentation" and "Chinese Moral Vision, Responsive Agency, and Factual Beliefs", *Journal of Chinese Philosophy* 1, 1980; "Practical Causation and Confucian Ethics" *Philosophy East and West* 25 (1975).

3. It is the thesis of *Privacy* that most of what we know of the privacies of people and what they privately do is learned from their publicly functioning in ways that cannot be accounted for by understanding how their bodies act as merely living or publicly conditioned units. Privacies are made evident by the differences they make to the functioning of bodies.

A state partially recognizes the distinction between what living human bodies do on their own and the difference made to that functioning by privacies, when it deals with them as being under the influence of uncontrollable passion, expressing malice aforethought, and the like. But it does not interest itself in those privacies as they are apart from what they publicly express in and through their bodies. Accepting the fact that there are such privacies and that they make a difference to what is bodily done, it takes only occasional and partial account of what these might be.

It is disheartening to hear of courts relying on the testimony of psychiatrists about the nature and functioning of privacies, and sometimes on what they think is being reported by "lie-detectors". These are surely not the ways to know what is privately being added to what people, as public units, might otherwise do. Such knowledge requires an understanding of the nature and functioning of at least the mind and the will as distinct activities, and not as reservoirs or just agencies for desires. An adequate grasp of what the mind and will are and do presupposes a knowledge of their natures and how they can be known to be acting well or poorly. Public evidence is needed, but it must be used properly. To get maximum knowledge of what is being evidenced of privacy at a particular time, it is necessary to move intensively and convergently into it, guided by a sound understanding of the kind of private act that could be and might most likely have been expressed.

What we know of privacies, we learn by making use of evidences. Most of these reflect a private involvement with what is outside the interests or of the reach of those who allow for no knowledge that is not publicly expressed. When a person engages in some act for no apparent reason, the tracing back of what was done should be guided by an understanding of the nature of that person's mind. What is to be discovered is how this functioned. To know that, we have to rely on other evidences. Only then would we be in a position to know if the person had reasoned well or poorly. Those evidences are used intensively and convergently. The same procedure is followed when attempts are made to learn what is believed. One should, though, avoid taking the usual step of supposing that a person drew a proper inference from that belief. At the very least, evidences should be obtained that such and such was believed, and still other evidences obtained showing that the belief was used in a particular way.

4. On the difference between selection and election, see particularly, *Privacy*, p. 149.

5. This account of reasonableness is quite close to what Aristotle spoke of as "practical wisdom". See particularly *Ethics*, 1103a 4-10; 1141b 8-23. Since he was concerned only with it as pertinent to and as practiced by those who govern, and because he also dealt with what transcended his categories, by means of inappropriate "amphibolous" terms, his account necessarily had a more limited scope than is needed and possible today.

Reasonableness harnesses the mind to expectations grounded in habit and justified by experience. It cannot therefore be identified with rationality, a readiness to accept what is logically necessitated. Courts use it as a measure of what is to be endorsed or disowned. When they have recourse to the opinions of experts to find out what someone "had in mind", they (and the experts) take the mind to be functioning properly only so far as it follows routes which are in accord with what reasonableness requires.

References to "intent", "malice", and the like refer to a readiness to do or not do what reasonableness endorses. The premises from which a rational mind draws conclusions are here either tacitly altered to reflect the mind's involvement with the body and what occurs in a world of reasonable people, or are used as the antecedents of reasonable moves. The one alternative depends on an endorsement of certain propensities to act; the other on an endorsement of qualifications to which an otherwise unsatisfactory beginning is subject. The first starts with what is acceptable, the second makes acceptable what might otherwise be undesirable. The one demands that a desirable malice, directed against enemies, be restrained; the other, that a regrettable malice be replaced by what is a better beginning for a reasonable act. While they both take a malice, directed at others inside a state, to be inappropriate, the one does so because the malice is not adequately modified, the other because it cannot be a part of what is reasonably done.

6. A better grip on the nature and roles of transcendents, and particularly of the nature of justice, would have compelled even a ruling Greek, whether active in politics or thinking about it, to realize that some of the

things commonly taken for granted by those who ruled should have been questioned and rejected. A mature reasonableness knows that it is beholden to what exists outside a state's provenance. Every once in a while reasonableness will take account of this; it will, therefore, modify the form it had unreflectingly assumed when it functioned within the limits of a state.

Genuinely reasonable people take note of what defenders of the idea of reasonableness often take to be nonexistent or impossible to know. They allow for the action of transcendent conditions which both govern a multiplicity of actual occurrences and can never be reduced to any or to all of them. It is not reasonable to pride oneself on having no knowledge and no way of knowing what one presupposes when trying to see that justice is being done.

7. This is close to the position at which John Stuart Mill arrived when he held that a Socrates dissatisfied is superior to a pig satisfied. He, though, did not recognize that he thereupon had given up the utilitarian theory so far as it applied to humans, perhaps because he did not deal with the question whether or not a Socrates dissatisfied was superior to a multiplicity of utilitarians satisfied.

Taking utilitarianism to be a theory, telling one how to deal with subhumans as quantified in relation to one another and for the benefit of people, denies it the status of an ethics. Ethics treats every being as unique, with an absolute value, unable to be quantified. Since every subhuman has a unique value, ethics must also take account of its rights and values, or these must come within its purview only when transformed into comparable values, with the status of means for preserving and enhancing people. The latter alternative grants ethics a universal application, but acknowledges only people to have unquantifiable rights, not to be denied without committing ethical wrong.

In a fire, we are to save the most hardened of criminals rather than the greatest of paintings, or a sickly, dying man instead of the noblest healthy horse or dog. The painting, horse, and dog have incomparable values in themselves. They also have comparable values in relation to the excellence people are to realize in themselves and in the complexes they help constitute. The values each has in itself must be respected, and preserved if possible, at the same time that it is recognized that it is ethically subordinate and can be instrumentally used on behalf of people. The value of these is both distinct and inseparable from them as present persons, no matter how incomplete, corrupt, or distorted they be.

A similar understanding of people as loci of only part of the good that is available in a state, allows one to understand why they should both promote and make room for what limits them. It is not necessary to suppose that their state embodies greater goods than they do in order to be warranted in holding that they can become as good as they possibly can only if they there make themselves be excellent, public, completed beings together.

As public beings who are irreducible private persons as well, people need to be cherished in a double way. Treated as means by a state, they cannot be denied their status as irreducible ends in themselves without the commission of an ethical wrong. Yet a state must at times allow ethics only the status of what adds limited qualifications to what is politically required. The conflict between the different demands of the two will not be overcome until one sees that a state must preserve and promote what ethics endorses, and that ethics takes account of the indispensable role that a state has in enabling people to be excellent together and to become enhanced privately. Each demands a price from the other, with people requiring the state to do more than what must be done to promote their living together, and the state requiring the acceptance of the fact that it is to be preserved and empowered, if only to enable people to be all they should be.

The ideal outcome is an ethics endorsing what must be publicly achieved in order for people to be able to exist and prosper as individuals, and for a state to respect people's irreducible value while enabling them to function well together. When, in the next chapter, account is taken of the presence of the state in larger contexts, a somewhat different but not unrelated approach to the problem of the relation of the state and ethics will become apparent.

Although each person is unique, with an irreplaceable superlative value, and although each is no less precious than all the others put together—for otherwise, one could be sacrificed to benefit "the greatest number"—the good of each must find a place alongside the goods of others. One does most justice to oneself, both privately and publicly, by promoting, allowing for, and benefiting from those others, since one's own good is enhanced by being joined with theirs. The good of all together is properly achieved and maintained only so far as it in turn promotes or at least allows for the good of each.

8. Unlike virtue—habits serving to make people readied to act as they ought—habits of obedience and submissiveness lead to a yielding to demands, whether or not this is desirable. When such habits are praised or spoken of as virtues, yielding is honored, regardless of the spirit of those who exhibit it.

Obedience is a desirable habit, but it could reveal an attitude toward authority grounded in fear rather than appreciation, in ignorance rather than in understanding. At its best, it joins respect for a common legitimate government to a respect for the rights of people. The product is as a derivative virtue, uniting a number of primary virtues to constitute a desirable attitude that is to be effectively expressed within a properly functioning state.

9. In *The Making of Men*, the nature of education was made the central topic, with particular emphasis put on what is to be taught at different ages, how different stages are to be related, and the outcome that is to be promoted. Although it is politically wise to have an independent educational system carry out that program, since the state will thereby gain in a way it otherwise could not, it is also true that the concerns of a sound education will not be limited to what is politically important or even politically desirable, and that it might therefore lay grounds for resistance and perhaps rebellion. A controlling state usually holds that some studies will work to its detriment then or eventually, and that others are of littie value, a waste of precious time and funds, despite their claims that the people and the state itself presuppose and need them. In fear of or in contempt for such studies, a state in control of education allows it only a limited independence.

A state's control over education can never be perfect. It has no way of assuring that what is taught will be taught or what is to be learned will be learned. It is naive to suppose that learning is entirely a function of teachers' acts, or that students simply absorb what they are told, adding no interpretations, engaging in no reflection, questioning, or criticism. No one knows how what is taught will be used. A state can surely block the process of education and, more likely than not, reduce or preclude the benefits that the studies it does not endorse or which it forbids might have produced. Speculative, historic, artistic, and mathematical inquiries, even questions about the ways a state carries out its functions, may yield desirable political results. To insist that envisaged political benefits or current political values be to the fore in education is to exclude possible political enrichments from unsuspected quarters; to tacitly suppose that the political is the highest good or proper measure of what is proper; and to deny to education its appropriate activity, scope, ends, and possible achievements.

10. When leaders believe that they alone know what should be done in every area, they are at a stage where they are ready to give way to those who can exploit their weakness, and prepare the way for the coming of another regime or state. It is necessary to let go in order to remain in control; only then will one be able to make best use of instruments for preserving and enhancing whatever is worth preserving. Those who cherish power, regardless of consequences, and in the face of the need to relax it in order to be more strongly entrenched, mistakenly believe that they never will face a greater counterforce, or that they are always able to generate the various kinds and degrees of support and help they need. It is sad that the lesson that has to be learned is one that those in control usually learn too late, with an unnecessary cost in lives, pain, and ugliness.

11. Undergraduates and graduates of Harvard asked the university to withdraw its investments in corporations which did business with South Africa. The students were expressing, and wanted the university to express, an opposition to the refusal of the South African government to recognize that blacks were private persons just as the whites were, and should be given a public status equal to that of the whites. The president of the university answered that such a withdrawal would do no practical good and might conceivably harm the blacks. He answered their ethical objection with an observation about practical wisdom.

The protestors were not proposing a practical answer to a practical problem; they were making an ethical observation and wanted some support for it. Conceivably, the withdrawal of Harvard's money from various corporations doing business with South Africa, might not make the government change its ways, and might even make for hardship for blacks beyond that which they are now suffering. A refusal to withdraw the money is, though, also a refusal to be financially involved with a country that was acknowledged, even by the president of the university, to be behaving in ethically indefensible ways. The courses in ethical thinking now required of undergraduates at Harvard, evidently, should also be required of its president. He seems to need it even more than they do.

12. In religious circles it is sometimes said that a person becomes perfected only when he or she accepts the will of a God, the source of a good

to which their own will is to yield. The reciprocal is rarely affirmed—God becomes perfected when he accepts the good of people as that which has the right to be together with his own and therefore, with his, to be brought under a common encompassing good. Of course, if a God accepted the good of people as worth being realized independently of himself, and also to be accommodated by him, his good and humanity's good would be taken by him to be subordinated to that single, all-encompassing good.

Although there could be a being whose value was greater than any other's, as long as there are others independent of it, with distinct values of their own, it cannot possess all the good there is. A God's supreme value is still one among many; it and the goods of other are subordinate to a final good. This, as existing apart from them, is also deficient. Were there only an x and a y and an ideal good distinct from them, their embodiment of this would either deny it its separate integrity or would allow for it. The first of these alternatives takes x and y to contain all that is valuable; the second reveals them to lack whatever value the ideal good itself possesses. The realities, x and y must embody the ideal, and still leave it distinct from them, still to be realized. This is but to say that the ideal always faces whatever there be, including itself as realized at any time.

Chapter Fourteen

1. If, in some accord with Plato, one were to suppose that the final good were the whole good, one would be faced with the fact that nothing, as apart from that good, would have any merit. The final good would then have to reach down to what exists apart from it, to make this attend to what is alien to it. It is with such existents that one should have begun, but that would not have allowed one to end with a good that was cut off from all else.

Because even the ideal final good is only a prospect, it is itself not perfect. Not perfect, it depends for its realization on the activities of present realities which enable it to be realized and thereby be in fact perfect. for each actuality, a limited form of the final good is a guiding prospect. That limited form of the prospect is realized by each at every moment, but in a fragmented and often a distorted form. Every actuality is better than the good it is to realize because it has a needed, desirable determinateness; every actuality is also less than it could be because it has realized that good in a contracted form.

2. Were one to remain within the compass of many current discussions, one would have to take ethics to be exclusively concerned with the decisions and actions of individuals, and would therefore not be able to pass ethical judgments on what they do together, or on what societies, governments, or states are or should do, except perhaps as agencies for helping individuals to carry out of their ethical tasks. There is surely an ethical judgment to be passed on unions, societies, and states, even apart from their affect on the way people can or do act ethically.

3. Inquiry takes its start in daily experience. from there it is possible to move on in a number of ways. One way is to progressively dissect what is encountered, and formulate what can be learned, at some particular stage, through reflection, theoretical formulation, or experiment. That is the course followed by philosophical analysis and the sciences. Recourse here is had to highly developed powers working on behalf of a rationalism, often without regard for the existence of that from which one began; or various established areas, such as economy, society, state, or history are distinguished and attempts made to understand these by examining their structures—or functionings. To avoid taking for granted what deserves examination and to accou nt for the presence of effective conditions governing what occurs, it will be necessary, sooner or later, to consider what can be known in other ways as well. Analysis and science are much too limited in procedures and scope to provide sufficiently pertinent bases and content for all other studies.

Suspicious of what has been assumed by formal enterprises, an attempt might be made to cling to insight, description, or the procedures of daily life, and to test every enterprise and deliverance in terms of its consonance with what these find congenial. A high price would be paid, one would then lose the guidance and help which reflection, plans, well-define methods, experiments, technology, and criticism provide.

Not only must ultimates be specialized so as to be appropriate to the conditions governing people together; attitudes successfully carried out in the course of the daily life must be merged with a knowledge of conditions. Only then will one be able to deal appropriately with social and poiitical topics. The outcome of that merger I have termed "sophisticated reasonableness". It cannot be fully ours unless we first attend to what is always being presupposed. A study of society and state, therefore, should come after one has engaged in the boldest speculative adventures. This is what Plato, and apparently Aristotle, did. It is the method also followed by Hobbes, Kant, and Hegel. Aristotle, in addition, saw that a distinctive method is to be employed when politics is not only to be practiced but understood. That method makes use of a chastened rationalism—or equally, a sophisticated reasonableness, or a judicious daily practice—and applies it in and to every society and state. It is not entirely suited to ethics, for this has to take account of ultimate realities, particularly of people's privacies, as well as of the rights of what is not human. Still, like even the most speculative of enterprises, ethics qualifies what it discerns of ultimates with what has been experientially learned, though only to that limited extent which assures that one is dealing with realities pertinent to what is daily encountered.

4. Even mathematical truths have conformal and embedded roles. A mathematical discovery about the properties of prime numbers or of algebras with an infinite number of variables is made in conformity with mathematical truths already discovered. Branches of mathematics are branches of a single subject, not separate domains having no bearing on or relation to one another. Mathematical truths are also embedded, perhaps in two places. They are grounded in a domain determining what constitutes an allowable hypothesis and proof, and play a role in daily experience.

Tacitly supposing that embedded truths need to be inseparable parts of actual occurrences, Dewey identified mathematical lines with the edges of objects. This is not yet to provide for lines infinite in length or subject to odd curvatures. To hold that such lines play variations on mathematical lines already found to be embedded is to beg the question whether those embedded lines are of interest to the mathematician, and whether variations on those lines are embedded in the same way the original lines were. Whatever the answer, it does not require one to deny that embedded truths are also conformal and objective.

Mature, reasonable people, occupied with affirming what may or may not be done in a state, are primarily occupied with embedded and conformal truths. That does not mean that what they say has no objectivity. An honest person can fit in with other honest people without thereby losing the status of one who can refer to what holds everywhere and forever. If one takes some act to be right in some situation, that will not prevent it from being right outside that setting. Nor does fitting in well with others, or doing what a state demands, thereupon preclude saying and doing what can be justified apart from these.

5. When one attempts to infer to what has been implied, a prospect is faced in two ways—as implicated, and as a possibility to be brought about through mental action. The two offer different routes to reach the same objective, the one doing this in such a way that the objective continues to be a possibility thought about, while the other makes it determinate and present. The latter is not subordinated to the former. Sometimes two different activities are carried out, in one of which a prospective conclusion is left indeterminate but endorsed, and in the other of which it is filled out, made present, asserted, replacing its antecedent.

6. The reasonable exhibits in one form the way in which conditions and people interplay to constitute an ongoing that is both guided by and embodies a prospect. Were one to deal with it in the spirit of pragmatism one would, with Peirce, leave Hegel behind to consider the ways in which people's laws were changed in import as they applied to people. If, instead, one followed the lead of Dewey, one would depart from Rousseau to consider the ways in which intelligence could order what People together did. james, in closer accord with actual political activity, emphasized the need to attend to the ways in which one had to work in and through what occurred in order to obtain satisfying outcomes. All three fragmented a primary fact: what occurs in the political world, like what goes on every day, is an ongoing produced by bringing together prescriptions and the efforts of people to constitute an activity incorporating an ideal guidance, thereby producing and perhaps maintaining their ongoing combination. The presence of reasonableness assures the presence and steadiness of the activity, as well as the effective presence of a desirable objective over an indefinite stretch of time. All the while, of course, individuals will persist and engage in their singular activities. Reasonableness expresses what they are as together inside a special combination of condition and conditioned.

Reasonableness does not exhaust itself in bringing about a steady, persistent combination of condition and conditioned; it also allows these to remain distinct and thereby able to benefit from what is achieved. Conditions

and conditioned remain outside the combinations they constitute. Reasonableness subjects the combination to demands affected by the past and the
future. The result is constancy amidst change; political action by actual people
under effective laws; activity of indefinite duration in a present enriched by
a past and future.

      7. Mankind, as well as what it presupposes and makes possible, is
within the universe. Each person is there as a real, distinctive, marked-off
part, subject to specializations of common conditions. The world known to
science also occurs within that universe; physical units and their combinations
are there subject to the same conditions which, in a different, specialized,
and limited form, are pertinent to people and their affairs. As distinguished
from all other kinds of being, the physical entities are only parts of a cosmos,
in a limited, specialized division of the universe.

    The objects of the sciences and those of the humanities exist in the same
universe. People, too, exist there with their possessions and their achievements. But at the same time that every occurrence is in the universe with a
limited number of others, it is also in the cosmos, history, and various complexes.

    For astronomers, the sun does not go round the earth; for most of the rest
it does. The fact has confused the Vatican, driving it from one extreme to the
other in the attempt to deal with Galileo's acceptance of the Copernican view
that the earth moves round the sun, and not conversely. Initially, it took the
Bible to provide the needed warrant for rejecting his view. Recently, it has
maintained that Galileo was right. The Vatican was wrong—or alternatively,
partly right—both times. For no people, whether or not they accept the Bible,
is there the slightest doubt but that the sun goes round the earth. Farmers,
sailors, and the families of astronomers take note of the fact daily. In the
mathematical reified Copernican cosmos of Galileo, the sun stands still, and
the "movement" of the earth is stated as a series of different positions at
which the earth can be taken to be at different times. Beyond, and specialized
by both the humanized world and the cosmos, is the universe. In that universe, sun and earth change positions relative to one another in a space and
time which are not reducible to those encountered by humans or exhausted
in mathematical formulae.

    Even the universe, precisely because it depends on the presence and ac-
tivities of privately acting actualities, final conditions, and a common ground,
contains less than all there is. It, together with these ultimates, which are
specialized in it and thereby govern limited numbers and kinds of entities,
are the topic of an ontology. Satisfactory accounts of humanity are at least
tacitly set within the frame which this provides.

    Embracing and constitutive of all interlocked particulars, the ultimates come
together to constitute the universe, and thereupon the cosmos and more
limited worlds. Economics, social occurrences, and political events are in the
humanized world; history extends over its entire career.

    People exist in a number of worlds. In the humanized world, they take
account of great works, and together help constitute various complexes; as
outside this, they are subject to conditions applicable to other beings, living
and nonliving, large and small. They can be in a number at the same time,

because the conditions governing the humanized world and those governing the others are themselves specializations of an even more basic ontology. The entities with which physics is occupied have a similar multiple status—at the very least, one in the cosmos where they are subject to conditions pertinent to them alone, and another in the universe where they are subject to conditions which also apply to people. A rejection of the world known to science is therefore as wrong-headed as is a rejection of the humanized world, or of any of the lesser complexes this contains.

Cosmology specializes ontology in one way; a study of the humanized world does so in another. Political theory attends to a part of what occurs within the latter.

Index of Names*

Adam 389n, 412n
Aeschylus 373
Alexander, S.A. 396n
Antisthenes 417n
Aristotle 26ff, 72, 74, 110, 128, 163, 165,
  192, 207ff, 218ff, 234ff, 306, 326ff,
  340, 348, 365, 373, 394n, 398n, 402n,
  405n, 410n, 417n, 427n, 432n
Augustine 408n

Bach, J.S. 373
Barker, E. 417n
Beethoven, L. 373
Bentham, J. 365
Bergson, H. 115, 211, 394n, 396n
Bernstein, R.J. 410n
Black, H.L. 282ff, 285, 407n

Cardoza, B.N. 282, 285
Casey, E. 388n, 394n
Castiglione, R. xii
Confucius 147, 241ff, 318, 426n
Copernicus 434n
Cua, A. S. xii, 388n, 426n

Dahlstrom, D. 388n
Dante 90
Descartes, R. 118, 399nff
Dewey, J. 93, 433n
Dougherty, J. xii, 388n

Ehrlich, E. 418n
Einstein, A. 373
Engels, F. 170

Frank, J. 418n

Galileo 400n, 434n
Gelasius, Pope 416n
Goffman, E. 331

Hamilton, A. 284ff, 292, 294
Hegel, G.W.F. 72, 106, 110, 119, 127ff,
  138, l7lff, 206, 208, 373, 390n, 400n,
  410n, 412n, 415n, 432nff
Heidegger, M. 411n
Hitler, A. 175, 362

Hobbes, T. 12, 72, 110, 203ff, 294, 365,
  389n, 432n
Homer 373
Hsün Tsu 426n
Hume D. 115, 418nff

James, W. 433n
Jay, J. 285, 291
Jung, C. 394n

Kant, I. 110, 115, 365, 373, 405n, 412n,
  432n
Kataoka, A. xii
Kierkegaard, S. 400n
Kuhn, T. 46

Leibniz, G. 400n
Lincoln, A. 254, 281
Locke, J. 138, 203ff, 247, 340

Madison, J. 285, 295, 305
Marcos, F. 209
Marshall, J. 407n
Marx, K. 49ff, 56, 170ff, 276ff, 314, 319,
  357, 393n
Mill, J.S. 275ff, 428n
Morgan, J. p. 244
Morgan, W.J. 393n

Neville, R. xii
Newton, I. 373, 400n
Nixon, R. 180
Northrop, F.S.C. 110, 394n, 418n

Peirce, C. S. 46, 93, 99, 108ff, 113, 343,
  392n, 402n, 413n, 418n
Plato 26, 141ff, 163, 206ff, 232, 348,
  356, 365, 373, 394n, 399n, 405n,
  431n-433n
Poe, E.A. 90
Popper, K. 110

Rawls, J. 39, 224, 288, 398n
Reichenbach, H. 115
Rotenstreich, N. 388n
Rousseau, J.J. 56, 106, 142, 165, 365,
  394nff, 433n
Royce, J. 342ff

*This and the Index of Subjects, were prepared by Mary Ducey.

Index of Subjects